Official Catholic Teachings

clergy & laity

Odile M. Liebard

 A Consortium Book

from McGrath Publishing Company
Wilmington, North Carolina 1978

Library of Congress Card Catalog Number: 78-53848
ISBN: 0-8434-0717-4
ISBN: 0-8434-0723-9 paper

The Publisher gratefully acknowledges permission to quote from the following
copyrighted publications.

AMERICA PRESS
  LUMEN GENTIUM; CHRISTUS DOMINUS; PRESBYTERORUM ORDINIS,
    "Documents of Vatican II" © 1966.

THE CATHOLIC MIND
  AD CATHOLICI SACERDOTII, Volume XXXIV, Number 3, February 8,
    1936.

THE DAUGHTERS OF SAINT PAUL
  *EST SANE MOLESTUM; SAPIENTIAE CHRISTIANAE; IL FERMO PRO-
    POSITO; QUAE NOBIS HAUD ITA; ADDRESS OF POPE PIUS XII TO
    THE CARDINALS AND BISHOPS;* "The Lay Apostolate", © 1961.

EDITIONS FLEURUS, PARIS
  HAERENT ANIMO, "The Catholic Priesthood", © 1957, published by the
    Newman Press, Md.

NATIONAL CATHOLIC WELFARE CONFERENCE
  MENTI NOSTRAE, 1950; *ADDRESS OF POPE PIUS XII TO THE WORLD
    CONGRESS OF THE LAY APOSTOLATE*, 1951; *ECCLESIAM SUAM*,
    1964; *DECLARATION ON THE QUESTION OF THE ADMISSION OF
    WOMEN TO THE MINISTERIAL PRIESTHOOD*, 1977.

OUR SUNDAY VISITOR
  *OPTATAM TOTIUS ECCLESIAE: THE DECREE ON TRAINING FOR THE
    PRIESTHOOD*, "The Pope Speaks", Volume 11, Number 1, © 1965.
  APOSTOLICAM ACTUOSITATEM, "The Pope Speaks", Volume 11, Number
    2 ©1966.
  SACRUM DIACONATUS ORDINEM, "The Pope Speaks", Volume 12, Num-
    ber 3, ©1967.
  *HOMILY OF POPE PAUL VI TO THE THIRD WORLD CONGRESS OF THE
    LAY APOSTOLATE*, "The Pope Speaks", Volume 12, Number 4, ©1967.
  ADDRESS OF POPE PAUL VI TO A GENERAL AUDIENCE", "The Pope
    Speaks", Volume 14, Number 2, © 1969.
  *SACRED CONGREGATION FOR THE CLERGY TO THE PRESIDENTS OF
    EPISCOPAL CONFERENCES*, "The Pope Speaks", Volume 15, Number
    2, ©1970.
  *ADDRESS OF POPE PAUL VI TO 21ST ITALIAN NATIONAL WEEK OF
    PASTORAL RENEWAL*, "The Pope Speaks", Volume 16, Number 3,
    © 1971.

Table of Contents

Introduction

The latter third of the twentieth century is highly paradoxical. The human being around whom the entire time process centers is at once incredibly strong and tragically weak, filled with the vigor of youth and bent over with old age, dancing a wild dance of joyous relationship and standing alone as the isolated being. Possibilities for achieving human perfection and for catching the elusive dream of human happiness seem greater than ever and yet, they are counterbalanced by moods of despair, of incertitude, of fear. Constantly drawn to dwell in time as the child of light, contemporary man holds tightly to the illusory security of darkness.

Much of the Second Vatican Council's greatness is due to its sensitivity to the present moods and situation of mankind. Its documents reveal a desire to experience with modern man all the joys and sorrows that constitute his world. The starting point for all that the Council has to say is the human condition as it really exists. As a result, the insights developed by the Council are highly relevant to the twentieth century. However, because of their very richness, they may be condemned to the level of "good ideas, but not very practical."

The Council proclaims the unity of all mankind to be a fact of existence. This means that all men, regardless of race, nationality, religion, financial status, history, language, and so forth are actually a single being moving through time. Until this is recognized by all men as the grounding fact of the human condition, goals such as perfection, harmony, peace and happiness simply cannot be realized. The theme of unity as fact runs counter to today's dominant mode of handling the human. Ours is a century which has preferred to dwell in division, disparity and separation.

Again, the Council declares the interrelatedness of all human beings. This is actually a correlate of the theme of unity. Thus humans do not merely happen to be bunched up on the earth in groups of various sizes. They are, by their very nature, related to one another, essential to one another's existence. There is no way that a given human being or even a nation can develop, mature, humanize without the support and presence of other human beings and nations. To the degree that mankind lives out relationship, to that degree is the human possible—a strange way of speaking if one has been trained to look upon the other as enemy.

In response to an industrial and technological age that has tended to gut human action of any meaning whatsoever, the Council firmly declares the value of human action. Involvement to any degree whatsoever in the process of shaping the earth means participation in shaping the history and destiny of mankind.

These particular insights, the unity and the interrelatedness of mankind along with the value of human action constitute the Council's proclamation of the dignity of the human person. This dignity manifests itself through human intelligence and human freedom which, together, give man the central role of responsibility in and for the world. The insights are not merely interesting ways to talk about the human. They are the basic facts of life. Without them there is no human—there is nothing to hope for, to work for, to look forward to. Lived out as dynamics, sought after as ideals, experienced as the human condition, they can bring mankind to fulfillment and reveal the mysterious dignity of the human person.

The decades that preceded the Council had, for all practical purposes, rejected these facts of unity, relationship and value. The end result is the pitiable condition of contemporary man; a being who cannot quite get hold of himself. And this includes the Christian in the twentieth century. Though his heritage contains the themes of a world unified in Christ, of universal brotherhood in Christ, of the sanctifying value of all human actions in Christ, his twentieth century history includes the two great world wars which were fought mostly on Christian soil between Christian nations in the name of truth and freedom. His lived experience is not one of unity but of division, not of relationship but of isolation, not of valued human action but of destruction. The Christ to whom he professes allegiance has been pushed somewhere into the background.

The Council boldly challenges all mankind, but especially all who profess Christianity, to overcome their own history and lived experience, and to become a new people of God, joined together in a common priesthood, to look upon one another as equals, as co-sharers of the mystery that is Christ, to recognize the value and the ordering of the whole of creation to the praise of God. It is a challenge anchored in the dynamics of faith, both in God and man, of hope and of a love that can shatter the bonds of history and let man be free. Should the People of God, as a People, ever respond and take up the challenge, the magnificence of the Christian person, in all of its unveiled beauty, will be for the first time.

It is only within the context of such insights and thought patterns that one can grasp the Council's perspective on the clergy and laity. For, though all the traditional terms were retained and all hierarchical structures respected, the Council looks at the clergy and laity in a new and fascinating manner.

The people of God are one. There is no better or worse, richer or poorer, more or less important. This unity precedes and supercedes all structures and classifications. If the tendency to categorize and rearrange humans by titles is permitted to control our understanding of the People of God, then the unity is immediately destroyed and there is no People of God. This means that every person who assumes the name Christian must strip down all the accidental trimmings of historic Christianity and return to the original simplicity of Christ. Then, terms such as hierarchy, bishop, clergy and laity, though practical and at times even necessary, are totally secondary.

According to the Council, all Christians share in the unique priesthood of Christ. This means that every Christian, regardless of life situation, must look upon himself and all other Christians as priests, that is, the one whose role in existence is to recreate the original harmony of the universe by bringing God to matter and matter to God. To behold oneself as any less than that, to see another Christian as less than that, is to back away from the challenge of the Council. Only after this perspective has been given ample freedom to shape Christianity can we begin to note that there are different types of priesthood, viz., the common priesthood of the faithful and the ministerial or hierarchical priesthood of the clergy. The oneness of Christ's priesthood as reality must precede the duality of organized priesthood. It is possible that this single point will be overlooked, with the result that the Council's true perspective will never see the light of day. Laity may find it difficult to look upon themselves as priests, for it is a word that traditionally has been reserved for a specially chosen few. Clergy may feel that a private domain has been invaded. Both clergy and laity may prefer to let well enough alone. And the starting point for a new day will have been missed.

"In the Church, not everyone marches along the same path, yet all are called to sanctity and have obtained an equal privilege of faith through the justice of God. Although by Christ's will, some are established as teachers, dispensers of the mysteries and pastors for the others, there remains, nevertheless, a true equality between all with regard to the dignity and to the activity which is common to all the faithful in the building up of the Body of Christ. The distinction which the Lord has made between the sacred ministers and the rest of the People of God involves union, for the pastors and the other faithful are joined together by a close relationship" *(Lumen Gentium)*.

If clergy and laity, and all other Christians as well, are to anchor their lives in the unity of Christ, no less are they to develop a set of relationships with one another that is most enriching. All are to look upon one another as brothers and sisters, as co-workers in the world and co-sharers in the grace of Christ. Though hierarchical terms continue in use, there is no longer any justification for arranging members of the Church in an ascending or descending order. Once one has grown accustomed to looking at another as above or below oneself, it is almost impossible to see that other, purely, simply, regardless of all terminology and traditions, as equal, as brother, as co-sharer. But it must be done.

All—bishops, laity, clergy, pope, cardinal, deacons—are one, equal, brothers, essentially interdependent in Christ. To treat any person as more or less than this is, again, to miss the Council's perspective. No one is more necessary, no one is a mere accessory.

Those who march along the path called clergy will have a specific formation, carry out specific functions and be expected to live up to certain commitments particular to the clergy. Likewise, those who are called laity have a specific task, viz., "to make the Church present and fruitful in those places and circumstances where it is only through them that she can become the salt of the earth" *(Lumen Gentium)*.

Throughout the Dogmatic Constitution on the Church, *Lumen Gentium,* the themes of unity and interrelationship repeatedly show up as the foundation for the life of the clergy and laity.

The insight is a simple one, almost too simple. It is the insight in the light of which all the other documents in this volume must be read. If it is not to be taken seriously and concretized, then all of the documents amount to no more than pious, irrelevant reading. Given the insight, it makes sense to speak of the priest as the minister of God's Word, of the Sacraments and Eucharist, as Ruler of God's People; it makes sense to ask him to live a life of holiness, of unity and harmony, of humility, obedience, celibacy, and poverty. Given the insight, it makes sense to tell the laity that theirs is the task of sanctifying and consecrating the world in Christ; it makes sense to ask them to anchor their lives in the liturgy; it makes sense to ask them to take on an active apostolate in modern society. But only given the insight.

Since the close of the Second Vatican Council, the American clergy and laity have been going through an unusual process. Conciliar documents have been met with enthusiasm and disdain. Groups calling themselves liberal or conservative have gone their separate ways, proclaiming their own versions of post conciliar Christianity. And no one knows how many clergy and laity have quietly left the institutional church, some to forget the whole scene, others to search out the meaning of Christ in their own private style. The diversity of reactions, no doubt, has many causes. I would like to suggest a few for reflection by the reader of this volume.

First, Christians may have missed the point of the Council. Its purpose was not to get rid of anything or to protect anything. The Council is simply a proclamation of good news, that there is a totally other way to dwell in time, viz., the way of Christ, which is the unity of an active and loving brotherhood. Located in time, humans always have difficulty in dealing with a totally other way. We want to reason our way into the future, bring our past with us. Entry into a totally other way demands the abandonment both of reason and of history. Most humans, American Christians included, cannot handle that. And so, one's existence, be it clergy or laity, continues on the same plane, with a few new documents to read.

Second, Christians may not have been sufficiently prepared for the richness and depth of the Council's insight. Indeed, a century of being told that you are the flock, that it is your duty to submit to the shepherds, to obey, to carry out their orders and to pay them honor (cf. Leo XIII, *Est sane molestum,* Dec. 17, 1888) hardly prepares the sheep to hear that they are incorporated into Christ and share in the priestly, prophetic and royal role of Christ Himself (cf. Paul VI, Homily to the Third World Congress of the Lay Apostolate, Oct. 15, 1967). The naked fact is that Catholic clergy and laity had, for too long, dwelt in a rigid structure which did not invite sufficient maturation and reflection. The capacity for change and creative freedom was highly limited. The typical response to the challenge of the Council was adolescent—noisy, superficial, short-lived and confusing. Suddenly the People of God was caught up in an identity crisis. What is it to be a Christian? A priest? A layperson?

Church leaders and thinkers have tried to respond to the questions arising from the post conciliar period. Naturally the quality of their responses is proportionate to their own grasp of the Council's insight. Pope Paul seems to long for the Christian existence of the pre-conciliar age and tends to offer conservative and paternal guidance to both clergy and laity as they seek their destiny. This is evidenced in the fact that he treats existential questions as problems. Yet he has earnestly struggled to understand the people for whom he is Pope and spokesman. The documents of Paul which were chosen for this volume reveal much of his ambivalence.

Third, Christians may be on the wrong path. Most of the last decade's effort at renewal was activity-oriented, a very common American approach. The assumption is that if the activities are changed or re-arranged, renewal has taken place. This is usually not true. Thus, the life styles of clergy and laity were revamped, new responsibilities were distributed or old ones redistributed, new liturgies involving laity were established, parish and diocesan structures were overhauled to give a greater voice to laity and clergy. The results, as far as Christian presence in the world is concerned, were minimal. Could it be that a change in activity never was necessary, that all that was called for was a new way of beholding oneself and the other?

Fortunately, Christians are hopeful beings and never panic in the face of history. I propose that we may still be in the pre-conciliar period existentially and are in need of a radical dissolution process. In some way, Christians must arrive at a point where all terms and structures cease to have a hold on the mystery of Christ. Christianity must overcome any word, title or category that keeps radical unity and relationship from being its sole foundation. Then and only then will it be ready for the Second Vatican Council's invitation, challenge, proclamation that we—hierarchy, clergy, laity—are no longer hierarchy, clergy and laity, but one in Christ.

James K. McGowan PhD
June 12th, 1978

A Note On the Selection of Documents

The selection of documents for this volume was a challenging task. Official writings, both before and after the Second Vatican Council, are more than abundant. Clergy and laity find their way into almost all papal documents.

I used several of the Council documents as the starting point, insofar as they signal the end of the era in which clergy and laity were fit into a linear and perpendicular model and the beginning of the new Christian age in which common and shared priesthood grounds the existence of all members of the Church. *Lumen Gentium,* the Dogmatic Constitution on the Church, presents the perspective in which all Christians, whether clergy or laity, can come to grasp the mystery of their own lives. The Decree on the Apostolate of Lay People, *Apostolicam Actuositatem,* and The Decree on the Ministry and Life of Priests, *Presbyterorum Ordinis,* are the Council's major statements on the laity and clergy. Though these documents stand on their own, they are better understood in relation to the Church hierarchy. Thus, I have included *Christus Dominus,* The Decree on the Pastoral Office of Bishops in the Church. *Optatam Totius,* The Decree on the Training of Priests, presents the Council's approach to the shaping of the priest of the future.

The temptation to include other documents of the Council, either in whole or in part, was great and it was with regret that I did not succumb. For example, The Pastoral Constitution on the Church in the Modern World, *Gaudium et Spes,* offers some beautiful insights on the clergy and laity. However, they do parallel what is said in the documents chosen for inclusion. Several areas, such as missions, ecumenism and relations with other religions, religious, and the social aspects of the apostolate, could all have justified inclusion of other conciliar documents. But each area is either treated in another volume of the series or merits separate consideration by itself.

Pope Paul VI, whose reign started during the Council, continues as the only post-Vatican II pope. Both during and since the close of the Council, he has issued documents of importance to the clergy and laity. I have included that portion of his encyclical *Ecclesiam Suam* (August 6, 1964) which discusses the Christian approach to dialogue. This timely statement indicated to the world that "dialogue with", not battle against, was to be the Church's way of dwelling in time. The conditions for and principles of true dialogue are essential to the new life of the clergy and laity.

The remaining statements of Paul VI which were chosen address particular issues, such as the permanent diaconate, lay apostolate, local church structures and ecclesial power. Statements from various sacred congregations complete the post conciliar selections. They also address issues of importance to the clergy and laity.

The nine pre-Vatican II documents which I have included span seventy-five years. My purpose was to present examples, by way of the most important documents from the reign of Pope Leo XIII to that of Pope Pius XII, of the predominant attitude toward and understanding of the clergy and laity before the Second Vatican Council. I believe that the documents selected do this well. There are two documents each from Leo XIII, Pius X, and Pius XI, and three from Pius XII.

The reader should be aware that there is a rich body of literature beyond this volume which relates to the clergy and laity. Encyclicals and other documents directed to religious naturally overlap with those directed to laity and clergy. But this literature calls for separate study. Consequently I did not include any of it here.

Two documents issued by the Sacred Congregation for Catholic education on the topic of priestly formation are of importance for anyone related to seminary training. They were issued on March 16, 1970 and February 22, 1976. Given that the emphasis in this volume is on the nature and role of the clergy, I judged it sufficient to include only the conciliar document mentioned above, without these additional documents.

It is difficult to speak of the clergy and laity today without immediately thinking of the many social justice issues

that confront contemporary man. Poverty, population con-
ʧrol, ecology war, communism and capitalism, right to life
and death—ᵗhese and many other key questions demand an
active response on the part of today's Christian. The volume
on *Social Justice* which is part of this series addresses all of
these issues and includes those documents which specifically
relate clergy and laity to them.

It is my hope that this volume will serve as a solid instrument for the person who is trying seriously to clarify the
identity and the role of clergy and laity in the world today.
There are obviously no set answers to the challenging questions that make up the lives of clergy and laity. But the
documents in this volume do offer rich insights into the
Church's thinking, suggest the historical thought patterns
of the last hundred years, show the attitudes and basic terms
which have shaped and continued to shape the lives of millions of people. Properly read and reflected upon, they can
free up the spirit of the clergy and laity and incorporate
them into the creative process of joyously consecrating the
world in Christ.

Odile M. Liébard

Subject Index

EST SANE MOLESTUM
Letter of Pope Leo XIII
on the Apostolate of the Laity
December 17, 1888

The Bishops form the most august body of the Church, that body which teaches and governs mankind by right divine; and whosoever resists them or obstinately refuses to obey their word separates himself from the Church.[1] But obedience should not limit itself to matters bearing upon faith; its sphere is much vaster; it extends to all matters which come under episcopal rule. For the Christian people, Bishops are not only masters in matters of faith, but they are placed above them to rule and to govern, being answerable to God to Whom one day they must render an account of their charge. Hence it is that the Apostle St. Paul delivers to Christians this exhortation: "Obey those who are over you, and be submissive to them, for they watch over you and have to give an account of your souls."[2]

It is indeed certain and clear that in the Church there are two orders very different from one another, the shepherds and the flock, that is, in other words, the leaders and the people. The first order has the duty to teach, to govern, to guide men through life, and to fix rules for them; the duty of the other is to submit to the first, to obey, to carry out its orders and to pay it honor. If then, the subjects usurp the place of the superior, it is not only an injurious act of rashness, but it is an attempt, so far as is possible for them, to overturn the order of things so wisely arranged by the providence of the Divine Founder of the Church. If by chance there should be in the ranks of the episcopacy a Bishop not sufficiently careful of his dignity, and apparently unfaithful to some of his sacred duties, he loses thereby none of his powers; and, as long as he is in communion with the Roman Pontiff, no one has a right to weaken in the smallest degree the respect and obedience due to his authority. On the other hand, to examine into and to criticize episcopal actions belongs to no individual, but it pertains only to those who, in the holy hierarchy, have a superior power, and, above all, to the Supreme Pontiff; for it is to him that Jesus Christ committed the charge of feeding not only the lambs but also the sheep. Nevertheless, when the faithful have a good cause to complain, it is indeed allowed to them to lay the whole case before the Roman Pontiff, provided that, having regard to the dictates of prudence and moderation, and being guided by the love of the public weal, they do not give way to outcries and local protestations, which tend rather to create divisions and hatreds or at least to increase them.

SAPIENTIAE CHRISTIANAE
Selection from Encyclical Letter of Pope Leo XIII
on the Chief Duties of Christian Citizens
January 10, 1890

To recoil before an emeny, or to keep silence when from all sides such clamors are raised against truth, is the part of a man either devoid of character or who entertains doubt as to the truth of what he professes to believe. In both cases such mode of behaving is base and is insulting to God, and both are incompatible with the salvation of mankind. This kind of conduct is profitable only to the enemies of the faith, for nothing emboldens the wicked so greatly as the lack of courage on the part of the good.

Moreover, want of vigor on the part of Christians is so much the more blameworthy, as not seldom little would be needed on their part to bring to naught false charges and refute erroneous opinions; and by always exerting themselves more strenuously they might reckon upon being successful. After all, no one can be prevented from manifesting that strength of soul which is the characteristic of true Christians; and very frequently by such display of courage our enemies lose heart and their designs are thwarted. Christians are, moreover, born for combat, whereof the greater the vehemence, the more assured, God aiding, the triumph: "Have confidence; I have overcome the world."[1] Nor is there any ground for alleging that Jesus Christ, the Guardian and Champion of the Church, needs not in any manner the help of men. Power certainly is not wanting to Him, but in His loving kindness He would assign to Us a share in obtaining and applying the fruits of salvation procured through His grace.

5   The chief elements of this duty consist in professing openly and unflinchingly the Catholic doctrine, and in propagating it to the utmost of Our power. For, as is often said, with the greatest truth, there is nothing so hurtful to Christian wisdom as that it should not be known, since it possesses, when loyally received, inherent power to drive away error. So as soon as Catholic truth is apprehended by a simple and unprejudiced soul, reason yields assent. Now faith, as a virtue, is a great boon of divine grace and goodness; nevertheless, the objects themselves to which faith is to be applied are scarcely known in any other way than through the hearing. "How shall they believe Him of Whom they have not heard? and how shall they hear without a preacher? Faith then cometh by hearing, and hearing by the word of Christ."[2] Since, then, faith is necessary for salvation, it follows that the word of Christ must be preached.

6   The office indeed of preaching, that is, of teaching, lies by divine right in the province of the pastors, namely of the bishops whom the Holy Ghost has placed to rule the Church of God.[3] It belongs above all to the Roman Pontiff, Vicar of Jesus Christ, established as head of the universal Church, teacher of all that pertains to morals and faith. No one, however, must entertain the notion that private individuals are prevented from taking some active part in this duty of teaching, especially those on whom God has bestowed gifts of mind with the strong wish of rendering themselves useful.

7   These, so often as circumstances demand, may take upon themselves, not indeed the office of the pastor, but the task of communicating to others what they have themselves received, becoming, as it were, living echoes of their masters in the faith. Such co-operation on the part of the laity seem to the Fathers of the Vatican Council so opportune and fruitful of good that they thought well to invite it. "All faithful Christians, but those chiefly who are in a prominent position, or engaged in teaching, we entreat, by the compassion of Jesus Christ, and enjoin by the authority of the same God and Savior, that they bring aid to ward off and eliminate these errors from

Holy Church, and contribute their zealous help in spreading abroad the light of undefiled faith."[4]

Let each one therefore bear in mind that he both can and   8 should, so far as can be, preach the Catholic faith by the authority of his example, and by open and constant profession of the obligations it imposes. In respect consequently to the duties that bind us to God and the Church, it should be borne earnestly in mind that in propagating Christian truth and warding off errors, the zeal of the laity should, as far as possible, be brought actively into play.

The faithful would not, however, so completely and advantageously satisfy these duties as is fitting they should, were   9 they to enter the field as isolated champions of the Faith. Jesus Christ, indeed, has clearly intimated that the hostility and hatred of men, which He first and foremost experienced, would be shown in like degree towards the work founded by Him, so that many would be barred from profiting by the salvation for which all are indebted to His loving kindness. Wherefore He willed not only to train disciples in His doctrine, but to unite them into one society, and closely conjoin them in one body, "which is the Church[5] whereof He would be the Head. The life of Jesus Christ pervades, therefore, the entire framework of this body, cherishes and nourishes its every member, uniting each with each, and making all work together to the same end, albeit the action of each be not the same.[6] Hence it follows that not only is the Church a perfect society far excelling every other, but it is enjoined by her Founder that for the salvation of mankind she is to contend "as an army drawn up in battle array."[7]

The organization and constitution of Christian society can   10 in no wise be changed, neither can any one of its members live as he may choose, nor elect that mode of fighting which best pleases him. For in effect he scatters and gathers not, who gathers not with the Chuch and with Jesus Christ, and all who fight not united with Him and with the Church are in very truth contending against God.

IL FERMO PROPOSITO
Encyclical Letter of Pope Pius X
on Catholic Action in Italy
June 11, 1905

We firmly resolved, at the very beginning of Our Pontificate, to consecrate all the strength which the Lord in His goodness has given Us, to the restoration of all things in Christ. This gives Us great confidence in the power of God's grace, without which here below We can neither conceive nor undertake any great or fruitful work for the salvation of souls. At the same time, We feel more strongly than ever, Venerable Brethren who are called to share Our pastoral office, the need of your united and constant cooperation in this noble purpose and the cooperation of all the clergy and faithful committed to your care. In truth, we are all called, in the holy Church of God, to build up that unique body of which Christ is the Head, a body which is highly organized, as the Apostle Paul teaches Us,[1] and well coordinated in all its movements. It is all this in virtue of the proper functioning of each member, by which the body takes its growth and gradually perfects itself in the bond of charity.

And if, in the work of the "edifying of the body of Christ,"[2] Our first duty is to teach, to indicate the method to be followed and the means to be used, to warn and paternally exhort, it is equally the duty of all Our well-beloved sons, throughout the whole world, to receive Our words, to put them into practice first in themselves and then to strive effectively that they may be put into practice by others, each one

according to the grace he has received from God, his state of
life and duties, and the zeal by which his heart is inflamed.

Here We will only call to mind the many good works under-   13
taken for the welfare of the Church, of society, and of individuals under the general name of *Catholic Action*, which by
the grace of God flourish throughout the world.

You well know how dear they are to Us and how ardently   14
We desire to see them strengthened and encouraged. We have
on this question, published, or caused to be authoritatively
published, certain documents which you all know. It is true
that some of these documents, by force of circumstances
bringing sorrow to Us, were meant rather to remove obstacles
which hindered the progress of Catholic action, and to condemn certain ill-regulated tendencies which were creeping in,
to the grave injury of the common cause.

Our heart longed to send to all a word of comfort and fa-   15
therly encouragement, so that, on the ground cleared, as far
as lay in Us, from every obstacle, good might continue to be
built up and largely increased. We are therefore very happy to
do so now by this letter, for the consolation of every one,
feeling sure that Our words will be heard and obeyed with
docility by all.

Immense is the field of Catholic action; it excludes abso-   16
lutely nothing which in any way, directly or indirectly, belongs to the divine mission of the Church.

It is plainly necessary to take part individually in a work so 17
important, not only for the sanctification of our own souls,
but also in order to spread and more fully open out the Kingdom of God in individuals, families, and society, each one
working according to his strength for his neighbor's good, by
the diffusion of revealed truth, the exercise of Christian virtue, and the spiritual and corporal works of charity and
mercy. Such is the conduct worthy of God to which St. Paul
exhorts us, "so as to please Him in all things, bringing forth
fruits of all good works, and increasing in the knowledge of
God: "That you may walk worthy of God in all things pleasing; being fruitful in every good work, and increasing in the
knowledge of God."[3]

18   Besides these benefits, there are many in the natural order, which, without being directly the object of the Church's mission, nevertheless flow from it as one of its natural consequences. Such is the light of Catholic revelation that it vividly illuminates all knowledge; so great is the strength of the Gospel maxims that the precepts of the natural law find in them a surer basis and a more energetic vigor; such, in fine, is the power of the truth and morality taught by Jesus Christ that even the material well-being of individuals, of the family, and of human society, receives from them support and protection.

19   The Church, while preaching Jesus crucified, "who was a stumbling-block and folly to the world,"[4] has been the first inspirer and promoter of civilization. She has spread it wherever her apostles have preached, preserving and perfecting what was good in ancient pagan civilization, rescuing from barbarism and raising to a form of civilized society the new peoples who took refuge in her maternal bosom, and giving to the whole of human society, little by little, no doubt, but with a sure and ever onward march, that characteristic stamp which it still everywhere preserves. The civilization of the world is Christian civilization; the more frankly Christian it is, so much is it more true, more lasting, and more productive of precious fruit; the more it withdraws from the Christian ideal, so much the feebler is it, to the great detriment of society.

20   Thus, by the intrinsic force of things, the Church became also in fact the guardian and protector of Christian civilization. This truth was recognized and admitted in former times; it even formed the immovable foundation of civil legislation. On it rested the relations of Chruch and States, the public recognition of the authority of the Church in all matters relating in any way to conscience, the subordination of all State laws to the divine laws of the Gospel, the harmony of the two powers, civil and ecclesiastical, for procuring the temporal well-being of the nations without injury to their eternal welfare.

21   It is unnecessary to tell you what prosperity and happiness, what peace and concord, what respectful submission to au-

thority, and what excellent government would be established and maintained in the world, if the perfect ideal of Christian civilization could be everywhere realized. But, given the continual welfare of the flesh with the spirit, of darkness with light, of Satan with God, we cannot hope for so great a good, at least in its full measure. Hence, against the peaceful conquests of the Church arose unceasing attacks, the more deplorable and fatal as human society tends more to govern itself by principles opposed to the Christian ideal, and to separate itself wholly from God.

This is not a reason for losing courage. The Church knows   22 that the gates of hell will never prevail against her; but she knows also that she will be oppressed in this world, that her apostles are sent like lambs among wolves, that her faithful children will ever be hated and despised, as her Divine Founder was covered with hatred and contempt. Nevertheless, the Church goes fearlessly on, and while extending the Kingdom of God in places where it has not yet been preached, she strives by every means to repair the losses inflicted on the Kingdom already acquired.

"To restore all things in Christ" has ever been the Church's   23 motto, and it is specially Ours, in the perilous times in which we live. To restore all things, not in any fashion, but in Christ; "that are in heaven, and on earth, in Him,"[5] adds the Apostle; to restore in Christ not only what directly depends on the divine mission of the Church to conduct souls to God, but also as We have explained, that which flows spontaneously from this divine mission, viz., Christian civilization in each and every one of the elements which compose it.

To dwell only on this last part of the desired restoration,   24 you see well what support is given to the Church by those chosen bands of Catholics whose aim is to unite all their forces in order to combat anti-Christian civilization by every just and lawful means, and to repair in every way the grievous disorders which flow from it; to reinstate Jesus Christ in the family, the school, and society; to re-establish the principle that human authority represents that of God; to take intimately to heart the interests of the people, especially those of the working and agricultural classes, not only by the inculcation of religion, the only true source of comfort in the sorrows of life, but also by striving to dry their tears, to soothe their sufferings, and by wise measures to improve their economic conditions; to endeavor, consequently, to make public laws conformable to justice, to amend or suppress those which are not so; finally, with a true Catholic spirit, to defend and support the rights of God in everything, and the no less sacred rights of the Church.

25   All these works, of which Catholic laymen are the principal supporters and promoters, and whose form varies according to the special needs of each nation, and the particular circumstances of each country, constitute what is generally known by a distinctive, and surely a very noble name: *Catholic Action* or *Action of Catholics*. This has always come to the aid of the Church, and the Church has always welcomed and blessed it, although it has acted in various ways in accordance with the age.

26   And here it must at once be observed that it is impossible at the present day to re-establish in the same form all the institutions which may have been useful, and were even the only efficient ones in past centuries, so numerous are the radical modifications which time has brought to society and public life, and so many are the fresh needs which changing circumstances cease not to call forth. But the Church, throughout her long history, has always and on every occasion luminously shown that she possesses a wonderful power of adaptation to the varying conditions of civil society; without injury to the integrity or immutability of faith or morals, and always safeguarding her sacred rights, she easily bends and adapts herself in all that is contingent and accidental, to the vicissitudes of time, and the fresh needs of society.

27   "Godliness," says St. Paul, "lends itself to everything, possessing divine promises as to the goods of this life as well as to those of the future": *Pietas autem ad omnia utilis est, promissionem habens vitae quae nunc est et futurae.*[6] And Catholic action also, while suitably varing its outward forms and methods, remains ever the same in the principles which guide it, and in the very noble end at which it aims. And in order that it may at the same time be really efficient, it will

be well to point out carefully the conditions it requires, if
its nature and object are well considered.

Before everything, people must be thoroughly convinced   28
that an instrument is useless if it is not suited to the work it
has to do. Catholic action (as is proved from what has already
been said), by proposing to restore all things in Christ, becomes a real apostolate for the honor and glory of Christ
Himself. To carry it out rightly, We must have divine grace,
and the apostle receives none if he is not united to Christ. Only
when we have formed Jesus Christ within us shall we more
easily be able to give Him back to the family and to society.
All, therefore, who are called upon to direct, or who devote
themselves to the promotion of the Catholic movement, ought
to be Catholics who are proof against everything, firm in
faith, solidly instructed in religious matters, truly submissive
to the Church and especially to this supreme Apostolic Chair
and to the Vicar of Jesus Christ on earth; they ought to be
men of real piety, of manly virtue, and of a life so chaste
and stainless that they are an efficacious example to all.

If the soul is not thus regulated, not only will it be difficult   29
to stir others to good, but almost impossible to act with a
right intention, and strength will fail for bearing perseveringly
the weariness which every apostolate brings with it, the cal-
umnies of enemies, the coldness and want of help from men
good in themselves, sometimes the jealousy of friends and
fellow-workers, excusable, doubtless, on account of the weakness of human nature, but very harmful, and a cause of discord,
offense and quarrels. Virtue, patient and strong, and at the
same time sweet and tender, is alone able to remove or lessen
these difficulties in such a way that the work to which Catholic energies are devoted may not be compromised. "The will
of God," said St. Peter to the first Christians, "is that by doing
good you may shut the mouths of the foolish": *Sic est voluntas
Dei, ut bene facientes, obmutescere faciatis imprudentiam
hominum ignorantiam.*[7]

It is also necessary to define clearly what are the works on   30
which Catholic strength should be energetically and perseveringly employed. These works must be of such evident importance, must bear such relation to the needs of modern society,

must be so well adapted to moral and material interests, especially those of the people and the poorer classes, that while arousing in promoters of Catholic action the greatest activity for obtaining the important and definite results which are to be looked for, they may also be readily understood and gladly welcomed by all.

31   Just because the grave problems of the social life of the present day demand a prompt and safe solution, every one is keenly desirous to know and understand the various ways in which these solutions are practical. Discussions of one kind or another are becoming more and more numerous, and are readily spread abroad by the press. It is therefore supremely necessary that Catholic activity should seize the opportune moment, should advance courageously, should bring forward its own solution and urge the recognition of it by means of a strong, active, intelligent and well-organized propaganda, so as to be able to confront directly the propaganda of the enemy.

32   The goodness and justice of Christian principles, the strict morality which Catholics profess, their entire disinterestedness in personal matters, the frankness and sincerity with which they seek only the true, solid and highest good of their neighbor; finally, their evident aptitude for promoting, even better than others, the real economic interests of the people—all this cannot fail to make an impression on the mind and heart of all who listen to them, and to swell their ranks in such a way as to form a solid and compact body, capable of vigorously resisting the contrary current, and of commanding the respect of hostile parties.

33   Our Predecessor Leo XIII, of holy memory, fully perceived this, and pointed out, notably in the famous Encyclical *Rerum Novarum*,[8] and in later documents, the object to which Catholic action should be specially devoted, namely, *the practical solution of the social question according to Christian principles.* And We Ourselves, following these wise rules, have, in Our *Motu proprio* of December 18, 1903,[9] given to Christian action for the people, which comprises the whole Catholic social movement, a fundamental constitution to be the practical rule of the common work, and the bound of union and

charity. On the basis, therefore, and with this very holy and very necessary aim, Catholic organizations ought before everything to group and strengthen themselves, various and multiform as they are, but all equally designed to promote efficciously the same social good.

But in order that this social action may continue and prosper   34
with the necessary cohesion of the different works which compose it, it is above all essential that all Catholics should preserve an exemplary harmony among themselves, and this will never be acquired if there is not in all a unity of design. As to the necessity of this, there can be no manner of doubt, so clear and evident are the teachings of this Apostolic Chair; so bright is the light which the most eminent Catholics of all countries have, by their writings, shed on this subject; so praiseworthy is the example, as We have often observed, of the Catholics of other countries, who, precisely by this harmony and unity of plan, have, in a short time, obtained abundant and very consoling results.

To secure this end, it has been stated elsewhere how remark-   35
ably efficient, among various undertakings equally worthy of praise, is an institution of a general character, which, under the the name of *People's Union*, is intended to unite Catholics of all social classes, but especially the great masses of the people, around a single and common center of teaching, propaganda, and social organization.

It meets, in fact, a want felt alike in almost every country;   36
the simplicity of its constitution arises from the very nature of things which are everywhere equally to be found; it cannot be said to suit one nation rather than another, but it is suitable to all which have the same needs and dangers. Its eminently popular character causes it to be readily appreciated and accepted; it does not interfere with, or obstruct, any other institution, but rather gives them strength and cohesion, because its strictly personal organization urges individuals to join special institutions, trains them to practical and really useful work, and unites all minds in a common aim and sentiment.

When once this social center is established, all other insti-   37
tutions of an economic character, designed to solve the social

problem practically in its various forms, find themselves, as it were, spontaneously grouped together for the common end which unites them; and this does not prevent them from taking various forms, and different methods of action, according to divers needs, and each one's special object.

38   And here it gives Us great pleasure to express Our great satisfaction at the great progress already achieved in Italy over this matter, and the confident hope that, with God's help, much more will be done in the future to consolidate the good achieved and to extend it with ever-growing zeal.

39   This line of conduct won the highest praise for the *Association of Catholic Congresses and Committees*, thanks to the intelligent activity of the excellent men who directed it, and who were at the head of its various special branches, or still direct them. That is why, as in virtue of Our own wish, a like center or union of organizations of an economic character has been purposely maintained since the dissolution of the above-mentioned association of Congresses, so too it must act in the future under the wise direction of those in charge of it.

40   Further, in order that Catholic action may be effectual on all points, it is not enough that it be adapted to actual social needs only; it ought also to be invigorated by all the practical methods furnished at the present day by progress in social and economic studies, by experience already gained elsewhere, by the condition of civil society, and even by the public life of States.

41   Otherwise there will be a risk of groping for a long time for new and hazardous things, while good and safe ones are ready on hand, and have been already well tried; or again, there will be the danger of proposing institutions and methods suitable, perhaps, in former times, but not understood by people of the present day; or finally, there will be the danger of stopping half-way by not using, in the measure in which they are granted, those rights of citizenship which modern constitutions offer to all, and therefore also to Catholics.

42   We dwell on this last point, for it is certain that the present constitutions of States offer to all without distinction the power of influencing public opinion, and Catholics, while recognizing the obligations imposed by the law of God and

the precepts of the Church, may with safe conscience enjoy this liberty, and prove themselves capable, as much as, and even more than others, of cooperating in the material and civil well-being of the people, thus acquiring that authority and respect which may even make it possible for them to defend and promote a higher good, namely, that of souls.

These civil rights are many and various, going as far as a   43
direct share in the political life of the country by representing the people in the legislature. Very grave reasons prevent Us, Venerable Brethren, from departing from that rule previously established by Our Predecessor Pius IX, of holy memory, and subsequently observed by Our other Predecessor Leo XIII, of holy memory; according to this rule, it is in general still forbidden for the Catholics of Italy to take part in the legislature.

However, other equally grave reasons, based on the supreme   44
welfare of society, which must be safeguarded at all cost, may cause the law to be dispensed in particular cares, especially when you, Venerable Brethren, consider this stricly necessary for the good of souls and the highest interests of your Churches, and ask for such a dispensation. This makes it incumbent on all Catholics to prepare themselves prudently and seriously for political life in case they should be called to it.

Hence it becomes necessary that this same activity, already   45
so laudably displayed by Catholics in preparing themselves by good electoral organization, for administrative life in parish and county councils, should be extended to a suitable preparation and organization for political life; this was opportunely recommended in the *Circular* issued on December 3, 1904, by the General Presidency of Economic Works in Italy.

At the same time the other principles which rule the con-   46
science of every true Catholic must be inculcated and put in practice. He should remember above all things to be and to show himself, in all circumstances, a true Catholic, undertaking and fulfilling public duties with the firm and constant intention of promoting, as much as he can, the social and economic welfare of his country, especially of the people, according to the maxims of a distinctly Christian civilization, at the same

time defending the supreme interests of the Church, which
are those of religion and justice.

47 Such are the characteristics, aims, and conditions of Catholic action considered in its more important part, namely, the
solution of the social question—a question worthy of the best
energy and perseverance of all Catholic forces.

48 This does not exclude the favoring and promotion of other
works of divers kinds and varied organizations, all equally
aiming at this or that particular good of society and of the
people, and at the revival of Christian civilization under various special aspects.

49 The works arise, for the most part, from the zeal of individuals; they are spread throughout separate dioceses and are
sometimes united in more extended federations. So long as
their object is praiseworthy, their Christian principles firm,
and the means they use are just, so much are they to be praised
and encouraged in every way.

50 A certain freedom of organization should be allowed them,
for it is not possible, when many persons meet together, that
all should be modelled on the same pattern or follow one single
direction. Their organization should spring spontaneously
from the works themselves; otherwise they will be like build-
ings of fine architecture, but without solid foundations, and
therefor quite unstable.

51 It is also necessary to take into account the natural disposition of different populations. Different usages and tendencies
are found in different places. The important thing is to have a
good foundation of solid principles, maintained with earnestness and constancy, and if this be the case, the method and
form of the various works will be only accidental.

52 Lastly, in order to renew and increase in all Catholic undertakings the necessary enthusiasm, to give to their promoters
and members an opportunity of seeing and becoming acquainted with each other, to draw ever more closely the bonds
of brotherly love, to enkindle in one another a more burning
zeal for effective action, and to provide for the better establishment and spread of the same works, a wonderful help will
be found in the meeting, from time to time, according to the
rules already given by the Holy See, of general or local Con-

gresses of Italian Catholics; and these ought to be a solemn manifestation of Catholic faith, and a common festival of harmony and peace.

It remains for Us to treat of another point of the highest 53 importance, namely, the relation which all the works of Catholic action should bear to ecclesiastical authority.

If the teaching unfolded in the first part of this letter be 54 well considered, it will easily be seen that all those works which are immediately in conjunction with the spiritual and pastoral ministry of the Church, and which have a religious aim intended directly for the good of souls, should submit in every smallest particular to the authority of the Church and to that of the bishops, who are appointed by the Holy Spirit to rule the Church of God in the dioceses assigned to them.

But those other works also, which, as We have said, are 55 designed chiefly to restore and promote in Christ true Christian civilization, and which constitute Catholic action in the sense explained, must by no means be considered independent of the advice and direction of ecclesiastical authority, inasmuch, especially, as they must all be conformed to the principles of Christian faith and morality; still less is it possible to imagine them in opposition, more or less open, to the same power.

It is certain that such works, from their very nature, ought 56 to move with a befitting and reasonable freedom, since they are held responsible for their acts, particularly in temporal and economic matters, and in those of public, administrative, or political life, all of which are foreign to a purely spiritual ministry. But as Catholics ever bear aloft the standard of Christ, for that very reason they bear aloft the standard of the Church; and so it is proper that they should receive it from the hands of the Church; that the Church should see that its honor is unstained; and that Catholics should submit, like docile, loving children, to this maternal vigilance.

Whence it is manifest how ill-advised were those, few indeed, 57 who, here in Italy and before Our very eyes, sought to take upon themselves a mission which they had received neither from Us, nor from any of Our brethren in the Episcopate, and set out to act upon it not only without the respect which is due to authority, but even by going openly against her wishes, seeking to render their disobedience lawful by futile distinctions. They said that they were raising aloft a banner in the name of Christ. But such a banner could not be Christ's, since it did not bear upon its folds the doctrine of the Divine Redeemer, which is most revelant to this matter. "He that heareth you heareth Me; and he that despiseth you despiseth Me"[10]; "he that is not with Me is against Me; and he that gathereth not with Me, scattereth;[11] a doctrine, therefore, of humility, submission and filial respect.

58   With extreme bitterness of heart, We were obliged to condemn such a tendency and to put an authoritative stop to the pernicious movement which was already emerging. And Our sorrow was all the greater because We saw a considerable number of young people who are very dear to Us, and many of whom have outstanding intelligence and ardent zeal, and are capable of achieving much good if properly directed.

59   While, however, We point out to all the right rule of Catholic action, We cannot disguise the no small danger to which the clergy of the present day are exposed; it is that of attaching an excessive importance to the material interest of the people, forgetting the much more serious ones of their sacred ministry.

60   The priest, raised higher than other men to fulfill the mission he has received from God, ought to keep himself equally above all human interests, all disputes, all classes of society. His proper field of action is the Church, where, as ambassador of God, he preaches the truth, and inculcates along with respect for the rights of God, respect also for the rights of every creature. Acting thus, he does not expose himself to opposition; he does not appear as a party man, supporting one side and going against another; nor, for the sake of avoiding collision with certain tendencies, and of not irritating by argument minds already embittered, does he put himself in danger of disguising the truth, or of suppressing it, which in both cases would be to fail in his duty; nor is it necessary to remark that having very often to treat of material things, he might find himself involved in responsible liabilities, hurtful alike to his person and to the dignity of the ministry. He ought not, there-

fore, to join an association of this kind except after mature consideration, with the approval of his bishop, and in those cases only where his assistance is safe from all danger and is evidently useful.

Nor does this in any way diminish his zeal. The true apostle   61
ought "to become all things to all men, to save all"[12]: like Our Divine Redeemer, he ought to be moved with compassion, "seeing the multitudes distressed, lying like sheep that have no shepherd."[13]

Let then each one strive by the efficacious propaganda of   62
the press, by the living exhortation of the spoken word, by direct help in the above-mentioned cases, to ameliorate, within the limits of justice and charity, the economic conditon of the people, supporting and promoting those institutions which conduce to this end, and those especially which aim at fortifying the multitude against the invasion of Socialism; thus to save them at once from economic ruin and from moral and religious destruction. In this way the cooperation of the clergy in the works of Catholic action has a deeply religious end; it will never become a hindrance, but will be a help to their spiritual ministry by enlarging its sphere and multiplying its fruits.

You see, Venerable Brethren, how anxious We have been   63
to explain and inculcate the manner in which Catholic action is to be supported and promoted in this Italy of ours.

It is not sufficient to point out what is good; it must be   64
put into practice. This will be very much helped by your exhortations, and by your paternal and immediate encouragement to well-doing. Beginnings may be very small, but provided we really do begin, Divine Grace will soon cause them to grow and prosper. And let all Our beloved sons, who are devoting themselves to Catholic action, listen again to the words which spring so spontaneously from Our heart. Amid the bitter sorrows which daily surround Us, We will say, with the Apostle St. Paul[14]: if there be any consolation in Christ, if any comfort comes to us from your charity, if any society of spirit, if any bowels of commiseration; fulfill ye Our joy, that you be of one mind, having the same charity, being of one accord, agreeing in sentiment, with humility and due submission, not

seeking one's own convenience, but the common good, and imprinting on your hearts the mind which was in Christ Jesus, our Savior. Let Him be the beginning of all your undertakings: "All whatsoever you do in word or in work all things do ye in the name of the Lord Jesus Christ,"[15] let Him be the end of your every word: "For of Him, and by Him, and in Him are all things: to Him be glory for ever."[16]

65   On this most happy day which recalls the moment when the Apostles, filled with the Holy Spirit, left the Cenacle to preach to the world the Kingdom of Christ, may the strength of the same Spirit descend likewise upon you all. May He soften all hardness, may He bring warmth to cold hearts and may He lead back to the right path all who have strayed: *Flecte quod est rigidum, fove quod est frigidum, rege quod est devium.*[17]

HAERENT ANIMO
Selection from Exhortation of Pope Pius X
to the Catholic Clergy
on Priestly Sanctity
August 4, 1908

Deeply imprinted upon our mind are those dread words which the Apostle of the gentiles wrote to the Hebrews to remind them of the obedience which they owed to their superiors: *They keep watch as having to render an account of your souls.*[1]

These grave words apply, no doubt, to all who have author- 67 ity in the Church, but they apply in a special way to us who, despite our unworthiness, by the grace of God exercise supreme power within the Church. Therefore, with unceasing solicitude, our thoughts and endeavours are constantly directed to the promotion of the well-being and growth of the flock of the Lord.

Our first chief concern is that all who are invested with 68 the priestly ministry should be in every way fitted for the discharge of their responsibilities. For we are fully convinced that it is here that hope lies for the welfare and progress of religious life.

Hence it is that, ever since our elevation to the office of 69 supreme Pontiff, we have felt it a duty, notwithstanding the manifest and numerous proofs of the high quality of the clergy as a whole, to urge with all earnestness our venerable brethren the bishops of the whole catholic world, to devote themselves unceasingly and efficaciously to the formation of Christ in those who, by their calling, have the responsibility of forming Christ in others.[2]

70   We are well aware of the eagerness with which the episcopate have carried out this task. We know the watchful care and unwearied energy with which they seek to form the clergy in the ways of virtue, and for this we wish not so much to praise them as to render them public thanks.

71   But though it is a matter for congratulation that, as a result of the diligence of the bishops, so many priests are animated by heavenly fervour to rekindle or strengthen in their souls the flame of divine grace which they received by the imposition of hands, we must deplore the fact that there are others in different countries who do not show themselves worthy to be taken as models by the christian people who rightly look to them for a genuine model of christian virtue.

72   It is to these priests that we wish to open our heart in this Letter; it is a father's loving heart which beats anxiously as he looks upon an ailing child. Our love for them inspires us to add our own appeal to the appeals of their own bishops. And while our appeal is intended above all to recall the erring to the right path and to spur the lukewarm to fresh endeavor, we would wish it to serve as an encouragement to others also. We point out the path which each one must strive to follow with constantly growing fervour, so that he may become truly a *man of God,*[3] as the Apostle so concisely expresses it, and fulfil the legitimate expectations of the Church.

73   We have nothing to say which you have not already heard, no doctrine to propound that is new to anyone; but we treat of matters which it is necessary for everyone to bear in mind, and God inspires us with the hope that our message will not fail to bear abundant fruit.

74   Our earnest appeal to you is this: *Be renewed in the spirit of your mind, and put on the new man, who according to God is created in justice and sanctity of truth;*[4] that will be the most excellent and most acceptable gift which you could offer to us on this fiftieth anniversary of our ordination.

75   For our own part, when we review before God *with a contrite heart and in a spirit of humility*[5] the years passed in the priesthood, we will feel that we are making reparation in some measure for the human frailties which we have cause to

regret, by thus admonishing and exhorting you to *walk worthily of God, in all things pleasing.*[6]

In this exhortation, it is not your personal welfare alone that   76
we are striving to secure, but the common welfare of catholic
peoples; the one cannot be separated from the other. For the
priest cannot be good or bad for himself alone; his conduct
and way of life have far-reaching consequences for the people. A truly good priest is an immense gift wherever he may
be.

I. The Obligation of Priestly Sanctity

Therefore, beloved sons, we will begin this exhortation by   77
stimulating you to that sanctity of life which the dignity of
your office demands.

Anyone who exercises the priestly ministry exercises it not   78
for himself alone, but for others. For every high priest taken
from among men is appointed for men in the things that pertain to God.[7] Christ himself taught that lesson when he compared the priest to salt and to light, in order to show the nature of the priestly ministry. The priest then is the light of
the world and the salt of the earth. Everyone knows that he
fulfils this function chiefly by the teaching of christian truth;
and who can be unaware that this ministry of teaching is
practically useless if the priest fails to confirm by the example of his life the truths which he teaches? Those who hear
him might say, insultingly it is true, but not without justification: *They profess that they know God but in their works
they deny him;*[8] they will refuse to accept his teaching and
will derive no benefit from the light of the priest.

Christ himself, the model of priests, taught first by example   79
of his deeds and then by his words: *Jesus began to do and
then to teach.*[9]

Likewise, a priest who neglects his own sanctification can   80
never be the salt of the earth; what is corrupt and contaminated is utterly incapable of preserving from corruption;
where sanctity is lacking, there corruption will inevitably find
its way. Hence Christ, continuing this comparison, calls such

priests salt that has lost its savour, *which is good for nothing any more, but to be cast out and to be trodden on by men.*[10]

81   These truths are all the more evident inasmuch as we exercise the priestly ministry not in our own name, but in the name of Jesus Christ. The Apostle said: *Let man so consider us as the ministers of Christ and the dispensers of the mysteries of God;*[11] *for Christ, therefore, we are ambassadors.*[12] This is the reason that Christ has numbered us not among his servants but as his friends. *I will not now call you servants; ... but I have called you friends, because all things whatsoever I have heard from my Father I have made known to you; ... I have chosen you and appointed you that you should go and bring forth fruit.*[13]

82   We have, therefore, to take the place of Christ: the mission which he has given to us we must fulfill with that same purpose that he intended. True friendship consists in unity of mind and will, identity of likes and dislikes; therefore, as friends of Jesus Christ, we are bound to have that mind in us which was in Jesus Christ who is *holy, innocent, undefiled.*[14] As his envoys, we must win the minds of men for his doctrine and his law by first observing them ourselves; sharing as we do in his power to deliver souls from the bondage of sin, we must strive by every means to avoid becoming entangled in these toils of sin.

83   But it is particularly as the ministers of Jesus Christ in the great sacrifice which is constantly renewed with abiding power for the salvation of the world, that we have the duty of conforming our minds to that spirit in which he offered himself as an unspotted victim to God on the altar of the Cross. In the Old Law, though victims were only shadowy figures and symbols, sanctity of a high degree was demanded of the priest; what then of us, now that the victim is Christ himself? "How pure should not he be who shares in this sacrifice! More resplendent than the sun must be the hand that divides this Flesh, the mouth that is filled with spiritual fire, the tongue that is reddened by this Blood!"[15]

84   Saint Charles Borromeo gave apt expression to this thought when, in his discourses to the clergy, he declared: "If we would only bear in mind, dearly beloved brethren, the exalted

character of the things that the Lord God has placed in our hands, what unbounded influence would not this have in impelling us to lead lives worthy of ecclesiastics! Has not the Lord placed everything in my hand, when he put there his only-begotten Son, coeternal and coequal with himself? In my hand he has placed all his treasures, his sacraments, his graces; he has placed there souls, than whom nothing can be dearer to him; in his love he has preferred them to himself, and redeemed them by his Blood; he has placed heaven in my hand, and it is in my power to open and close it to others ... How, then, can I be so ungrateful for such condescension and love as to sin against him, to offend his honour, to pollute this body which is his? How can I come to defile this high dignity, this life consecrated to his service?"

It is well to speak at greater length on this holiness of life, 85 which is the object of the unfailing solicitude of the Church. This is the purpose for which seminaries have been founded; within their walls young men who hope to be priests are trained in letters and other branches of learning, but even more important is the training in piety which they also receive there from their tender years. And then, when the Church gradually and at long intervals promotes candidates to Orders, like a watchful parent she never fails to exhort them to sanctity.

It is a source of joy to recall her words on these occasions. 86

When we were first enrolled in the army of the Church, she 87 sought from us the formal declaration: *The Lord is the portion of my inheritance and of my cup: it is thou that wilt restore my inheritance to me.*[16] St. Jerome tells us that with these words "the cleric is reminded that one who is the portion of the Lord, or who has the Lord as his portion, must show himself to be such a one as possesses the Lord and is possessed by him."[17]

How solemnly the Church addresses those who are about 88 to be promoted sub-deacons! "You must consider repeatedly and with all attention the office which of your own volition you see today ... if you receive this Order, you cannot afterwards revoke your decision, you must remain always in the service of God and, with his help, observe chastity." And finally: "If up to now you have been negligent in relation to the Church, henceforth you must be diligent; if hitherto you have been somnolent, henceforth you must be vigilant . . . if up to now your life has been unseemly, henceforth you must be chaste; . . . Consider the ministry which is entrusted to you!"

89   For those who are about to be raised to the diaconate, the Church prays to God through the mouth of the bishop: "May they have in abundance the pattern of every virtue, authority that is unassuming, constancy in chastity, the purity of innocence, and the observance of spiritual discipline. May thy commands shine forth through their conduct, and may the people find a saintly model in their exemplary chastity."

90   The admonition addressed to those who are about to be ordained priests is even more moving: "It is with great fear that one must approach this high dignity, and care must be taken that those chosen for it are recommended by heavenly wisdom, blameless life and sustained observance of justice . . . Let the fragrance of your life be a joy to the Church of Christ, so that by your preaching and example you may build up the house, that is, the family of God." Above all the Church stresses the solemn words: *Imitate that which you handle,* an injunction which fully agrees with the command of St. Paul: *That we may present every man perfect in Jesus Chirst.*[18]

91   Since this is the mind of the Church on the life of a priest, one cannot be surprised at the complete unanimity of the Fathers and Doctors on this matter; it might indeed be thought that they are guilty of exaggeration, but a careful examination will lead to the conclusion that they taught nothing that was not entirely true and correct. Their teaching can be summarized thus: there should be as much difference between the priest and any other upright man as there is between heaven and earth; consequently, the priest must see to it that his life is free not merely from grave faults but even from the slightest faults.[19] The Council of Trent made the teaching of these venerable men its own when it warned clerics to avoid "even venial faults which in their case would be very grave."[20] These faults are grave, not in themselves, but in relation to the one

who commits them; for to him, even more than to the sacred
edifice, are applicable the words: *Holiness becometh thy
house.*[21]

II. Nature of Priestly Holiness

We must now consider what is the nature of this sanctity,   92
which the priest cannot lack without being culpable; ignorance
or misunderstanding of it leaves one exposed to grave peril.

There are some who think, and even declare openly, that   93
the true measure of the merits of a priest is his dedication to
the service of others; consequently, with an almost complete
disregard for the cultivation of the virtues which lead to the
personal sanctification of the priest (these they describe as
passive virtues), they assert that all his energies and fervour
should be directed to the development and practice of what
they call the *active* virtues. One can only be astonished by
this gravely erroneous and pernicious teaching.

Our predecessor of happy memory in his wisdom spoke as   94
follows of this teaching:[22] "To maintain that some christian
virtues are more suited to one period than to another is to
forget the words of the Apostle: *Those whom he foreknew he
also predestined to be conformed to the image of his Son.*[23]
Chirst is the teacher and the model of all sanctity; all who desire to take their place in the abode of the blessed must adapt
their conduct to the standard which he has laid down. Now
Christ does not change with the passing of the centuries: *He
is the same yesterday and today and forever.*[24] The words:
Learn of me because I am meek and humble of heart,[25] apply
to men of every age; at all times Christ reveals himself *obedi-
dent unto death;*[26] true for every age are the words of the
Apostle: *They that are Christ's have crucified the flesh, with
the vices and concupiscences.*"[27]

These passages apply, no doubt, to all the faithful, but   95
they apply more especially to priests. Let priests take as directed particularly to themselves the further words which were
spoken by our predecessor in his apostolic zeal: "Would that
at the present day there were many more who cultivated these
virtues as did the saints of former times, who by their humility,

their obedience, their abstinence, were mighty in work and word, to the great benefit not only of religion but also of public and civil life."[28]

96   It is not irrelevant to note here that Leo XIII in his wisdom made special mention of the virtue of abstinence, which we call self-denial, in the words of the Gospel. He was quite right to do so, for it is from self-denial chiefly that the strength and power and fruit of every priestly function derive; it is when this virtue is neglected that there appears in the priest's conduct whatever may be of a nature to cause offence to the eyes and hearts of the faithful. If one acts for the sake of filthy lucre, or becomes involved in worldly affairs,[29] or seeks for the highest places and despises others, or follows merely human counsel, or seeks to please men, or trusts in the persuasive words of human wisdom, this is the result of neglect of the command of Christ and of the refusal to accept the condition laid down by him: *If anyone will come after me, let him deny himself.*[30]

97   While insisting on these truths, we would likewise admonish the priest that in the last analysis, it is not for himself alone that he has to sanctify himself, for he is the workman whom Christ *went out . . . to hire into his vineyard.*[31] Therefore, it is his duty to uproot unfruitful plants and to sow useful ones, to water the crop and to guard lest the enemy sow cockle among it. Consequently, the priest must be careful not to allow an unbalanced concern for personal perfection to lead him to overlook any part of the duties of his office which are conducive to the welfare of others. These duties include the preaching of the word of God, the hearing of confessons, assisting the sick, especially the dying, the instruction of those who are ignorant of the faith, the consolation of the sorrowing, leading back the erring, in a word, the imitation in every respect of Christ *who went about doing good and healing all that were oppressed by the devil.*[32]

98   In the midst of all these duties, the priest shall have ever present to his mind the striking admonition given by St. Paul: *Neither he who plants is anything, nor he who waters, but God who gives the increase.*[33] it may be that we go and sow the seed with tears; it may be that we tend its growth at the

cost of heavy labour; but to make it germinate and yield the
hoped for fruit, that depends on God alone and his powerful
assistance. This further point also is worthy of profound consideration, namely that men are but the instruments whom
God employs for the salvation of souls; they must, therefore,
be instruments fit to be employed by God. And how is this
to be achieved? Do we image that God is influenced by any
inborn or acquired excellence of ours, to make use of our
help for the extension of his glory; By no means; for it is
written: *God has chosen the foolish things of the world to
confound the wise, and the weak things of the world God has
chosen to counfound the strong, and the humble and con-
temptible things of the world God has chosen, the things that
are not, in order to bring to nought the things that are.*[34]

There is, indeed, only one thing that unites man to God,   99
one thing that makes him pleasing to God and not a unworthy
dispenser of his mercy; and that one thing is holiness of life
and conduct. If this holiness, which is the true supereminent
knowledge of Jesus Christ, is wanting in the priest, then
everything is wanting. Without this, even the resources of profound learning (which we strive to promote among the clergy),
or exceptional competence in practical affairs, though they
may bring some benefit to the Church or to individuals, are
not infrequently the cause of deplorable damage to them.

On the other hand, there is abundant evidence from every   100
age that even the humblest priest, provided his life has the
adornment of overflowing sanctity, can undertake and accomplish marvellous works for the spiritual welfare of the people
of God; an outstanding example in recent times is John Baptist Vianne, a model pastor of souls, to whom we are happy
to have decreed the honours of the Blessed in heaven.[35]

Sanctity alone makes us what our divine vocation demands,   101
men crucified to the world and to whom the world has been
crucified, men walking in newness of life who, in the words
of St. Paul, show themselves as ministers of God *in labours,
in vigils, in fasting, in chastity, in knowledge, in long-suffering,
in kindness, in the Holy Spirit, in sincere charity, in the
word of truth;*[36] men who seek only heavenly things and
strive by every means to lead others to them.

Letter of Pope Pius XI
to Cardinal Bertram
on the Origins of Catholic Action
November 13, 1928

To tell the truth, We are dealing with activity which was not unknown in apostolic times. In his Epistle to the Philippians, St. Paul indeed mentions "his fellow laborers" and his desire that help should be given to "those women who have labored with me in the Gospel."[1] But in our own time especially, when the integrity of faith and morals is more seriously threatened each day, and the lack of priests, to Our great sorrow, renders the clergy absolutely unable to meet the needs of souls, more reliance must be placed upon Catholic Action; it will help the priests and will make up for their small numbers by multiplying their helpers among the laity. The idea of furthering the Catholic cause in this way has been urged and put into practice by Our Predecessors; they even succeeded in achieving this object when, in the midst of the most terrible circumstances for the Church and for humanity, they "sounded the call to arms" exhorting all the faithful most strongly to fight the good fight, under the direction of their Bishops, and to devote themselves according to their ability to the eternal salvation of their neighbor.[2]

103   We Ourselves, from the beginning of Our Pontificate, have been no less anxious to promote Catholic Action. Already in the Encyclical *Ubi arcano*,[3] We clearly affirmed that it cannot in any way be separated from the pastoral ministry and from the Christian life. Since then, on several occasions, We have defined with ever greater care its nature and purposes. The

latter, if well considered, show that Catholic Action has no other purpose than the participation of the laity in the apostolate of the hierarchy.

Catholic Action, indeed, does not simply consist in the application of each individual to his own Christian perfection, although this is the first and principal purpose; it is also a true apostolate, shared in by Catholics of all classes who unite themselves in thought and action to centers of sound doctrine and multifarious social activity, legitimately set up and in consequence assisted and supported by the authority of the Bishops. Thus grouped and gathered together under the direction of the ecclesiastical hierarchy, the Catholic elite receives therefrom not only a mandate, but also impetus and encouragement.[4] Also, like the mandate entrusted to the Church by God, and like the apostolate of the hierarchy itself, this Catholic Action is spiritual, not temporal, supernatural, not of this world, religious, not political.

104

However, it deserves no less because of this to be called social action; for its purpose is precisely to extend the kingdom of Christ and by this extension to procure for society the greatest of all benefits, from which all others spring, that is to say all those which concern the organization of a nation and which are termed political, benefits which are not the personal property of individuals but the common possession of all citizens. All this, Catholic Action can and must achieve, if it obeys with docility the laws of God and the Church, avoiding entirely the preoccupations of political parties. Animated and upheld by this spirit, those Catholics who participate in the apostolate of the hierarchy cannot fail to achieve their most immediate purpose, which is to promote the union of the faithful of all nations in religious and moral questions, and most important, to spread widely the principles of Christian faith and teaching, to defend them and to cause them to prevail more fully in public and private life.

105

Catholic Action must indeed be the universal and concerted action of all Catholics, regardless of age, sex, condition and culture, without distincition of race or party, provided that these latter do not depart in any way from the teaching of the Gospel and Christian law, and do not lead their adherents

106

to renounce that teaching and law; in short, action which embraces the whole man, in his private as well as his public life, by assuring him a better religious and civic formation, that is to say, solid piety, deep knowledge of religious truth, perfect integrity in life, all virtues without which the apostolate of the hierarchy cannot be fruitfully exercised.

107   From this it is easy to understand that, in practice, Catholic Action must adapt itself to difference of age, sex, and circumstances of time and place, but always in such a way that the young people's organizations concentrate on the work of formation and preparation for their future labors, while those already mature dedicate themselves generously to the apostolate in a broader field, without excluding or neglecting any form of good works, provided that they are in keeping with the divine mission of the Church.

108   Does this mean that Catholic Action constitutes an exclusive and special form of activity? On the contrary, it utilizes and directs towards the social apostolate all organizations, especially those of a religious nature, whether they specialize in the education of youth and in the furthering of Christian piety, or whether their purposes are social and economic. Moreover, by that wise allocation of works and deployment of forces which procures for Catholic Action its harmony and unity of direction and which governs the various elements of the whole—associations of men, women, boys and girls,—that same Catholic Action will derive benefit from the religious or economic associations, and at the same time will not fail to afford them support and ensure their progress; for among them all, it maintains mutual good will and guarantees cordial relations between them; it encourages mutual collaboration to the great advantage of the Church and human society, as is quite evident to all.

109   To obtain this purpose, which is above all moral and religious, Catholic Action does not forbid its members to participate as fully as possible in public life; on the contrary, it will render them better fitted to fill public offices, thanks to strict training in holiness of life and the fulfillment of the duties of Christians. It is not destined to provide society with its best

citizens, and the State with its most upright and skillful magistrates?

Who then would dare to assert that it betrays the true inter- 110
ests of the nation, interests which cannot in any case prevail outside the domain of Christian charity, to which it belongs to promote public welfare in all its forms? Does not Catholic Action contribute to this welfare, which is the primary purpose of civil society, by ordering its members to respect lawful authority and to obey the law, to maintain and defend the foundations of the happiness and salvation of nations, namely, the integrity of morals, the purity of family life, the harmony and unity of the social classes, in a word, all that can help to guarantee peace and security for society?

Catholic Action will obtain all this, all the more surely if it 111
remains aloof, as We have said, from the interests of parties, even those formed by Catholics—who are not forbidden to differ in controversial questions left open to free discussion— and if it conforms more faithfully to the instructions and advice of the hierarchy, even if these regulations should be opposed in reality or in appearance, to the discipline and particular interests of parties.

From all that We have said up to the present, dear children, 112
it becomes clear that Catholic Action rightly deserves to be considered as a means by which the Church can bestow upon the nations benefits of all kinds: a means which seems to be given by God in His wisdom and goodness to enable the Church to draw and lead to the teaching and law of the Gospel those who, because they lack any contact or link with the priest, might easily fall into the evil snares and traps of seditious men.

Such are the principles and general foundations of all 113
forms of Catholic Action, although different effects will flow from one and the same cause, according to the different genius and circumstances of nations. It is therefore clear that Catholic Action deserves the support not only of Bishops and priests—who know quite well that it is the apple of Our eye— but also of the heads and rulers of every State. If it comes to enjoy everywhere such support, it will certainly bring a won-

derful abundance of benefits upon the Catholic nations; but everywhere too, by reawakening souls to the Faith, it will greatly contribute to civil prosperity. That is precisely what We desire so fervently to see realized.

AD CATHOLICI SACERDOTII
Selection from Encyclical Letter of Pope Pius XI
on the Catholic Priesthood
December 20, 1935

I

The human race has always felt the need of a priesthood: of men, that is, who have the official charge to be mediators between God and humanity, men who should consecrate themselves entirely to this mediation, as to the very purpose of their lives, men set aside to offer to God public prayers and sacrifices in the name of human society. For human society as such is bound to offer to God public and social worship. It is bound to acknowledge in Him its Supreme Lord and first beginning, and to strive toward Him as to its last end, to give Him thanks and offer Him propitiation. In fact, priests are to be found among all peoples whose customs are known, except those compelled by violence to act against the most sacred laws of human nature. They may, indeed, be in the service of false divinities; but wherever religion is professed, wherever altars are built, there also is a priesthood surrounded by particular marks of honor and veneration.

Yet in the splendor of Divine Revelation the priest is seen invested with a dignity far greater still. This dignity was foreshadowed of old by the venerable and mysterious figure of Melchisedech, Priest and King, whom St. Paul recalls as prefiguring the Person and Priesthood of Christ Our Lord Himself.

115

116   The priest, according to the magnificent definition given
by St. Paul is indeed a man *Ex hominibus assumptus*, "taken
from amongst men," yet *pro hominibus constituitur in his
quae sunt ad Deum*, "ordained for men in the things that
appertain to God": his office is not for human things, and
things that pass away, however lofty and valuable these may
seem; but for things divine and enduring. These eternal things
may, perhaps, through ignorance, be scorned and contemned,
or even attacked with diabolical fury and malice, as sad experience has often proved, and proves even today; but they
always continue to hold the first place in the aspirations,
individual and social, of humanity, because the human heart
feels irresistibly it is made for God and is restless till it rests
in Him.

117   The Old Law, inspired by God and promulgated by Moses,
set up a priesthood, which was, in this manner, of divine institution; and determined for it every detail of its duty,
residence and rite. It would seem that God, in His great care
for them, wished to impress upon the still primitive mind of
the Jewish people one great central idea. This idea throughout
the history of the chosen people, was to shed its light over all
events, laws, ranks and offices: the idea of sacrifice and
priesthood. These were to become, through faith in the
future Messias, a source of hope, glory, power and spiritual
liberation. The temple of Solomon, astonishing in richness
and splendor, was still more wonderful in its rites and ordinances. Erected to the one true God as a tabernacle of the
divine Majesty upon earth, it was also a sublime poem sung to
that sacrifice and that priesthood, which, though type and
symbol, was still so august, that the sacred figure of its High
Priest moved the conqueror Alexander the Great, to bow in
reverence; and God Himself visited His wrath upon the im-
pious king Balthasar because he made revel with the sacred
vessels of the temple. Yet that ancient priesthood derived its
greatest majesty and glory from being a foretype of the Christian priesthood; the priesthood of the New and eternal
Covenant sealed with the Blood of the Redeemer of the
world, Jesus Christ, true God and true Man.

The Apostle of the Gentiles thus perfectly sums up what   **118**
may be said of the greatness, the dignity and the duty of the
Christian priesthood: *Sic nos existimet homo ut ministros
Christi et dispensatores mysteriorum Dei*—"Let a man so
account of us as of the ministers of Christ and the dispensers
of the mysteries of God." The priest is the minister of Christ,
an instrument, that is to say, in the hands of the Divine
Redeemer. He continues the work of the Redemption in all
its world-embracing universality and divine efficacy, that
work that wrought so marvellous a transformation in the
world. Thus the priest, as is said with good reason, is indeed
"another Christ"; for, in some way, he is himself a continuation of Christ. "As the Father hath sent Me, I also send you,"
is spoken to the priest, and hence the priest, like Christ,
continues to give "glory to God in the highest and on earth
peace to men of good will."

For in the first place, as the Council of Trent teaches,   **119**
Jesus Christ at the Last Supper instituted the Sacrifice and
the priesthood of the New Covenant: "our Lord and God,
although once and for all, by means of His death on the altar
of the cross, He was to offer Himself to God the Father, that
thereon He might accomplish eternal Redemption; yet, because death was not to put an end to His priesthood, at the
Last Supper, the same night in which He was betrayed, in
order to leave to His beloved spouse the Church, a sacrifice
which should be visible (as the nature of man requires),
which should represent that bloody sacrifice, once and for all
to be completed on the cross, which should perpetuate His
memory to the end of time, and which should apply its saving
power unto the remission of the sins we daily commit, showing Himself made a priest forever according to the order of
Melchisedech, offered to God the Father, under the appearance of bread and wine, His Body and Blood, giving them to
the Apostles (whom He was then making priests of the New
Covenant) to be consumed under the signs of these same
things, and commanded the Apostles and their successors in
the priesthood to offer them, by the words 'Do this in com-
memoration of Me.' "

120   And thenceforth, the Apostles, and their successors in the priesthood, began to lift to heaven that "clean oblation" foretold by Malachy, through which the name of God is great among the gentiles. And now, that same oblation in every part of the world and at every hour of the day and night, is offered and will continue to be offered without interruption till the end of time: a true sacrificial act, not merely symbolical, which has a real efficacy unto the reconciliation of sinners with the Divine Majesty.

121   "Appeased by this oblation, the Lord grants grace and the gift of repentance, and forgives iniquities and sins, however great." The reason of this is given by the same Council in these words: "For there is one and the same Victim, there is present the same Christ who once offered Himself upon the Cross, who now offers Himself by the ministry of priests, only the manner of the offering being different."

122   And thus the ineffable greatness of the human priest stands forth in all its splendor; for he has power over the very Body of Jesus Christ, and makes It present upon our altars. In the name of Christ Himself he offers It a victim infinitely pleasing to the Divine Majesty. "Wondrous things are these," justly exclaims St. John Chrysostom, "so wonderful, they surpass wonder."

123   Besides this power over the real Body of Christ, the priest has received other powers, august and sublime, over His Mystical Body. There is no need, My Venerable Brethren, to enlarge upon the beautiful doctrine of the Mystical Body of Christ, a doctrine so dear to St. Paul; this beautiful doctrine that shows us the Person of the Word-made-Flesh in union with all His brethren. For from Him to them comes a supernatural influence, so that they, with Him as Head, form a single Body of which they are the members. Now a priest is the appointed "dispenser of the mysteries of God," for the benefit of the members of the Mystical Body of Christ; since he is the ordinary minister of nearly all the Sacraments,— those channels through which the grace of the Saviour flows for the good of humanity. The Christian, at almost every important stage of his mortal career, finds at his side the priest with power received from God, in the act of communi-

cating or increasing that grace which is the supernatural life of his soul.

Scarcely is he born before the priest baptizing him, brings   124
him by a new birth to a more noble and precious life, a supernatural life, and makes him a son of God and of the Church of Jesus Christ. To strengthen him to fight bravely in spiritual combats, a priest invested with special dignity makes him a soldier of Christ by holy chrism. Then, as soon as he is able to recognize and value the Bread of Angels, the priest gives It to him, the living and life-giving Food come down from Heaven. If he fall, the priest raises him up again in the name of God, and reconciles him to God with the Sacrament of Penance. Again, if he is called by God to found a family and to collaborate with Him in the transmission of human life throughout the world, thus increasing the number of the faithful on earth and, thereafter, the ranks of the elect in Heaven, the priest is there to bless his espousals and unblemished love; and when, finally, arrived at the portals of eternity, the Christian feels the need of strength and courage before presenting himself at the tribunal of the Divine Judge, the priest with the holy oils anoints the failing members of the sick or dying Christian, and reconsecrates and comforts him.

Thus the priest accompanies the Christian throughout the   125
pilgrimage of this life to the gates of Heaven. He accompanies the body to its resting place in the grave with rites and prayers of immortal hope. And even beyond the threshold of eternity he follows the soul to aid it with Christian suffrages, if need there be of further purification and alleviation. Thus, from the cradle to the grave the priest is ever beside the faithful, a guide, a solace, a minister of salvation and dispenser of grace and blessing.

But among all these powers of the priest over the Mystical   126
Body of Christ for the benefit of the faithful, there is one of which the simple mention made above will not content Us. This is that power which, as St. John Chrysostom says: "God gave neither to Angels nor Archangels"—the power to remit sins. "Whose sins you shall forgive they are forgiven them: and whose sins you shall retain they are retained"; a tremendous power, so peculiar to God that even human pride could

not make the mind conceive that it could be given to man. "Who can forgive sins but God alone?" And, when we see it exercised by a mere man there is reason to ask ourselves, not, indeed, with pharisaical scandal, but with reverent surprise at such a dignity: "Who is this that forgiveth sins also?" But it is so: the God-Man who possessed the "power on earth to forgive sins" willed to hand it on to His priests; to relieve, in His divine generosity and mercy, the need of moral purification which is rooted in the human heart.

127   What a comfort to the guilty, when, stung with remorse and repenting of his sins, he hears the word of the priest who says to him in God's name: "I absolve thee from thy sins!" These words fall, it is true, from the lips of one who, in his turn, must needs beg the same absolution from another priest. This does not debase the merciful gift; but makes it, rather, appear greater; since beyond the weak creature is seen more clearly the hand of God through whose power is wrought this wonder. As an illustrious layman has written, treating with rare competence of spiritual things: ". . . when a priest, groaning in spirit at his own unworthiness and at the loftiness of his office, places his consecrated hands upon our heads; when, humiliated at finding himself the dispenser of the Blood of the Covenant; each time amazed as he pronounces the words that give life; when a sinner has absolved a sinner; we, who rise from our knees before him, feel we have done nothing debasing. . . . We have been at the feet of a man who represented Jesus Christ, . . . we have been there to receive the dignity of free men and of sons of God."

128   These august powers are conferred upon the priest in a special Sacrament designed to this end: they are not merely passing or temporary in the priest, but are stable and perpetual, united as they are with the indelible character imprinted on his soul whereby he becomes "a priest forever"; whereby he becomes like unto Him in whose eternal priesthood he has been made a sharer. Even the most lamentable downfall, which, through human frailty, is possible to a priest, can never blot out from his soul the priestly character. But along with this character and these powers, the priest through the Sacrament of Orders receives new and special grace with

special helps. Thereby, if only he will loyally further, by his free and personal cooperation, the divinely powerful action of the grace itself, he will be able worthily to fulfill all the duties, however arduous, of his lofty calling. He will not be overborne, but will be able to bear the tremendous responsibilities inherent to his priestly duty; responsibilities which have made fearful even the stoutest champions of the Christian priesthood, men like St. John Chrysostom, St. Ambrose, St. Gregory the Great, St. Charles and many others.

The Catholic priest is minister of Christ and dispenser of the mysteries of God in another way, that is, by his words. The "ministry of the word" is a right which is inalienable; it is a duty which cannot be disallowed; for it is imposed by Jesus Christ Himself: "Going, therefore, teach ye all nations . . . teaching them to observe all things whatsoever I have commanded you." The Church of Christ, depository and infallible guardian of divine revelation, by means of her priests, pours out the treasures of heavenly truth; she preaches Him who is "the true Light which enlighteneth every man that cometh into this world"; she sows with divine bounty that seed which is small and worthless to the profane eyes of the world, but which is like the mustard seed of the Gospel. For it has within itself power to strike strong deep roots in souls which are sincere and thirsting for the truth, and make them like sturdy trees able to withstand the wildest storms. 129

Amidst all the aberrations of human thought, infatuated by a false emancipation from every law and curb; and amidst the awful corruptions of human malice, the Church rises up like a bright lighthouse warning by the clearness of its beam every deviation to right or left from the way of truth, and pointing out to one and all the right course that they should follow. Woe if ever this beacon should Be—We do not say extinguished, for that is impossible owing to the unfailing promises on which it is founded—but if it should be hindered from shedding far and wide its beneficent light! We see already with Our own eyes whither the world has been brought by its arrogant rejection of divine revelation, and its pursuit of false philosophical and moral theories that bear the specious name of "science." That it has not fallen still lower down the 130 slope of error and vice is due to the guidance of the light of Christian truth that always shines in the world. Now the Church exercises her "ministry of the word" through her priests of every grade of the Hierarchy, in which each has his wisely allotted place. These she sends everywhere as unwearied heralds of the good tidings which alone can save and advance true civilization and culture, or help them to rise again. The word of the priest enters the soul and brings light and power; the voice of the priest rises calmly above the storms of passion, fearlessly to proclaim the truth, and exhort to the good; that truth which elucidates and solves the gravest problems of human life; that good which no misfortune can take from us, which death but secures and renders immortal.

131   Consider the truths themselves which the priest if faithful to his ministry, must frequently inculcate. Ponder them one by one and dwell upon their inner power; for they make plain the influence of the priest, and how strong and beneficent it can be for the moral education, social concord and peaceful development of peoples. He brings home to young and old the fleeting nature of the present life; the perishableness of earthly goods; the value of spiritual goods and of the immortal soul; the severity of divine judgment; the spotless holiness of the divine gaze that reads the hearts of all; the justice of God, which "will render to every man according to his works." These and similar lessons the priest teaches; a teaching fitted indeed to moderate the feverish search for pleasure, and the uncontrolled greed for worldly goods, that debase so much of modern life, and spur on the different classes of society to fight one another like enemies, instead of helping one another like friends. In this clash of selfish interest, and unleashed hate, and dark plans of revenge, nothing could be better or more powerful to heal, than loudly to proclaim the "new commandment" of Christ. That commandment enjoins a love which extends to all, knows no barriers nor national boundaries, excludes no race, excepts not even its own enemies.

132   The experience of twenty centuries fully and gloriously reveals the power for good of the word of the priest. Being the faithful echo and reëcho of the "word of God," which

"is living and effectual and more piercing than any two-edged sword," it too reaches "unto the division of the soul and spirit"; it awakens heroism of every kind, in every class and place, and inspires the self-forgetting deeds of the most generous hearts. All the good that Christian civilization has brought into the world is due, at least radically, to the word and works of the Catholic priesthood. Such a past might, of itself, serve as sufficient guarantee for the future; but we have a still more secure guarantee, "a more firm prophetical word" in the infallible promises of Christ.

The work, too, of the Missions manifests most vividly the   133 power of expansion given by divine grace to the Church. This work is advanced and carried on principally by priests. Pioneers of faith and love, at the cost of innumerable sacrifices, they extend and widen the Kingdom of God upon earth.

Finally, the priest, in another way, follows the example of   134 Christ. Of Him it is written that He "passed the whole night in the prayer of God" and "ever lives to make intercession for us"; and like Him, the priest, is public and official intercessor of humanity before God; he has the duty and commission of offering to God in the name of the Church, over and above sacrifice strictly so-called, the "sacrifice of praise," in public and official prayer; for several times each day, with psalms, prayers and hymns taken in great part from the inspired books, he pays to God this dutiful tribute of adoration and thus performs his necessary office of interceding for humanity. And never did humanity, in its afflictions, stand more in need of intercession and of the divine help which it brings. Who can tell how many chastisements priestly prayer wards off from sinful mankind, how many blessings it brings down and secures?

If Our Lord made such magnificent and solemn promises   135 even to private prayers, how much more powerful must be that prayer which is said *ex officio* in the name of the Church, the beloved Spouse of the Saviour? The Christian, though in prosperity so often forgetful of God, yet in the depth of his heart keeps his confidence in prayer, feels that prayer is all powerful, and as by a holy instinct, in every distress, in every peril whether private or public, has recourse with special trust to the prayer of the priest. To it the unfortunate of every sort look for comfort; to it they have recourse, seeking divine aid in all the vicissitudes of this exile here on earth. Truly does the "priest occupy a place midway between God and human nature: from Him bringing to us absolving beneficence, offering our prayers to Him and appeasing the wrathful Lord."

136   A last tribute to the priesthood is given by the enemies of the Church. For as We have said on a previous page, they show that they fully appreciate the dignity and importance of the Catholic priesthood, by directing against it their first and fiercest blows; since they know well how close is the tie that binds the Church to her priests. The most rabid enemies of the Catholic priesthood are today the very enemies of God; a homage indeed to the priesthood, showing it the more worthy of honor and veneration.

II

137   Most sublime, then, Venerable Brethren, is the dignity of the priesthood. Even the falling away of the few unworthy in the priesthood, however deplorable and distressing it may be, cannot dim the splendor of so lofty a dignity. Much less can the unworthiness of a few cause the worth and merit of so many to be overlooked; and how many have been, and are, in the priesthood, preëminent in holiness, in learning, in works of zeal, nay, even in martyrdom.

138   Nor must it be forgotten that personal unworthiness does not hinder the efficacy of a priest's ministry. For the unworthiness of the minister does not make void the Sacraments he administers; since the Sacraments derive their efficacy from the Blood of Christ, independently of the sanctity of the instrument, or, as scholastic language expresses it, the Sacraments work their effect *ex opere operato*.

139   Nevertheless, it is quite true that so holy an office demands holiness in him who holds it. A priest should have a loftiness of spirit, a purity of heart and a sanctity of life befitting the solemnity and holiness of the office he holds. For this, as We have said, makes the priest a mediator between God and man;

a mediator in the place, and by the command, of Him who is "the one mediator of God and men, the man Jesus Christ." The priest must, therefore, approach as close as possible to the perfection of Him whose vicar he is, and render himself ever more and more pleasing to God, by the sanctity of his life and of his deeds; because more than the scent of incense, or the beauty of churches and altars, God loves and accepts holiness. "They who are the intermediaries between God and His people," says St. Thomas, "must bear a good conscience before God, and a good name among men." On the contrary, whosoever handles and administers holy things, while blameworthy in his life, profanes them and is guilty of sacrilege: "They who are not holy ought not to handle holy things."

For this reason even in the Old Testament God commanded   140
His priests and levites: "Let them therefore be holy because I am also holy: the Lord who sanctify them." In his canticle for the dedication of the temple, Solomon the Wise made this same request to the Lord in favor of the sons of Aaron: "Let Thy priests be clothed with justice: and let Thy saints rejoice." So, Venerable Brethren, may we not ask with St. Robert Bellarmine: "If so great uprightness, holiness and lively devotion was required of priests who offered sheep and oxen, and praised God for temporal blessings; what, I ask, is required of those priests who sacrifice the Divine Lamb and give thanks for eternal blessings?" "A great dignity," exclaims St. Laurence Justinian, "but great too is the responsibility; placed high in the eyes of men they must also be lifted up to the peak of virtue before the eye of Him who seeth all; otherwise their elevation will be not to their merit but to their damnation."

And surely every reason We have urged in showing the   141
dignity of the Catholic priesthood does but reinforce its obligation of singular holiness; for as the Angelic Doctor teaches: "To fulfill the duties of Holy Orders, common goodness does not suffice; but excelling goodness is required; that they who receive Orders and are thereby higher in rank than the people, may also be higher in holiness." The Eucharistic Sacrifice in which the Immaculate Victim who taketh away the sins of the world is immolated, requires in a special way

that the priest, by a holy and spotless life, should make himself as far as he can, less unworthy of God, to whom he daily offers that adorable Victim, the very Word of God incarnate for love of us. *Agnoscite quod agitis, imitamini quod tractatis,* "realize what you are doing, and imitate what you handle," says the Church through the Bishop to the deacons as they are about to be consecrated priests. The priest is also the almoner of God's graces of which the Sacraments are the channels; how grave a reproach would it be, for one who dispenses these most precious graces, were he himself without them, or were he even to esteem them lightly and guard them with little care.

142   Moreover, the priest must teach the truths of faith; but the truths of religion are never so worthily and effectively taught as when taught by virtue; because, in the common saying: "Deeds speak louder than words." The priest must preach the law of the Gospel; but for that preaching to be effective, the most obvious and, by the Grace of God, the most persuasive arguments, is to see the actual practice of the law in him who preaches it. St. Gregory the Great gives the reason: "The voice which penetrates the hearts of the hearers, is the voice commended by the speaker's own life; because what his word enjoins, his example helps to bring about." This exactly is what Holy Scripture says of our Divine Saviour: He "began to do and to teach." And the crowds hailed Him, not so much because "never did man speak like this man," but rather because "He hath done all things well." On the other hand, they who "say and do not," practising not what they preach, become like the Scribes and Pharisees. And Our Lord's rebuke to the other hand, they who "say and do not," practising not what they preach, the word of God, was yet administered publicly, in the presence of the listening crowd: "The Scribes and Pharisees have sitten on the chair of Moses. All things therefore whatsoever they shall say to you observe and do: but according to their works do ye not." A preacher who does not try to ratify by his life's example the truth he preaches, only pulls down with one hand what he builds up with the other. On the contrary, God greatly blesses the labor of those heralds of the Gospel who attend first to their own

holiness; they see their apostolate flourishing and fruitful, and in the day of the harvest, "coming they shall come with joyfulness carrying in their sheaves."

It would be a grave error fraught with many dangers should   143
the priest, carried away by false zeal, neglect his own sanctification, and become over immersed in the external works, however holy, of the priestly ministry. Thereby, he would run a double risk. In the first place he endangers his own eternal salvation, as the great Apostle of the Gentiles feared for himself: "But I chastise my body, and bring it into subjection: lest perhaps, when I have preached to others, I myself should become a castaway." In the second place he might lose, if not divine grace, certainly that unction of the Holy Spirit which gives such a marvellous force and efficacy to the external apostolate.

Now to all Christians in general it has been said: "Be ye   144
perfect as your Heavenly Father is perfect"; how much more then should the priest consider these words of the Divine Master as spoken to himself, called as he is by a special vocation to follow Christ more closely. Hence the Church publicly urges on all her clerics this most grave duty, placing it in the code of her laws: "Clerics must lead a life, both interior and exterior, more holy than the laity, and be an example to them by excelling in virtue and good works." And since the priest is an ambassador for Christ, he should so live as to be able with truth to make his own the words of the Apostle: "Be ye followers of me, as I also am of Christ"; he ought to live as another Christ who by the splendor of His virtue enlightened and still enlightens the world.

It is plain, then, that all Christian virtues should flourish   145
in the soul of the priest. Yet there are some virtues which in a very particular manner attach themselves to the priest as most befitting and necessary to him. Of these the first is piety, or godliness, according to the exhortation of the Apostle to his beloved Timothy: *Exerce . . . teipsum ad pietatem,* "exercise thyself unto godliness." Indeed the priest's relations with God are so intimate, so delicate and so frequent, that clearly they should ever be graced by the sweet odor of piety; if "godliness is profitable to all things," it is

especially profitable to a right exercise of the priestly charge. Without piety the holiest practices, the most solemn rites of the sacred ministry, will be performed mechanically and out of habit; they will be devoid of spirit, unction and life. But remark, Venerable Brethren, the piety of which We speak is not that shallow and superficial piety which attracts but does not nourish, is busy but does not sanctify. We mean that solid piety which is not dependent upon changing mood or feeling. It is based upon principles of sound doctrine; it is ruled by staunch convictions; and so it resists the assaults and the illusions of temptation. This piety should primarily be directed towards God our Father in Heaven; yet it should be extended also to the Mother of God. The priest even more than the faithful should have devotion to Our Lady, for the relation of the priest to Christ is more deeply and truly like that which Mary bears to her Divine Son.

146   It is impossible to treat of the piety of a Catholic priest without being drawn on to speak, too, of another most precious treasure of the Catholic priesthood, that is, of chastity; for from piety springs the meaning and the beauty of chastity. Clerics of the Latin Church in higher Orders are bound by a grave obligation of chastity; so grave is the obligation in them of its perfect and total observance that a transgression involves the added guilt of sacrilege.

MENTI NOSTRAE
Apostolic Exhortation of Pope Pius XII
on the Development of Holiness in Priestly Life
September 23, 1950

INTRODUCTION

The words of the Divine Redeemer to Peter keep coming to Our mind: "Simon, son of John, dost thou love me more than these do? . . . feed my lambs, feed my sheep";[1] and also those words spoken by the same Prince of the Apostles exhorting the Bishops and priests of his time: "Tend the flock of God which is among you . . . becoming from the heart a pattern to the flock".[2]

2. Carefully pondering over these words, We deem it the chief duty of Our supreme ministry to do Our utmost to help to make the work of pastors and priests daily more efficacious in encouraging the faithful to avoid evil, to overcome dangers and to acquire perfection. This is all the more necessary in our days when people and nations, as a result of the recent terrible war, are not only harassed by serious material difficulties but are suffering in the depths of their souls while the enemies of Catholicism, becoming bolder, owing to the state of civil society, are striving with deadly hate and subtle snares to separate men from God and Jesus Christ.   148

3. The necessity for this Christian renewal, which all men of good will appreciate, urges Us to turn Our thoughts and affections in a special way to the priests of the whole world because We know that their humble, vigilant and painstaking work among the people, whose difficulties, sufferings and   149

bodily as well as spiritual needs they realize, is capable of restoring morals through the practice of the precepts of the Gospel and of establishing firmly on earth the Kingdom of Christ, "a Kingdom of justice, love and peace".[3]

150   4. But the priesthood cannot in any way procure the full effects which are demanded by the needs of the present time unless the priests shine forth among the people with the marks of sanctity, as worthy "ministers of Christ," faithful "dispensers of the mysteries of God",[4] "God's helpers,"[5] and ready for every noble work.[6]

151   5. We think there is no more fitting way in which We can show Our gratitude to the clergy of the world who, on the occasion of Our golden jubilee as a priest, showed their filial affection for Us by offering prayers to God on Our behalf, than by exhorting all the clergy in fatherly manner to attain that sanctity of life without which their ministry cannot be fruitful. We desire that the first fruit of the Holy Year, which We proclaimed for the renewal of morals in keeping with the teachings of the Gospel, should be that the leaders of the faithful strive to acquire greater perfection so that, thus inspired and thus prepared, they may renew in their flock the spirit of Jesus Christ.

152   6. It must be recalled that, even though the increasing needs of Christian society today more urgently demand personal holiness in priests, they are already obliged by the very nature of the high ministry confided to them by God to work unceasingly for their own sanctification always and everywhere.

153   7. As our predecessors taught, especially Pius X[7] and Pius XI[8], and as We referred to in the encyclicals *Mystici Corporis*[9] and *Mediator Dei*[10], the priesthood is a great gift of the Divine Redeemer, Who, in order to perpetuate the work of redemption of the human race which He completed on the Cross, confided His powers to the Church which He wished to be a participator in His unique and everlasting Priesthood. The priest is like "another Christ" because he is marked with an indelible character making him, as it were, a living image of our Saviour. The priest represents Christ Who said "As the Father has sent me, I also send you";[11] "he who

hears you, hears me".[12] Admitted to this most sublime ministry by a call from heaven, "he is appointed for men in the things pertaining to God, that he may offer gifts and sacrifices for sins".[13] To him must come anyone who wishes to live the life of the Divine Redeemer and who desires to receive strength, comfort and nourishment for his soul; from him the salutary medicine must be sought by anyone who wishes to rise from sin and lead a good life. Hence all priests may apply to themselves with full right the words of the Apostle of the Gentiles: "We are God's helpers".[14]

8. This lofty dignity demands from priests that they react   154
to their exalted office with the strictest fidelity. Since they are destined to promote the glory of God on earth and to cherish and increase the Mystical Body of Christ, they must be outstanding by the sanctity of their lives in order that through them the "fragrance of Christ" may be spread everywhere.[15]

9. Beloved sons, on the very day that you were raised to   155
the sacerdotal dignity, the Bishop, in the name of God, solemnly pointed out to you your fundamental duty in the following words: "Understand what you do, imitate the things you deal with; and celebrating the mystery of the death of the Lord, strive to mortify in your members all vice and concupiscence. May your doctrine be the spiritual medicine for the people of God; let the fragrance of your life of virtue be an ornament of the Church of Christ; and by your preaching and example may you build the house, that is the family of God".[16] Your life, which should be completely immune from sin, should be even more hidden with Christ in God[17] than the lives of Christian layfolk. Advance then, thus adorned with that high virtue which your dignity demands, to the work of completing the redemption of man for which your priestly ordination has destined you.

10. This is the undertaking which you have freely and   156
spontaneously assumed; be holy because, as you know, your ministry is holy.

PART I

Sanctity of Life

157   11. According to the teaching of the Divine Master, the perfection of Christian life consists especially in the love of God and of one's neighbor,[18] a love that is fervent, devoted, and painstaking. If it has these qualities it can be said to embrace all virtues;[19] and can rightly be called the "bond of perfection".[20] In whatever circumstances a man is placed he should direct his intentions and his actions towards this end.

158   12. However, the priest is bound to do this by his very office. By its very nature every priestly action necessarily tends to this end since the priest is called to this by divine vocation, destined for it by his divine office and confirmed by a divine grace. For he must cooperate with Christ, the only and eternal Priest; he must follow Him and imitate Him, Who during His life on earth had no other purpose than to bear witness to His most ardent love for His Father and to bestow on men the infinite treasure of His Heart.

Imitation of Christ

159   13. The first striving of a priestly soul should be towards the closest union with the Divine Redeemer, towards the complete and humble acceptance of the precepts of Christian doctrine, and towards such a diligent application of those precepts at every moment of his life that his faith will illumine his conduct and his conduct will be a reflection of his faith.

160   14. Led by the light of this virtue, let him keep his eyes fixed on Christ. Let him follow closely His Teaching, His actions and His example, convincing himself that it is not sufficient for him to accomplish the duties enjoined on the ordinary faithful. He must strive with ever increasing efforts to tend to perfection of life in keeping with the high dignity of the priesthood according to the warning of the Church: "Clerics must live both interiorly and exteriorly a holier life

than lay people, and must excel them in giving an example of virtue and good deeds".[21]

15. The priestly life, since it arises from Christ should always and in everything be directed towards Him. Christ is the Word of God and did not disdain to assume human nature. He lived a life on earth in order to obey the will of the Eternal Father. He spread around Himself the fragrance of the lily. He lived in poverty, and "went about doing good and healing all."[22] Finally, He offered Himself as a victim for the salvation of His brethren. That, beloved sons, is the summary of the wonderful life proposed to you. Strive with all your strength to reproduce it in yourselves and recall His words of exhortation: "For I have given you an example, that as I have done to you, so you also should do."[23]   161

16. The beginning of Christian perfection stems from humility. "Learn from Me, for I am meek and humble of heart."[24] The consideration of the high dignity to which we are called by Baptism and Holy Orders and the knowledge of our own spiritual need ought to induce us to meditate on the words of Christ: "Without Me you can do nothing."[25]   162

17. Let the priest not trust in his own strength nor be complacent in his own gifts nor seek the esteem and praise of men but let him imitate Christ, Who "did not come to be served but to serve,"[26] let him deny himself according to the teaching of the Gospel,[27] detaching himself from the things of the earth in order to follow the Divine Master more easily and more readily. Whatever he has, whatever he is, is due to the goodness and power of God; if he wishes to glory in this let him remember the words of the Apostle of the Gentiles: "For myself I will glory in nothing save in my infirmities."[28]   163

18. The spirit of humility, illumined by faith, disposes the soul to the immolation of the will by means of obedience. Christ Himself established in the society He founded a legitimate authority which is a continuation of His own. Hence he who obeys the authorities of the church is obeying the Redeemer Himself.   164

19. In an age like ours, in which the principle of authority is grievously disturbed, it is absolutely necessary that the priest, keeping the precepts of faith firmly in mind, should   165

consider and duly accept this same authority, not only as the bulwark of the social and religious order, but also as the foundation of his own personal sanctification. While the enemies of God, with criminal astuteness, are trying to incite and solicit people's unruly passions, to make them rise up against the commands of Holy Mother Church, We wish to give due praise to, and animate with paternal encouragement that vast army of ministers of God, who, in order to manifest openly their Christian obedience and to preserve intact their fidelity to Christ and to the legitimate authority established by Him, "have been counted worthy to suffer disgrace for the name of Jesus,"[29] and not only disgrace, but persecutions and prison and even death.

166
20. The priest has as the proper field of his activity everything that pertains to the supernatural life, since it is he who promotes the increase of this supernatural life and communicates it to the Mystical Body of Jesus Christ. Consequently, it is necessary that he renounce "the things of the world," in order to have care only for "the things of the Lord."[30] And it is precisely because he should be free from preoccupation with worldly things to dedicate himself entirely to the divine service, that the Church has established the law of celibacy, thus making it ever more manifest to all peoples that the priest is a minister of God and the father of souls. By his law of celibacy, the priest, so far from losing the gift and duties of fatherhood, rather increases them immeasurably, for, although he does not beget progeny for this passing life of earth, he begets children for that life which is heavenly and eternal.

167
21. The more resplendent priestly chastity is, so much the more does the sacred minister become, together with Christ, "a pure victim, a holy victim, an immaculate victim."[31]

168
22. In order carefully to preserve unstained this inestimable treasure of our chastity, it is suitable and necessary to be obedient to that exhortation of the Prince of Apostles, which we daily repeat in the Divine Office, "Be ye sober, and watch."[32]

169
23. Yes, watch, beloved sons, because priestly chastity is exposed to so many dangers, whether by reason of laxity in

public morals, or because of the allurements of vice which
you find so easily seductive in these days, or, finally, because
of that excessive liberty in relations between the sexes which
at times dares to insinuate itself even into the exercise of the
sacred ministry. "Watch and pray,"[33] mindful that your
hands touch those things which are most holy, that you have
been consecrated to God and are to serve Him alone. The
very habit which you wear, reminds you that you should live
not to the world, but to God. Therefore, trusting in the protection of the Virgin Mother of God, generously make every
effort to preserve yourselves "clean, unstained, pure and
chaste, as becomes the ministers of Christ and the dispensers
of the mysteries of God."[34]

24. To this end We deem it opportune to address to you a   170
special exhortation as regards your direction of associations
and sodalities of women, that you show yourselves as becomes
a priest; avoid every familiarity; when you must give your
services, give them in a way that is befitting sacred ministers.
Moreover, in directing these associations, let your interest be
confined to the demands of the sacred ministry.

25. Nor should you consider it sufficient to renounce   171
earthly pleasures through chastity and to submit in generous
obedience to your superiors; to these you must also unite
daily a detachment of your hearts from riches and from the
things of earth. Reverently take as your models those great
saints of ancient and modern times who joined this essential
detachment from material goods to a profound trust in Divine
Providence and a most ardent priestly zeal; as a result, they
produced works that are truly marvelous, confiding solely in
God who, assuredly, is never found wanting in our needs.
Even priests who do not make a profession of poverty by a
special vow, must always be guided by the love of this virtue,
a love that ought to show itself in the simplicity and modesty
of their manner of life, in their living quarters, and in their
generosity to the poor. Let them especially refrain from
those economic enterprises which would impede the fulfillment of their pastoral duties, and lessen the respect which is
due to them from the faithful. Since it is the office of the
priest to spend every effort to obtain the salvation of souls,

he must apply to himself those words of St. Paul, "I do not seek yours, but you."[3][5]

172   26. Many things occur to Our mind which We might say if there were an opportunity here of giving a detailed treatment of all the virtues by which the priest should reproduce in himself as faithfully as possible the Divine Model, Jesus Christ. But We have chosen to concentrate Our attention on those things which seemed to be specially necessary in our times. As for other virtues, let it suffice that We now recall to your minds the words of that golden book, *The Imitation of Christ*, "The priest should be adorned with all the virtues, and give an example to others of a righteous life. Let his conversation be not according to the common and vulgar ways of men, but with the angels and with men that are perfect."[3][6]

Necessity of Grace for Sanctification

173   27. Everyone knows, beloved brethren, that it is impossible for a Christian and, in a special way, a priest, to imitate the admirable example of the Divine Master in daily life without the help of grace, and without the use of those instruments of grace which He Himself has placed at our disposal: a use which is as much more necessary as the grade of perfection to which we are bound to attain is higher, and as the difficulties which arise from our natural inclination to evil are greater. For this reason, We judge it opportune to pass on to the consideration of certain other truths, as sublime as they are consoling, from which should appear still more clearly how deep should be the sanctity of the priest, and how efficacious are the helps given to us by the Lord to enable us to fulfill in ourselves the designs of His divine mercy.

174   28. As the whole life of the Saviour was directed toward the sacrifice of Himself, so the life of the priest, which should reproduce in itself the image of Christ, ought also to be with Him, and through Him, and in Him, a pleasing sacrifice.

175   29. Indeed, the sacrifice which the Lord made upon Calvary, hanging on the cross, was not only the immolation of His own Body; for He offered Himself, a Victim of expiation, as the Head of the human race and, therefore, "while com-

mending His Spirit into the hands of the Father, He commends Himself to God as man, in order to commend to the Eternal Father all mankind."[37]

30. The very same thing occurs in the Sacrifice of the   176
Eucharist, which is the unbloody renewal of the Sacrifice of the Cross: Christ offers Himself to the Eternal Father for His glory and for our salvation. And in so far as He, the Priest and Victim, acts in His capacity as Head of the Church, He offers and immolates not only Himself, but all Christians, and in a certain manner, all of mankind.[38]

31. Now if this holds true for all Christians, much more   177
does it hold for priests, who are the ministers of Christ, principally in order to celebrate the Eucharistic Sacrifice. And precisely in the Eucharistic Sacrifice, when "in the person of Christ", he consecrates bread and wine, which become the Body and Blood of Christ, the priest can draw from that same fountain of the supernatural life the inexhaustible treasures of salvation and all those helps which he needs for himself personally and for the fulfillment of his mission.

32. Being in such close contact with the divine mysteries,   178
the priest cannot but be hungry and thirsty after justice,[39] or not feel inspired to assimilate his life to his exalted dignity, and orient his life towards that sacrifice in which he must needs offer and immolate himself with Christ. Consequently, he will not merely celebrate Holy Mass, but will live it out intimately in his daily life; in no other way can he obtain that supernatural vigor which will transform him and make him a sharer in the life of sacrifice of the Redeemer.

33. St. Paul sets down as the basic principle of Christian   179
perfection, the precept, "Put on the Lord Jesus Christ."[40] Again if this precept applies to all Christians, it applies in a particular way to priests. But putting on Jesus Christ does not mean merely adapting one's mind to His doctrine; it means that a person enters upon a new life which, in order to shine with the splendor of Thabor, must first be conformed to the sufferings and trials of our Redeemer suffering on Calvary. This involves long and arduous labor, by which the soul is transformed to the state of victim, in order that it may participate intimately in the sacrifice of Christ. However, this

arduous and assiduous labor is not to be accomplished through empty velleity, nor achieved through mere desires and promises; it must be an indefatigable and continuous exercise, which aims at a fruitful renovation of spirit; it must be an exercise of piety, which refers all things to the glory of God; it must be an exercise of penance, which tempers and checks the immoderate movements of the soul; it must be an act of charity, which inflames the soul with love of God and the neighbor, and which effectuates works of mercy; it must, in fine, be that active and ready willingness by which we strive and struggle to accomplish whatsoever is most perfect.

180

34. The priest should, therefore, study to reproduce in his own soul the things that are effected upon the Altar. As Jesus Christ immolates Himself, so His minister should be immolated with Him; as Jesus expiates the sins of men, so he, by following the hard road of Christian asceticism, should labor at the purification of himself and of others. Hence the admonition of St. Peter Chrysologus: "Be you the priest and the sacrifice of God; do not lose that which has been given to you by the authority of God. Clothe yourself with the garment of sanctity, gird yourself with the cincture of chastity; let Christ be the covering for your head; let the cross of Christ be the protection before your face; instill in your breast the sacrament of divine wisdom; constantly burn the incense of prayer; grasp the sword of the Spirit; let your heart be, as it were, an altar, on which you may safely offer your body as a victim to God . . . Offer Him your faith, for the chastisement of perfidy; offer Him your fasting, that gluttony may cease; offer your chastity as a sacrifice that passion may die; place on the Altar your piety, that impiety be put away; call upon mercy, that avarice may be overcome; and that folly may disappear, the immolation of sanctity is called for. In this way shall your body be also your victim, if it has not been wounded by any dart of sin."[4][1]

181

35. We wish to repeat here in a special manner for priests, what We have already proposed to the meditation of all the faithful in the Encyclical *Mediator Dei*: "It is quite true that Christ is a priest; but He is a priest not for Himself but for us, when in the name of the whole human race He offers our

prayers and religious homage to the eternal Father; He is also a victim since He substitutes Himself for sinful man. Now the exhortation of the Apostle, 'Let this mind be in you which was also in Christ Jesus,' requires that all Christians should possess, as far as is humanly possible, the same dispositions as those which the divine Redeemer had when He offered Himself in sacrifice: that is to say, they should, in a humble attitude of mind, pay adoration, honor, praise and thanksgiving to the supreme majesty of God. Moreover, it means that they must assume to some extent the character of a victim, that they deny themselves as the Gospel commands, that freely and of their own accord they do penance and that each detests and satisfies for his sins. It means, in a word, that we must all undergo with Christ a mystical death on the cross so that we can apply to ourselves the words of St. Paul, 'With Christ I am nailed to the cross.' "

36. Priests and beloved sons, we hold in our hands a great   182
treasure, a precious pearl, the inexhaustible riches of the Blood of Jesus Christ; let us use them even to prodigality, so that, by the complete sacrifice of ourselves offered with Christ to the Eternal Father, we may become, in truth, mediators of justice, "in the things which appertain to God,"[43] and that we may deserve to have our prayers accepted and obtain a super-abundance of graces which may refresh and make more fruitful the Church and the souls of all men. Only when we have become one with Christ through His oblation and ours and when we have raised our voice with the choir of the inhabitants of the heavenly Jerusalem, as we read, "We join ourselves in song with them, our hopes in Holy Sion,"[44] only then, strengthened by the virtue of our Savior, shall we be able to descend in safety from the heights of sanctity to which we have attained, to bring to all men the life and the light of God by means of our priestly ministry.

Necessity of Prayer and Piety

37. Perfect sanctity also demands a continual communica-   183
tion with God; and because this intimate contact which the priestly soul should enjoy with God, ought never be inter-

rupted in the succession of days and hours, the Church obliges
the priest to recite the Divine Office. In this manner, she has
been faithfully obedient to the injunction of the Lord, "That
they must always pray and not lose heart."[45]

184   38. Just as the Church herself never ceases praying, so she
ardently desires that her children should do the same, repeating the words of the Apostle, "Through Him (Jesus), therefore, let us offer up a sacrifice of praise always to God, that
is, fruit of lips praising His name."[46] To priests, she has committed the special duty of consecrating to God, praying also
in the name of the people, every period of the day and every
circumstance of life.

185   39. Obedient to this duty, the priest continues to do down
the course of the ages, that which Christ Himself had done,
who "in the days of His earthly life, with a loud cry and tears,
offered up prayers and supplications . . . and was heard because of His reverent submission."[47] This prayer has, without
doubt, a singular efficacy because it is done in the name of
Christ, "through our Lord Jesus Christ," who is our Mediator
with the Father, presenting to Him incessantly, His own satisfaction, His merits, and the infinite price of His Blood. It is
truly "the voice of Christ," who "prays for us as our Priest,
prays among us as our Head."[48] By the same token, it is
always "the voice of the Church," which takes up the sentiments and desires of all the faithful who unite their voices to
the prayers and faith of the priest in praising Jesus Christ and,
through Him, render thanks to the Eternal Father, obtaining
from Him the assistance which they need in their lives every
day and every hour. In this wise there is repeated daily, by
means of the priests, what Moses once did on the mountain
top, when, with his arms lifted up to heaven, he spoke to
God and earnestly begged of Him mercy and favor for his
people, who were suffering trials in the valley below.

186   40. Moreover, the Divine Office is a most efficacious
means of sanctification. Certainly it is not a mere recitation
of formularies or of artistically executed chants; it is not just
a question of respect for certain norms, called rubrics, or for
external ceremonies of worship; it is above all a matter of
elevating the mind and heart to God, in unison with the

blessed spirits,[49] who eternally sing praises to God. Therefore, the canonical hours should be recited "worthily, attentively, and with devotion," as we are reminded at the beginning of the Office.

41. Consequently, the priest ought to pray with the same intention as the Redeemer. So that his voice is, as it were, the voice of the Lord who, by means of the priest, continues to implore from the most merciful Father the benefits of the Redemption; it is the very voice of the Lord with which are associated the armies of the angels and saints in heaven and of all the faithful on earth, to render due glory to God; it is the voice of Christ our Advocate, by which we receive the immense treasure of His merits.   187

42. Meditate with care and attention on these fertile truths which the Holy Spirit has disclosed to us in the Sacred Scriptures and upon which the writings of the Fathers and Doctors are commentary explanations. As your lips repeat the words dictated by the Holy Spirit, try not to lose anything of this great treasure, and, that your souls may be responsive to the voice of God, put away from your minds with all effort and zeal whatever might distract you and recollect your thoughts, that you may thus more easily and with greater fruit attend to the contemplation of the eternal truths.   188

43. In the Encyclical *Mediator Dei*, We have explained at great length why the Church, through the course of the liturgical year, recalls to mind and represents before our eyes, in orderly fashion, all the mysteries of Jesus Christ and bids us celebrate the feasts of the Virgin Mary and of the Saints. Those lessons, which We there imparted to all Christians because they are eminently useful for all, should be especially meditated upon by you priests; you, who through the Sacrifice of the Eucharist and the Divine Office, play such an important role in the development of the liturgical cycle.   189

44. In order that we may progress all the more speedily day by day along the road of sanctity, the Church heartily recommends to us, besides the celebration of Mass and the recitation of the Divine Office, also other exercises of piety. Regarding these, it is in place here to propose certain points for your consideration.   190

191   45. Above all else, the Church exhorts us to the practice of meditation, which raises the mind to the contemplation of heavenly things, which influences the heart with love of God and guides it on the straight path to Him. This meditation on sacred things offers the best means of preparation before and of thanksgiving after the celebration of the Eucharistic Sacrifice. Meditation also disposes the soul to savor and to comprehend the beauties of the liturgy, and leads us to the contemplation of the eternal verities, and of the marvelous examples and teachings of the Gospel.

192   46. It behooves the sacred ministers, therefore, to strive to reproduce in themselves the examples of the Gospel and the virtues of the Divine Redeemer. However, just as the food of the body does not nourish, sustain or develop our life unless, after being digested and assimilated, it be changed into our own substance, so the priest cannot acquire dominion over himself and his senses, cannot purify his spirit, cannot strive for virtue as he should, cannot, in brief, fulfill faithfully, generously, or fruitfully the duties of his sacred ministry, unless his life becomes one with the life of the Lord through assiduous and unceasing meditation on the mysteries of the Divine Redeemer, the supreme model of perfection and the inexhaustible source of sanctity.

193   47. We therefore consider it Our grave duty to exhort you in a special manner to the practice of daily meditation, a practice recommended to all the clergy also by Canon Law.[50] For just as the desire for priestly perfection is nourished and strengthened by daily meditation, so its neglect is the source of distaste for spiritual things, through which piety is lessened and grows languid, and the impulse towards personal sanctification is not only weakened or ceases altogether, but the entire priestly ministry suffers great harm. It must therefore be stated without reservation that no other means has the unique efficacy of meditation, and that, as a consequence, its daily practice can in no wise be substituted for.

194   48. From mental prayer cannot be separated vocal prayer, and those other forms of private prayer which, according to each one's peculiar needs, help in uniting the soul with God. Let this be remembered, however: more than a mere multi-

plicity of prayers, is to be valued piety and the true and ardent spirit of prayer. If ever before, in our days especially is this ardent spirit of prayer necessary, when the so-called "naturalism" has invaded men's minds and hearts and when virtue is exposed to every kind of danger, dangers which not infrequently meet one in the very exercise of one's ministry. Is there anything which can more securely protect you against these snares, anything which can more surely elevate your souls to heavenly things and keep them united with God, than assiduous prayer and supplication for Divine help?

49. Inasmuch as priests can be called by a very special title, **195** sons of the Virgin Mary, they will never cease to love her with an ardent piety, invoke her with perfect confidence, and frequently implore her strong protection. So that every day, as the Church herself recommends,[51] they will recite the holy rosary, which, by proposing for our meditation the mysteries of the Redeemer, leads us "to Jesus through Mary."

50. Also, before closing his day's work, the priest will be- **196** take himself to the Tabernacle, and spend at least a little time there to adore Jesus in the Sacrament of His love, to make reparation for the ingratitude of so many men, to enkindle in himself ever more the love of God, and to remain, in some sense, even during the time of repose at night, which recalls to our minds the silence of death, present in His Most Sacred Heart.

51. Let him also not omit his daily examination of con- **197** science which is undoubtedly the most efficacious means we have for taking account of the conduct of our spiritual life during the day, for removing the obstacles which hinder or retard one's progress in virtue, and finally, for determining on the most suitable means to assure to our sacred ministry greater fruitfulness and to implore from the Heavenly Father indulgence upon so many of our deeds wretchedly done.

52. This indulgence and the remission of our sins are given **198** to us in a special manner in the Sacrament of Penance, the masterpiece of God's goodness, by which our weakness is fortified. Let it never happen that the very minister of this Sacrament of reconciliation, himself does not use it. The Church, as you know, declares as follows in this respect: "Let

The Ordinaries be vigilant to see that all their clergy frequently cleanse the stains of their conscience in the Sacrament of Penance."⁵² Though we are the ministers of Christ, we are, nevertheless, wretched and weak; how then can we ascend to the Altar and handle the Sacred Mysteries unless we make a frequent effort to expiate our sins and cleanse ourselves? By means of frequent Confession, "The right knowledge of one's self is increased, Christian humility is developed, perverse moral habits are uprooted, negligence and spiritual torpor are resisted, the conscience is purified, the will is fortified, salutary self-control is obtained, and an increase of grace is secured by the very fact that the Sacrament is received."⁵³

199　　53. Still another recommendation, we feel, is in place here: that, in undertaking and advancing in the spiritual life, you do not trust too much to yourselves, but with docile simplicity seek and accept the help of someone who, with wise moderation, can guide your soul, point out to you the dangers, suggest suitable remedies, and in every internal and external difficulty can guide you in the right way towards an ever greater perfection, according to the example of the saints and the teachings of Christian asceticism. Without these prudent guides for one's conscience, it is often very difficult to be duly responsive to the impulses of the Holy Spirit and of the grace of God.

200　　54. Finally, We wish to recommend heartily to all the practice of Retreats. When we seclude ourselves for some days from our accustomed occupations and habitual environment, and retire into solitude and silence, we are then more attentive to give ear to the voice of God, which consequently penetrates more deeply into our soul. Retreats, while they call us to a more holy fulfillment of the duties of our ministry, and to the contemplation of the Mysteries of the Redeemer, give new strength to our will, that we may "serve Him without fear, in holiness and justice before Him all our days."⁵⁴

PART II

The Holiness of the Sacred Ministry

55. The Redeemer's Side was pierced on Mount Calvary   201
and from it flowed His Precious Blood running like a torrent
in flood through the centuries to cleanse men's consciences,
expiate their sins, impart to them the treasures of salvation.

56. It is the priests who are destined to carry out this   202
mystery so sublime. Not only do they procure and communicate Christ's grace to the members of His Mystical Body, but
they are also the organs whereby this Mystical Body develops
because they must ever give the Church new sons, bring them
up, educate them, and guide them. Priests are "the stewards
of the mysteries of God;"[55] therefore they must serve Jesus
Christ with perfect charity and consecrate all their strength
to the salvation of their brethren. They are the apostles of
light; therefore they must illuminate the world with the teachings of the Gospel and be so strong in the Christian faith as to
be able to communicate it to others, and follow the example
and doctrine of the Divine Master in order to lead everyone
to Him. They are the apostles of grace and pardon: therefore
they must consecrate themselves entirely to the salvation of
men and draw them to the altar of God in order that they
may nourish themselves with the bread of eternal life. They
are the apostles of charity: therefore they must promote
works of charity, all the more urgent today when the needs
of the indigent have grown enormously.

57. The priest must also strive to see that the faithful have   203
a correct understanding of the doctrine of the "Communion
of Saints," and that they feel and live it. For this purpose let
him zealously recommend those institutions known as the
Liturgical Apostolate and the Apostleship of Prayer. In like
manner, he must promote all those forms of the apostolate
which today, on account of the special needs of the Christian
people, are so very important and urgent. Let him, therefore,
labor most diligently for the diffusion of instruction in the

Catechism, the development and diffusion of Catholic Action and Missionary Action, and, with the assistance of well prepared and trained laymen, let him increase those projects of the social apostolate which are demanded by our time.

204   58. But the priest must remember that the closer he is united to Christ and guided in his activities by the spirit of Christ, the more fruitful his ministry will be. Thus, his priestly work will not be reduced to a purely natural activity which tires the body and mind and draws the priest himself away from the right path with no little detriment both to himself and to the Church. But his work and his labor will be fruitful and corroborated by those gifts of grace that God denies to the proud but concedes generously to those working humbly in "the Vineyard of the Lord," not seeking themselves and their own interests[56] but the glory of God and the salvation of souls. Hence, faithful to the teaching of the Gospel, let him not trust in himself, as we have said, and in his own strength but let him place his faith in the help of the Lord. "So then neither he who plants is anything, nor he who waters, but God Who gives the growth."[57]

205   59. When the apostolate is directed and inspired in this manner, it is impossible that the priest should not attract the souls of everyone to himself with an almost divine strength. By his reproducing in his habits and his life a living image of Christ, all those who turn to him as a master will recognize, thanks to some inward conviction, that the words he speaks are not his but God's and that he does not act of his own accord but by the virtue of God: "If anyone speaks, let it be as with words of God. If anyone ministers, let it be as from the strength that God furnishes . . ."[58] In striving towards holiness and in exercising his ministry with the greatest diligence, the priest must spend himself to represent Christ so perfectly as, in all modesty, to be able to repeat the words of the Apostle of the Gentiles, "Be imitators of me, as I am of Christ."[59]

206   60. For these reasons, while giving due praise to those who in the years which have followed the long and terrible war, urged by the love of God and of doing good to their neighbor under the guidance and following the example of their Bish-

ops, have consecrated their entire strength to the relief of so much misery, We cannot abstain from expressing our preoccupation and our anxiety for those who on account of the special circumstances of the moment have become so engulfed in the vortex of external activity that they neglect the chief duty of the priest, his own sanctification. We have already stated publicly in writing[60] that those who presume that the world can be saved by what has been rightly called "the heresy of action" must be made to exercise better judgment. The heresy of action is that activity which is not based upon the help of grace and does not make constant use of the means necessary to the pursuit of sanctity given us by Christ. In the same way, nevertheless, We have deemed it timely to stimulate to the activities of the ministry those who, shut up in themselves and almost diffident of the efficacy of divine aid, do not labor to the best of their ability to make the spirit of Christianity penetrate daily life in all those ways demanded by our times.[61]

61. We earnestly exhort you, therefore, to labor with all solicitude for the salvation of those whom Providence has entrusted to your care, closely united to the Redeemer with whose strength we can do all things.[62] How ardently We desire, O beloved sons, that you emulate those saints who in past times, by their great deeds, have shown what the might of Divine Grace can do in this world. May you one and all, in humility and sincerity, always be able to attribute to yourselves—with your spiritual charges as witnesses—the words of the Apostle, "But I will most gladly for my part, spend and be spent myself for your souls."[63] Enlighten the minds, guide the consciences, comfort and sustain the souls who are struggling with doubt and groaning with sorrow. To these forms of apostolate, add also all those others which the needs of the times demand. But let it always be clear to everybody that the priest in all his activities seeks nothing beyond the good of souls, and looks toward no one but Christ to Whom he consecrates his energies and his whole self.

62. In the same way that, in order to urge you to personal sanctification, We have exhorted you to reproduce in yourselves the living image of Christ, so now for the sanctifying

207

208

efficacy of your ministry We excite you to follow constantly the example of the Divine Redeemer. Full of the Holy Ghost, He "went about doing good and healing all who were in the power of the devil; for God was with Him."[64] Strengthened by the same Spirit and encouraged by His Strength, you will be able to exercise a ministry which, nourished and enkindled by Christian charity, will be rich in Divine virtue and capable of communicating this virtue to others. May your apostolic zeal be animated by that divine charity which bears everything with peace of mind, which does not let itself be overcome by adversity, and which embraces all, rich and poor, friends and enemies, faithful and unfaithful. This daily effort and these daily hardships are demanded of you by souls for whose salvation Our Saviour patiently suffered grief and torment unto death in order to restore us to the Divine Friendship. This is, and well you know it, the greatest good of all. Do not allow yourselves, therefore, to be carried away by the immoderate desire for success, do not allow yourselves to be dismayed if, after assiduous labor, you do not gather the desired fruits. "One sows, another reaps."[65]

209   63. Furthermore, let your apostolic zeal shine with benign charity. If it be necessary—and it is everyone's duty—to fight error and repel vice, the soul of the priest must be ever open to compassion. Error must be fought with all our might, but the brother who errs must be loved intensely and brought to salvation. How much good have the saints not done, how many admirable deeds have they not performed by their kindness even in circumstances and in environments penetrated by lies and degraded by vice? Of a truth, he who to please men would gloss over their evil inclinations or be indulgent about their incorrect ways of thinking or acting, thereby prejudicing Christian teaching and integrity of morals, would be betraying his ministry. But when the teachings of the Gospel are preserved and those who stray are moved by the sincere desire to return to the right path, the priest must remember the reply of Our Lord to St. Peter when he asks Him how many times he must forgive his neighbor. "I do not say to thee seven times, but seventy times seven."[66]

64. The object of your zeal must not be earthly and tran- 210
sient things but things eternal. The resolution of priests
aspiring to holiness must be this: to labor solely for the glory
of God and the salvation of souls. How many priests, even in
the straitened circumstances of our time, have taken the
example and the warnings of the Apostle of the Gentiles as a
rule of conduct! The Apostle of the Gentiles, content with
the indispensible minimum, declared: ". . . but having food
and sufficient clothing, with these let us be content."⁶ ⁷

65. Through this disinterestedness and this detachment 211
from earthly things worthy of the highest praise, in conjunction with trust in Divine Providence, the priestly ministry
has given the Church ripe fruits of spiritual and social good.

66. Finally, this industrious zeal must be illuminated by 212
the light of wisdom and discipline and inflamed by the fire of
charity. Whoever sets before himself his own sanctification
and that of other people must be equipped with solid learning
that comprises not only theology but also the results of
modern science and discovery so that, like a good father, he
may draw "from his storeroom things new and old"⁶ ⁸ and
make his ministry always more appreciated and fruitful. In
the first place, let your activities be inspired by and remain
faithful to the prescriptions of this Apostolic See and the
directives of the Bishops. May it never happen, beloved sons,
that those new forms and methods of the apostolate, so
opportune today especially in regions where the clergy is not
sufficiently numerous, remain dead or, through poor direction, not correspond to the needs of the faithful.

67. May your zeal increase every day, therefore, sustain 213
the Church of God, be an example to the faithful, and constitute a powerful bulwark against which the assaults of the
enemies of God may be broken.

68. We desire likewise, in this paternal exhortation of Ours, 214
to give special mention to those priests who, in humility and
burning charity, labor prudently for the sanctification of
their brother-priests as counsellors, confessors, or spiritual
directors. The incalculable good they render the Church remains hidden for the greater part, but it will one day be
revealed in the glory of God's kingdom.

215   69. Not many years ago, with great satisfaction, We decreed the honors of the altar to the Turinese priest, Giuseppe Cafasso who, as you know, in a most difficult period, was the wise and holy spiritual guide of not a few priests whom he helped to progress in virtue and whose sacred ministry he rendered particularly fruitful. We are fully confident that, through his powerful patronage, our Divine Redeemer will raise up many priests of like sanctity who will bring themselves and their brethren in the ministry to such a height of perfection in their lives that the faithful, admiring their example, will feel themselves moved spontaneously to imitate it.

PART III

Practical Rules

216   70. Up to the present we have set forth the chief truths and the basic principles on which the Catholic priesthood and the exercise of its ministry are founded. In daily practice, all holy priests conform diligently to these truths and principles while all those who, alas, have deserted or renounced the priesthood have violated the obligations contracted by sacred ordination.

217   71. Now, however, in order that this Our paternal exhortation may be more efficacious, We deem it opportune to indicate in greater detail some of the things which refer to the practice of daily life. This is all the more necessary because in modern life there are a number of situations and problems presented in a new way demanding more diligent examination and more attention. It is Our intention, therefore, to exhort all priests, especially Bishops, to expend all their solicitude in promoting all that is necessary in our times and in bringing all those who withdraw from the right path back to truth, goodness, and virtue.

Formation of the Clergy

72. As you well know, after the long and varied upheavals   218
of the recent war, the number of priests both in Catholic
countries and in the missions has often fallen behind the ever-
growing needs. For this reason, We exhort all priests, both
those of the diocesan clergy and those belonging to religious
orders or congregations, to go forward, bound close together
with bonds of fraternal charity, in union of strength and will,
toward the common goal: the good of the Church, personal
sanctification, and the sanctification of the faithful. All, even
Religious who live apart from the world and in silence, can
contribute to the efficacy of the priestly apostolate with
prayer, sacrifice and also with ready and generous action, in
so far as they can.

73. But it is also necessary to recruit new workers, with   219
the help of divine grace. Therefore, We draw the attention
especially of the Ordinaries and of those engaged in any way
in the care of souls to this most important question which is
intimately connected with the future of the Church. It is true
that the Society founded by Christ will never lack the priests
necessary for its mission. Nevertheless, it is necessary for all
to be watchful and to exert themselves, mindful of the words
of Our Lord, "the harvest indeed is abundant but the laborers
are few,"[69] and to be as diligent as possible in giving the
Church numerous and holy ministers.

74. Our Lord Himself shows us the surest way of having   220
numerous vocations, "Pray therefore the Lord of the harvest
to send forth laborers into his harvest:"[70] humble prayer
trusting in God.

75. But it is also necessary that the souls of those called by   221
God be prepared for the impulse and the invisible action of
the Holy Ghost. The contribution that Christian parents,
pastors, confessors, superiors of seminaries, all priests, and all
the faithful who have the needs and the growth of the Church
at heart can give is precious to this end. Let the ministers of
God seek not only by preaching and catechetical instruction

but also in private conversations to dissipate the prejudices now so widespread against the priestly state by showing its lofty dignity, its beauty, its necessity and its great merit. Every Christian mother and father, whatever their social status, must pray to God to make them worthy to have at least one of their children called to His service. Finally, all Christians must deem it their duty to encourage and aid those who feel called to the priesthood.

222   76. The choice of candidates for the priesthood recommended by Canon Law[71] to pastors of souls must be the particular task of all priests, who have not only to render humble and generous thanks to God for the inestimable gift they have received but in like manner must hold nothing dearer or more pleasing than to find and prepare a successor for themselves among those young men whom they know to be equipped with the necessary qualifications. To succeed more efficaciously in this, every priest must make an effort to be and to show himself an example of the priestly life which for the young men whom he approaches and among whom he looks for signs of the divine call can constitute an ideal for imitation.

223   77. This wise and prudent selection must go on always and in all places not only among the young men who are already in the seminary but also among those who are studying elsewhere, and particularly among those who partake in the various activities of the Catholic apostolate. These last, even though they enter the priesthood at a later age, are often equipped with greater and more solid virtues because they have already been tried and have strengthened their souls by contact with the difficulties of life and have already collaborated in a field which is also the realm of priestly activity.

224   78. But it is always necessary to investigate individual aspirants to the priesthood with diligence, to ascertain the intentions and the reasons with which they have taken this resolution. Particularly, when it is a question of boys, it is necessary to find out if they are furnished with the necessary moral and physical qualifications and whether they aspire to the priesthood solely for its dignity and the spiritual profit of themselves and other people.

79. You know well, venerable brethren, what are the con-   225
ditions of mental and moral fitness the Church requires in
young men who aspire to the priesthood. We deem it superfluous to detain you with this subject. On the other hand, We
rather deem it useful to exhort you to examine with your
acknowledged prudence and with care whether those who
wish to receive Orders are physically fit, all the more so because the recent war has not infrequently left deadly traces
on the rising generation and has disturbed them in many
ways. For this reason, these candidates should be carefully
examined and, where necessary, the judgment of a good
physician should be sought.

80. With this choice of vocations made with zeal and pru-   226
dence, We trust that there will arise on all sides a numerous
and select force of candidates for the priesthood.

The Care of Vocations

81. But if many pastors are preoccupied about the decrease   227
of vocations, they are no less disturbed when it is a question
of handling the young men who have already entered the
seminary. We are aware, venerable brethren, how arduous this
labor is and how many great difficulties it presents. But the
carrying out of so serious a duty will give you the greatest
consolation insofar as, as Our predecessor Leo XIII said:
"From the cares and solicitude imposed by the training of
priests, you will have results most ardently to be desired and
you will experience that your episcopal office will be easier
in its exercise and much more fruitful in its results."[7][2]

82. We deem it opportune, therefore, to give you some   228
rules suggested by the necessity, greater today than ever, of
training holy priests.

83. In the first place, it is necessary to remember that   229
pupils in minor seminaries are adolescents separated from the
natural environment of their home. It is necessary, therefore,
that the life the boys lead in the seminaries corresponds as
far as possible to the normal life of boys. Great importance
will be given to spiritual life, but in a manner suited to their
capacity and their degree of development. Everything must

be carried out in a healthy and calm atmosphere. Nevertheless, even here it must be observed that "the just measure is moderation" in order that it may not happen that those who have to be trained to sacrifice and the evangelical virtues "live in sumptuous houses with attendance paid to their taste and comfort."[7 3]

230   84. Particular attention must be paid to character formation in each boy by developing in him the sense of responsibility, the capacity to use his judgment concerning men and events, and the spirit of initiative. For this reason, directors of seminaries must use moderation in the employment of coercive means, gradually lightening the system of rigorous control and restrictions as the boys grow older, by helping the boys themselves to stand on their own feet and to feel responsibility for their own actions. Directors should give a certain liberty of action in some kinds of projects habituating their pupils to reflect so that the assimilation of theoretical and practical truths may become easier for them. Let directors have no fear in keeping them in contact with the events of the day which apart from furnishing them with the necessary material for forming and expressing a good judgment can form material for discussions to help them and accustom them to form judgments and reach balanced conclusions.

231   85. In this way young men are put on the path of honesty and loyalty, of esteem for firmness and uprightness of character and aversion for falsehood and every kind of duplicity. The more sincere and upright they are, the better can they be known and guided by their superiors who must judge whether they are called by God to undertake the burdens of the sacred ministry.

232   86. If young men—especially those who have entered the seminary at a tender age—are educated in an environment too isolated from the world, they may, on leaving the seminary, find serious difficulty in their relations with either the ordinary people or the educated laity, and it may happen that they either adopt a misguided and false attitude toward the faithful or that they consider their training in an unfavorable light. For this reason, it is necessary that the students come in closer contact, gradually and prudently, with the judg-

ments and tastes of the people in order that when they receive
Holy Orders and begin their ministry they will not feel themselves disorientated—a thing that would not only be harmful
to their souls but also injure the efficacy of their work.

87. Another serious duty of Superiors is the intellectual   233
training of students. You have in mind, venerable brethren,
norms and prescriptions given by this Apostolic See on this
subject and We Ourselves from Our first meeting with the
students of the seminaries and colleges of Rome at the beginning of Our pontificate have recommended these directives
to all.[74]

88. In the first place We urge that the literary and scien-   234
tific education of future priests be at least not inferior to that
of laymen who take similar courses of study. In this way, not
only will the seriousness of the intellectual training be assured
but the choice of subjects also will be facilitated. Seminarians
will feel themselves freer in the choice of their vocation and
there will be warded off the danger that, through lack of sufficient cultural preparation which can assure a position in the
world, one or the other student may feel himself in some way
driven to take a path that is not his by following the reasoning of the unfaithful steward: "To dig I am not able, to beg I
am not ashamed."[75] If, then, it should happen that some
student about whom good hopes were formed for his entering
the Church should leave the seminary, this would not be a
source of preoccupation, because later on the young man
who succeeds in finding his path, would not be able to forget
the benefits received in the seminary and by his activity would
be able to make a notable contribution to the work of the
Catholic laity.

89. In the intellectual training of young seminarians—   235
although other studies especially those relating to social questions, so necessary today, should not be overlooked—the
greatest importance must be given to philosophical and theological teaching "according to the method of the Angelic
Doctor"[76] brought up to date and adapted to meet modern
errors. Study of these subjects is of maximum importance
and usefulness both for the priest himself and for the people.
The masters of the spiritual life state that the study of the

sacred sciences, provided they be imparted in the right way and according to correct systems, is a most efficacious help in preserving and nourishing the spirit of faith, checking the passions, and maintaining the soul united to God. It must be added that the priest who is the "salt of the earth" and "the light of the world"[7][7] must labor mightily for the defense of the Faith by preaching the Gospel and confuting the doctrinal errors opposed to it which are disseminated today among the people by every possible means. But these errors cannot be efficaciously fought if the unassailable principles of Catholic philosophy and theology are not thoroughly known.

236   90. In this connection, it is not out of place to recall that the method of teaching which has long been in use in Catholic schools is of particular efficacy in giving clear concepts and showing how doctrines entrusted as sacred deposit to the Church, teacher of Christians, are organically connected and clear. Today, there are not lacking those who, departing from the teachings of the Church and overlooking clarity and precision of ideas, not only depart from the correct method of our schools but open the way to errors and confusion, as sad experience shows.

237   91. In order to prevent wavering and uncertainty where ecclesiastical studies are concerned, We, strongly exhort you, venerable brethren, to watch carefully that the precise rules laid down by this Apostolic See for such studies be faithfully received and translated into action.

Spiritual and Moral Training

238   92. If, with so much solicitude, We have, in the discharge of Our Apostolic office, recommended solid intellectual training among the clergy, it is easy to understand how much We have at heart the spiritual and moral training of young clerics without which even outstanding knowledge can bring incalculable harm on account of arrogant pride which easily enters the heart. Therefore, Mother Church primarily and anxiously wishes that in seminaries solid foundations be laid for the holiness that the minister of God must develop and practice all his life.

93. As We have already written regarding priests, we now   239
insist that clerical students be deeply convinced of the necessity of striving to acquire those ornaments of the soul which
are the virtues and, after acquiring them, to preserve them
with the desire of increasing them.

94. In the course of the day, following the more or less   240
uniform program, clerics perform the same spiritual exercises.
There is ready danger that the external exercises of piety may
not be accompanied by an interior movement of the soul, a
thing which can become habitual and even grow worse when,
outside the seminary, the minister of God is often carried
away by the necessary performance of his duties.

95. For this reason, let every care be given to the training   241
of future clerics for the interior life which is the life of the
spirit and according to the spirit. Let them do everything in
the light of divine Faith and in union with Christ, convinced
that there is no other kind of life possible for him who one
day must receive the priestly character and represent the
Divine Master in the Church. For seminarians, the interior
life is the most efficacious means of acquiring the priestly
virtues, of overcoming difficulties and carrying out salutary
resolutions.

96. Those who are responsible for the moral training of   242
seminarians must always aim at making them acquire all the
virtues the Church demands in priests. Of these virtues We
have already spoken in another part of this Exhortation and,
therefore, there is no reason to return to the subject here.
But We cannot refrain from indicating and recommending
among all virtues that aspirants to the priesthood must firmly
possess those upon which the moral structure of the priest is
built, as upon solid pillars.

97. It is necessary that young men acquire the spirit of   243
obedience by accustoming themselves to submit their own
will sincerely to that of God manifested through the legitimate authority of the superiors. Nothing can be lamented
more in the conduct of the future priest than that it is not in
conformity with the Will of God. This obedience must always
be inspired by the perfect model, the Divine Teacher Who on
earth had but one single program "to do thy will, O God."[78]

244   98. From the seminary on, the future priest must learn to give filial and sincere obedience to his superiors in order to be always ready later on to obey his Bishop docilely according to the teaching of the invincible Athlete of Christ, Ignatius of Antioch: "Obey ye all the bishop as Jesus Christ obeyed the Father."[79] "He who honors the bishop is honored by God." "He who does anything without the Bishop's knowledge, serves the devil."[80] "Do nothing without the bishop, keep your body like the temple of God, love union, flee discord, be an imitator of Jesus Christ as He was an imitator of His Father."[81]

245   99. Every care and solicitude must be used to have the young soldiers of the sacred army appreciate, love, and preserve chastity, because the choice of the priestly state and perseverance in it depend in great part on this virtue. Being exposed to greater dangers, chastity must be solidly possessed and proved at length. Let seminarians, therefore, inform themselves about the nature of ecclesiastical celibacy, of the chastity that they must observe and of the obligations it brings with it,[82] and let them be warned of the dangers they may meet. Let them take heed to defend themselves against these dangers from a tender age, having recourse faithfully to the means offered by Christian asceticism for bridling the passions, because the more strongly and efficaciously they control them, the further the soul will progress in the other virtues and the surer will be the fruit of their priestly ministry. Hence, whenever young seminarians show evil tendencies in this regard and, after a due trial, show themselves incorrigible, it is absolutely necessary to dismiss them from the seminary before they receive Holy Orders.

246   100. These and all the other priestly virtues can be easily acquired and firmly possessed by seminarians if from the beginning they have acquired and cultivated a sincere and tender devotion to Christ Jesus present "truly, really, and substantially" in our midst in the most august Sacrament, and if they make of Him the inspiration and the end of all their actions and their aspirations. And, if to devotion to the Blessed Sacrament they unite filial devotion to the Most Blessed Virgin Mary, full of trust and abandonment to the Mother of God

and urging the soul to imitate her virtues, then the Church will be supremely happy, because the fruit of an ardent and zealous ministry can never be wanting in a priest whose adolescence has been nourished with the love of Jesus and Mary.

101. Here We cannot refrain from strongly urging you, venerable brethren, to take particular care of the young priests.   247

102. The passage from the sheltered and tranquil life of the seminary to the active ministry may be dangerous for the priest who enters the open field of the apostolate if he has not been prudently prepared for the new life. You should realize that the many hopes placed in young priests may fail if they are not gradually introduced to the work, wisely watched, and paternally guided in the first steps of their ministry.   248

103. We approve, therefore, the gathering of young priests when possible for some years in special institutions where, under the guidance of experienced superiors, they can develop their piety and perfect themselves in sacred studies and be put on the path toward that form of the ministry more closely corresponding to their temperaments and aptitudes.   249

104. For this reason We would like to see institutions of this nature established in every diocese or, according to circumstances, for a number of dioceses together.   250

105. In Our own Beloved City, We Ourselves did this when, on the 50th anniversary of Our priesthood, We erected the St. Eugene Institute for young priests.[83]   251

106. We exhort you, venerable brethren, to avoid so far as it is possible placing still inexperienced priests into full pastoral activity or sending them into places far removed from the See of the diocese or from other larger centers. In this situation—isolated, inexperienced, exposed to dangers, lacking prudent advisors,—they themselves and their ministry would certainly suffer harm.   252

107. It is particularly recommended that young priests live with some pastor and his assistants, for, in this way, with the guidance of older people, they can more easily adjust themselves to the sacred ministry and perfect the spirit of piety.   253

254   108. We remind all pastors of souls that the future of newly ordained priests is to a great extent in their hands. The burning zeal and the generous resolutions with which they are animated at the beginning of their ministry can be spent and certainly weakened by the example of their seniors if these latter do not shine with the splendor of virtue or if, under the pretext of not changing old customs, they show themselves inclined to idleness.

255   109. We approve and strongly recommend what is already the wish of the Church[84] that the custom of community life be introduced and extended among the priests of the same parish or of nearby parishes.

256   110. If the practice of community life brings with it some sacrifice, there is, however, no doubt that great advantages derive from it. In the first place, it daily nourishes the spirit of charity and zeal among the priests. Then, it gives an admirable example to the faithful of the detachment of the ministers of God from their own interests and from their families. Finally, it is a testimony of the scrupulous care with which they safeguard priestly chastity.

257   111. Moreover, priests must cultivate study as Canon Law wisely prescribes: "Clerics must not suspend their studies, especially those of a sacred nature, after having received the priesthood."[85] The Code, besides requiring that examinations be undergone "every year for at least three years"[86] where new priests are concerned, also prescribes that the clergy should hold meetings several times a year "to promote knowledge and piety."[87]

258   112. To encourage these studies, sometimes rendered difficult by the precarious economic conditons of the clergy, it would be most opportune if Ordinaries, according to the splendid tradition of the Church, were to restore dignity and efficiency to cathedral, collegiate, and parochial libraries.

259   113. Despite the despoiling and destruction they have undergone, many ecclesiastical libraries often possess a precious heritage of parchments, of books in manuscript or print, "eloquent testimony of the activity and influence of the Church, of the faith and generous piety of our ancestors, their studies and their good taste."[88]

114. These libraries must not be neglected receptacles for   260
books but living structures with a room for reference and
reading. Above all, however, let them be up to date and enriched with works of every kind, especially those relating to
the religious and social questions of our times, so that teachers,
parish priests, and particularly young priests may find there
the doctrine necessary for diffusing the truth of the Gospel
and for fighting error.

PART IV

Current Problems

115. Finally, venerable brethren, We deem it Our office to   261
give you a warning about the difficulties proper to our time.

116. You are already aware that among priests, especially   262
those less equipped with doctrine and of less strict lives, a
certain spirit of novelty is being diffused in an ever graver and
more disturbing manner.

117. Novelty is never in itself a criterion of truth and it   263
can be worthy of praise only when it confirms the truth and
leads to righteousness and virtue.

118. The age in which we live suffers from serious errors   264
indeed: philosophical systems which are born and die without improving morals in any way; monstrosities of art which
even pretend to call themselves Christian; standards of government in many countries which are aimed at the personal
interests of individuals rather than at the common prosperity
of all; methods of living and economic and social relations
which threaten honest men more than the cunning. From this
it follows almost naturally that there are not lacking in our
times priests, infected in some way by this contagion, who
imbibe opinions and follow a mode of life even in dress and
the care of their person alien to both their dignity and their
mission; priests who allow themselves to be led astray by the
mania for novelty whether it be in their preaching to the
faithful or in combating the errors of adversaries; priests who
compromise not only their consciences but also their good
name and the efficacy of their ministry.

265   119. We earnestly call your attention to all this, venerable brethren, confident that, between widespread passion for the new and exaggerated attachment to the past, you will use a prudence which is circumspect and vigilant even when it tries fresh paths of activity and struggle for the triumph of the truth. We are far from holding that the apostolate must not be in keeping with the reality of modern life and that projects adapted to the needs of our time should not be promoted. But since the whole apostolate carried on by the Church is by its essence under the control of the Hierarchy, new forms must not be introduced save with the Bishop's approval. Ordinaries of one and the same region or one and the same country must strive in this matter to establish an understanding among themselves in order to provide for the needs of their districts and to study the methods best suited to and in keeping with the modern apostolate.

266   120. In this way, all will be done in an orderly and disciplined manner and the efficacy of priestly action will be assured. Let everyone be persuaded of this: that it is necessary to follow the Will of God and not that of the world, and to regulate the activity of the apostolate according to the directives of the Hierarchy and not according to personal opinions. It is a vain illusion to think oneself able to hide one's own inner poverty and still cooperate effectively in spreading the Kingdom of Christ by novelties in his method of action.

The Clergy and the Social Question

267   121. Similarly, a correct attitude is required with regard to the social doctrine of our times.

268   122. There are some who show themselves fearful and uncertain when faced with the wickedness of communism which aims to rob of their faith the very ones to whom it promises material prosperity. But documents recently issued by this Holy See have shown clearly the way to be followed, the path from which no one must stray unless he wishes to fail in his duty.

269   123. Others show themselves no less timid and uncertain in the face of that economic system which derives its name from

the excessive amassing of private wealth, the serious effects of which the Church has never ceased to denounce. The Church has not only indicated the abuses of capital and the right to property promoted and defended by this system, but has insisted just as much that capital and private property must be instruments of production for the benefit of the whole of society and the means of sustaining and defending the freedom and dignity of the human person. Errors of both economic systems and the harmful results deriving from them must persuade everyone, especially priests, to remain faithful to the social teaching of the Church, to spread the knowledge of it and, to the extent of their power, to reduce it to practical application. This teaching unites and perfects the demands of justice and the duties of charity and promotes a social order which does not oppress individuals and isolate them in a blind selfishness but unites everyone in harmonious relations and the bond of fraternal solidarity.

124. Following the example of the Divine Master, the priest must help the poor, the working class, all those who are in difficulties and misery, which includes also many of the middle class and not a few brother priests. But he must not overlook those who, although well off as far as worldly goods are concerned, are often the poorest in soul and have need of being called to spiritual renovation in order to do as did Zacchaeus, who said: "I give one-half of my possessions to the poor, and if I have defrauded anyone of anything, I restore it fourfold."[89] Where struggling society is concerned, therefore, the priest must never lose sight of the purpose of his mission. Zealously and fearlessly, he must explain the correct principles regarding property, wealth, social justice and Christian charity among the different classes, and give to all an obvious example of their application.   **270**

125. Ordinarily, carrying out of these Christian social principles in public life is the task of the laity, but where no capable lay Catholics are found, the priest should make every effort to train some adequately.   **271**

The Holy Father's Solicitude for Impoverished Priests

272   126. This subject gives Us the opportunity of saying a word about the economic conditions in which, during the postwar period, very many priests find themselves, especially those in regions which have felt more seriously the consequences of the way and of the political situation brought about by the recent conflict. This state of affairs distresses Us profoundly and We leave nothing undone in order to relieve to the best of Our ability the hardship, misery, and extreme want experienced by many.

273   127. You especially, venerable brethren, are well aware how, in places where there was extreme need, We intervened through the Sacred Congregation of the Council and gave extraordinary faculties to the Bishops and established special norms to eliminate glaring economic inequalities among priests of the same diocese. We observe that, in some places, priests have answered their Pastor's call in a praiseworthy manner. In other places, it has not been possible to carry out fully the regulations laid down, because of serious difficulties encountered.

274   128. For this reason, We exhort you to continue in paternal fashion on the path you have taken and to notify Us of the results of your efforts, for it is inadmissible that the worker who has been sent into the vineyard of the Lord should go without his daily bread.

275   129. Moreover, venerable brethren, We strongly praise all joint efforts you make so that priests not only do not lack for their daily needs but also that their future is provided for, following the social security system which is already in force in other classes of society, which We praise so much and which assures proper assistance in case of sickness, invalidism and old age. In this way you will relieve the anxieties of priests about an insecure future.

276   130. In this connection, We express Our paternal gratitude to all those priests who, even at considerable sacrifice, have helped and still help their brethren, especially the sick and aged. By acting in this manner, they give a shining proof

of that mutual charity which Jesus Christ has laid down as the distinctive mark of His disciples: "By this will all men know that you are my disciples, if you have love for one another."[90] We trust that these ties of brotherly love will become ever closer among priests of all nations so that it may become ever more obvious that they, ministers of God the Universal Father, are united by the bond of charity, wherever they live.

131. But you well understand that such a problem cannot be adequately resolved unless the faithful feel the obligation to help the clergy according to their ability and to take every step needed to achieve this end.   **277**

132. Therefore, instruct the faithful under your care on their obligation to help their priests in want. Our Lord's words always hold true: "The laborer deserves his wages."[91] How can you expect fervent and energetic work from priests when they lack the necessities of life? Those faithful who overlook this duty open the way, although involuntarily, to the Church's enemies who in a number of countries seek to reduce the clergy to want in order to deprive the people of their lawful pastors.   **278**

133. Public authorities also, according to the conditions prevailing in each country, have the duty of providing for the needs of the clergy, from whose activity society derives incalculable spiritual and moral benefits.   **279**

Final Exhortation

134. Finally, before closing Our exhortation, We cannot refrain from recapitulating and repeating how much We desire to impress Our words deeper and deeper on your minds as a program of life and work.   **280**

135. We are priests of Christ. Therefore we must labor with all our strength to see that the fruits of His Redemption be most efficaciously applied to every soul. Consider the immense need of our time. We must make every effort to lead back to Christian principles those brethren who have strayed through error or been blinded by passions, to enlighten nations with the light of Christian doctrine, to guide them   **281**

according to Christian norms and to form in them more Christian consciences, and lastly to urge them to struggle for the triumph of truth and justice.

282 136. We shall reach our goal only when we have so sanctified ourselves that we are able to transmit to others the life and virtue we have received from Christ.

283 137. For this reason, We remind every priest of the words of the Apostle: "Do not neglect the grace that is in thee, granted to thee by reason of prophecy with the laying on of hands of the presbyterate."[92] "Show thyself in all things an example of good works, in teaching, in integrity and dignity; let thy speech be sound and blameless, so that anyone opposing may be put to shame, having nothing bad to say of us."[93]

284 138. Take the greatest heed of your vocation, beloved sons, and live it so as to produce abundant fruit for the edification of the Church and the conversion of her enemies.

285 139. In order that this Our paternal exhortation may achieve the desired result, We repeat to you these words which, in view of the Holy Year, are more opportune than ever before: "But be renewed in the spirit of your mind, and put on the new man, which has been created according to God in justice and holiness of truth."[94] "Be you, therefore, imitators of God, as very dear children and walk in love, as Christ also loved us and delivered himself up for us an offering and a sacrifice to God to ascend in fragrant odor."[95] "But be filled with the Spirit, speaking to one another in psalms and hymns and spiritual songs, singing and making melody in your hearts to the Lord."[96] "Be vigilant in all perseverance and supplication for all the saints."[97]

286 140. Reflecting upon these incentives given by the Apostle of the Gentiles, We think it opportune to suggest that during the course of this Holy Year you make an extraordinary Retreat so that, full of renewed fervor and piety, you can incite other souls to acquire the treasures of divine indulgence.

287 141. When you meet very serious difficulties in the path of holiness and the exercise of your ministry, turn your eyes and your mind trustfully to her who is the Mother of the Eternal Priest and therefore the loving Mother of all Catholic

priests. You are well aware of the goodness of this Mother. In many regions you have been the humble instruments of the mercy of the Immaculate Heart of Mary in wonderfully reviving the faith and charity of the Christian people.

142. Our Lady loves everyone with a most tender love, but   288
She has a particular predilection for priests who are the living image of Jesus Christ. Take comfort in the thought of the love of the Divine Mother for each of you and you will find the labors of your sanctification and priestly ministry much easier.

143. To the Beloved Mother of God, mediatrix of heavenly   289
graces, We entrust the priests of the whole world in order that, through her intercession, God will vouchsafe a generous outpouring of His Spirit which will move all ministers of the altar to holiness and, through their ministry, will spiritually renew the face of the earth.

144. Trusting in the powerful patronage of the Immaculate   290
Virgin Mary as far as the realization of these wishes is concerned, We implore an abundance of divine graces on all, but especially on the Bishops and priests who suffer persecution, imprisonment and exile because of their dutiful defense of the rights and the freedom of the Church. We express Our most tender affection to them and exhort them paternally to continue to give an example of priestly courage and virtue.

145. May the Apostolic Blessing that We lovingly impart to   291
each and all of you, venerable brethren, and to all your priests, be the earnest of these heavenly graces and a proof of Our paternal benevolence.

146. Given at Rome, in Saint Peter's in the twenty-third   292
day of September in the year of the Great Jubilee, 1950, the twelfth year of Our Pontificate.

Address of Pope Pius XII
to the World Congress
of the Lay Apostolate
on Its Need Today
October 14, 1951

What consolation and what joy overflows Our heart at the sight of this imposing assembly, where We see you gathered together before Our eyes, you Our venerable brothers in the Episcopate, and you also, dear sons and daughters, come together from all continents and regions to the center of the Church, to celebrate here this World Congress of the Lay Apostolate.

2. You have studied its nature and object. You have considered its present state. You have meditated on the important duties which are incumbent upon it in view of the future. These have been for you days of constant prayer, of serious examination of conscience, of exchanges of views and experiences. To conclude all this, you have come to renew the expression of your faith, of your devotion and of your fidelity to the Vicar of Jesus Christ, and to beg Him to make fruitful by His blessing your resolutions and activity.

3. Frequently, indeed, in the course of Our pontificate, We have spoken of this apostolate of the laity under the most diverse circumstances and varied aspects—in Our messages to all the faithful, or in addressing Ourselves to Catholic Action, to Marian congregations, to workers and teachers, both male and female, to doctors and jurists, to women's organizations and to other groups—always stressing their present-day duties, even in public life. These were for Us so many opportunities to treat, either incidentally or expressly,

of questions which this week have found their well-defined place on your agenda.

4. This time, in the present of so distinguished and numerous a group of priests and faithful, all most justly conscious of their responsibility in or toward this apostolate, We would wish, in a very brief word, to define its place and its role today in the light of the past history of the Church. It has never been absent from it. It will be interesting and instructive to follow the development of this apostolate in the course of times past.   296

5. It is often said that during the past four centuries the Church has been exclusively "clerical" as a reaction against the crisis, which in the 16th century had tried to achieve the abolition, pure and simple, of the hierarchy. In this regard it is insinuated that it is time for the Church to enlarge its framework.   297

6. Such a judgment is so far from the reality that it is precisely since the sacred Council of Trent that the laity has taken rank and progressed in apostolic activity. The thing is easily noted. It here suffices to recall two patent historic facts from among so many others; the Marian congregations of men actively exercising the apostolate of the laity in all the domains of public life and the progressive introduction of women in the modern apostolate.   298

7. It is fitting, on this point, to recall two outstanding figures of Catholic history: one is Mary Ward, that incomparable woman whom, in the most somber and bloody times, Catholic England gave to the Church; the other, St. Vincent de Paul, unquestionably in the first rank among the founders and promoters of the works of Catholic charity.   299

8. Nor can one let pass unnoticed or without recognition its beneficent influence that close union which, until the French Revolution, marked the mutual relations, in the Catholic world, of the two divinely established authorities: the Church and the State. The intimacy of their relations on the common ground of public life generally created an atmosphere of Christian spirit, which rendered largely unnecessary that delicate work which priest and laity must under-   300

take today in order to safeguard the faith and assure its practical value.

301   9. At the end of the 18th century, a new factor came into play. On the one hand the Constitution of the United States of America—a country which had an extraordinarily rapid development and where the Church soon began to grow considerably in life and vigor—and on the other hand the French Revolution with its consequences in Europe as well as overseas led to the detachment of the Church from the State. Without taking effect everywhere at the same time and in the same degree, this separation everywhere had for its logical conclusion: leaving the Church to assure by her own means freedom of action, accomplishment of her mission and defense of her rights and liberty.

302   10. This was the origin of what is called the Catholic movements which, under the direction of priests and the laity and strong in their compact units and sincere loyalty, led the large mass of believers on to combat and to victory. Do we not see here already an initiation and introduction of the laity into the apostolate?

303   11. On this solemn occasion it is a sweet duty for Us to address a word of gratitude to all, priests and faithful, men and women, who are engaged in these movements for the cause of God and the Church and whose names deserve to be mentioned everywhere with honor.

304   12. They worked hard and fought, uniting as best they could their scattered efforts. The times were not yet ripe for a congress such as the one you have just held. How, then, have they matured in the course of this half century? You know the answer well. Following a swifter and swifter rhythm, the cleavage which long had separated spirits and hearts into two parties, for or against God. Church and religion, was enlarged and deepened. It established, perhaps not everywhere with equal clarity, a line of division in the very heart of peoples and families.

305   13. There is, it is true, a confused number of tepid, irresolute and wavering souls, for whom perhaps religion still means something, but only something vague, without any influence in their lives. This amorphous mass may, as exper-

ience teaches, find itself constrained unexpectedly, one day or another to take a decision.

14. As far as the Church is concerned, she has a three-   306
fold mission to fulfill for all: to raise up the fervent believers to the level of present day needs; to introduce those
who hesitate on the threshold to the warm and salutary
intimacy of the hearth and to lead back those who have
separated themselves from religion and whom she cannot
abandon to their miserable fate.

15. An inspiring task for the Church! But it is one ren-   307
dered more difficult by the fact that, while the Church as a
whole has grown greatly, the number of clergy has not increased in proportion. Besides, the clergy must above all
keep themselves free for the exercise of the sacred ministry
proper to the sacerdotal state, which no one else can do for
them.

16. For that reason, assistance rendered by the laity to the   308
apostolate is an indispensable necessity. The experience of
those who were comrades in arms, in captivity, or in other
trails of war bears testimony that this support is truly valuable. Especially in matters of religion there is evidence of the
profound and efficacious influence of those who are companions in a profession or condition of life. These factors,
and others besides, according to the circumstances of places
and persons, have opened wider the doors for the collaboration of the laity in the apostolate of the Church.

17. The great numbers of suggestions and experiences ex-   309
changed in the course of your congress, besides what We have
said on the occasions already mentioned, makes it unneces-
ary for Us to enter into more detail regarding the present-
day apostolate of the laity. We shall content Ourselves,
therefore, with giving a few consideration which can throw a
little more light on one or other of the problems that present themselves.

18. (1) All the faithful, without exception, are members of   310
the Mystical Body of Christ. It follows that the law of nature, and still more pressing, the law of Christ, imposes upon
them the obligation of giving a good example by a truly Christian life: "For we are the fragrance of Christ for God, alike as

regards those who are saved and those who are lost" (2 *Cor.*
2, 15). Today, all are more and more concerned in their prayer and sacrifice not only about their own private needs, but
also about the great intentions of the reign of God in the
world according to the spirit of the Our Father, which Jesus
Christ Himself has taught us.

311   19. Can we say that everyone is called to the Apostolate in
the strict sense of the word? God has not given to everyone
either the possibility or the aptitude. One can hardly ask a
wife and mother, who has to look after the Christian up-
bringing of her children and has to work at home besides to
help her husband feed their little ones, to do apostolic work
of this kind. The vocation to be an apostle is, therefore, not
addressed to all alike.

312   20. It is certainly not easy to draw an exact line of de-
marcation showing precisely where the true apostolate of the
laity begins. Should it include, for example, the education
given by the mother of a family, or by the men and women
teachers engaged with holy zeal in the practice of their profession? Or the conduct of a reputable and openly Catholic
doctor whose conscience never wavers when there is question
of the natural and divine law and who fights with all his
might in defense of the Christian dignity of married persons
and the sacred rights of their offspring? Should it include
even the action of the Catholic statesman who sponsors a
generous housing policy in favor of the less fortunate?

313   21. Many would be inclined to answer in the negative, seeing in all these examples merely the accomplishment, very
laudable in itself but obligatory, of the duties of one's state.

314   22. We recognize, however, the powerful and irreplaceable
value, for the good of souls, of this ordinary performance of
the duties of one's state by so many millions of conscientious
and exemplary faithful.

315   23. The apostolate of the laity, in its proper sense, is without doubt to a large extent organized in Catholic Action and
in other forms of apostolic activity approved by the Church;
but, apart from these, there can be and actually are, lay
apostles, those men and women who see all the good to be
done and the possibilities and means of doing it; and they do

it with only one desire: the winning of souls to truth and grace.

24. We also have in mind so many excellent lay people in   316
countries where the Church is being persecuted today as she
was in the first centuries of Christianity, who are doing their
best, at the peril of their very lives, to fill the place of impris-
oned priests, by teaching Christian doctrine and instructing
others in the religious way of life and in true Catholic
thought, and by encouraging the frequentation of the Sacrament. All these lay people, you see them at work; do not
concern yourself to ask to which organization they belong;
but rather admire and heartily recognize the good they accomplish.

25. It is far from Our thoughts to belittle organization or   317
to underestimate its value as a factor in the apostolate. On
the contrary, We hold it in the highest esteem, especially in
a world in which the adversaries of the Church descend upon Her will all the compact mass of their organizations. But
it must not lead to mean exclusivism, to what the apostle
called "explorare libertatem": "to spy upon our liberty"
(*Gal.* 2, 4). Within the framework of your organization, allow great latitude for each member to develop his personal
qualities and gifts in all that can conduce to doing good and
to edification (*Rom.* 15, 2), and rejoice when you see others,
outside your ranks, who "led by the spirit of God" (*Gal.* 5,
18) win their brethren to Christ.

26. (2) It is self-evident that the apostolate of the laity is   318
subordinated to the ecclesiastical hierarchy; for the hierarcy
is of divine institution. The apostolate, then, cannot be independent with regard to it. To think otherwise would be to
undermine the very wall on which Christ Himself has built
His Church.

27. Granted this, it would still be erroneous to believe   319
that, within the confines of the diocese, the traditional structure and present form of the Church places the lay apostolate
in an essential parallel with the hierarchical apostolate, in
such a manner than even the Bishop himself could not make
the parish apostolate of the laity subject to the pastor. This
the Bishop can do; and he can establish the rule that the

works of the lay apostolate which are destined for the good of the parish itself should be under the pastor's authority. The Bishop has constituted the pastor shepherd of the whole parish, and as such he is responsible for the salvation of all his sheep.

320   28. On the other hand, there may exist works of the lay apostolate which are extra-parochial or even extra-diocesan —We should, rather, say supra-parochial and supra-diocesan— according as the common good of the Church demands. That is equally true and it is not necessary to repeat it.

321   29. In Our allocution of last May 3 to Italian Catholic Action, We made it clear that the dependence of the lay apostolate with respect to the hierarchy admits of gradations. Such dependence is strictest for Catholic Action, for Catholic Action, indeed, represents the official lay apostolate, it is an instrument in the hands of the hierarchy. It must be, as it were, a prolongation of its arm; it is, by that very fact, essentially subject to the direction of the ecclesiastical superior. Other works of the lay apostolate, organized or not, may be left more to their free initiative, with all the latitude required by the ends to be attained. It is self-evident, however, that the initiative of the laity in the exercise of the apostolate must always remain within the bounds of orthodoxy and not oppose the lawful prescriptions of the competent ecclesiastical authorities.

322   30. In comparing the lay apostle, or more precisely the layman of Catholic Action, to an instrument in the hands of the hierarchy, according to the expression which has become current, We understand the comparison in this sense: namely, that the ecclesiastical superiors use him in the manner in which the Creator and Lord uses rational creatures as instruments, as second causes, "disposing (of them) with great favor" (*Wisd.* 12, 18). Let them use those instruments, then, with a consciousness of their grave responsibility; let them encourage them, suggesting enterprises to them and welcoming with good will the enterprises which they suggest, approving them in broadmindedness according to their opportuneness. In decisive battles, it is often at the front that the most use-

ful initiatives arise. The history of the Church offers us sufficiently numerous examples of this.

31. In a general way, in apostolic work it is to be desired   323
that the most cordial relations reign between priests and laity.
The apostolate of the one is not in competition with that of
the other. Indeed, to tell the truth, the expression "emancipation of the laity" which is heard here and there is hardly
pleasing to Us. It has rather an unpleasant sound; it is, moreover, historically inexact. Were they children or minors, did
they have to await their emancipation, those great "trail
blazers" to whom We referred when speaking of the Catholic
movement of the past 150 years? Moreover, in the kingdom
of grace all are regarded as adults. And it is that which counts.

32. The appeal for the help of the laity is not due to the   324
failure or frustration of the clergy in the face of their present
task. That there are individual failures is the inevitable result
of the wretchedness of human nature, and they are found
here and there. But, generally speaking, the priest has as good
a sight as the layman to discern the signs of the times, and his
ear is not less sensitive to hear the human heart. The layman
is called to the apostolate as the collaborator of the priest—
often a most precious, even necessary collaborator, because
of the shortage of clergy, too few, as We have said, to be able
to complete their mission unaided.

33. (3) We cannot conclude, beloved sons and daughters,   325
without recalling the practical work which the lay apostolate
has accomplished and is accomplishing throughout the whole
world in all the domains of individual and social human life;
a work the results and experience of which you have compared
and discussed among yourselves during these days; the apostolate at the service of Christian marriage, the family, the
child, education and the school; for young men and young
women; an apostolate of charity and aid under the number-
less aspects it assumes today; an apostolate for practical
betterment of social disorders and misery; an apostolate of
the missions, or for emigrants and immigrants; an apostolate
in the field of intellectual and cultural life; an apostolate of
games and sports; finally, and it is not the least of these, the
apostolate of public opinion.

326   34. We recommend and We praise your efforts and your work, and above all the vigor of the good will and apostolic zeal which inspires you and which you have spontaneously manifested during the Congress itself, and which, like abundant springs of life-giving waters, have made its deliberations fertile.

327   35. We congratulate you on your resistance to that noxious tendency which exists even among Catholics and which would like to confine the Church to those questions said to be "purely religious"—not that pains are taken to know exactly what is meant by that phrase: provided the Church keeps to the sanctuary and the sacristy, and slothfully lets humanity struggle outdoors in its distress and needs, no more is asked of her.

328   36. It is only too true; in certain countries the Church is constrained thus to cloister herself. Even in this case, within the four walls of the temple, she must still do, as best she can, the little that remains possible for her. She does not withdraw spontaneously or voluntarily.

329   37. Necessarily and continually, human life—both private and social—finds itself in contact with the law and spirit of Christ. Consequently, by force of circumstances, there arises reciprocal compenetration between the religious apostolate and political action. "Political," in the highest sense of the word, means nothing else but collaboration for the good of the state. But this "good of the state" is to be understood in a very wide sense. Consequently it is on the political level that there are debated and enacted laws of the greatest import, such as those concerning marriage, the family, the child, the school, to confine Ourselves to these examples. Are these not questions which primarily interest religion? Can they leave an apostole indifferent, apathetic?

330   38. We have traced, in the allocution already cited (May 3, 1951), the boundary between Catholic Action and political action. Catholic Action must not become a litigant in party politics. But, as We have already said to the members of the Olivaint Conference, "to the extent that it is praiseworthy to remain above contingent quarrels which poison the struggles of parties . . . to that same extent would it be blameworthy

to leave the field free to persons unworthy or incapable of directing the affairs of State." (Disc. March 28, 1948).

39. Up to what point can and should the apostle keep him-   331
self at a distance from this limit? It is difficult to formulate an uniform rule for all on this point. The circumstance and the mentality are not the same everywhere.

40. We receive your resolutions with pleasure. They ex-   332
press your firm good will to extend your hand, one to the other, beyond national frontiers, in order to achieve in practice a full and efficacious collaboration in universal charity. If there is a power in the world capable of overthrowing the petty barriers of prejudices and of partisan spirit, and to dispose souls for a frank reconciliation and for a fraternal union among peoples, it is, indeed, the Catholic Church. You can rejoice in it with pride. It is for you to contribute to it with all your strength.

41. Could We give to your Congress a better conclusion   333
than in repeating to you the admirable words of the Apostle of the Nations: "In conclusion, brethren, rejoice, be perfected, be comforted, be of the same mind, be at peace and the God of peace and love will be with you." (*2 Cor.* 13, 11). And then the Apostle ends: "The grace of our Lord Jesus Christ, and the charity of God, and the fellowship of the Holy Spirit be with you all." (*2 Cor.* 13, 13). It expresses all that which your action seeks to carry to men. May this gift fill also your own hearts and souls.

42. Let this be Our final wish! May God deign to hear it   334
and pour out upon you and the whole Catholic world, His best graces. In testimony of this We impart to you, with all Our heart, Our Apostolic Benediction.

Address of Pope Pius XII
to the Cardinals and Bishops
on the Role of the Laity
November 2, 1954

Role of the Celebrant, Role of the Faithful

The Apostles, therefore, and not all the faithful, did Christ ordain and appoint priests; to them He gave the power to offer sacrifice. Concerning this noble duty of offering the sacrifice of the New Law, the Council of Trent taught: "In this divine sacrifice which takes place at Mass, the same Christ is present and is immolated in an unbloody manner, Who once on the Cross offered Himself in a bloody manner. For the victim is one and the same, now offering through the ministry of priests, Who then offered Himself on the Cross; only the manner of offering is different."[1] Thus the priest-celebrant, putting on the person of Christ, alone offers sacrifice, and not the people, nor clerics, nor even priests who reverently assist. All however, can and should take an active part in the Sacrifice. "The Christian people, though participating in the Eucharistic Sacrifice, do not thereby possess a priestly power," We stated in the Encyclical "Mediator Dei."

We realize, Venerable Brethren, that what We have just said is quite familiar to you; yet we wished to recall it, since it is the basis of, and motive for, what We are about to say. For there are some who have not ceased claiming a certain true power to offer sacrifice on the part of all, even laymen, who piously assist at the sacrifice of the Mass. Opposing them We must distinguish truth from error, and do away with all confusion. Seven years ago, in the same Encyclical We just quoted, We reproved the error of those who did not hesitate to state that Christ's command, "do this in remembrance of Me," refers directly to the entire assembly of the faithful, and only afterwards did a hierarchical priesthood follow. Hence, they say, the people possess a true sacerdotal power, the priest acts only on an authority delegated by the community. Wherefore they think that "concelebration" is the true Eucharistic Sacrifice, and that it is more fitting for priests and people together to "concelebrate" than to offer the Sacrifice in private, with "no congregation present." We also recalled to mind, in that Encyclical, in what sense the celebrating priest can be said "to take the place of the people"; namely "because he bears the person of Jesus Christ our Lord, Who is the head of all the Members, and offers Himself for them; thus the priest goes to the altar as a minister of Christ, subordinate to Christ, but ranking above the people. The people, however, since they in no way bear the person of our Divine Redeemer, and are not mediators between themselves and God, cannot in any way share in sacerdotal rights."

In considering this matter, it is not only a question of   337
measuring the fruit that is derived from the hearing or offering of the Eucharistic Sacrifice—it is indeed possible that one derive more fruit from a Mass devoutly and religiously heard than from a Mass celebrated with casual negligence—but of establishing the *nature of the act* of hearing and celebrating Mass, from which the other fruits of the sacrifice flow. Omitting any mention of the acts of worship of God, and thanksgiving to Him, We refer to those fruits of propitiation and impetration on behalf of those for whom the Sacrifice is offered, even though they are not present; likewise the fruits "for the sins, penalties, satisfactions and other needs of the faithful still alive, as well as for those who have died in Christ, but are not yet fully purified."[2] When the matter is thus regarded, an assertion which is being made today, not only by laymen but also at times by certain theologians and priests and spread about by them, ought to be rejected as an erroneous opinion: namely, that the offering of one Mass, at which a hundred priests assist with religious devotion, is the same as

a hundred Masses celebrated by a hundred priests. That is not true. With regard to the offering of the Eucharistic Sacrifice, the actions of Christ, the High Priest, are as many as are the priests celebrating not as many as are the priests reverently hearing the Mass of a Bishop or a priest; for those present at the Mass in no sense sustain, or act in, the person of Christ sacrificing, but are to be compared to the faithful layfolk who are present at the Mass.

338   On the other hand, it should not be denied or called in question that the faithful have a kind of "priesthood," and one may not depreciate or minimize it. For the Prince of the Apostles, in his first Letter, addressing the faithful, uses these words: "You, however, are a chosen race, a royal priesthood, a holy nation, a purchased people,"[3] and just before this, he asserts that the faithful possess "a holy priesthood, to offer spiritual sacrifices, acceptable to God through Jesus Christ."[4] But whatever is the full meaning of this honorable title and claim, it must be firmly held that the "priesthood" common to all the faithful, profound and incomprehensible as it is, differs not only in degree, but in essence also, from priesthood fully and properly so called, which lies in the power of offering the sacrifice of Christ Himself, since he bears the person of Christ, the supreme High Priest.

339   But it is not our present purpose, Venerable Brethren, while We are addressing you, the shepherds of your flocks, to sketch again the noble image of the saintly Pontiff and shepherd. We wish rather—as We did with the teaching power and priesthood of Bishops—to mention some points which, especially in our times, demand the interest, voice and activity of the pastor of souls.

340   And first, there are some noticeable attitudes and tendencies of mind which presume to check and set limits to the power of Bishops (the Roman Pontiff not excepted), as being strictly the shepherds of the flock entrusted to them. They fix their authority, office and watchfulness within certain bounds, which concern strictly religious matters, the statement of the truths of the faith, the regulation of devotional practices, administration of the Sacraments of the Church, and the carrying out of liturgical ceremonies. They wish to

restrain the Church from all undertakings and matters which concern life as it is really conducted—"the realities of life," as they say. In short, this way of thinking in the official statements of some lay Catholics, even those in high positions, is sometimes shown when they say: "We are perfectly willing to see, to listen to, and to approach Bishops and priests in their churches, and regarding matters within their authority; but in places of official and public business, where matters of this life are dealt with and decided, we have no wish to see them or to listen to what they say. For there, it is we laymen, and not the clergy—no matter of what rank or qualification— who are the legitimate judges."

We must take an open and firm stand against errors of this   341
kind. The power of the Church is not bound by the limits of "matters strictly religious," as they say, but the whole matter of the natural law, its foundation, its interpretation, its application, so far as their moral aspects extend, are within the Church's power. For the keeping of the natural law, by God's appointment, has reference to the road by which man has to approach his supernatural end.

But, on this road, the Church is man's guide and guardian in   342
what concerns his supreme end. The Apostles observed this in times past, and afterwards, from the earliest centuries, the Church has kept to this manner of acting, and keeps to it today, not indeed like a private guide or adviser, but by virtue of the Lord's command and authority. Therefore, when it is a question of instructions and propositions which the properly constituted shepherds (i.e. the Roman Pontiff for the whole Church and the Bishops for the faithful entrusted to them) publish on matters within the natural law, the faithful must not invoke that saying (which is wont to be employed with respect to the opinions of individuals): "the strength of the authority is no more than the strength of the arguments." Hence, even though to someone, certain declarations of the Church may not seem proved by the arguments put forward, his obligation to obey still remains. This was the mind, and these are the words of St. Pius X in his Encyclical Letter *Singulari Quadam* of September 24th, 1912: "Whatever a Christian may do, even in affairs of this world, he may not ignore the

supernatural, nay, he must direct all to the highest good as to his last end, in accordance with the dictates of Christian wisdom; but all his actions, insofar as they are morally good or evil, that is, agree with, or are in opposition to, divine and natural law, are subject to the judgment and authority of the Church." And he immediately transfers this principle to the social sphere: "The social question and the controversies underlying that question . . . are not merely of an economic nature, and consequently such as can be settled while the Church's authority is ignored, since, on the contrary, it is most certain that it (the social question) is primarily a moral and religious one, and on that account must be settled chiefly in accordance with the moral law and religion."

343 Many and serious are the problems in the social field—whether they be merely social or socio-political, they pertain to the moral order, are of concern to conscience and the salvation of men; they cannot be declared outside the authority and care of the Church. Indeed, there are problems outside the social field, not strictly "religious," political problems, of concern either to individual nations, or to all nations, which belong to the moral order, weigh on the conscience and can, and very often do, hinder the attainment of man's last end. Such are: the purpose and limits of temporal authority; the relations between the individual and society, the so-called "totalitarian state," whatever be the principle it is based on; the "complete laicization of the State" and of public life; the complete laicization of the schools; war, its morality, liceity or nonliceity when waged as it is today, and whether a conscientious person may give or withhold his cooperation in it; the moral relationships which bind and rule the various nations.

344 Common sense, and truth as well, are contradicted by whoever asserts that these and like problems are outside the field of morals, and hence are, or at least can be, beyond the influence of that authority established by God to see to a just order and to direct the consciences and actions of men along the path to their true and final destiny. This she is certainly to do not only "in secret," within the walls of the Church and sacristy, but also in the open, crying "from the rooftops"

(to use the Lord's words),[5] in the front line, in the midst of the struggle that rages between truth and error, virtue and vice, between the "world" and the kingdom of God, between the prince of this world and Christ its Savior.

We must add a few remarks on ecclesiastical discipline.   345
Clergy and laity must realize that the Church is fitted and authorized, as also are the Bishops for the faithful entrusted to them, in accordance with Canon Law, to promote ecclesiastical discipline and see to its observance, i.e., to establish an external norm of action and conduct for matters which concern public order and which do not have their immediate origin in natural or divine law. Clerics and laity may not exempt themselves from this discipline; rather all should be concerned to obey it, so that by the loyal observance of the Church's discipline the action of the shepherd may be easier and more efficacious, and the union between him and his flock stronger; that within the flock harmony and cooperation may reign, and each be an example and support to his fellow men.

Yet, these points We have just mentioned in connection   346
with the jurisdiction of Bishops, who are shepherds of the souls committed to their care in all those matters which have to do with religion, moral law and ecclesiastical discipline, are subjected to criticism, often not above a whisper, and do not receive the firm assent they deserved. Hence, some proud, modern spirits provoke serious and dangerous confusion, traces of which are more or less clear in various regions. The awareness, daily more strongly insisted on, of having reached maturity produces in them an agitated and febrile spirit. Not a few moderns, men and women, think that the leadership and vigilance of the Church is not to be suffered by one who is grown up; they not only say it, but they hold it as a firm conviction. They are unwilling to be, like children "under guardians and stewards."[6] They wish to be treated as adults who are in full possession of their rights, and can decide for themselves what they must, or must not, do in any given situation. Let the Church—they do not hesitate to say—propose her doctrine, pass her laws as norms of our actions. Still, when there is question of practical application to each individual's life, the Church must not interfere; she should let each one

of the faithful follow his own conscience and judgment. They declare this all the more necessary because the Church and her ministers are unaware of certain sets of circumstances, either personal or extrinsic to individuals; in them each person has been placed, and must take his own counsel and decide what he must do. Such people, moreover, are unwilling in their final personal decisions to have any intermediary or intercessor placed between themselves and God, no matter what his rank or title. Two years ago, in Our allocutions of March 23rd and April 18th, 1952, We spoke about these reprehensible theories and We examined their arguments.

347   Concerning the importance given to the attainment of a person's majority this assertion is correct: it is just and right that adults should not be ruled as children. The Apostle speaking of himself says, "When I was a child, I spoke as a child, I felt as a child, I thought as a child. Now that I have become a man, I have put away the things of a child."[7] That is not a true art of education which follows any other principle or procedure, nor is he a true shepherd of souls who pursues any other purpose than to elevate the faithful entrusted to his care "to perfect manhood, to the mature measure of the fullness of Christ."[8] But to be an adult and to have put off the things of childhood is one thing, and quite another to be an adult and not to be subject to the guidance and government of legitimate authority. For government is not a kind of nursery for children, but the effective direction of adults toward the end proposed to the state.

Duties of Bishops

348   Since We are speaking to you, Venerable Brothers, and not to the faithful, when these ideas begin to appear and to take root in your flocks, remind the faithful: 1) that God placed shepherds of souls in the Church not to put a burden on the flock, but to help and protect it; 2) that the true liberty of the faithful is safeguarded by the guidance and vigilance of pastors; that they are protected from the slavery of vice and error, they are strengthened against the temptations which come from bad example and from the customs of evil men

among whom they must live; 3) and therefore they act contrary to the prudence and charity which they owe themselves if they spurn this protection of God and his most certain help.

If among clergy and priests you find some infected with this false zeal and attitude, set before them the grave warnings which Our Predecessor, Benedict XV, uttered: "There is one thing which should not be passed over in silence: We want to warn all priests, who are Our dearly beloved sons, how absolutely necessary it is, not only for their own salvation, but for the fruitfulness of their sacred ministry, that each be most devoted and obedient to his own Bishop. As We deplored in passing, not all dispensers of the sacred mysteries are free from that proud and arrogant spirit which is characteristic of our times; and it frequently happens that shepherds of the Church are grieved and opposed, where they might rightly expect comfort and help."[9]   349

Thus far We have spoken of pastoral care, about the persons for whose benefit it is exercised. It is not right to end Our discourse without turning Our attention to the pastors themselves. To Us and to you shepherds the holy words of the Eternal Shepherd are pertinent: "I am the good shepherd. I came that they may have life, and have it more abundantly."[10] To Peter the Lord said: "If you love me, feed my lambs, feed my sheep."[11] With these good shepherds He contrasts the hireling, who seeks himself and his own interests and is not ready to give his life for his flock.[12] He contrasts them with the Scribes and Pharisees, who, greedy for power and domination and seeking their own glory, were seated on the chair of Moses, amassing heavy and oppressive burdens and imposing them on the shoulders of men.[13] Of his own yoke the Lord said: "Take my yoke upon you! For my yoke is easy and my burden light."[14]   350

Frequent and mutual communication among Bishops is very helpful for the fruitful and effective exercise of the pastoral office. Thus one perfects the other in assaying the lessons of past experience; government is made more uniform, the wonder of the faithful is avoided, for often they do not understand why in one diocese a certain policy is followed, while in another, which is perhaps adjacent, a different or   351 even a quite contrary policy is followed. To realize these purposes, general assemblies, which are now held almost everywhere, are very helpful, and also the more solemnly convened Provincial and Plenary Councils, for which the Code of Canon Law provides, and which are governed by definite laws.

352   In addition to this union and intercourse among brothers in the episcopacy there should be added close union and frequent communication with this Apostolic See. The custom of consulting the Holy See, not only in doctrinal matters, but also in affairs of government and discipline, has flourished from the earliest days of Christianity. Many proofs and examples are to be found in ancient historical records. When asked for their decision, the Roman Pontiffs did not answer as private theologians, but in virtue of their authority and conscious of the power which they received from Christ to rule over the whole flock and each of its parts. The same is deduced from the instances in which the Roman Pontiffs, unasked, settled disputes that had arisen or commanded that "doubts" be brought to them to be resolved.

353   This union, therefore, and harmonious communication with the Holy See arise not from a kind of desire to centralize and unify everything, but by divine right and by reason of an essential element of the constitution of the Church of Christ. The result of this is not detrimental but advantageous to the Bishops, to whom is entrusted the governing of individual flocks. For from communication with the Apostolic See they gain light and assurance "in doubts," advice and strength in difficulties, assistance in labors, comfort and solace in distress. On the other hand, from the "reports" of the Bishops to the Apostolic See, the latter attains a wider knowledge of the state of the whole flock, learns more quickly and more accurately what dangers are threatening and what remedies can be applied to cure the evils.

ECCLESIAM SUAM
Selection from Encyclical Letter of Pope Paul VI
on the Ways in which the Church Must Carry Out
Its Mission in the Contemporary World
August 6, 1964

III

The Dialogue

There is a third attitude which the Catholic Church should adopt at this period in the history of the world, an attitude characterized by study of the contacts which the Church ought to maintain with humanity. If the Church acquires an ever-growing awareness of itself, and if the Church tries to model itself on the ideal which Christ proposes to it, the result is that the Church becomes radically different from the human environment in which it, of course, lives or which it approaches.

59. The Gospel makes us recognize such a distinction when   355
it speaks to us of "the world," i.e., of humanity opposed both to the light of faith and to the gift of grace, of humanity which exalts itself in a naive optimism which believes that its own energies suffice to give man complete, lasting, and beneficient self-expression. Or, finally, of humanity which plunges itself into a crude form of pessimism which declares its own vices, weaknesses and moral ailments to be fatal, incurable, and perhaps even desirable as manifestations of freedom and of authenticity.

The Gospel, which recognizes, denounces, pities and cures   356
human misfortunes with penetrating and sometimes with

heartrending sincerity, does not yield to any illusions about the natural goodness of man (as if he were sufficient unto himself and as if he needed nothing else than to be left free to express himself according to his whims), nor to any despairing resignation to the incurable corruption of human nature.

357   The Gospel is light, it is newness, it is energy, it is rebirth, it is salvation. Hence, it both creates and defines a type of new life, about which the New Testament teaches us a continuous and remarkable lesson which is expressed in the warning of St. Paul: "You must not fall in with the manners of this world; there must be an inward change, a remaking of your minds, so that you can satisfy yourselves what is God's will, the good thing, the desirable thing, the perfect thing."[36]

358   60. This distinction between the life of the Christian and the life of the worldling also derives from the reality and from the consequent recognition of the sanctification produced in us by our sharing in the paschal mystery and, above all, in holy baptism, which, as was said above, is and ought to be considered a true rebirth. Again St. Paul reminds us of this truth: "We who were taken up into Christ by baptism have been taken up, all of us, into His death. In our baptism, we have been buried with Him, died like Him, that is, just as Christ was raised up by His Father's power from the dead, we too might live and move in a new kind of existence."[37]

359   61. It will not be amiss if the Christian of today keeps always in view his original and wondrous form of life which should not only sustain him with the happiness that results from his dignity but also protect him from an environment which threatens him with the contagion of human wretchedness and with the seduction of human glory.

360   62. See how St. Paul himself formed the Christians of the primitive church: "You must not consent to be yokefellows with unbelievers. What has innocence to do with lawlessness? What is there in common between light and darkness? How can a believer throw in his lot with an infidel?"[38] Christian education will always have to remind the student today of his privileged position and of his resultant duty to live in the world but not in the way of the world, according to the above-mentioned prayer of Jesus for His disciples: "I am not

asking that thou shouldst take them out of the world, but that thou shouldst keep them clear of what is evil. They do not belong to the world, as I, too, do not belong to the world."[39]

63. But this distinction is not a separation. Neither is it indifference or fear or contempt. When the Church distinguishes itself from human nature, it does not oppose itself to human nature, but rather unites itself to it. Just as the doctor who, realizing the danger inherent in a contagious disease, not only tries to protect himself and others from such infection, but also dedicates himself to curing those who have been stricken, so too the Church does not make an exclusive privilege of the mercy which the divine goodness has shown it, nor does it distort its own good fortune into a reason for disinterest in those who have not shared it. Rather in its own salvation it finds an argument for interest in and for love for anyone who is either close to it and can at least be approached through universal effort to share its blessings.

361

64. If, as we said before, the Church has a true realization of what the Lord wishes it to be, then within the Church there arises a unique sense of fullness and a need for outpouring, together with the clear awareness of a mission which transcends the Church, of a message to be spread. It is the duty of evangelization. It is the missionary mandate. It is the apostolic commission.

362

An attitude of preservation of the faith is insufficient. Certainly we must preserve and also defend the treasure of truth and of grace which has come to us by way of inheritance from the Christian tradition. "Keep safe what has been entrusted to thee," warns St. Paul.[40] But neither the preservation nor the defense of the faith exhausts the duty of the Church in regard to the gifts which it possesses.

363

The duty consonant with the patrimony received from Christ is that of spreading, offering, announcing it to others. Well do we know that "going, therefore, make disciples of all nations"[41] is the last command of Christ to His Apostles. By the very term "apostles" these men define their inescapable mission. To this internal drive of charity which tends to become the external gift of charity we will give the name of dialogue, which has in these days come into common usage.

364

365   65. The Church should enter into dialogue with the world in which it exists and labors. The Church has something to say; the Church has a message to deliver; the Church has a communication to offer.

366   66. It is no secret that this important facet of the contemporary life of the Church will be specially and fully studied by the Ecumenical Council, and we have no desire to undertake the concrete examination of the themes involved in such study, in order to leave to Fathers of the Council full freedom in discussing them. We wish only to invite you, Venerable Brethren, to preface such study with certain considerations in order that we see more clearly the motives which impel the Church toward the dialogue, the methods to be followed, and the goals to be achieved. We wish to give, not full treatment to topics, but proper dispositions to hearts.

367   67. Nor can we do otherwise in our conviction that the dialogue ought to characterize our Apostolic Office, heirs as we are of such a pastoral approach and method as has been handed down to us by our predecessors of the past century, beginning with the great, wise Leo XIII. Almost as a personification of the Gospel character of the wise scribe, who, like the father of a family, "knows how to bring both new and old things out of his treasure-house,"[42] in a stately manner he assumed his function as teacher of the world by making the object of his richest instruction the problems of our time considered in the light of the Word of Christ.

368   Thus, also, did his successors, as you well know.

369   68. Did not our predecessors, especially Pope Pius XI and Pope Pius XII, leave us a magnificently rich patrimony of teaching which was conceived in the loving and enlightened attempt to join divine to human widom, not considered in the abstract, but rather expressed in the concrete language of modern man? And what is this apostolic endeavor if not a dialogue? And did not John XXIII, our immediate predecessor of venerable memory, place an even sharper emphasis on its teaching in the sense of approaching as close as possible to the experience and the understanding of the contemporary world? And was not the Council itself assigned—and justly so—a pastoral function which would be completely focused on

the injection of the Christian message into the stream of the thought, of the speech, of the culture, of the customs, of the strivings of man as he lives today and acts in this life? Even before converting the world, nay, in order to convert it, we must meet the world and talk to it.

69. Concerning our lowly self, although we are reluctant to speak of it and would prefer not to attract to it the attention of others, we cannot pass over in silence, in this deliberate communication to the Episcopal Hierarchy and to the Christian people our resolution to persevere, so far as our weak energies will permit and, above all, so far as the grace of God will grant us the necessary means, in the same direction and in the same effort to approach the world in which Providence has destined us to live, with all due reverence to be observed in this approach, and with all due solicitude and love, in order that we may understand it and offer it the gifts of truth and of grace of which Christ has made us custodians in order that we may communicate to the world our wonderful destiny of redemption and of hope. Deeply engraved on our heart are those words of Christ which we would humbly but resolutely make our own: "When God sent His Son into the world, it was not to reject the world, but so that the world might find salvation through Him."[43]   370

70. See, then, Venerable Brethren, the transcendent origin of the dialogue. It is found in the very plan of God. Religion, of its very nature, is a relationship between God and man. Prayer expresses such a relationship in dialogue. Revelation, i.e., the supernatural relationship which God Himself, on His own initiative, has established with the human race, can be represented as a dialogue in which the Word of God is expressed in the Incarnation and therefore in the Gospel.   371

The fatherly and holy conversation between God and man, interrupted by original sin, has been marvelously resumed in the course of history. The history of salvation narrates exactly this long and changing dialogue which begins with God and brings to man a many-splendored conversation. It is in this conversation of Christ among men[44] that God allows us to understand something of Himself, the mystery of His life, unique in its essence, trinitarian in its persons; and He tells   372 us finally how He wishes to be known; He is Love; and how He wishes to be honored and served by us: Love is our supreme commandment. The dialogue thus takes on full meaning and offers grounds for confidence. The child is invited to it; the mystic finds a full outlet in it.

373   71. We need to keep ever present this ineffable, yet real relationship of the dialogue, which God the Father, through Christ in the Holy Spirit, has offered to us and established with us, if we are to understand the relationship which we, i.e., the Church, should strive to establish and to foster with the human race.

374   72. The dialogue of salvation was opened spontaneously on the intiative of God: "He (God) loved us first;"[45] it will be up to us to take the initiative in extending to men this same dialogue, without waiting to be summoned to it.

375   73. The dialogue of salvation began with charity, with the divine goodness: "God so loved the world as to give His only-begotten Son;"[46] nothing but fervent and unselfish love should motivate our dialogue.

376   74. The dialogue of salvation was not proportioned to the merits of those toward whom it was directed, nor to the results which it would achieve or fail to achieve: "Those who are healthy need no physician;"[47] so also our own dialogue ought to be without limits or ulterior motives.

377   75. The dialogue of salvation did not physically force anyone to accept it; it was a tremendous appeal of love which, although placing a vast responsibility on those toward whom it was directed,[48] nevertheless left them free to respond to it or to reject it. Even the number of miracles[49] and their demonstrative power[50] were adapted to the spiritual needs and dispositions of the recipients, in order that their free consent to the divine revelation might be facilitated, without, however, their losing the merit involved in such a consent. So, too, although our own mission is the announcement of the truth which is both indisputable and necessary for salvation, that mission will not be introduced in the armor of external force, but simply through the legitimate means of human education, of interior persuasion, of ordinary conversa-

tion, and it will offer its gift of salvation with full respect for personal and civic freedom.

76. The dialogue of salvation was made accessible to all; it was destined for all without distinction;[51] in like manner our own dialogue should be potentially universal, i.e. all-embracing and capable of including all, excepting only one who would either absolutely reject it or insincerely pretend to accept it.

77. The dialogue of salvation normally experienced a gradual development, successive advances, humble beginnings before complete success.[52] Ours, too, will take cognizance of the slowness of psychological and historical maturation and of the need to wait for the hour when God may make our dialogue effective. Not for this reason will our dialogue postpone till tomorrow what it can accomplish today; it ought to be eager for the opportune moment; it ought to sense the preciousness of time.[53] Today, i.e. every day, our dialogue should begin again; we, rather than those toward whom it is directed, should take the initiative.

78. As is clear, the relationships between the Church and the world can assume many mutually different aspects. Theoretically speaking, the Church could set its mind on reducing such relationships to a minimum, endeavoring to isolate itself from dealings with secular society; just as it could set itself the task of pointing out the evils that can be found in secular society, condemning them and declaring crusades against them, so also it could approach so close to secular society as to strive to exert a preponderant influence on it or even to exercise a theocratic power over it, and so on.

But it seems to us that the relationship of the Church to the world, without precluding other legitimate forms of expression, can be represented better in a dialogue, not, of course, a dialogue in a univocal sense, but rather a dialogue adapted to the nature of the interlocutor and to factual circumstances (the dialogue with a chiild differs from that with an adult; that with a believer from that with an unbeliever). This has been suggested by the custom, which has by now become widespread, of conceiving the relationships between the

378

379

380

381

sacred and the secular in terms of the transforming dynamism
of modern society, in terms of the pluralism of its manifestations, likewise in terms of the maturity of man, be he religious
or not, enabled through secular education to think, to speak
and to act through the dignity of dialogue.

382   79. This type of relationship indicates a proposal of cour-
teous esteem, of understanding and of goodness on the part
of the one who inaugurates the dialogue; it excludes the *a
priori* condemnation, the offensive and time worn polemic
and emptiness of useless conversation. If this approach does
not aim at effecting the immediate conversion of the interlocutor, inasmuch as it respects both his dignity and his freedom,
nevertheless it does aim at helping him, and tries to dispose
him for a fuller sharing of sentiments and convictions.

383   80. Hence, the dialogue supposes that we possess a state of
mind which we intend to communicate to others and to foster
in all our neighbors: It is a state of mind of one who feels
within himself the burden of the apostolic mandate, of one
who realizes that he can no longer separate his own salvation
from the endeavor to save others, of one who strives constantly to put the message of which he is custodian into the
mainstream of human discourse.

384   81. The dialogue is, then, a method of accomplishing the
apostolic mission. It is an example of the art of spiritual communication. Its characteristics are the following:

(1) Clearness above all; the dialogue supposes and demands
comprehensibility. It is an outpouring of thought; it is an
invitation to the exercise of the highest powers which man
possesses. This very claim would be enough to classify the
dialogue among the best manifestations of human activity
and culture. This fundamental requirement is enough to en-
list our apostolic care to review every angle of our language
to guarantee that it be understandable, acceptable, and well-
chosen.

(2) A second characteristic of the dialogue is its meekness,
the virtue which Christ sets before us to be learned from Him:
"Learn of me, because I am meek and humble of heart."[54]
The dialogue is not proud, it is not bitter, it is not offensive.

Its authority is intrinsic to the truth it explains, to the charity it communicates, to the example it proposes; it is not a
command, it is not an imposition. It is peaceful; it avoids
violent methods; it is patient; it is generous.

(3) Trust, not only in the power of one's words, but also
in an attitude of welcoming the trust of the interlocutor.
Trust promotes confidence and friendship. It binds hearts
in mutual adherence to the good which excludes all self-
seeking.

(4) Finally, pedagogical prudence, which esteems highly
the psychological and moral circumstances of the listener,[55]
whether he be a child, uneducated, unprepared, diffident,
hostile. Prudence strives to learn the sensitivities of the hearer
and requires that we adapt ourselves and the manner of our
presentation in a reasonable way lest we be displeasing and
incomprehensible to him.

82. In the dialogue, conducted in this manner, the union   385
of truth and charity, of understanding and love is achieved.

83. In the dialogue one discovers how different are the   386
ways which lead to the light of faith, and how it is possible to
make them converge on the same goal. Even if these ways are
divergent, they can become complementary by forcing our
reasoning process out of the worn paths and by obliging it to
deepen its research, to find fresh expressions.

The dialectic of this exercise of thought and of patience   387
will make us discover elements of truth also in the opinions
of others, it will force us to express our teaching with great
fairness, and it will reward us for the work of having explained
it in accordance with the objections of another or despite his
slow assimilation of our teaching. The dialogue will make us
wise; it will make us teachers.

84. And how is the dialogue to be carried on?   388

85. Many, indeed, are the forms that the dialogue of salva-   389
tion can take. It adapts itself to the needs of a concrete situation, it chooses the appropriate means, it does not bind itself
to ineffectual theories and does not cling to hard and fast
forms when these have lost their power to speak to men and
move them.

390   86. The question is of great importance, for it concerns the relation of the Church's mission to the lives of men in a given time and place, in a given culture and social setting.

391   87. To what extent should the Church adapt itself to the historic and local circumstances in which its mission is exercised? How should it guard against the danger of a relativism which would falsify its moral and dogmatic truth? And yet, at the same time, how can it fit itself to approach all men so as to save all, according to the example of the Apostle: "I became all things to all men that I might save all"?[56]

392   The world cannot be saved from the outside. As the Word of God became man, so must a man to a certain degree identify himself with the forms of life of those to whom he wishes to bring the message of Christ. Without invoking privileges which would but widen the separation, without employing unintelligible terminology, he must share the common way of life—provided that it is human and honorable—especially of the most humble, if he wishes to be listened to and understood.

393   And before speaking, it is necessary to listen, not only to a man's voice, but to his heart. A man must first be understood; and, where he merits it, agreed with. In the very act of trying to make ourselves pastors, fathers and teachers of men, we must make ourselves their brothers. The spirit of dialogue is friendship and, even more, is service. All this we must remember and strive to put into practice according to the example and commandment that Christ left to us.[57]

394   88. But the danger remains. The apostle's art is a risky one. The desire to come together as brothers must not lead to a watering-down or subtracting from the truth. Our dialogue must not weaken our attachment to our faith. In our apostolate we cannot make vague compromises about the principles of faith and action on which our profession of Christianity is based.

395   An immoderate desire to make peace and sink differences at all costs is, fundamentally, a kind of skepticism about the power and content of the Word of God which we desire to preach. Only the man who is completely faithful to the teaching of Christ can be an apostle. And only he who lives his

Christian life to the full can remain uncontaminated by the errors with which he comes into contact.

89. We believe that the Council, when it comes to deal   396
with questions on the Church's activity in the modern world, will indicate a number of theoretical and practical norms for the guidance of our dialogue with men of the present-day. We believe, too, that in matters concerning the apostolic mission of the Church, on the one hand, and, on the other, the diverse and changing circumstances in which that mission is exercised, it will be for the wise, attentive government of the Church to determine, from time to time, the limits and forms and paths to be followed in maintaining and furthering a living and fruitful dialogue.

90. Accordingly, let us leave this aspect of the subject and   397
confine ourselves to stressing once again the supreme importance which Christian preaching maintains, an importance which grows greater daily, for the Catholic Apostolate and specifically for the dialogue. No other form of communication can take its place; not even the enormously powerful technical means of press, radio and television. In a sense, the apostolate and preaching are the same.

Preaching is the primary apostolate. Our apostolate, Vener-   398
able Brothers, is above all the ministry of the Word. We know this very well, but it seems good to remind ourselves of it now, so as to direct our pastoral activities aright. We must go back to the study, not of human eloquence or empty rhetoric, but of the genuine art of the Sacred Word.

91. We must search for the laws of its simplicity and clari-   399
ty, for its power and authority, so as to overcome our natural lack of skill in the use of the great and mysterious spiritual instrument of speech and to enable us worthily to compete with those who today exert so much influence through their words by having access to the organs of public opinion.

We must beg the Lord for the great and uplifting gift of   400
speech,[58] to be able to confer on faith its practical and efficacious principle,[59] and to enable our words to reach out to the ends of the earth.[60]

May we carry out the prescriptions of the Council's Consti-   401
tution on Sacred Liturgy with zeal and ability. And may the

catechetical teaching of the Faith to the Christian people, and to as many others as possible, be marked by the aptness of its language, the wisdom of its method, the zeal of its exercise supported by the evidence of real virtues, and may it strive ardently to lead its hearers to the security of the faith, to a realization of the intimate connection between the Divine Word and life, and to the illumination of the living God.

402   92. We must, finally, refer to those to whom our dialogue is directed. But, even on this point, we do not intend to forestall the Council, which, please God, will soon make its voice heard.

403   93. Speaking in general on the role of partner in dialogue, a role which the Catholic Church must take up with renewed fervor today, we should like merely to observe that the Church must be ever ready to carry on the dialogue with all men of good will, within and without its own sphere.

404   94. There is no one who is a stranger to its heart, no one in whom its ministry has no interest. It has no enemies, except those who wish to be such. Its name of Catholic is not an idle title. Not in vain has it received the commission to foster in the world unity, love and peace.

405   95. The Church is not unaware of the formidable dimensions of such a mission; it knows the disproportion in numbers between those who are its members and those who are not; it knows the limitations of its power. It knows, likewise, its own human weaknesses and failings. It recognizes, too, that the acceptance of the Gospel depends, ultimately, not upon any apostolic efforts of its own nor upon any favorable temporal conditions, for faith is a gift of God and God alone defines in the world the times and limits of salvation.

406   But the Church knows that it is the seed, the leaven, the salt and light of the world. It sees clearly enough the astounding newness of modern times, but with frank confidence it stands upon the path of history and says to men: "I have that for which you search, that which you lack."

407   It does not thereby promise earthly felicity, but it does offer something—its light and its grace—which makes the attainment as easy as possible; and then it speaks to men of their transcendent destiny. In doing this it speaks to them of

truth, justice, freedom, progress, concord, peace and civilization.

These are words whose secret is known to the Church, for Christ has entrusted the secret to its keeping. And so the Church has a message for every category of humanity: For children, for youth, for men of science and learning, for the world of labor and for every social class, for artists, for statesmen and for rulers. Most of all, the Church has words for the poor, the outcasts, the suffering and the dying; for all men.   408

96. In speaking in this way, we may seem to be allowing ourselves to be carried away in the contemplation of our mission and to be out of touch with reality as regards the actual relations of mankind with the Catholic Church. But that is not so. We see the concrete situation quite clearly. To give a brief idea of it, we think it can be described as consisting of a series of concentric circles around the central point in which God has placed us.   409

97. The first of these circles is immense. Its limits stretch beyond our sight and merge with the horizon. It is that of mankind as such, the world. We gauge the distance that lies between us and the world; yet we do not consider the world a stranger. All things human are our concern.   410

We share with the whole of mankind a common nature; human life with all its gifts and problems. In this primary universal reality we are ready to play our part, to acknowledge the deep-seated claims of its fundamental needs, to applaud the new, and sometime sublime, expressions of its genius.   411

We possess, too, vital moral truths, to be brought to men's notice and to be corroborated by their conscience, to the benefit of all. Wherever men are trying to understand themselves and the world, we can communicate with them. Wherever the councils of nations come together to establish the rights and duties of man, we are honored when they allow us to take our seat among them. If there exists in men "a soul which is naturally Christian," we desire to show it our respect and to enter into conversation with it.   412

98. Our attitude in this, as we remind ourselves and everyone else, is, on the one hand, entirely disinterested. We have   413

no temporal or political aim whatever. On the other hand, its purpose is to raise up and elevate to a supernatural and Christian level every good human value in the world. We are not civilization, but we promote it.

414   99. We realize, however, that in this limitless circle there are many—very many, unfortunately—who profess no religion. We are aware also that there are many who profess themselves, in various ways, to be atheists. We know that some of these proclaim their godlessness openly and uphold it as a program of human education and political conduct, in the ingenuous but fatal belief that they are setting men free from false and outworn notions about life and the world and are, they claim, putting in their place a scientific conception that is in conformity with the needs of modern progress.

415   100. This is the most serious problem of our time. We are firmly convinced that the theory on which the denial of God is based is utterly erroneous.

416   This theory is not in keeping with the basic, undeniable requirements of thought. It deprives the reasonable order of the world of its genuine foundation. This theory does not provide human life with a liberating formula but with a blind dogma which degrades and saddens it. This theory destroys, at the root, any social system which attempts to base itself upon it. It does not bring freedom. It is a sham, attempting to quench the light of the living God.

417   We shall, therefore, resist with all our strength the assaults of this denial. This we do in the supreme cause of truth and in virtue of our sacred duty to profess Christ and His Gospel, moved by deep, unshakable love for men and in the invincible hope that modern man will come again to discover, in the religious ideals that Catholicism sets before him, his vocation to the civilization that does not die, but ever tends to the natural and supernatural perfection of the human spirit, and in which the grace of God enables man to possess his temporal goods in peace and honor, and to live in hope of attaining eternal goods.

418   101. These are the reasons which compel us, as they compelled our predecessors and, with them, everyone who has religious values at heart, to condemn the ideological systems

which deny God and oppress the church-systems which are often identified with economic, social and political regimes, amongst which atheistic communism is the chief. It could be said that it is not so much that we condemn these systems and regimes as that they express their radical opposition to us in thought and deed. Our regret is, in reality, more sorrow for a victim than the sentence of a judge.

102. Dialogue in such conditions is very difficult, not to say impossible, although, even today, we have no preconceived intention of excluding the persons who profess these systems and belong to these regimes. For the lover of truth discussion is always possible.   419

The difficulties are enormously increased by obstacles of the moral order: The absence of sufficient freedom of thought and action, and the perversion of discussion so that the latter is not made use of to seek and express objective truth but to serve predetermined utilitarian ends.   420

103. This is what puts an end to dialogue. The Church of Silence, for example, speaks only by sufferings, and with her speaks also the suffering of an oppressed and degraded society, in which the rights of the spirit are crushed by those who control its fate. If we begin to speak in such a state of affairs, how can we offer dialogue, when we cannot be anything more than a "voice crying in the wilderness"?[61] Silence, groaning, patience and always love, in such conditions, are the witness that the Church can still offer, and not even death can silence it.   421

104. But though we must speak firmly and clearly in declaring and defending religion and the human values which it proclaims and upholds, we are moved by our pastoral office to seek in the heart of the modern atheist the motives of his turmoil and denial.   422

His motives are many and complex, so that we must examine them with care if we are to answer them effectively. Some of them arise from the demand that divine things be presented in a worthier and purer way than is, perhaps, the case in certain imperfect forms of language and worship, which we ought to try to purify so that they express as perfectly and clearly as possible the sacred reality of which they are the sign.   423

424   We see these men full of yearning, prompted sometimes by passion and desire for the unattainable, but often also by great-hearted dreams of justice and progress. In such dreams noble social aims are set up in the place of the absolute and necessary God, testifying thereby to the ineradicable need for the Divine Source and End of all things, whose transcendence and immanence it is the task of our teaching office to reveal with patience and wisdom.

425   Again, we see them, sometimes with ingenuous enthusiasm, having recourse to human reason, with the intention of arriving at a scientific explanation of the universe. This procedure is all the less reprehensible in that it is often based upon laws of logical thought not unlike those of our classical school. It is a procedure which leads in a direction quite contrary to the will of those who use it, thinking to find in it an unanswerable proof of their atheism and its own intrinsic validity, for it leads them onward towards the new and final metaphysical and logical assertion of the existence of the Supreme God.

426   In this cogent process of reasoning the atheistic politico-scientist stops short wilfully at a certain point and so extinguishes the sovereign light of the intelligibility of the universe. Is there no one among us who could help him to reason on to a realization of the objective reality of the cosmic universe, a realization which restores to man the sense of the Divine Presence, and brings to his lips the humble, halting words of a consoling prayer?

427   Sometimes, too, the atheist is spurred on by noble sentiments and by impatience with the mediocrity and self-seeking of so many contemporary social settings. He knows well how to borrow from our Gospel modes and expressions of solidarity and human compassion. Shall we not be able to lead him back one day to the Christian source of such manifestations of moral worth?

428   105. Accordingly, bearing in mind the words of our predecessor of venerable memory, Pope John XXIII, in his encyclical *Pacem in Terris* to the effect that the doctrines of such movements, once elaborated and defined, remain always the same, whereas the movements themselves cannot help but evolve and undergo changes, even of a profound nature,[62] we

do not despair that they may one day be able to enter into a more positive dialogue with the Church than the present one which we now of necessity deplore and lament.

106. But we cannot turn our gaze away from the contemporary world without expressing a cherished desire, namely that our intention of developing and perfecting our dialogue in the varied and changing facets which it presents, may assist the cause of peace between men, by providing a method which seeks to order human relationships in the sublime light of the language of reason and sincerity, and by making a contribution of experience and wisdom which can stir up all men to the consideration of the supreme values.   429

The opening of a dialogue, such as ours would be, disinterested, objective and sincere, is in itself a decision in favor of a free and honorable peace. It excludes pretense, rivalry, deceit and betrayal. It cannot do other than condemn, as a crime and destruction, wars of aggression, conquest or domination. It cannot confine itself to relationships with the heads of nations, but must set them up also with the body of the nation and with its foundations, whether social, family or individual, so as to diffuse in every institution and in every soul the understanding, the relish and the duty of peace.   430

107. Then we see another circle around us. This, too, is vast in its extent, yet it is not so far away from us. It is made up of the men who above all adore the one, Supreme God whom we too adore.   431

We refer to the children, worthy of our affection and respect, of the Hebrew people, faithful to the religion which we call that of the Old Testament. Then to the adorers of God according to the conception of Monotheism, the Moslem religion especially, deserving of our admiration for all that is true and good in their worship of God. And also to the followers of the great Afro-Asiatic religions.   432

Obviously we cannot share in these various forms of religion nor can we remain indifferent to the fact that each of them, in its own way, should regard itself as being the equal of any other and should authorize its followers not to seek to discover whether God has revealed the perfect and definitive form, free from all error, in which He wishes to be known,   433 loved and served. Indeed, honesty compels us to declare openly our conviction that there is but one true religion, the religion of Christianity. It is our hope that all who seek God and adore Him may come to acknowledge its truth.

434   108. But we do, nevertheless, recognize and respect the moral and spiritual values of the various non-Christian religions, and we desire to join with them in promoting and defending common ideals of religious liberty, human brotherhood, good culture, social welfare and civil order. For our part, we are ready to enter into discussion on these common ideals, and will not fail to take the initiative where our offer of discussion in genuine, mutual respect, would be well received.

435   109. And so we come to the circle which is nearest to us, the circle of Christianity.

436   In this field the dialogue, which has come to be called ecumenical, has already begun, and in some areas is making real headway. There is much to be said on this complex and delicate subject, but our discourse does not end here. For the moment we limit ourself to a few remarks—none of them new.

437   The principle that we are happy to make our own is this: Let us stress what we have in common rather than what divides us. This provides a good and fruitful subject for our dialogue. We are ready to carry it out wholeheartedly. We will say more: On many points of difference regarding tradition, spirituality, canon law, and worship, we are ready to study how we can satisfy the legitimate desires of our Christian brothers, still separated from us. It is our dearest wish to embrace them in a perfect union of faith and charity.

438   But we must add that it is not in our power to compromise with the integrity of the faith or the requirements of charity. We foresee that this will cause misgiving and opposition, but now that the Catholic Church has taken the initiative in restoring the unity of Christ's fold, it will not cease to go forward with all patience and consideration.

439   It will not cease to show that the prerogatives, which keep the separated brothers at a distance, are not the fruits of historic ambition or of fanciful theological speculation, but

derive from the will of Christ and that, rightly understood, they are for the good of all and make for common unity, freedom and Christian perfection. The Catholic Church will not cease, by prayer and penance, to prepare herself worthily for the longed-for reconciliation.

110. In reflecting on this subject, it distresses us to see   440
how we, the promoter of such reconciliation, are regarded by many of the separated brethren as being its stumbling-block, because of the primacy of honor and jurisdiction which Christ bestowed upon the Apostle Peter, and which we have inherited from him.

Do not some of them say that if it were not for the primacy   441
of the Pope, the reunion of the separated churches with the Catholic Church would be easy?

We beg the separated brethren to consider the inconsistency   442
of this position, not only in that, without the Pope the Catholic Church would no longer be Catholic, but also because, without the supreme, efficacious and decisive pastoral office of Peter the unity of the Church of Christ would utterly collapse.

It would be vain to look for other principles of unity in   443
place of the one established by Christ Himself. As St. Jerome justly wrote: "There would arise in the Church as many sects as there are priests."[63] We should also like to observe that this fundamental principle of Holy Church has not as its objective a supremacy of spiritual pride and human domination. It is a primacy of service, of ministration, of love. It is not empty rhetoric which confers upon the Vicar of Christ the title of "Servant of the Servants of God."

111. It is along these lines that our dialogue is alert, and,   444
even before entering into fraternal conversation, it speaks in prayer and hope with the heavenly Father.

112. We must observe, Venerable Brethren, with joy and   445
confidence, that the vast and varied circle of separated Christians is pervaded by spiritual activities which seem to promise consoling developments in regard to their reunion in the one Church of Christ. We beg that the Holy Spirit will breathe upon the "ecumenical movement," and we recall the emotion

and joy we felt at Jerusalem in our meeting, full of charity and new hope, with the Patriarch Athenagoras.

446   We wish to greet with gratitude and respect the participation of so many representatives of separated churches in the Second Vatican Ecumenical Council.

447   We want to give our assurance, once again, that we have an attentive, reverent interest in the spiritual movements connected with the problem of unity, which are stirring up vital and noble religious sentiments in various individuals, groups and communities. With love and reverence we greet all these Christians, in the hope that we may promote together, even more effectively, the cause of Christ and the unity which He desired for His Church, in the dialogue of sincerity and love.

448   113. And lastly we turn to speak with the children of the House of God, the one, holy, catholic and apostolic Church, of which this Roman Church is "mother and head." It is our ardent desire that this conversation with our own children should be full of faith, of charity, of good works, should be intimate and familiar.

449   We would have it responsive to all truth and virtue and to all the realities of our doctrinal and spiritual inheritance. Sincere and sensitive in genuine spirituality, ever ready to give ear to the manifold voice of the contemporary world, ever more capable of making Catholics truly good men, men wise, free, serene and strong; that is what we earnestly desire our family conversation to be.

450   114. This desire to impress upon the internal relationships of the Church the character of a dialogue between members of a body, whose constitutive principle is charity, does not do away with the exercise of the virtue of obedience where the right order necessary in all well-constructed societies, and above all, the hierarchic constitution of the Church requires that, on the one side, authority should be exercised according to its proper function and that, on the other side, there should be submission.

451   The Church's authority is instituted by Christ; it is, indeed, representative of Him; it is the authorized channel of His Word; it is the expression of His pastoral charity. Obedience, therefore, is motivated by faith, develops into a school of

cvangclical humility, and links the obedient man to the wisdom, unity, constructiveness and charity by which the body
of the Church is sustained. It confers upon him who imposes
it and upon him who conforms himself to it the merit of being
like Christ who was "made obedient unto death."[64]

115. By obedience, therefore, in the context of dialogue,   452
we mean the exercise of authority in the full awareness of its
being a service and ministry of truth and charity, and we
mean the observance of canonical regulations and respect for
the government of legitimate superiors in the spirit of un-
troubled readiness as becomes free and loving children.

The spirit of independence, of criticism, of rebellion ill   453
accords with the charity which gives life to the Church's
solidarity, concord and peace, and easily transforms the dialogue into argument, dispute and disagreement. This most
regrettable attitude, so easy, alas, to produce, is condemned
by the Apostle Paul in his warning words: "Let there be no
divisions among you."[65]

116. It is, therefore, our ardent desire that the dialogue   454
within the Church should take on new fervor, new themes
and speakers, so that the holiness and vitality of the Mystical
Body of Christ on earth may be increased.

Anything that makes known the teachings of which the   455
Church is both custodian and dispenser receives our approba-
tion. We have already mentioned the liturgy, the interior life
and preaching. We could add also: schools, the press, the
social apostolate, the missions, the exercise of charity.

All these are themes to which the Council will direct our   456
attention. And we bless and encourage all those who, under
the guidance of competent authority, take part in the life-
giving dialogue of the Church, priests especially and religious,
and our well-loved laity, dedicated to Christ in Catholic
action and in so many other associations and activities.

117. It is a cause of joy and comfort for us to see that such 457
a dialogue is already in existence in the Church and in the
areas which surround it. The Church today is more than ever
alive. But it seems good to consider that everything still remains to be done; the work begins today and never comes to
an end. This is the law of our temporal, earthly pilgrimage.

This is the ordinary task, Venerable Brothers, of our ministry, which everything today stimulates us to renew and to make more devoted and intense.

458   118. As for ourself in speaking to you of these things, we are pleased to trust in your cooperation and offer you our own in return. This union of aims and labor we ask for and offer not long after our elevation to the Chair of the Apostle Peter, bearing the name and sharing, please God, something of the spirit of the Apostle of the Gentiles.

459   And so in celebrating the unity of Christ among us, we send to you with this, our first letter, in the name of the Lord, our blessing as Brother and Father, a blessing which we gladly extend to the whole church and to all mankind.

460   From the Vatican, 6 August 1964.

461   On the Feast of the Transfiguration of Our Lord Jesus Christ.

LUMEN GENTIUM
Selections from the Dogmatic Constitution
on the Church
November 21, 1964

Chapter II

The People of God

At all times and among every people, God has given welcome to whosoever fears Him and does what is right (cf. *Acts* 10:35). It has pleased God, however, to make men holy and save them not merely as individuals without any mutal bonds, but by making them into a single people, a people which acknowledges Him in truth and serves Him in holiness. He therefore chose the race of Israel as a people unto Himself. With it He set up a convenant. Step by step He taught this people by manifesting in its history both Himself and the decree of His will, and by making it holy unto Himself. All these things, however, were done by way of preparation and as a figure of that new and perfect covenant which was to be ratified in Christ, and of that more luminous revelation which was to be given through God's very Word made flesh.

"Behold the days shall come, saith the Lord, and I will 463 make a new covenant with the house of Israel, and with the house of Judah. . . . I will give my law in their bowels, and I will write it in their heart: and I will be their God, and they shall be my people. . . . For all I shall know me, from the least of them even to the greatest, saith the Lord" (*Jer.* 31:31-34).

Christ instituted this new covenant, that is to say, the new testament, in His blood (cf. 1 *Cor.* 11:25), by calling together a people made up of Jew and Gentile, making them one, not according to the flesh but in the Spirit.

464   This was to be the new People of God. For, those who believe in Christ, who are reborn not from a perishable but from an imperishable seed through the Word of the living God (cf. 1 *Pet.* 1:23), not from the flesh but from water as "a chosen race, a royal priesthood, a holy nation, a purchased people. . . You who in times past were not a people, but are now the people of God" (1 *Pet.* 2:9-10).

465   That messianic people has for its head Christ, "who was delivered up for our sins, and rose again for our justification" (*Rom.* 4:25), and who now, having won a name which is above all names reigns in glory in heaven. The heritage of this people are the dignity and freedom of the sons of God, in whose hearts the Holy Spirit dwells as in His Temple. Its law is the new commandment to love as Christ loved us (cf. *Jn.* 13:34). Its goal is the kingdom of God, which has been begun by God Himself on earth, and which is to be further extended until it is brought to perfection by Him at the end of time. Then Christ our life (cf. *Col.* 3:4), will appear, and "creation itself also will be delivered from its slavery to corruption into the freedom of the glory of the sons of God" (*Rom.* 8:21).

466   So it is that this messianic people, although it does not actually include all men, and may more than once look like a small flock, is nonetheless a lasting and sure seed of unity, hope, and salvation for the whole human race. Established by Christ as a fellowship of life, charity, and truth, it is also used by Him as an instrument for the redemption of all, and is sent forth into the whole world as the light of the world and the salt of the earth (cf. *Mt.* 5:13-16).

467   Israel according to the flesh, which wandered as an exile in the desert, was already called the Church of God (2 *Esd.* 13:1; cf. *Num.* 20:4; *Dt.* 23:1 ff). Likewise the new Israel which, while going forward in this present world, goes in search of a future and abiding city (cf. *Heb.* 13:14) is also called the Church of Christ (cf. *Mt.* 16:18). For He has

bought it for Himself with His blood (cf. *Acts* 20:28), has
filled it with His Spirit, and provided it with those means
which befit it as a visible and social unity. God has gathered
together as one all those who in faith look upon Jesus as the
author of salvation and the source of unity and peace, and
has established them as the Church, that for each and all she
may be the visible sacrament of this saving unity.[1]

While she transcends all limits of time and of race, the   468
Church is destined to extend to all regions of the earth and
so to enter into the history of mankind. Moving forward
through trial and tribulation, the Church is strengthened
by the power of God's grace promised to her by the Lord,
so that in the weakness of the flesh she may not waver from
perfect fidelity, but remain a bride worthy of her Lord; that
moved by the Holy Spirit she may never cease to renew herself, until through the cross she arrives at the light which
knows no setting.

10. Christ the Lord, High Priest taken from among men   469
(cf. *Heb.* 5:1-5), "made a kingdom and priests to God his
Father" *Apoc.* 1:6; cf. 5:9-10) out of this new people. The
baptized, by regeneration and the anointing of the Holy Spirit,
are consecrated into a spiritual house and a holy priesthood.
Thus through all those works befitting Christian men they can
offer spiritual sacrifices and proclaim the power of Him who
has called them out of darkness into His marvelous light (cf. 1
Pet. 2:4-10). Therefore all the disciples of Christ, persevering
in prayer and praising God (cf. *Acts* 2:42-47), should present
themselves as living sacrifice, holy and pleasing to God (cf.
Rom. 12:1). Everywhere on earth they must bear witness to
Christ and give an answer to those who seek an account of
that hope of eternal life which is in them (cf. 1 *Pet.* 3:15).

Though they differ from one another in essence and not
only in degree, the common priesthood of the faithful and the   470
ministerial or hierarchical priesthood are nonetheless interrelated. Each of them in its own special way is a participation in
the one priesthood of Christ.[2] The ministerial priest, by the
sacred power he enjoys, molds and rules the priestly people.
Acting in the person of Christ, he brings about the Eucharistic
Sacrifice, and offers it to God in the name of all the people.

For their part, the faithful join in the offering of the Eucharist by virtue of their royal priesthood.[3] They likewise exercise that priesthood by receiving the sacraments, by prayer and thanksgiving, by the witness of a holy life, and by self-denial and active charity.

471   11. It is through the sacraments and the exercise of the virtues that the sacred nature and organic structure of the priestly community is brought into operation. Incorporated into the Church through baptism, the faithful are consecrated by the baptismal character to the exercise of the cult of the Christian religion. Reborn as sons of God, they must confess before men the faith which they have received from God through the Church.[4] Bound more intimately to the Church by the sacrament of confirmation, they are endowed strictly obliged to spread and defend the faith both by word and by deed as true witness of Christ.[5]

472   Taking part in the Eucharistic Sacrifice, which is the fount and apex of the whole Christian life, they offer the divine Victim to God, and offer themselves along with It.[6] Thus, both by the act of oblation and through holy Communion, all perform their proper part in this liturgical service, not, indeed, all in the same way but each in that way which is appropriate to himself. Strengthened anew at the holy table by the Body of Christ, they manifest in a practical way that unity of God's People which is suitably signified and wondrously brought about by this most awesome sacrament.

473   Those who approach the sacrament of penance obtain pardon from the mercy of God for offenses committed against Him. They are at the same time reconciled with the Church, which they have wounded by their sins, and which by charity, example, and prayer seeks their conversion. By the whole Church commends those who are ill to the suffering and glorified Lord, asking that He may lighten their suffering and save them (cf. *Jas.* 5:14-16). She exhorts them, moreover, to contribute to the welfare of the whole People of God by associating themselves freely with the passion and death of Christ (cf. *Rom.* 8:17; *Col.* 1:24; *2 Tim.* 2:11-12); holy orders are appointed to feed the Church in Christ's name with the Word and the grace of God.

Finally, Christian spouses, in virtue of the sacrament of   474
matrimony, signify and partake of the mystery of that unity
and fruitful love which exists between Christ and His Church
(cf. *Eph.* 5:32). The spouses thereby help each other to attain to holiness in their married life and by the rearing and
education of their children. And so, in their state and order
of life, they have their own special gift among the People of
God (cf. 1 *Cor.* 7:7).[7]

For from the wedlock of Christians there comes the family,   475
in which new citizens of human society are born. By the
grace of the Holy Spirit received in baptism these are made
children of God, thus perpetuating the People of God through
the centuries. The family is, so to speak, the domestic Church.
In it parents should, by their word and example, be the first
preachers of the faith to their children. They should encourage
them in the vocation which is proper to each of them, fostering with special care any religious vocation.

Fortified by so many and such powerful means of salva-   476
tion, all the faithful, whatever their condition or state, are
called by the Lord, each in his own way, to that perfect holiness whereby the Father Himself is perfect.

12. The holy People of God shares also in Christ's pro-   477
phetic office. It spreads abroad a living witness to Him, especially by means of a life of faith and charity and by offering
to God a sacrifice of praise, the tribute of lips which give honor
to His name (cf. *Heb.* 13:15). The body of the faithful as
a whole, anointed as they are by the Holy One (cf. *Jn.* 2:20,
27), cannot err in matters of belief. Thanks to a supernatural
sense of the faith which characterizes the People as a whole,
it manifests this unerring quality when, "from the bishops
down to the last member of the laity,"[8] it shows universal
agreement in matters of faith and morals.

For, by this sense of faith which is aroused and sustained   478
by the Spirit of truth, God's People accepts not the word of
men but the very Word of God (cf. 1 *Th.* 2:13). It clings
without fail to the faith once delivered to the saints (cf. *Jude*
3), penetrates it more deeply by accurate insights, and applies
it more thoroughly to life. All this it does under the lead of a
sacred teaching authority to which it loyally defers.

479   It is not only through the sacraments and Church ministries that the same Holy Spirit sanctifies and leads the People of God and enriches it with virtues. Allotting His gifts "to everyone according as he will" (1 *Cor.* 12:11), He distributes special graces among the faithful of every rank. By these gifts He makes them fit and ready to undertake the various tasks or offices advantageous for the renewal and upbuilding of the Church, according to the words of the Apostle: "The manifestation of the Spirit is given to everyone for profit" (1 *Cor.* 12:7). These charismatic gifts, whether they be the most outstanding or the more simple and widely diffused, are to be received with thanksgiving and consolation, for they are exceedingly suitable and useful for the needs of the Church.

480   Still, extraordinary gifts are not to be rashly sought after, nor are the fruits of apostolic labor to be presumptuously expected from them. In any case, judgment as to their genuineness and proper use belongs to those who preside over the Church, and to whose special competence it belongs, not indeed to extinguish the Spirit, but to test all things and hold fast to that which is good (cf. 1 *Th.* 5:12, 19-21).

481   13. All men are called to belong to the new People of God. Wherefore this People, while remaining one and unique, is to be spread throughout the whole world and must exist in all ages, so that the purpose of God's will may be fulfilled. In the beginning God made human nature one. After His children were scattered, He decreed that they should at length be unified again (cf. *Jn.* 11:52). It was for this reason that God sent His Son, whom He appointed heir of all things (cf. *Heb* 1:2), that He might be Teacher, King, and Priest of all, the Head of the new and universal people of the sons of God. For this God finally sent His Son's Spirit as Lord and Lifegiver. He it is who, on behalf of the whole Church and each and every one of those who believe, is the principle of their coming together and remaining together in the teaching of the apostles and in fellowship, in the breaking of bread and in prayers (cf. *Acts* 2:42, Greek text).

482   It follows that among all the nations of earth there is but one People of God, which takes its citizens from every race, making them citizens of a kingdom which is of a heavenly

and not an earthly nature. For all the faithful scattered throughout the world are in communion with each other in the Holy Spirit, so that "he who occupies the See of Rome knows the people of India are his members."[9] Since the kingdom of Christ is not of this world (cf. *Jn.* 18:36), the Church or People of God takes nothing away from the temporal welfare of any people by establishing that kingdom. Rather does she foster and take to herself, insofar as they are good, the ability, resources, and customs of each people. Taking them to herself she purifies, strengthens, and ennobles them. The Church in this is mindful that she must harvest with that King to whom the nations were given for an inheritance (cf. *Ps.* 2:8) and into whose city they bring gifts and presence (cf. *Ps.* 71[72]:10; *Is.* 60: 4-7; *Apoc.* 21:24). This characteristic of universality which adorns the People of God is a gift from the Lord Himself. By reason of it, the Catholic Church strives energetically and constantly to bring all humanity with all its riches back to Christ its Head in the unity of His Spirit.[10]

In virtue of this catholicity each individual part of the   **483** Church contributes through its special gifts to the good of the other parts and of the whole Church. Thus through the common sharing of gifts and through the common effort to attain fullness in unity, the whole and each of the parts receive increase. Not only, then, is the People of God made up of different peoples but even in its inner structure it is composed of various ranks. This diversity among its members arises either by reason of their duties, as is the case with those who exercise the sacred ministry for the good of their brethren, or by reason of their situation and way of life, as is the case with those many who enter the religious state and, tending toward holiness by a narrower path, stimulate their brethren by their example.

Moreover, within the Church particular Churches hold a   **484** rightful place. These Churches retain their own traditions without in any way lessening the primacy of the Chair of Peter. This Chair presides over the whole assembly of charity[11] and protects legitimate differences, while at the same time it sees that such differences do not hinder unity but rather contribute toward it. Finally, between all the parts of the Church there remains a bond of close communion with respect to spiritual riches, apostolic workers, and temporal resources. For the members of the People of God are called to share these goods, and to each of the Churches the words of the Apostle apply: "According to the gift that each has received, administer it to one another as good stewards of the manifold grace of God" (1 *Pet.* 4:10).

485   All men are called to be part of this catholic unity of the People of God, a unity which is harbinger of the universal peace it promotes. And there belong to it or are related to it in various ways, the Catholic faithful as well as all who believe in Christ, and indeed the whole of mankind. For all men are called to salvation by the grace of God.

486   14. This sacred Synod turns its attention first to the Catholic faithful. Basing itself upon sacred Scripture and tradition, it teaches that the Church, now sojourning on earth as an exile, is necessary for salvation. For Christ, made present to us in His Body, which is the Church, is the one Mediator and the unique Way of salvation. In explicit terms He Himself affirmed the necessity of faith and baptism (cf. *Mk.* 16:16; *Jn.* 3:5) and thereby affirmed also the necessity of the Church, for through baptism as through a doctor men enter the Church. Whosoever, therefore, knowing that the Catholic Church was made necessary by God through Jesus Christ, would refuse to enter her or to remain in her could not be saved.

487   They are fully incorporated into the society of the Church who, possessing the Spirit of Christ, accept her entire system and all the means of salvation given to her, and through union with her visible structure are joined to Christ, who rules her through the Supreme Pontiff and the bishops. This joining is effected by the bonds of professed faith, of the sacraments, of ecclesiastical government, and of communion. He is not saved, however, who, though he is part of the body of the Church, does not persevere in charity. He remains indeed in the bosom of the Church, but, as it were, only in a "bodily" manner and not "in his heart."[1][2] All the sons of the Church should remember that their exalted status is to be attributed

not to their own merits but to the special grace of Christ. If they fail moreover to respond to that grace in thought, word, and deed, not only will they not be saved but they will be the more severely judged.[13]

Catechumens who, moved by the Holy Spirit, seek with explicit intention to be incorporated into the Church are by that very intention joined to her. With love and solicitude Mother Church already embraces them as her own.   488

15. The Church recognizes that in many ways she is linked with those who, being baptized, are honored with the name of Christian, though they do not profess the faith in its entirety or do not preserve unity of communion with the successor of Peter.[14] For there are many who honor sacred Scripture, taking it as a norm of belief and of action, and who show a true religious zeal. They lovingly believe in God the Father Almighty and in Christ, Son of God and Savior.[15] They are consecrated by baptism, through which they are united with Christ. They also recognize and receive other sacraments within their own Churches or ecclesiastical communities. Many of them rejoice in the episcopate, celebrate the Holy Eucharist, and cultivate devotion toward the Virgin Mother of God.[16] They also share with us in prayer and other spiritual benefits.   489

Likewise, we can say that in some real way they are joined with us in the Holy Spirit, for to them also He gives His gifts and graces, and is thereby operative among them with His sanctifying power. Some indeed He has strengthened to the extent of the shedding of their blood. In all of Christ's disciples the Spirit arouses the desire to be peacefully united, in the manner determined by Christ, as one flock under one shepherd, and He prompts them to pursue this goal.[17] Mother Church never ceases to pray, hope, and work that they may gain this blessing. She exhorts her sons to purify and renew themselves so that the sign of Christ may shine more brightly over the face of the Church.   490

16. Finally, those who have not yet received the gospel are related in various ways to the People of God.[18] In the first place there is the people to whom the covenants and the promises were given and from whom Christ was born accord-   491

ing to the flesh (cf. *Rom.* 9:4-5). On account of their fathers, this people remains most dear to God, for God does not repent of the gifts He makes nor of the calls He issues (cf. *Rom.* 11:28-29).

492   But the plan of salvation also includes those who acknowledge the Creator. In the first place among these there are the Moslems, who, professing to hold the faith of Abraham, along with us adore the one and merciful God, who on the last day will judge mankind. Nor is God Himself far distant from those who in shadows and images seek the unkown God, for it is He who gives to all men life and breath and every other gift (cf. *Acts* 17:25-28), and who as Savior wills that all men be saved (cf. 1 *Tim.* 2:4).

493   Those also can attain to everlasting salvation who through no fault of their own do not know the gospel of Christ or His Church, yet sincerely seek God and, moved by grace strive by their deeds to do His will as it is known to them through the dictates of conscience.[19] Nor does divine Providence deny the help necessary for salvation to those who, without blame on their part, have not yet arrived at an explicit knowledge of God, but who strive to live a good life, thanks to His grace. Whatever goodness or truth is found among them is looked upon by the Church as a preparation for the gospel.[20] She regards such qualities as given by Him who enlightens all men so that they may finally have life.

494   But rather often men, deceived by the Evil One, have become caught up in futile reasoning and have exchanged the truth of God for a lie, serving the creature rather than the Creator (cf. *Rom.* 1:21, 25). Or some there are who, living and dying in a world without God, are subject to utter hopelessness. Consequently, to promote the glory of God and procure the salvation of all such men, and mindful of the command of the Lord, "Preach the gospel to every creature" (*Mk.* 16:16), the Church painstakingly fosters her missionary work.

495   17. Just as the Son was sent by the Father, so He too sent the apostles (cf. *Jn.* 20:21), saying: "Go, therefore, and make disciples of all nations, baptizing them in the name of the Father and of the Son and of the Holy Spirit, teaching them

to oberserve all that I have commanded you; and behold, I am with you all days even unto the consummation of the world" (*Mt.* 28:18-20).

The Church has received from the apostles as a task to be discharged even to the ends of the earth this solemn mandate of Christ to proclaim the saving truth (cf. *Acts* 1:8). Hence she makes the words of the Apostle her own: "Woe to me, if I do not preach the gospel" (1 *Cor.* 9:16), and continues unceasingly to send heralds of the gospel until such time as the infant churches are fully established and can themselves carry on the work of evangelizing. For the Church is compelled by the Holy Spirit to do her part towards the full realization of the will of God, who has established Christ as the source of salvation for the whole world. By the proclamation of the gospel, she prepares her hearers to receive and profess the faith, disposes them for baptism, snatches them from the slavery of error, and incorporates them into Christ so that through charity they may grow up into full maturity in Christ.

Through her work, whatever good is in the minds and hearts of men, whatever good lies latent in the religious practices and cultures of diverse peoples, is not only saved from destruction but is also healed, ennobled, and perfected unto the glory of God, the confusion of the devil, and the happiness of man. The obligation of spreading the faith is imposed on every disciple of Christ, according to his ability.[21] Though all the faithful can baptize, the priest alone can complete the building up of the Body in the Eucharistic Sacrifice. Thus are fulfilled the Words of God, spoken through His prophet: "From the rising of the sun even to the going down, my name is great among the Gentiles, and in every place there is sacrifice, and there is offered to my name a clean oblation" (*Mal.* 1:11).[22] In this way the Church simultaneously prays and labors in order that the entire world may become the People of God, the Body of the Lord, and the Temple of the Holy Spirit, and that in Christ, the Head of all, there may be rendered to the Creator and Father of the Universe all honor and glory.

496

497

Chapter III

The Hierarchical Structure of the Church
with Special Reference to the Episcopate

498   18. For the nurturing and constant growth of the People of God, Christ the Lord instituted in His Church a variety of ministries, which work for the good of the whole body. For those ministers who are endowed with sacred power are servants of their brethren, so that all who are of the People of God, and therefore enjoy a true Christian dignity, can work toward a common goal freely and in an orderly way, and arrive at salvation.

499   This most sacred Synod, following in the footsteps of the First Vatican Council, teaches and declares with that Council that Jesus Christ, the eternal Shepherd, established His holy Church by sending forth the apostles as He Himself had been sent by the Father (cf. *Jn.* 20:21). He willed that their successors, namely the bishops, should be shepherds in His Church even to the consummation of the world.

500   In order that the episcopate itself might be one and undivided, He placed blessed Peter over the other apostles, and instituted in him a permanent and visible source and foundation of unity of faith and fellowship.[23] And all this teaching about the institution, the perpetuity, the force and reason for the sacred primacy of the Roman Pontiff and of his infallible teaching authority, this sacred Synod again proposes to be firmly believed by all the faithful.

501   Continuing in the same task of clarification begun by Vatican I, this Council has decided to declare and proclaim before all men its teaching concerning bishops, the successors of the apostles, who together with the successor of Peter, the Vicar of Christ[24] and the visible Head of the whole Church, govern the house of the living God.

502   19. The Lord Jesus, after praying to the Father and calling to Himself those whom He desired, appointed twelve men who would stay in His company, and whom He would send to preach the kingdom of God (cf. *Mk.* 3:13-19; *Mt.*

10:1-42). These apostles (cf. *Lk.* 6:13) He formed after the manner of a college or a fixed group, over which He placed Peter, chosen from among them (cf. *Jn.* 21:15-17). He sent them first to the children of Israel and then to all nations (cf. *Rom.* 1:16), so that as sharers in His power they might make all peoples His disciples, sanctifying and governing them (cf. *Mt.* 28: 16-20; *Mk.* 16:15; *Lk.* 24:45-48; *Jn.* 20: 21-23). Thus they would spread His Church, and by ministering to it under the guidance of the Lord, would shepherd it all days even to the consummation of the world (cf. *Mt.* 28:20).

They were fully confirmed in this commission on the day   503
of Pentecost (cf. *Acts* 2:1-26) in accordance with the Lord's promise: "You shall receive power when the Holy Spirit comes upon you, and you shall be witnesses for me in Jerusalem and in all Judea and in Samaria and even to the very ends of the earth" (*Acts* 1:8). By everywhere preaching the gospel (cf. *Mk.* 16:20), which was accepted by their hearers under the influence of the Holy Spirit, the apostles gathered together the universal Church, which the Lord established on the apostles and built upon blessed Peter, their chief, Christ Jesus Himself remaining the supreme cornerstone (cf. *Apoc.* 21:14; *Mt.* 16:18; *Eph.* 2:20).[25]

20. That divine mission, entrusted by Christ to the apostles,   504
will last until the end of the world (*Mt.* 28:20), since the gospel which was to be handed down by them is for all time the source of all life for the Church. For this reason the apostles took care to appoint successors in this hierarchically structured society.

For they not only had helpers in their ministry,[26] but also,   505
in order that the mission assigned to them might continue after their death, they passed on to their immediate cooperators, as a kind of testament, the duty of perfecting and consolidating the work begun by themselves,[27] charging them to attend to the whole flock in which the Holy Spirit placed them to shepherd the Church of God (cf. *Acts* 20:28). They therefore appointed such men, and authorized the arrangement that, when these men should have died, other approved men would take up their ministry.[28]

506   Among those various ministries which, as tradition witnesses, were exercised in the Church from the earliest times, the chief place belongs to the office of those who, appointed to the episcopate in a sequence running back to the beginning,[29] are the ones who pass on the apostolic seed.[30] Thus, as St. Irenaeus testifies, through those who were appointed bishops by the apostles, and through their successors down to our own time, the apostolic tradition is manifested[31] and preserved[32] throughout the world.

507   With their helpers, the priests and deacons, bishops have therefore taken up the service of the community,[33] presiding in place of God over the flock[34] whose shepherds they are, as teachers of doctrine, priests of sacred worship, and officers of good order.[35] Just as the role that the Lord gave individually to Peter, the first among the apostles, is permanent and was meant to be transmitted to his successors, so also the apostles' office of nurturing the Church is permanent, and was meant to be exercised without interruption by the sacred order of bishops.[36] Therefore, this sacred Synod teaches that by divine institution bishops have succeeded to the place of the apostles[37] as shepherds of the Church, and that he who hears them, hears Christ, while he who rejects them, rejects Christ and Him who sent Christ (cf. *Lk.* 10:16).[38]

508   21. In the bishops, therefore, for whom priests are assistants, our Lord Jesus Christ, the supreme High Priest, is present in the midst of those who believe.[39] For sitting at the right hand of God the Father, He is not absent from the gathering of His high priests,[40] but above all through their excellent service He is preaching the Word of God to all nations, and constantly administering the sacraments of faith to those who believe. By their paternal role (cf. 1 *Cor.* 4:15). He incorporates new members into His body by a heavenly regeneration, and finally by their wisdom and prudence He Directs and guides the people of the New Testament in its pilgrimage toward eternal happiness.

509   These pastors, selected to shepherd the Lord's flock, are servants of Christ and stewards of the mysteries of God (cf. 1 *Cor.* 4:1). To them has been assigned the bearing of witness to the gospel of God's grace (cf. *Rom.* 15:16; *Acts* 20:24),

and to the ministration of the Spirit and of God's glorious power to make men just (cf. *2 Cor.* 3:8-9).

For the discharging of such great duties, the apostles were enriched by Christ with a special outpouring of the Holy Spirit, who came upon them (cf. *Acts* 1:8; 2:4; *Jn.* 20:22-23). This spiritual gift they passed on to their helpers by the imposition of hands (cf. 1 *Tim.* 4:14; 2 *Tim.* 1:6-7), and it has been transmitted down to us in episcopal consecration.[41] This sacred Synod teaches that by episcopal consecration is conferred the fullness of the sacrament of orders, that fullness which in the Church's liturgical practice and in the language of the holy Fathers of the Church is undoubtedly called the high priesthood, the apex of the sacred ministry.[42]

510

But episcopal consecration, together with the office of sanctifying, also confers the offices of teaching and of governing. (These, however, of their very nature, can be exercised only in hierarchical communion with the head and the members of the college.) For from tradition, which is expressed especially in liturgical rites and in the practice of the Church both of the East and of the West, it is clear that, by means of the imposition of hands and the words of consecration, the grace of the Holy Spirit is so conferred,[43] and the sacred character so impressed,[44] that bishops in an eminent and visible way undertake Christ's own role as Teacher, Shepherd, and High Priest, and that they act in His person.[45] Therefore it devolves on the bishops to admit newly elected members into the episcopal body by means of the sacrament of orders.

511

22. Just as, by the Lord's will, St. Peter and the other apostles constituted one apostolic college, so in a similar way the Roman Pontiff as the successor of Peter, and the bishops as the successors of the apostles are joined together. The collegial nature and meaning of the episcopal order found expression in the very ancient practice by which bishops appointed the world over were linked with one another and with the Bishop of Rome by the bonds of unity, charity, and peace,[46] also, in the conciliar assemblies[47] which made common judgments about more profound matters[48] in decisions reflecting the views of many.[49] The ecumenical

512

councils held through the centuries clearly attest this collegial aspect. And it is suggested also in the practice, introduced in ancient times, of summoning several bishops to take part in the elevation of someone newly elected to the ministry of the high priesthood. Hence, one is constituted a member of the episcopal body by virtue of sacramental consecration and by hierarchical communion with the head and members of the body.

513   But the college or body of bishops has no authority unless it is simultaneously conceived of in terms of its head, the Roman Pontiff, Peter's successor, and without any lessening of his power of primacy over all, pastors as well as the general faithful. For in virtue of his office, that is, as Vicar of Christ and pastor of the whole Church, the Roman Pontiff has full, supreme, and universal power over the Church. And he can always exercise this power freely.

514   The order of bishops is the successor to the college of the apostles in teaching authority and pastoral rule; or, rather, in the episcopal order the apostolic body continues without a break. Together with its head, the episcopal order is the subject of supreme and full power over the universal Church.[50] But this power can be exercised only with the consent of the Roman Pontiff. For our Lord made Simon Peter alone the rock and keybearer of the Church (cf. *Mt.* 16: 18-19), and appointed him shepherd of the whole flock (cf. *Jn.* 21:15 ff.).

515   It is definite, however, that the power of binding and loosing, which was given to Peter (*Mt.* 16:19), was granted also to the college of apostles, joined with their head (*Mt.* 18:18; 28:16-20).[51] This college, insofar as it is composed of many, expresses the variety and universality of the People of God, but insofar as it is assembled under one head, it expresses the unity of the flock of Christ. In it, the bishops, faithfully recognizing the primacy and pre-eminence of their head, exercise their own authority for the good of her own faithful, and indeed of the whole Church, with the Holy Spirit constantly strengthening its organic structure and inner harmony.

516   The supreme authority with which this college is empowered over the whole Church is exercised in a solemn way

through an ecumenical council. A council is never ecumenical unless it is confirmed or at least accepted as such by the successor of Peter. It is the prerogative of the Roman Pontiff to convoke these councils, to preside over them, and to confirm them.[52] The same collegiate power can be exercised in union with the Pope by the bishops living in all parts of the world, provided that the head of the college calls them to collegiate action, or at least so approves so freely accepts the united action of the dispersed bishops, that it is made a true collegiate act.

23. This collegial union is apparent also in the mutual relations of the individuals bishops with particular churches and with the universal Church. The Roman Pontiff, as the successor of Peter, is the perpetual and visible source and foundation of the unity of the bishops and of the multitude of the faithful.[53] The individual bishop, however, is the visible principle and foundation of unity in his particular church,[54] from such individual churches there comes into being the one and only Catholic Church.[55] For this reason each individual bishop represents his own church, but all of them together in union with the Pope represent the entire Church joined in the bond of peace, love, and unity.   **517**

The individual bishops, who are placed in charge of particular churches, exercise their pastoral government over the portion of the People of God committed to their care, and not over other churches nor over the universal Church. But each of them, as a member of the episcopal college and a legitimate successor of the apostles, is obliged by Christ's decree and command[56] to be solicitous for the whole Church.   **518**

This solicitude, though it is not exercised by an act of jurisdiction, contributes immensely to the welfare of the universal Church. For it is the duty of all bishops to promote and to safeguard the unity of faith and the discipline common to the whole Church, to instruct the faithful in love for the whole Mystical Body of Christ, especially for its poor and sorrowing members and for those who are suffering persecution for justice' sake (cf. *Mt.* 5:10), and, finally, to foster every activity which is common to the whole Church, especially efforts to spread the faith and make the light of full truth   **519** dawn on all men. For the rest, it is a sacred reality that by governing well their own church as a portion of the universal Church, they themselves are effectively contributing to the welfare of the whole Mystical Body, which is also the body of the churches.[57]

520   The task of proclaiming the gospel everywhere on earth devolves on the body of pastors, to all of whom in common Christ gave His command, thereby imposing upon them a common duty, as Pope Celestine in his time reminded the Fathers of the Council of Ephesus.[58] From this it follows that the individual bishops, insofar as the discharge of their duty permits, are obliged to enter into a community of effort among themselves and with the successor of Peter, upon whom was imposed in a special way the great duty of spreading the Christian name.[59] With all their energy, therefore, they must supply to the missions both workers for the harvest and also spiritual and material aid, both directly and on their own account, as well as by arousing the ardent cooperation of the faithful. And finally, in a universal fellowship of charity, bishops should gladly extend their fraternal aid to other churches, especially to neighboring and more needy dioceses, in accordance with the venerable example of antiquity.

521   By divine Providence it has come about that various churches established in diverse places by the apostles and their successors have in the course of time coalesced into several groups, organically united, which, preserving the unity of faith and the unique divine constitution of the universal Church, enjoy their own discipline, their own liturgical usage, and their own theological and spiritual heritage. Some of these churches, notably the ancient patriarchical churches, as parent-stocks of the faith, so to speak, have begotten others as daughter churches. With these they are connected down to our own time by a close bond of charity in their sacramental life and in their mutual respect for rights and duties.[60]

522   This variety of local churches with one common aspiration is particularly splendid evidence of the catholicity of the undivided Church. In like manner the episcopal bodies of today are in a position to render a manifold and fruitful assistance,

so that this collegiate sense may be put into practical application.

24. To the Lord was given all power in heaven and on earth.   523
As successors of the apostles, bishops receive from Him the
mission to teach all nations and to preach the gospel to every
creature, so that all men may attain to salvation by faith, baptism, and the fulfillment of the commandments (cf. *Mt.* 28:18;
Mk. 16:15-16; *Acts* 26:17 f.). To fulfill this mission, Christ
the Lord promised the Holy Spirit from heaven. By His power
they were to be witnesses to Christ before the nations and
peoples and kings, even to the ends of the earth (cf. *Acts*
1:8; 2: 1 ff.; 9:15). Now, that duty, which the Lord committed to the shepherds of His people, is a true service, and in
sacred literature is significantly called "diakonia" or ministry
(cf. *Acts* 1:17, 25; 21:19; *Rom.* 11:13; 1 *Tim.* 1:12).

The canonical mission of bishops can come about by legi-   524
timate customs which have not been revoked by the supreme
and universal authority of the Church, or by laws made or
recognized by that same authority, or directly through the
successor of Peter himself. If the latter refuses or denies
apostolic communion, a bishop cannot assume office.[61]

25. Among the principal duties of bishops, the preaching   525
of the gospel occupies an eminent place.[62] For bishops are
preachers of the faith who lead new disciples of Christ. They
are authentic teachers, that is, teachers endowed with the
authority of Christ, who preach to the people committed to
them the faith they must believe and put into practice. By
the light of the Holy Spirit, they make that faith clear, bringing forth from the treasury of revelation new things and old
(cf. *Mt.* 13:52), making faith bear fruit and vigilantly warding
off any errors which threaten their flock (cf. 2 *Tim.* 4:1-4).

Bishops, teaching in communion with the Roman Pontiff,   526
are to be respected by all as witnesses to divine and Catholic
truth. In matters of faith and morals, the bishops speak in
the name of Christ and the faithful are to accept their teaching and adhere to it with a religious assent of soul. This religious submission of will and of mind must be shown in a
special way to the authentic teaching authority of the Roman
Pontiff, even when he is not speaking ex cathedra. That is, it

must be shown in such a way that his supreme magisterium is acknowledged with reverence, the judgments made by him are sincerely adhered to, according to his manifest mind and will. His mind and will in the matter may be known chiefly either from the character of the documents, from his frequent repetition of the same doctrine, or from his manner of speaking.

527   Although the individual bishops do not enjoy the prerogative of infallibility, they can nevertheless proclaim Christ's doctrine infallibly. This is so, even when they are dispersed around the world, provided that while maintaining the bond of unity among themselves and with Peter's successor, and while teaching authentically on a matter of faith or morals, they concur in a single viewpoint as the one which must be held conclusively.[63] This authority is even more clearly verified when, gathered together in an ecumenical council, they are teachers and judges of faith and morals for the universal Church. Their definitions must then be adhered to with the submission of faith.[64]

528   This infallibility with which the divine Redeemer willed His Church to be endowed in defining a doctrine of faith and morals extends as far as extends the deposit of divine revelation, which must be religiously guarded and faithfully expounded. This is the infallibility which the Roman Pontiff, the head of the college of bishops, enjoys in virtue of his office, when, as the supreme shepherd and teacher of all the faithful, who confirms his brethren in their faith (cf. *Lk.* 22: 32), he proclaims by a definitive act some doctrine of faith or morals.[65] Therefore his definitions, of themselves, and not from the consent of the Church, are justly styled irreformable, for they are pronounced with the assistance of the Holy Spirit, an assistance promised to him in blessed Peter. Therefore they need no approval of others, nor do they allow an appeal to any other judgment. For then the Roman Pontiff is not pronouncing judgment as a private person. Rather, as the supreme teacher of the universal Church, as one in whom the charism of the infallibility of the Church herself is individually present, he is expounding or defending a doctrine of Catholic faith.[66]

The infallibility promised to the Church resides also in the body of bishops when that body exercises supreme teaching authority with the successor of Peter. To the resultant definitions the assent of the Church can never be wanting, on account of the activity of that same Holy Spirit, whereby the whole flock of Christ is preserved and progresses in unity of faith.[67]

529

But when either the Roman Pontiff or the body of bishops together with him formulates a definition, they do so in accord with revelation itself. All are obliged to maintain and be rules by this revelation, which, as written or preserved by tradition, is transmitted in its entirety through the legitimate succession of bishops and especially through the care of the Roman Pontiff himself.

530

Under the guiding light of the Spirit of truth, revelation is thus religiously preserved and faithfully expounded in the Church.[68] The Roman Pontiff and the bishops, in conformity with their duty and as befits the gravity of the matter, strive painstakingly and by appropriate means to inquire properly into that revelation and to give apt expression to its contents.[69] But they do not accept any new public revelation as part of the divine deposit of faith.[70]

531

26. A bishop, marked with the fullness of the sacrament of orders, is "the steward of the grace of the supreme priesthood,"[71] especially in the Eucharist, which he offers or causes to be offered,[72] and by which the Church constantly lives and grows. This Church of Christ is truly present in all legitimate local congregations of the faithful which, united with their pastors, are themselves called churches in the New Testament.[73] For in their own locality these are the new people called by God, in the Holy Spirit and in much fullness (cf. 1 *Th.* 1:5). In them the faithful are gathered together by the preaching of the gospel of Christ, and the mystery of the Lord's Supper is celebrated, "that by the flesh and blood of the Lord's body the whole brotherhood may be joined together."[74]

532

In any community existing around an altar, under the sacred ministry of the bishop,[75] there is manifested a symbol of that charity and "unity of the Mystical Body, without

533

which there can be no salvation."[76] In these communities, though frequently small and poor, or living far from any other, Christ is present. By virtue of Him the one, holy, catholic, and apostolic Church gathers together.[77] For "the partaking of the Body and Blood of Christ does nothing other than transform us into that which we consume."[78]

534   Every legitimate celebration of the Eucharist is regulated by the bishop, to whom is committed the office of offering the worship of Christian religion to the divine Majesty and of administering it in accordance with the Lord's commandments and with the Church's laws, as further defined by his particular judgment for his diocese.

535   By thus praying and laboring for the people, bishops channel the fullness of Christ's holiness in many ways and abundantly. By the ministry of the word they communicate God's power to those who believe unto salvation (cf. *Rom.* 1:16). Through the sacraments, the regular and fruitful distribution of which they direct by their authority,[79] they sanctify the faithful. They govern the conferring of baptism, by which a sharing in the kingly priesthood of Christ is granted. They are the original ministers of confirmation, dispensers of sacred orders, and the moderators of penitential discipline. They earnestly exhort and instruct their people to carry out with faith and reverence their part in the liturgy and especially in the holy Sacrifice of the Mass. Finally, by the example of their manner of life they must be an influence for good on those over whom they preside, by refraining from all evil and, as far as they are able with God's help, turning evil to good. Thus, together with the flock committed to their care, they can arrive at eternal life.[80]

536   27. Bishops govern the particular churches entrusted to them as the vicars and ambassadors of Christ.[81] This they do by their counsel, exhortations, and example, as well, indeed, as by their authority and sacred power. This power they use only for the edification of their flock in truth and holiness, remembering that he who is greater should become as the lesser and he who is the more distinguished, as the servant (cf. *Lk.* 22:26-27). This power, which they personally exercise in Christ's name, is proper, ordinary, and immediate,

although its exercise is ultimately regulated by the supreme authority of the Church, and can be circumscribed by certain limits, for the advantage of the Church or of the faithful. In virtue of this power, bishops have the sacred right and the duty before the Lord to make laws for their subjects, to pass judgment on them, and to moderate everything pertaining to the ordering of worship and the apostolate.

The pastoral office or the habitual and daily care of their 537 sheep is entrusted to them completely. Nor are they to be regarded as vicars of the Roman Pontiff, for they exercise an authority which is proper to them, and are quite correctly called "prelates," heads of the people whom they govern.[82] Their power, therefore, is not destroyed by the supreme and universal power. On the contrary it is affirmed, strengthened, and vindicated thereby,[83] since the Holy Spirit unfailingly preserves the form of government established by Christ the Lord in His Church.

Since he is sent by the Father to govern His family, a bish- 538 op must keep before his eyes the example of the Good Shepherd, who came not to be ministered unto but to minister (cf. *Mt.* 20:28; *Mk.* 10:45), and to lay down His life for His sheep (cf. *Jn.* 10:11). Taken from among men, and himself beset with weakness, he is able to have compassion on the ignorant and erring (cf. *Heb.* 5:1-2). Let him not refuse to listen to his subjects, whom he cherishes as his true sons and exhorts to cooperate readily with him. As having one day to render to God an account for their souls (cf. *Heb.* 13:17), he takes care of them by his prayer, preaching, and all the works of charity, and not only of them, but also of those who are not yet of the one flock. For these also are commended to him in the Lord.

Since, like Paul the Apostle, he is debtor to all men, let 539 him be ready to preach the gospel to all (cf. *Rom.* 1:14-15), and to urge his faithful to apostolic and missionary activity. For their part, the faithful must cling to their bishop, as the Church does to Christ, and Jesus Christ to the Father, so that everything may harmonize in unity,[84] and abound to the glory of God (cf. 2 *Cor.* 4:15).

540   28. Christ, whom the Father sanctified and sent into the world (*Jn.* 10:36) has, through His apostles, made their successors, the bishops, partakers of His consecration and His mission.[85] These in their turn have legitimately handed on to different individuals in the Church various degrees of participation in this ministry. Thus the divinely established ecclesiastical ministry is exercised on different levels by those who from antiquity have been called bishops, priests, and deacons.[86] Although priests do not possess the highest degree of the priesthood, and although they are dependent on the bishops in the exercise of their power, they are nevertheless united with the bishops in sacerdotal dignity.[87] By the power of the sacrament of orders,[88] and in the image of Christ the eternal High Priest (*Heb.* 5:1-10; 7 24; 9:11-28), they are consecrated to preach the gospel, shepherd the faithful, and celebrate divine worship as true priests of the New Testament.[89] Partakers of the function of Christ the sole Mediator (1 *Tim.* 2:5) on their level of ministry, they announce the divine word to all. They exercise the sacred function of Christ most of all in the Eucharistic liturgy or synaxis. There, acting in the person of Christ,[90] and proclaiming His mystery, they join the offering of the faithful to the sacrifice of their Head. Until the coming of the Lord (cf. 1 *Cor.* 11:26), they re-present and apply in the Sacrifice of the Mass the one sacrifice of the New Testament, namely the sacrifice of Christ offering Himself once and for all to His Father as a spotless victim (cf. *Heb.* 9:11-28).[91]

541   For the penitent or ailing among the faithful, priests exercise fully the ministry of reconciliation and alleviation, and they present the needs and the prayers of the faithful to God the Father (cf. *Heb.* 5:1-4). Exercising within the limits of their authority the function of Christ as Shepherd and Head, [92] they gather together God's family as a brotherhood all of one mind[93] and lead them in the Spirit, through Christ, to God the Father. In the midst of the flock they adore Him in spirit and in truth (cf. *Jn.* 4:24). Finally, they labor in word and doctrine (cf. *Tim.* 5:17), believing what they have read and meditated upon in the law of the Lord, teaching what they believe, and practicing what they teach.[94]

Priests, prudent cooperators with the episcopal order[95]   542
as well as its aids and instruments, are called to serve the People of God. They constitute one priesthood[96] with their
bishop, although that priesthood is comprised of different
functions. Associated with their bishop in a spirit of trust and
generosity, priests make him present in a certain sense in the
individual local congregations of the faithful, and take upon
themselves, as far as they are able, his duties and concerns,
discharging them with daily care. As they sanctify and govern
under the bishop's authority that part of the Lord's flock entrusted to them, they make the universal Church visible in
their own locality and lend powerful assistance to the upbuilding of the whole body of Christ (cf. *Eph.* 4:12). Intent
always upon the welfare of God's children, they must strive
to lend their effort to the pastoral work of the whole diocese,
and even of the entire Church.

On account of this sharing in his priesthood and mission,   543
let priests sincerely look upon the bishop as their father, and
reverently obey him. And let the bishop regard his priests,
who are his co-workers, as sons and friends, just as Christ
called His disciples no longer servants but friends (cf. *Jn.*
15:15). All priests, both diocesan and religious, by reason of
orders and ministry, are associated with this body of bishops,
and serve the good of the whole Church according to their
vocation and the grace given to them.

In virtue of their common sacred ordination and mission,   544
all priests are bound together in an intimate brotherhood,
which should naturally and freely manifest itself in mutual
aid, spiritual as well as material, pastoral as well as personal,
in meetings and in a community of life, of labor, of charity.

Let them, as fathers in Christ, take care of the faithful   545
whom they have spiritually begotten by baptism and by their
teaching (cf. 1 *Cor.* 4:15; 1 *Pet.* 1:23). Having become from
the heart a pattern to the flock (1 *Pet.* 5:3), let them so lead
and serve their local community that it may worthily be called
by that name by which the one and entire People of God is
distinguished, namely, the Church of God (cf. 1 *Cor.* 1:2; 2
Cor. 1:1 and passim). They should remember that by their
daily life and interests they are showing the face of a truly

priestly and pastoral ministry to the faithful and the unbeliever, to Catholics and non-Catholics, and that to all men
they should bear witness about truth and life, and as good
shepherds, go after those also (cf. *Lk*. 15:4-7) who, though
baptized in the Catholic Church, have fallen away from the
sacraments, or even from the faith.

546 		Because the human race today is joining more and more
into a civic, economic, and social unity, it is that much more
necessary that priests, united in concern and effort, under
the leadership of the bishops and the Supreme Pontiff, wipe
out every kind of division, so that the whole human race may
be brought into the unity of the family of God.

547 		29. At a lower level of the hierarchy are deacons, upon
whom hands are imposed "not unto the priesthood, but unto
a ministry of service."[97] For strengthened by sacramental
grace, in communion with the bishop and his group of priests,
they serve the People of God in the ministry of the liturgy,
of the word, and of charity. It is the duty of the deacon, to
the extent that he has been authorized by competent authority, to administer baptism solemnly, to be custodian and
dispenser of the Eucharist, to assist at and bless marriages in
the name of the Church, to bring Viaticum to the dying, to
read the sacred Scripture to the faithful, to instruct and exhort the people, to preside at the worship and prayer of the
faithful, to administer sacramentals, and to officiate at funeral and burial services. Dedicated to duties of charity and
of administration, let deacons be mindful of the admonition
of Blessed Polycarp: "Be merciful, diligent, walking according
to the truth of the Lord, who became the servant of all."[98]

548 		These duties, so very necessary for the life of the Church,
can in many areas be fulfilled only with difficulty according
to the prevailing discipline of the Latin Church. For the reason, the diaconate can in the future be restored as a proper
and permanent rank of the hierarchy. It pertains to the competent territorial bodies of bishops, of one kind or another,
to decide, with the approval of the Supreme Pontiff, whether
and where it is opportune for such deacons to be appointed
for the care of souls. With the consent of the Roman Pontiff,
this diaconate will be able to be conferred upon men of

more mature age, even upon those living in the married state. It may also be conferred upon suitable young men. For them, however, the law of celibacy must remain intact.

Chapter IV

The Laity

30. Having set forth the functions of the hierarchy, this   549
holy Synod gladly turns its attention to the status of those
faithful called the laity. Everything which has been said so
far concerning the People of God applies equally to the laity,
religious, and clergy. But there are certain things which pertain in a particular way to the laity, both men and women,
by reason of their situation and mission. Because of the special circumstances of our time the foundations of these par-
ticularities must be examined more thoroughly.

For their sacred pastors know how much the laity contri-   550
bute to the welfare of the entire Church. Pastors also know
that they themselves were not meant by Christ to shoulder
alone the entire saving mission of the Church toward the
world. On the contrary, they understand that it is their noble
duty so to shepherd the faithful and recognize their services
and charismatic gifts that all according to their proper roles
may cooperate in this common undertaking with one heart.
For we must all "practice the truth in love, and so grow up
in all things in him who is head, Christ. For from him the
whole body (being closely joined and knit together through
every joint of the system according to the functioning in
due measure of each single part) derives its increase to the
building up of itself in love" (*Eph.* 4:15-16).

31. The term laity is here understood to mean all the faith-   551
ful except those in holy orders and those in a religious state
sanctioned by the Church. These faithful are by baptism
made one body with Christ and are established among the
People of God. They are in their own way made sharers in
the priestly, prophetic, and kingly functions of Christ. They
carry out their own part in the mission of the whole Christian people with respect to the Church and the world.

552   A secular quality is proper and special to laymen. It is true that those in holy orders can at times engage in secular activities, and even have a secular profession. But by reason of their particular vocation they are chiefly and professedly ordained to the sacred ministry. Similarly, by their state in life, religious give splendid and striking testimony that the world cannot be transfigured and offered to God without the spirit of the beatitudes.

553   But the laity, by their very vocation, seek the kingdom of God by engaging in temporal affairs and by ordering them according to the plan of God. They live in the world, that is, in each and in all of the secular professions and occupations. They live in the ordinary circumstances of family and social life, from which the very web of their existence is woven.

554   They are called there by God so that by exercising their proper function and being led by the spirit of the gospel they can work for the sanctification of the world from within, in the manner of leaven. In this way they can make Christ known to others, especially by the testimony of a life reinvolved in temporal affairs of every sort. It is therefore his special task to illumine and organize these affairs in such a way that they may always start out, develop, and persist according to Christ's mind, to the praise of the Creator and the Redeemer.

555   32. By divine institution Holy Church is structured and governed with a wonderful diversity. "For just as in one body we have many members, yet all the members have not the same function, so we, the many, are one body in Christ, but severally members one of another" (*Rom.* 12:4-5).

556   Therefore, the chosen People of God is one: "one Lord, one faith, one baptism" (*Eph.* 4:5). As members they share a common dignity from their rebirth in Christ. They have the same filial grace and the same vocation to perfection. They possess in common one salvation, one hope, and one undivided charity. Hence, there is in Christ and in the Church no inequality on the basis of race or nationality, social condition or sex, because "there is neither Jew nor Greek; there is neither slave nor freeman; there is neither male nor female.

For you are all 'one' in Christ Jesus" (*Gal.* 3:28, Greek text; cf. *Col.* 3:11).

If therefore everyone in the Church does not proceed by   557
the same path, nevertheless all are called to sanctity and have received an equal privilege of faith through the justice of God (cf. 2 *Pet.* 1:1). And if by the will of Christ some are made teachers, dispensers of mysteries, and shepherds on behalf of others, yet all share a true equality with regard to the dignity and to the activity common to all the faithful for the building up of the Body of Christ.

For the distinction which the Lord made between sacred   558
ministers and the rest of the People of God entails a unifying purpose, since pastors and the other faithful are bound to each other by a mutual need. Pastors of the Church, following the example of the Lord, should minister to one another and to the other faithful. The faithful in their turn should enthusiastically lend their cooperative assistance to their pastors and teachers. Thus in their diversity all bear witness to the admirable unity of the Body of Christ. This very diversity of graces, ministries, and works gathers the children of God into one, because "all these things are the work of one and the same Spirit" (1 *Cor.* 12:11).

Therefore, by divine condescension the laity have Christ   559
for their brother who, though He is the Lord of all, came not to be served but to serve (cf. *Mt.* 20:28). They also have for their brothers those in the sacred ministry who by teaching, by sanctifying, and by ruling with the authority of Christ so feed the family of God that the new commandment of charity may be fulfilled by all. St. Augustine puts this very beautifully when he says: "What I am for you terrifies me; what I am with you consoles me. For you I am a bishop; but with you I am a Christian. The former is a title of duty; the latter, one of grace. The former is a danger; the latter, salvation.[99]

33. The laity are gathered together in the People of God   560
and make up the Body of Christ under one Head. Whoever they are, they are called upon, as living members, to expend all their energy for the growth of the Church and its continu-

ous sanctification. For this very energy is a gift of the Creator and a blessing of the Redeemer.

561   The lay apostolate, however, is a participation in the saving mission of the Church itself. Through their baptism and confirmation, all are commissioned to that apostolate by the Lord Himself. Moreover, through the sacraments, especially the Holy Eucharist, there is communicated and nourished that charity toward God and man which is the soul of the entire apostolate. Now, the laity are called in a special way to make the Church present and operative in those places and circumstances where only through them can she become the salt of the earth.[100] Thus every layman, by virtue of the very gifts bestowed upon him, is at the same time a witness and a living instrument of the mission of the Church herself, "according to the measure of Christ's bestowal" (*Eph.* 4:7).

562   Besides this apostolate, which pertains to absolutely every Christian, the laity can also be called in various ways to a more direct form of cooperation in the apostolate of the hierarchy.[101] This was the case with certain men and women who assisted Paul the Apostle in the gospel, laboring much in the Lord (cf. *Phil.* 4:3; *Rom.* 16:3 ff). Further, laymen have the capacity to be deputed by the hierarchy to exercise certain church functions for a spiritual purpose.

563   Upon all the laity, therefore, rests the noble duty of working to extend the divine plan of salvation ever increasingly to all men of each epoch and in every land. Consequently, let every opportunity be given them so that, according to their abilities and the needs of the times, they may zealously participate in the saving work of the Church.

564   34. Since the supreme and eternal Priest, Christ Jesus, wills to continue His witness and serve through the laity too, He vivifies them in His Spirit and unceasingly urges them on to every good and perfect work.

565   For besides intimately associating them with His life and His mission, Christ also gives them a share in His priestly function of offering spiritual worship for the glory of God and the salvation of men. For this reason the laity, dedicated to Christ and anointed by the Holy Spirit, are marvelously called and equipped to produce in themselves ever more

abundant fruits of the Spirit. For all their works, prayers, and apostolic endeavors, their ordinary married and family life, their daily labor, their mental and physical relaxation, if carried out in the Spirit, and even the hardships of life, if patiently borne—all of these become spiritual sacrifices ac- ᛙ ceptable to God through Jesus Christ (cf. 1 *Pet.* 2:5). During the celebration of the Eucharist, these sacrifices are most lovingly offered to the Father along with the Lord's body. Thus, as worshipers whose every deed is holy, the laity consecrate the world itself to God.

35. Christ, the great Prophet, who proclaimed the kingdom   566
of His Father by the testimony of His life and the power of His words, continually fulfills His prophetic office until His full glory is revealed. He does this not only through the hierarchy who teach in His name and with His authority, but also through the laity. For that very purpose He made them His witnesses and gave them understanding of the faith and the grace of speech (cf. *Acts* 2:17-18; *Apoc.* 19:10), so that the power of the gospel might shine forth in their daily social and family life.

They show themselves to be children of the promise, if   567
strong in faith and in hope, they make the most of the present time (cf. *Eph.* 5:16; *Col.* 4:5), and with patience await the glory that is to come (cf. *Rom.* 8:25). Let them not, then, hide this hope in the depths of their hearts, but even in the framework of secular life let them express it by a continual turning toward God and by wrestling "against the world-rulers of this darkness, against the spiritual forces of wickedness" (*Eph.* 6:12).

The sacraments of the New Law, by which the life and   568
the apostolate of the faithful are nourished, prefigure a new heaven and a new earth (cf. *Apoc.* 21:1). So too the laity go forth as powerful heralds of a faith in things to be hoped for (cf. *Heb.* 11:1) provided they steadfastly join to their profession of faith a life springing from faith. This evangelization, that is, this announcing of Christ by a living testimony as well as by the spoken word, takes on a specific quality and a special force in that it is carried out in the ordinary surroundings of the world.

569   In connection with this function, that state of life which is sanctified by a special sacrament is obviously of great value, namely, married and family life. For where Christianity pervades a whole way of life and ever increasingly transforms it, there will exist both the practice and an excellent school of the lay apostolate. In such a home, husband and wife find their proper vocation in being witnesses to one another and to their children of faith in Christ and love for Him. The Christian family loudly proclaims both the present virtues of the kingdom of God and the hope of a blessed life to come. Thus by its example and its witness it accuses the world of sin and enlightens those who seek the truth.

570   Consequently, even when preoccupied with temporal cares, the laity can and must perform eminently valuable work on behalf of bringing the gospel to the world. Some of them do all they can to provide sacred services when sacred ministers are lacking or are blocked by a persecuting regime. Many devote themselves entirely to apostolic work. But all ought to cooperate in the spreading and intensifying of the kingdom of Christ in the world. Therefore, let the laity strive skillfully to acquire a more profound grasp of revealed truth, and insistently beg of God the gift of wisdom.

571   36. Christ obeyed even at the cost of death, and was therefore raised up by the Father (cf. *Phil.* 2:8-9). Thus He entered into the glory of His kingdom. To Him all things are made subject until He subjects Himself and all created things to the Father, that God may be all (cf. 1 *Cor.* 15:27-28). Now, Christ has communicated this power of subjection to His disciples that they might be established in royal freedom and that by self-denial and a holy life they might conquer the reign of sin in themselves (cf. *Rom.* 6:12). Further, He has shared this power so that by serving Him in their fellow men they might through humility and patience lead their brother men to that King whom to serve is to reign.

572   For the Lord wishes to spread His kingdom by means of the laity also, a kingdom of truth and life, a kingdom of holiness and grace, a kingdom of justice, love, and peace.[102] In this kingdom, creation itself will be delivered out of its slavery to corruption and into the freedom of the glory of

the sons of God (cf. *Rom.* 8:21). Clearly then a great promise and a great mandate are committed to the disciples: "For all are yours, and you are Christ's, and Christ is God's" (1 *Cor.* 3:23).

The faithful, therefore, must learn the deepest meaning and the value of all creation, and how to relate it to the praise of God. They must assist one another to live holier lives even in their daily occupations. In this way the world is permeated by the spirit of Christ and more effectively achieves its purpose in justice, charity, and peace. The laity have the principal role in the universal fulfillment of this purpose.   573

Therefore, by their competence in secular fields and by their personal activity, elevated from within by the grace of Christ, let them labor vigorously so that by human labor, technical skill, and civic culture created goods may be perfected for the benefit of every last man, according to the design of the Creator and the light of His Word. Let them work to see that created goods are more fittingly distributed among men, and that such goods in their own way lead to general progress in human and Christian liberty. In this manner, through the members of the Church, Christ will progressively illumine the whole of human society with His saving light.   574

Moreover, let the laity also by their combined efforts remedy any institutions and conditions of the world which are customarily an inducement to sin, so that all such things may be conformed to the norms of justice and may favor the practice of virtue rather than hinder **it**. By so doing, laymen will imbue culture and human activity with moral values. They will better prepare the field of the world for the seed of the Word of God. At the same time they will open wider the Church's doors, through which the message of peace can enter the world.   575

Because the very plan of salvation requires it, the faithful should learn how to distinguish carefully between those rights and duties which are theirs as members of the Church, and those which they have as members of human society. Let them strive to harmonize the two, remembering that in every temporal affair they must be guided by a Christian   576 conscience. For even in secular affairs there is no human activity which can be withdrawn from God's dominion. In our own time, however, it is most urgent that this distinction and also this harmony should shine forth as radiantly as possible in the practice of the faithful, so that the mission of the Church may correspond more adequately to the special conditions of the world today. For while it must be recognized that the temporal sphere is governed by its own principles, since it is properly concerned with the interests of this world, that ominous doctrine must rightly be rejected which attempts to build a society with no regard whatever for religion, and which attacks and destroys the religious liberty of its citizens.[103]

577   37. The laity have the right, as do all Christians, to receive in abundance from their sacred pastors the spiritual goods of the Church, especially the assistance of the Word of God and the sacraments.[104] Every layman should openly reveal to them his needs and desires with that freedom and confidence which befits a son of God and a brother in Christ. An individual layman, by reason of the knowledge, competence, or outstanding ability which he may enjoy, is permitted and sometimes even obliged to express his opinon on things which concern the good of the Church.[105] When occasions arise, let this be done through the agencies set up by the Church for this purpose. Let it always be done in truth, in courage, and in prudence, with reverence and charity toward those who by reason of their sacred office represent the person of Christ.

578   With ready Christian obedience, laymen as well as all disciples of Christ should accept whatever their sacred pastors, as representatives of Christ, decree in their role as teachers and rulers in the Church. Let laymen follow the example of Christ, who, by His obedience even at the cost of death, opened to all men the blessed way to the liberty of the children of God. Nor should they omit to pray to God for those placed over them, who keep watch as having to render an account of their souls, so that they may render this account with joy and not with grief (cf. *Heb.* 13:17).

Let sacred pastors recognize and promote the dignity as   579
well as the responsibility of the layman in the Church. Let
them willingly make use of his prudent advice. Let them confidently assign duties to him in the service of the Church, allowing him freedom and room for action. Further, let them
encourage the layman so that he may undertake tasks on his
own initiative. Attentively in Christ, let them consider with
fatherly love the projects, suggestions, and desires proposed
by the laity.[106] Furthermore, let pastors respectfully acknowledge that just freedom which belongs to everyone in
this earthly city.

A great many benefits are to be hoped for from this famil-   580
iar dialogue between the laity and their pastors: in the laity,
a strengthened sense of personal responsibility, a renewed
enthusiasm, a more ready application of their talents to the
projects of their pastors. The latter, for their part, aided by
the experience of the laity, can more clearly and more
suitably come to decisions regarding spiritual and temporal
matters. In this way, the whole Church, strengthened by each
one of its members, can more effectively fulfill its mission for
the life of the world.

38. Each individual layman must stand before the world   581
as a witness to the resurrection and life of the Lord Jesus and
as a sign that God lives. As a body and individually, the laity
must do their part to nourish the world with spiritual fruits
(cf. *Gal.* 5:22), and to spread abroad in it that spirit by which
are animated those poor, meek, and peacemaking men whom
the Lord in the gospel calls blessed (cf. *Mt.* 5:3-9). In a word,
"what the soul is to the body, let Christians be to the
world."[107]

Chapter V

The Call of the Whole Church to Holiness

39. Faith teaches that the Church, whose mystery is being   582
set forth by this sacred Synod, is holy in a way which can
never fail. For Christ, the Son of God, who with the Father

and the Spirit is praised as being "alone holy,"[108] loved the Church as His Bride, delivering Himself up for her. This He did that He might sanctify her (cf. *Eph.* 5:25-26). He united her to Himself as His own body and crowned her with the gift of the Holy Spirit, for God's glory. Therefore in the Church, everyone belonging to the hierarchy, or being cared for by it, is called to holiness, according to the saying of the Apostle: "For this is the will of God, your sanctification" (1 *Th.* 4:3; cf. *Eph.* 1:4).

583   Now, this holiness of the Church is unceasingly manifested, as it ought to be, through those fruits of grace that the Spirit produces in the faithful. It is expressed in multiple ways by those individuals who, in their walk of life, strive for the perfection of charity, and thereby help others to grow. In a particularly appropriate way this holiness shines out in the practice of the counsels customarily called "evangelical." Under the influence of the Holy Spirit, the practice of these counsels is undertaken by many Christians, either privately or in some Church-approved situation or state, and produces in the world, as produce it should a shining witness and model of holiness.

584   40. The Lord Jesus, the divine Teacher and Model of all perfection, preached holiness of life to each and every one of His disciples, regardless of their situation: "You therefore are to be perfect, even as your heavenly Father is perfect" (*Mt.* 5:48).[109] He Himself stands as the Author and Finisher of this holiness of life. For He sent the Holy Spirit upon all men that He might inspire them from within to love God with their whole heart and their whole soul, with all their mind and all their strength (cf. *Mk.* 12:30) and that they might love one another as Christ loved them (cf. *Jn.* 13:34; 15:12).

585   The followers of Christ are called by God, not according to their accomplishments, but according to his own purpose and grace. They are justified in the Lord Jesus, and through baptism sought in faith they truly become sons of God and sharers in the divine nature. In this way they are really made holy. Then, too, by God's gifts they must hold on to and complete in their lives this holiness which they have received.

They are warned by the Apostle to live "as becomes saints" (*Eph.* 5:3), and to put on "as God's chosen ones, holy and beloved, a heart of mercy, kindness, humility, meekness, patience" (*Col.* 3:12), and to possess the fruits of the Spirit unto holiness (cf. *Gal.* 5:22; *Rom.* 6:22). Since we all truly offend in many things (cf. *Jas.* 3:2), we all need God's mercy continuously and must daily pray: "Forgive us our debts" (*Mt.* 6:12).[110]

Thus it is evident to everyone that all the faithful of Christ   586
of whatever rank or status are called to the fullness of the Christian life and to the perfection of charity.[111] By this holiness a more human way of life is promoted even in this earthly society. In order that the faithful may reach this perfection, they must use their strength according as they have received it, as a gift from Christ. In this way they can follow in His footsteps and mold themselves in His image, seeking the will of the Father in all things, devoting themselves with all their being to the glory of God and the People of God will grow into an abundant harvest of good, as is brilliantly proved by the lives of so many saints in Church history.

41. In the various types and duties of life, one and the same   587
holiness is cultivated by all who are moved by the Spirit of God, and who obey the voice of the Father, worshiping God the Father in spirit and in truth. These souls follow the poor Christ, the humble and cross-bearing Christ, in order to be made worthy of being partakers in His glory. Every person should walk unhesitatingly according to his own personal gifts and duties in the path of a living faith which arouses hopes and works through charity.

In the first place, the shepherds of Christ's flock ought to   588
carry out their ministry with holiness, eagerness, humility, and courage, in imitation of the eternal High Priest, the Shepherd and Guardian of our souls. They will thereby make this ministry the principal means of their own sanctification. Those chosen for the fullness of the priesthood are gifted with sacramental grace enabling them to exercise a perfect role of pastoral charity through prayer, sacrifice, and preaching, as through every form of a bishop's care and service.[112] They are enabled to lay down their life for their sheep fear-

lessly, and, made a model for their flock (cf. 1 *Pet.* 5:3), can lead the Church to ever-increasing holiness through their own example.

589   Thanks to Christ, the eternal and sole Mediator, priests share in the grace of the bishop's rank and form his spiritual crown.[113] Like bishops, priests should grow in love for God and neighbor through the daily exercise of their duty. They should preserve the bond of priestly fraternity, abound in every spiritual good, and give living evidence of God to all men.[114] Let their heroes be those priests who have lived during the course of the centuries, often in lowly and hidden service, and have left behind them a bright pattern of holiness. Their praise lives on the Church.

590   A priest's task is to pray and offer sacrifice for his own people and indeed the entire People of God, realizing what he does and reproducing in himself the holiness of the things he handles.[115] Let him not be undone by his apostolic cares, dangers, and toils, but rather led by them to higher sanctity. His activities should be fed and fostered by a wealth of meditation, to the delight of the whole Church of God. All priests, especially those who are called diocesan in view of the particular title of their ordination, should bear in mind how much their sanctity profits from loyal attachment to the bishop and generous collaboration with him.

591   In their own special way, ministers of lesser rank also share in the mission and grace of the supreme priest. First among these are deacons. Since they are servants of the mysteries of Christ and the Church,[116] they should keep themselves free from every fault, be pleasing to God, and be a source of all goodness in the sight of men (cf. 1 *Tim.* 3:8-10, 12-13).

592   Called by the Lord and set aside as His portion, other clerics prepare themselves for various ministerial offices under the watchful eye of pastors. They are bound to bring their hearts and minds into accord with the splendid calling which is theirs, and will do so by constancy in prayer, burning love, and attention to whatever is true, just, and of good repute, all for the glory and honor of God. In addition, there are laymen chosen by God and called by the bishop to devote themselves

exclusively to apostolic labors, working with great fruitfulness in the Lord's field.[117]

Married couples and Christian parents should follow their own proper path to holiness by faithful love, sustaining one another in grace throughout the entire length of their lives. They should imbue their offspring, lovingly welcomed from God, with Christian truths and evangelical virtues. For thus they can offer all men an example of unwearying and generous love, build up the brotherhood of charity, and stand as witnesses to and cooperators in the fruitfulness of Holy Mother Church. By such lives, they signify and share in that very love with which Christ loved His bride and because of which He delivered Himself up on her behalf.[118] A like example, but one given in a different way, is that offered by widows and single people, who are able to make great contirbutions toward holiness and apostolic endeavor in the Church.

Finally, laborers, whose work is often toilsome, should by their human exertions try to perfect themselves, aid their fellow citizens, and raise all of society, and even creation itself, to a better mode of existence. By their lively charity, joyous hope, and sharing of one another's burdens, let them also truly imitate Christ, who roughened His hands with carpenter's tools, and who in union with His Father is always at work for the salvation of all men. By their daily work itself laborers can achieve greater apostolic sanctity.

Those who are oppressed by poverty, infirmity, sickness, or various other hardships, as well as those who suffer persecution for justice' sake—may they all know that in a special way they are united with the suffering Christ for the salvation of the world. The Lord called them blessed in His gospel. They are those whom "the God of all grace, who has called us unto his eternal glory in Christ Jesus, will himself, after we have suffered a little while, perfect, strengthen, and establish" (1 *Pet.* 5:10).

All of Christ's faithful, therefore, whatever be the conditions, duties, and circumstances of their lives, will grow in holiness day by day through these very situations, if they accept all of them with faith from the hand of their heavenly

593

594

595

596

Father, and if they cooperate with the divine will by showing
every man through their earthly activities the love with which
God has loved the world.

597   42. "God is love, and he who abides in love abides in God,
and God in him" (1 *Jn.* 4:16). God pours out His love into
our hearts through the Holy Spirit, who has been given to us
(cf. *Rom.* 5:5). Thus the first and most necessary gift is
that charity by which we love God above all things and our
neighbor because of God. If that love, as good seed, is to
grow and bring forth fruit in the soul, each one of the faithful must willingly hear the Word of God and with the help
of His grace act to fulfill His will.

598   Each must share frequently in the sacraments, the Eucharist
especially, and in liturgical rites. Each must apply himself
constantly to prayer, self-denial, active brotherly service, and
the exercise of all the virtues. For charity, as the bond of perfection and the fulfillment of the law (cf. *Col.* 3:14; *Rom.*
13:10), rules over all the means of attaining holiness, gives
life to them, and makes them work.[119] Hence it is the love
of God and of neighbor which points out the true disciple
of Christ.

599   Since Jesus, the Son of God, manifested His charity by
laying down His life for us, no one has greater love than he
who lays down his life for Christ and his brothers (cf. 1 *Jn.*
3:16; *Jn.* 15:13). From the earliest times, then, some Christians have been called upon—and some will always be called
upon—to give this supreme testimony of love to all men, but
especially to persecutors. The Church, therefore, considers
martyrdom as an exceptional gift and as the highest proof of
love.

600   By martyrdom a disciple is transformed into an image of
his Master, who freely accepted death on behalf of the world's
salvation; he perfects that image even to the shedding of
blood. Though few are presented with such an opportunity,
nevertheless all must be prepared to confess Christ before
men, and to follow Him along the way of the cross through
the persecutions which the Church will never fail to suffer.

601   The holiness of the Church is also fostered in a special way
by the observance of the manifold counsels proposed in the

gospel by our Lord to His disciples.[120] Outstanding among them is that precious gift of divine grace which the Father gives to some men (cf. *Mt.* 19:11; 1 *Cor.* 7:7) so that by virginity, or celibacy, they can more easily devote their entire selves to God alone with undivided heart (cf. 1 *Cor.* 7:32-34).[121] This total continence embraced on behalf of the kingdom of heaven has always been held in particular honor by the Church as being a sign of charity and stimulus towards it, as well as a unique fountain of spiritual fertility in the world.

The Church also keeps in mind the advice of the Apostle, who summoned the faithful to charity by exhorting them to share the mind of Christ Jesus—He who "emptied himself, taking the nature of a slave. . . becoming obedient to death" (*Phil.* 2:7-8), and, because of us, "being rich, he became poor" (2 *Cor.* 8:9).   602

Since the disciples must always imitate and give witness to this charity and humility of Christ, Mother Church rejoices at finding within her bosom men and women who more closely follow and more clearly demonstrate the Savior's self-giving by embracing poverty with the free choice of God's sons, and by renouncing their own wills. They subject the latter to another person on God's behalf, in pursuit of an excellence surpassing what is commanded. Thus they liken themselves more thoroughly to Christ in His obedience.[122]   603

All of Christ's followers, therefore, are invited and bound to pursue holiness and the perfect fulfillment of their proper state. Hence, let them all see that they guide their affections rightly. Otherwise, they will be thwarted in the search for perfect charity by the way they use earthly possessions and by a fondness for riches which goes against the gospel spirit of poverty. The Apostle has sounded the warning: let those who make use of this world not get bogged down in it, for the structure of this world is passing away (cf. 1 *Cor.* 7:31, Greek text). [23]   604

Chapter VI

Religious

605   43. The evangelical counsels of chastity dedicated to God, poverty, and obedience are based upon the words and example of the Lord. They were further commended by the apostles and the Fathers, and other teachers and shepherds of the Church. The counsels are a divine gift, which the Church has received from her Lord and which she ever preserves with the help of His grace. Church authority has the duty, under the inspiration of the Holy Spirit, of interpreting these evangelical counsels, of regulating their practice, and finally of establishing stable forms of living according to them.

606   Thus it has come about that various forms of solitary and community life, as well as different religious families have grown up. Advancing the progress of their members and the welfare of the whole body of Christ,[124] these groups have been like branches sprouting out wondrously and abundantly from a tree growing in the field of the Lord from a seed divinely planted.

607   These religious families give their members the support of greater stability in their way of life, a proven method of acquiring perfection, fraternal association in the militia of Christ, and liberty strengthened by obedience. Thus these religious can securely fulfill and faithfully observe their religious profession, and rejoicing in spirit make progress on the road of charity.[125]

608   From the point of view of the divine and hierarchical structure of the Church, the religious state of life is not an intermediate one between the clerical and lay states. Rather, the faithful of Christ are called by God from both these latter states of life so that they may enjoy this particular gift in the life of the Church and thus each in his own way can forward the saving mission of the Church.[126]

609   44. The faithful of Christ can bind themselves to the three previously mentioned counsels either by vows, or by other sacred bonds which are like vows in their purpose. Through

such a bond a person is totally dedicated to God by an act of supreme love, and is committed to the honor and service of God under a new and special title.

It is true that through baptism he has died to sin and has   610
been consecrated to God. However, in order to derive more abundant fruit from this baptismal grace, he intends, by the profession of the evangelical counsels in the Church, to free himself from those obstacles which might draw him away from the fervor of charity and the perfection of divine worship. Thus he is more intimately consecrated to divine service.[127] This consecration gains in perfection since by virtue of firmer and steadier bonds it serves as a better symbol of the unbreakable link between Christ and His Spouse, the Church.

By the charity to which they lead,[128] the evangelical   611
counsels join their followers to the Church and her mystery in a special way. Since this is so, the spiritual life of these followers should be devoted to the welfare of the whole Church. Thence arises their duty of working to extend that kingdom to every land. This duty is to be discharged to the extent of their capacities and in keeping with the form of their proper vocation. The chosen means may be prayer or active undertakings. It is for this reason that the Church preserves and fosters the special character of her various religious communities.

The profession of the evangelical counsels, then, appears   612
as a sign which can and ought to attract all the members of the Church to an effective and prompt fulfillment of the duties of their Christian vocation. The People of God has no lasting city here below, but looks forward to one which is to come. This being so, the religious state by giving its members greater freedom from earthly cares more adequately manifests to all believers the presence of heavenly goods already possessed here below.

Furthermore, it not only witnesses to the fact of a new   613
and eternal life acquired by the redemption of Christ. It foretells the resurrected state and the glory of the heavenly kingdom. Christ also proposed to His disciples that form of life which He, as the Son of God, accepted in entering this world

to do the will of the Father. In the Church this same state of life is imitated with particular accuracy and perpetually exemplified. The religious state reveals in a unique way that the kingdom of God and its overmastering necessities are superior to all earthly considerations. Finally, to all men it shows wonderfully at work within the Church the surpassing greatness of the force of Christ the King and the boundless power of the Holy Spirit.

614   Thus, although the religious state constituted by the profession of the evangelical counsels does not belong to the hierarchical structure of the Church, nevertheless it belongs inseparably to her life and holiness.

615   45. Since it is the duty of the hierarchy of the Church to nourish the People of God and lead them to the choicest pastures (cf. *Ezek.* 34:14), it devolves on the same hierarchy to govern with wise legislation[129] the practice of the evangelical counsels. For by that practice is uniquely fostered the perfection of love for God and neighbor.

616   Submissively following the promptings of the Holy Spirit, the hierarchy also endorses rules formulated by eminent men and women, and authentically approves later modifications. Moreover, by its watchful and shielding authority, the hierarchy keeps close to communities established far and wide for the upbuilding of Christ's body, so that they can grow and flourish in accord with the spirit of their founders.

617   Any institute of perfection and its individual members can be removed from the jurisdiction of the local Ordinaries by the Supreme Pontiff and subjected to himself alone. This is possible by virtue of his primacy over the entire Church. He does so in order to provide more adequately for the necessities of the entire flock of the Lord and in consideration of the common good.[130] In like manner, these communities can be left or committed to the charge of their proper patriarchical authorities. In fulfilling their duty toward the Church in accord with the special form of their life, the members of these communities should show toward bishops the reverence and obedieince required by canonical laws. For bishops possess pastoral authority over individual churches, and apostolic labor demands unity and harmony.[131]

By her approval the Church not only raises the religious   618
profession to the dignity of a canonical state. By the liturgical setting of that profession she also manifests that it is a
state consecrated to God. The Church herself, by the authority given to her by God, accepts the vows of those professing
them. By her public prayer she begs aid and grace from God
for them. She commends them to God, imparts a spiritual
blessing to them, and accompanies their self-offering with the
Eucharistic sacrifice.

46. Religious should carefully consider that through them,   619
to believers and non-believers alike, the Church truly wishes
to give an increasingly clearer revelation of Christ. Through
them Christ should be shown contemplating on the mountain,
announcing God's kingdom to the multitude, healing the sick
and the maimed, turning sinners to wholesome fruit, blessing
children, doing good to all, and always obeying the will of
the Father who sent Him.[132]

Finally, everyone should realize that the profession of the   620
evangelical counsels, though entailing the renunciation of
certain values which undoubtedly merit high esteem, does
not detract from a genuine development of the human person. Rather by its very nature it is most beneficial to that
development. For the counsels, voluntarily undertaken according to each one's personal vocation, contribute greatly
to purification of heart and spiritual liberty. They continually
kindle the fervor of charity. As the example of so many
saintly founders shows, the counsels are especially able to
pattern the Christian man after that manner of virginal and
humble life which Christ the Lord elected for Himself, and
which His Virgin Mother also chose.

Let no one think that by their consecration religious have   621
become strangers to their fellow men or useless citizens of
this earthly city. For even though in some instances religious
do not directly mingle with their contemporaries, yet in a
more profound sense these same religious are united with
them in the heart of Christ and cooperate with them spiritually. In this way the work of building up the earthly city
can always have its foundation in the Lord and can tend

toward Him. Otherwise, those who build this city will perhaps have labored in vain.[133]

622   In summary, therefore, this sacred Synod encourages and
praises the men and women, brothers and sisters, who in
monasteries, or in schools and hospitals, or on the missions,
adorn the Bride of Christ. They do so by their unswerving
and humble loyalty to their chosen consecration, while rendering to all men generous services of every variety.

623   47. Let all who have been called to the profession of the
vows take painstaking care to persevere and excel increasingly
in the vocation to which God has summoned them. Let their
purpose be a more vigorous flowering of the Church's holiness
and the greater glory of the one and undivided Trinity, which
in Christ and through Christ is the fountain and the wellspring
of all holiness.

Vatican II
CHRISTUS DOMINUS
Decree on the Bishops' Pastoral Office
in the Church
October 28, 1965

PREFACE

Christ the Lord, Son of the living God, came that He might save His people from their sins[1] and that all men might be made holy. Just as He Himself was sent by the Father, so He also sent His apostles.[2] Therefore, He sanctified them, conferring on them the Holy Spirit, so that they too might glorify the Father upon earth and save men, "for the building up of the body of Christ" (*Eph.* 4:12), which is the Church.

2. In this Church of Christ the Roman Pontiff is the successor of Peter, to whom Christ entrusted the feeding of His sheep and lambs. Hence by divine institution he enjoys supreme, full, immediate, and universal authority over the care of souls. Since he is pastor of all the faithful, his mission is to provide for the common good of the universal Church and for the good of the individual churches. He holds, therefore, a primacy of ordinary power over all the churches.

For their part, the bishops too have been appointed by the Holy Spirit, and are successors of the apostles as pastors of souls.[3] Together with the Supreme Pontiff and under his authority, they have been sent to continue throughout the ages the work of Christ, the eternal pastor.[4] Christ gave the apostles and their successors the command and the power to teach all nations, to hallow men in the truth, and to feed

625

626

them. Hence, through the Holy Spirit who has been given to them, bishops have been made true and authentic teachers of the faith, pontiffs, and shepherds.[5]

627   3. Sharing in solicitude for all the churches, bishops exercise this episcopal office of theirs, received through episcopal consecration,[6] in communion with and under the authority of the Supreme Pontiff. All are united in a college or body with respect to teaching the universal Church of God and governing her as shepherds.

628   They exercise this office individually over the portions of the Lord's flock assigned to them, each one taking care of the particular church committed to him. On occasion some of them jointly provide for certain common needs of their various dioceses.

629   This most sacred Synod, therefore, attentive to the developments in human relations which have brought about a new order of things in our time,[7] and wishing to determine more exactly the pastoral office of bishops, issues the following decrees.

CHAPTER I

The Relationship of Bishops to the Universal Church

I. The Role of the Bishops in the Universal Church

630   4. By virtue of sacramental consecration and hierarchical communion with the head and other members of the college, a bishop becomes a part of the episcopal body.[8] "The order of bishops is the successor to the college of the apostles in teaching authority and pastoral rule; or, rather, in the episcopal order the apostolic body continues without a break. Together with its head, the Roman Pontiff, and never without this head, the episcopal order is the subject of supreme and full power over the universal Church. But this power can be exercised only with the consent of the Roman Pontiff."[9] This power "is exercised in a solemn manner in an Ecumenical Council."[10] Therefore, this most sacred Synod decrees

that all bishops who are members of the episcopal college have the right to be present at an Ecumenical Council.

"The same collegiate power can be exercised in union with   631
the Pope by the bishops living in all parts of the world, provided that the head of the college calls them to collegiate action, or provided that at least he so approves or freely accepts the united action of the dispersed bishops that it is made a true collegiate act."[11]

5. Bishops from various parts of the world, chosen through   632
ways and procedures established or to be established by the Roman Pontiff, will render especially helpful assistance to the supreme pastor of the Church in a council to be known by the proper name of Synod of Bishops.[12] Since it will be acting in the name of the entire Catholic episcopate, it will at the same time demonstrate that all the bishops in hierarchical communion share in the responsibility for the universal Church.[13]

6. As lawful successors of the apostles and as members of   633
the episcopal college, bishops should always realize that they are linked one to the other, and should show concern for all the churches. For by divine institution and the requirement of their apostolic office, each one in concert with his fellow bishops is responsible for the Church.[14] They should be especially concerned about those parts of the world where the Word of God has not yet been proclaimed or where, chiefly because of the small number of priests, the faithful are in danger of departing from the precepts of the Christian life, and even of losing the faith itself.

Let bishops, therefore, make every effort to have the faith-   634
ful actively support and promote works of evangelization and the apostolate. Let them strive, moreover, to see to it that suitable sacred ministers as well as assistants, both religious and lay, are prepared for the missions and other areas suffering from a lack of clergy. As far as possible, they should also arrange for some of their own priests to go to such missions or dioceses to exercise the sacred ministry permanently or at least for a set period of time.

Moreover, in administering ecclesiastical assets, bishops   635
should think not only of the needs of their own dioceses, but

of other ones as well, for these too are part of the one Church of Christ. Finally, in proportion to their means, bishops should give attention to relieving the disasters which afflict other dioceses and regions.[15]

636   7. Above all, let them unite themselves in brotherly affection with those bishops, who, for the sake of Christ, are harassed by false accusations and by restrictions, detained in prisons, or prevented from exercising their ministry. They should take an active fraternal interest in them so that their sufferings may be assuaged and alleviated through the prayers and good works of their confreres.

II. Bishops and the Apostolic See

637   8. (a) As successors of the apostles, bishops automatically enjoy in the dioceses entrusted to them all the ordinary, proper, and immediate authority required for the exercise of their pastoral office. But this authority never in any instance infringes upon the power which the Roman Pontiff has, by virtue of his office, of reserving cases to himself or to some other authority.

638   (b) Except when it is a question of matters reserved to the supreme authority of the Church, the general law of the Church gives each diocesan bishop the faculty to grant dispensations in particular cases to the faithful over whom he exercises authority according to the norm of law, provided he judges it helpful for their spiritual welfare.

639   9. In exercising supreme, full, and immediate power over the universal Church, the Roman Pontiff makes use of the departments of the Roman Curia. These, therefore, perform their duties in his name and with his authority for the good of the churches and in the service of the sacred pastors.

640   The Fathers of this most sacred Council, however, strongly desire that these departments—which have rendered exceptional assistance to the Roman Pontiff and to the pastors of the Church—be reorganized and better adapted to the needs of the times, and of various regions and rites. This task should give special thought to their number, name, competence, and particular method of procedure, as well as to the

coordination of their activities.[16] The Fathers also eagerly desire that, in view of the pastoral role proper to bishops, the office of legates of the Roman Pontiff be more precisely determined.

10. Furthermore, since these departments are established   641 for the good of the universal Church, this Council wishes that their members, officials, and consultors, as well as legates of the Roman Pontiff, be drawn more widely from various geographical areas of the Church, insofar as it is possible. In such a way the offices and central agencies of the Catholic Church will exhibit a truly universal character.

It is also desired that into the membership of these de-   642 partments there be brought other bishops, especially diocesan ones, who can more adequately apprise the Supreme Pontiff of the thinking, the desires, and the needs of all the churches.

Finally, the Fathers of the Council believe it would be   643 most advantageous if these same departments would give a greater hearing to laymen who are outstanding for their virtue, knowledge, and experience. Thus they, too, will have an appropriate share in Church affairs.

CHAPTER II

Bishops and their Particular Churches or Dioceses

I. Diocesan Bishops

11. A diocese is that portion of God's people which is   644 entrusted to a bishop to be shepherded by him with the cooperation of the presbytery. Adhering thus to its pastor and gathered together by him in the Holy Spirit through the gospel and the Eucharist, this portion constitutes a particular church in which the one, holy, catholic, and apostolic Church of Christ is truly present and operative.

The individual bishops, to each of whom the care of a   645 particular church has been entrusted, are, under the authority of the Supreme Pontiff, the proper, ordinary, and immediate pastors of these churches. They feed their sheep in the name of the Lord, and exercise in their regard the office of teaching, sanctifying, and governing. Yet they should acknowledge the rights which lawfully belong to patriarchs and other hierarchical authorities.[17]

646   Bishops should dedicate themselves to their apostolic office as witnesses of Christ before all men. Not only should they look after those who already follow the Prince of Pastors, but they should also devote themselves wholeheartedly to those who have strayed in any way from the past of truth or who are ignorant of the gospel of Christ and His saving mercy. Their ultimate goal as bishops is that all men may walk "in all goodness and justice and truth" (*Eph.* 5:9).

647   12. In exercising their duty of teaching, they should announce the gospel of Christ to men, a task which is eminent among the chief duties of bishops.[18] They should, in the power of the Spirit, summon men to faith or confirm them in a faith already living. They should expound the whole mystery of Christ to them, namely, those truths the ignorance of which is ignorance of Christ. At the same time they should point out the divinely revealed way to give glory to God and thus attain to everlasting bliss.[19]

648   They should show, moreover, that earthly goods and human institutions structured according to the plan of God the Creator are also related to man's salvation, and therefore can contribute much to the upbuilding of Christ's Body.

649   Hence let them teach with what seriousness the Church believes these realities should be regarded: the human person with his freedom and bodily life, the family and its unity and stability, the procreation and education of children, civil society with its laws and professions, labor and leisure, the arts and technical inventions, poverty and affluence. Finally, they should set forth the ways by which are to be solved the very grave questions concerning the ownership, increase, and just distribution of material goods, peace and war, and brotherly relations among all peoples.[20]

650   13. The bishops should present Christian doctrine in a manner adapted to the needs of the times, that is to say, in a manner corresponding to the difficulties and problems by which people are most vexatiously burdened and troubled. They should also guard that doctrine, teaching the faithful

to defend and spread it. In propounding it, bishops should manifest the Church's maternal solicitude for all men, believers or not. With a special concern they should attend upon the poor and the lower classes to whom the Lord sent them to preach the gospel.

Since it is the mission of the Church to converse with the human society in which she lives,[21] bishops especially are called upon to approach men, seeking and fostering dialogue with them. These conversations on salvation ought to be distinguished for clarity of speech as well as for humility and gentleness so that truth may always be joined with charity, and understanding with love. Likewise they should be characterized by due prudence allied, however, with that trustfulness which fosters friendship and thus is naturally disposed to bring about a union of minds.[22]   651

They should also strive to use the various means at hand today for making Christian doctrine known: namely, first of all, preaching and catechetical instruction which always hold pride of place, then the presentation of this doctrine in schools, academies, conferences, and meetings of every kind, and finally its dissemination through public statements made on certain occasions and circulated by the press and various other media of communication, which should certainly be used to proclaim the gospel of Christ.[23]   652

14. Catechetical training is intended to make men's faith become living, conscious, and active, through the light of instruction. Bishops should see to it that such training be painstakingly given to children, adolescents, young adults, and even grownups. In this instruction a proper sequence should be observed as well as a method appropriate to the matter that is being treated and to the natural disposition, ability, age, and circumstances of life of the listener. Finally, they should see to it that this instruction is based on sacred Scripture, tradition, the liturgy, the teaching authority, and life of the Church.   653

Moreover, they should take care that catechists be properly trained for their task, so that they will be thoroughly acquainted with the doctrine of the Church and will have both   654 a theoretical and a practical knowledge of the laws of psychology and of pedagogical methods.

655   Bishops should also strive to reestablish or better adapt the instruction of adult catechumens.

656   15. In fulfilling their duty to sanctify, bishops should be mindful that they have been taken from among men and appointed their representatives before God in order to offer gifts and sacrifices for sins. Bishops enjoy the fullness of the sacraments of orders, and all priests as well as deacons are dependent upon them in the exercise of authority. For the "presbyters" are prudent fellow workers of the episcopal order and are themselves consecrated as true priests of the New Testament, just as deacons are ordained for service and minister to the People of God in communion with the bishop and his presbytery. Therefore bishops are the principal dispensers of the mysteries of God, just as they are the governors, promoters, and guardians of the entire liturgical life in the church committed to them.[24]

657   Hence, they should constantly exert themselves to have the faithful know and live the paschal mystery more deeply through the Eucharist and thus become a firmly knit body in the solidarity of Christ's love.[25] "Intent upon prayer and the ministry of the word" (*Acts* 6:4), they should devote their labor to this end, that all those committed to their care may be of one mind in prayer[26] and through the reception of the sacraments may grow in grace and be faithful witnesses to the Lord.

658   As those who lead others to perfections, bishops should be diligent in fostering holiness among their clerics, religious, and laity according to the special vocation of each.[27] They should also be mindful of their obligation to give an example of holiness through charity, humility, and simplicity of life. Let them so hallow the churches entrusted to them that the true image of Christ's universal Church may shine forth fully in them. For that reason they should foster priestly and religious vocations as much as possible, and take a special interest in missionary vocations.

659   16. In exercising his office of father and pastor, a bishop should stand in the midst of his people as one who serves.[28]

Let him be a good shepherd who knows his sheep and whose sheep know him. Let him be a true father who excels in the spirit of love and solicitude for all and to whose divinely conferred authority all gratefully submit themselves. Let him so gather and mold the whole family of his flock that everyone, conscious of his own duties, may live and work in the communion of love.

To accomplish these things effectively, a bishop, "ready for every good work" (*2 Tim.* 2:21) and "enduring all things for the sake of the chosen ones" (*2 Tim.* 2:10), should arrange his life in such a way as to accommodate it to the needs of the time.   660

A bishop should always welcome priests with a special love since they assume in part the bishop's duties and cares and carry the weight of them day by day so zealously. He should regard his priests as sons and friends.[29] Thus by his readiness to listen to them and by his trusting familiarity, a bishop can work to promote the whole pastoral work of the entire diocese.   661

He should be concerned about the spiritual, intellectual, and material condition of his priests, so that they can live holy and pious lives and fulfill their ministry faithfully and fruitfully. For this reason, he should encourage institutes and hold special meetings in which priests can gather from time to time for the performance of lengthier spiritual exercises by way of renewing their lives and for the acquisition of deeper knowledge of ecclesiastical subjects, especially sacred Scripture and theology, the social questions of major.importance, and the new methods of pastoral activity. With active mercy a bishop should attend upon priests who are in any sort of danger or who have failed in some respect.   662

In order to be able to consult more suitably the welfare of the faithful according to the condition of each one, a bishop should strive to become duly acquainted with their needs in the social circumstances in which they live. Hence, he ought to employ suitable methods, especially social research. He should manifest his concern for all, no matter what their age, condition, or nationality, be they natives, strangers, or foreigners. In exercising this pastoral care he   663 should preserve for his faithful the share proper to them in Church affairs; he should also recognize their duty and right to collaborate actively in the building up of the Mystical Body of Christ.

664   He should deal lovingly with the separated brethren, urging the faithful also to conduct themselves with great kindness and charity in their regard, and fostering ecumenism as it is understood by the Church.[30] He should also have the welfare of the non-baptized at heart so that upon them too there may shine the charity of Christ Jesus, to whom the bishop is a witness before all men.

665   17. Various forms of the apostolate should be encouraged, and in the whole diocese or in given areas of it the coordination and close interconnection of all apostolic works should be fostered under the direction of the bishop. In this way, all undertakings and organizations, whether catechetical, missionary, charitable, social, family, educational, or any other program serving a pastoral goal, will be brought into harmonious action. At the same time the unity of the diocese will thereby be made more evident.

666   The faithful should be vigorously urged to assume their duty of carrying on the apostolate, each according to his state in life and his ability. They should be invited to join or assist the various works of the lay apostolate, especially Catholic Action. Those associations should also be promoted and supported which either directly or indirectly pursue a supernatural goal, for example, attaining a saintlier life, spreading the gospel of Christ to all men, promoting Christian doctrine or the liturgical apostolate, pursuing social aims, or performing works of piety and charity.

667   The forms of the apostolate should be properly adapted to current needs not only in terms of spiritual and moral conditions, but also of social, demographic, and economic ones. Religious and social surveys, made through offices of pastoral sociology, contribute greatly to the effective and fruitful attainment of that goal, and they are cordially recommended.

668   18. Special concern should be shown for those among the faithful who, on account of their way or condition of life,

cannot sufficiently make use of the common and ordinary
pastoral services of parish priests or are quite cut off from
them. Among this group are very many migrant, exiles and
refugees, seamen, airplane personnel, gypsies, and others of
this kind. Suitable pastoral methods should also be developed
to sustain the spiritual life of those who journey to other
lands for a time for the sake of recreation.[31]

Episcopal conferences, especially national ones, should pay   669
energetic attention to the more pressing problems confront-
ing the aforementioned groups. Through common agreement
and united efforts, such conferences should look to and promote the spiritual care of these people by means of suitable
methods and institutions. They should first bear in mind the
special rules already laid down or due to be laid down by the
Apostolic See.[32] These can be suitably adapted to the circumstances of time, place, and persons.

19. In discharging their apostolic office, which concerns   670
the salvation of souls, bishops of themselves enjoy full and
perfect freedom, and independence from any civil authority.
Hence, the exercise of their ecclesiastical office may not be
hindered, directly or indirectly, nor may they be forbidden
to communicate freely with the Apostolic See, with ecclesiastical authorities, or with their subjects.

Assuredly, while sacred pastors devote themselves to the   671
spiritual care of their flock, they are also in fact having regard for social and civil progress and prosperity. According
to the nature of their office and as behooves bishops, they
collaborate actively with public officials for this purpose, and
advocate obedience to just laws and reverence for legitimately
constituted authorities.

20. Since the apostolic office of bishops was instituted by   672
Christ the Lord and serves a spiritual and supernatural purpose, this most sacred Ecumenical Synod declares that the
right of nominating and appointing bishops belongs properly,
peculiarly, and of itself exclusively to the competent ecclesiastical authority.

Therefore, for the purpose of duly protecting the freedom   673
of the Church and of promoting more suitably and efficiently
the welfare of the faithful, this most holy Council desires

that in the future no rights or privileges of election, nomination, presentation, or designation for the office of bishop be any longer granted to civil authorities. Such civil authorities, whose favorable attitude toward the Church this most sacred Synod gratefully acknowledges and very warmly appreciates, are most kindly requested to make a voluntary renunciation of the above-mentioned rights and privileges which they presently enjoy by reason of a treaty or custom. The matter, however, should first be discussed with the Apostolic See.

674   21. Since the pastoral office of bishops is so important and weighty, when diocesan bishops and others, regarded in law as their equals, have become less capable of fulfilling their duties properly because of the increasing burden of age or some other serious reason, they are earnestly requested to offer their resignation from office either on their own initiative or upon invitation from the competent authority. If the competent authority accepts the resignation, it will make provision for the suitable support of those who have resigned and for special rights to be accorded them.

II. Diocesan Boundaries

675   22. For a diocese to fulfill its purpose, the nature of the Church must be clearly evident to the People of God who belong to that diocese. Likewise, bishops must be able to carry out their pastoral duties effectively among their people. Finally, the welfare of the People of God must be served as perfectly as possible.

676   These requirements, then, demand a proper determination of the boundaries of dioceses and a distribution of clergy and resources which is reasonable and in keeping with the needs of the apostolate. All these things will truly benefit not only the clergy and Christian people directly involved, but also the entire Catholic Church.

677   Concerning diocesan boundaries, therefore, this most sacred Synod decrees that, to the extent required by the good of souls, a fitting revision of diocesan boundaries be undertaken prudently and as soon as possible. This mandate can be

met by dividing, dismembering, or uniting dioceses, or by changing their boundaries, or by determining a better place for the episcopal see or, finally, by providing them with a new internal organization, especially when they are composed of rather large cities.

23. In revising diocesan boundaries, the very first concern must be with the organic unity of each diocese, whose personnel, offices, and institutions must operate like a properly functioning body. In individual cases, all circumstances should be carefully studied and the general criteria which follow should be kept in mind. 678

1.) In fixing a diocesan boundary, as much consideration as possible should be given to the variety in composition of the People of God. Such provision can contribute greatly to a more effective exercise of the pastoral office. At the same time, population clusterings, together with the civil jurisdictions and social institutions which give an organic structure, should be preserved as units to the extent possible. For this reason the territory of each diocese should be continuous. 679

Provision should also be made, if necessary, for civil boundaries and the special characteristics of regions and peoples. They may be psychological, economic, geographic and historical. 680

2.) The extent of the diocesan boundaries and the number of its inhabitants should generally be such that, on the one hand, though he may be helped by others, the bishop can exercise his pontifical functions and suitably carry out pastoral visitations, can properly direct and coordinate all the works of the apostolate in his diocese, be especially well acquainted with his priests and with the religious and laity who have some part in diocesan enterprises. On the other hand, an adequate and suitable area should be provided so that bishop and clergy can usefully devote all their energies to the ministry, while the needs of the Church at large are not overlooked. 681

3.) Finally, in order that the ministry of salvation be more suitably carried out in each diocese, each diocese should regularly have clergy of at least sufficient number and quality for the proper care of the People of God. Also, there should be no lack of the offices, institutions, and organizations 682 which are proper to the particular church and which experience has shown necessary for its efficient government and apostolate; finally, resources for the support of personnel and institutions should be on hand or at least should be prudently foreseen as available elsewhere.

683   For the same reasons, where there are faithful of a different rite, the diocesan bishop should provide for their spiritual needs either through priests or parishes of that rite or through an episcopal vicar endowed with the necessary faculties. Wherever it is fitting, the latter should also have episcopal rank. Or, the Ordinary himself may perform the office of an Ordinary of different rites. If for certain reasons, these arrangements are not feasible in the eyes of the Apostolic See, then a proper hierarchy for the different rites is to be established.[33]

684   Also, in similar circumstances, provision should be made for the faithful of different language groups, either through priests or parishes of the same language, or through an episcopal vicar well versed in the language, and, if need be, endowed with the episcopal dignity; or, in some other more appropriate way.

685   24. By way of effecting the changes and alterations in dioceses, as set forth in Articles 22 and 23, and without prejudice to the discipline of the Oriental Churches, it is desirable that the competent episcopal conferences examine these matters, each for its respective territory. If deemed opportune, a special episcopal commission may be employed for this purpose. But account must always be taken of the opinions of the bishops of the provinces or regions concerned. Finally, these conferences should propose their recommendations and wishes to the Apostolic See.

III. Those Who Cooperate with the Diocesan Bishop in His Pastoral Task

1. Coadjutor and Auxiliary Bishops

686   25. In the government of dioceses, the welfare of the Lord's flock must be the prime concern in any provisions relating to

the pastoral office of bishops. That this welfare may be duly secured, auxiliary bishops must frequently be appointed because the diocesan bishop cannot personally fulfill all his episcopal duties as the good of souls demands. The problem may be the vast extent of the diocese, the great number of its inhabitants, the special nature of the apostolate, or other reasons of a different nature. Sometimes, in fact, a particular need requires that a coadjutor bishop be appointed to assist the diocesan bishop. Coadjutor and auxiliary bishops should be granted those faculties necessary for rendering their work more effective and for safeguarding the dignity proper to bishops. These purposes should always be accomplished without detriment to the unity of the diocesan administration and the authority of the diocesan bishop.

Since coadjutor and auxiliary bishops are called to share   687
part of the burden of the diocesan bishop, they should exercise their office in such a way that they may proceed in all matters in single-minded agreement with him. In addition, they should always manifest obedience and reverence toward the diocesan bishop. He, in turn, should have a fraternal love for coadjutor and auxiliary bishops and hold them in esteem.

26. When the good of souls demands, the diocesan bishop   688
should not decline to ask the competent authority for one or more auxiliaries who will be appointed for the diocese without the right of succession.

If there is no provision for it in the letter of nomination,   689
the diocesan bishop should appoint his auxiliary or auxiliaries as vicars general or at least as episcopal vicars. They shall be dependent upon his authority only, and he may wish to consult them in examining questions of major importance, especially of a pastoral nature.

Unless competent authority has otherwise determined, the   690
powers and faculties which auxiliary bishops have by law do not cease when the administration of a diocesan bishop comes to an end. Unless some serious reasons persuade otherwise, it is also desirable that when the See is vacant the office of ruling the diocese should be committed to the auxiliary bishop or, when there are more than one, to one of the auxiliaries.

691   A coadjutor bishop, appointed with the right of succession, must always be named vicar general by the diocesan bishop. In particular cases the competent authority can grant him even more extensive faculties.

692   In order to provide as far as possible for the present and future good of the diocese, the diocesan bishop and his coadjutor should not fail to consult with one another on matters of major importance.

2. The Diocesan Curia and Councils

693   27. The most important office in the diocesan curia is that of vicar general. However, as often as the proper government of the diocese requires it, one or more episcopal vicars can be named by the bishop. These automatically enjoy for a certain part of the diocese, or for a determined type of activity, or for the faithful of a determined rite, the same authority which the common law grants the vicar general.

694   Included among the collaborators of the bishop in the government of the diocese are those priests who constitute his senate or council, such as the cathedral chapter, the board of consultors, or other committees established according to the circumstances or nature of various localities. To the extent necessary, these institutions, especially the cathedral chapters, should be reorganized in keeping with present-day needs.

695   Priests and lay people who belong to the diocesan curia should realize that they are making a helpful contribution to the pastoral ministry of the bishop.

696   The diocesan curia should be so organized that it is an appropriate instrument for the bishop, not only for administering the diocese but also for carrying out the works of the apostolate.

697   It is highly desirable that in each diocese a pastoral council be established over which the diocesan bishop himself will preside and in which specially chosen clergy, religious, and lay people will participate. The function of this council will be to investigate and to weigh matters which bear on pastoral activity, and to formulate practical conclusions regarding them.

3. The Diocesan Clergy

28. All priests, both diocesan and religious, participate in 698
and exercise with the bishop the one priesthood of Christ and
are thereby meant to be prudent cooperators of the episcopal
order. In securing the welfare of souls, however, the first
place is held by diocesan priests who are incardinated or attached to a particular church, and who fully dedicate themselves to its service by way of pasturing a single portion of
the Lord's flock. In consequence, they form one presbytery
and one family, whose father is the bishop. In order to distribute the sacred ministries more equitably and properly
among his priests, the bishop should possess a necessary freedom in assigning offices and benefices. Therefore, rights or
privileges which in any way limit this freedom are to be suppressed.

The relationships between the bishop and his diocesan 699
priests should rest above all upon the bonds of supernatural
charity so that the harmony of the will of the priests with
that of their bishop will render their pastoral activity more
fruitful. Hence, for the sake of greater service to souls, let
the bishop engage in discussion with his priests, even col-
lectively, especially about pastoral matters. This he should do
not only occasionally but, as far as possible, at fixed intervals.

Furthermore, all diocesan priests should be united among 700
themselves and thereby develop a pressing concern for the
spiritual welfare of the whole diocese. They should also be
mindful that the benefits which they receive by reason of
their ecclesiastical office are closely bound up with their sacred work. Therefore, they should contribute generously
according to their means to the material needs of the diocese
as the bishop's program provides for them.

29. Collaborating even more closely with the bishop are 701
those priests charged with a pastoral office or apostolic works
of a supraparochial nature, whether in a certain area of the
diocese or among special groups of the fruitful or with respect to a specific kind of activity.

702   Priests assigned by the bishop to various works of the apostolate, whether in schools or in other institutions or associations, contribute an exceedingly valuable assistance. Those priests also who are engaged in supradiocesan works are commended to the special consideration of the bishop in whose diocese they reside, for they perform outstanding works of the apostolate.

703   30. Pastors, however, cooperate with the bishop in a very special way, for as shepherds in their own right they are entrusted with the care of souls in a certain part of the diocese under the bishop's authority.

704   1.) In exercising this care of souls, pastors and their assistants should so fulfill their duty of teachings, sanctifying, and governing that the individual parishioners and the parish communities will really feel that they are members of the diocese and of the universal Church. To this end, they should collaborate with other pastors, and with priests who exercise a pastoral office in the area (such as vicars forane and deans), as well as with those engaged in works of a supraparochial nature. In this way the pastoral work in the diocese will be unified and made more effective.

705   Moreover, the care of souls should always be infused with a missionary spirit so that it reaches out in the proper manner to everyone living within the parish boundaries. If the pastor cannot contact certain groups of people, he should seek the help of others, including laymen, who can assist him in the apostolate.

706   To render the care of souls more efficacious, community life for priests is strongly recommended, especially for those attached to the same parish. While this way of living encourages apostolic action, it also affords an example of charity and unity to the faithful.

707   2.) In the exercise of their teaching office it is the duty of pastors to preach God's word to all the Christian people so that, rooted in faith, hope, and charity, they may grow in Christ, and that the Christian community may bear witness to that charity which the Lord commended.[34] Pastors should bring the faithful to a full knowledge of the mystery of salvation through a catechetical instruction which is adapted to

each one's age. In imparting this instruction, they should seek not only the assistance of religious but also the cooperation of the laity, and should establish the Confraternity of Christian Doctrine.

In discharging their duty to sanctify their people, pastors should arrange for the celebration of the Eucharistic Sacrifice to be the center and culmination of the whole life of the Christian community. They should labor to see that the faithful are nourished with spiritual food through the devout and frequent reception of the sacraments and through intelligent and active participation in the liturgy. Pastors should also be mindful of how much the sacrament of penance contributes to developing the Christian life and, therefore, should make themselves available to hear the confessions of the faithful. If necessary, they should invite the assistance of priests who are experienced in various languages. 708

In fulfilling the office of shepherd, pastors should first take pains to know their own flock. Since they are the servants of all the sheep, they should foster growth in Christian living among the individual faithful and also in families, in associations especially dedicated to the apostolate, and in the whole parish community. Therefore, they should visit homes and schools to the extent that their pastoral work demands. They should pay special attention to adolescents and youth, devote themselves with a paternal love to the poor and the sick, and have a particular concern for working men. Finally, they should encourage the faithful to assist in the works of the apostolate. 709

3.) As cooperators with the pastor, assistant pastors make an outstanding and active contribution to the pastoral ministry under the authority of the pastor. Therefore, there should always be fraternal association, mutual charity, and respect between the pastor and his assistants. They should assist one another with counsel, help, and example, furthering the welfare of the parish with united purpose and energy. 710

31. In making a judgment on the suitability of a priest for the administration of any parish, the bishop should take into consideration not only his knowledge of doctrine but also 711

his piety, apostolic zeal, and other gifts and qualities necessary for the proper exercise of the care of souls.

712   The parish exists solely for the good of souls. Therefore, by way of enabling the bishop to provide more easily and effectively for pastorates, all rights whatsoever of presentation, nomination, reservation are to be suppressed, including any general or particular law of concursus.[35] The rights of religious, however, are to be maintained.

713   Pastors should enjoy in their respective parishes that stability of office which the good of souls demands. Hence, although the distinction between removable and irremovable pastors is to be abrogated, the procedure for transferring and removing pastors is to be re-examined and simplified. In this way, while natural and canonical equity are preserved, the bishop can better provide for the needs of the good of souls.

714   Pastors who are unable to fulfill their office properly and fruitfully because of the increasing burden of age or some other serious reason are urgently requested to tender their resignation voluntarily or upon invitation from the bishop. The bishop should see to the suitable support of those who have resigned.

715   32. Finally, the same concern for souls should be the basis for determining or reconsidering the erection or suppression of parishes and any other changes of this kind, which the bishop will be able to bring about on his own authority.

4. Religious

716   33. All religious have the duty, each according to his proper vocation, of cooperating zealously and diligently in building up and increasing the whole Mystical Body of Christ and for the good of the particular churches. (In this section of the present document, it should be noted, the word religious includes members from other institutes who make a profession of the evangelical counsels.)

717   It is their duty to foster these objectives primarily by means of prayer, works of penance, and the example of their own life. This most sacred Synod strongly urges them ever to increase their esteem and zeal for these means. With due con-

sideration for the character proper to each religious community, they should also enter more vigorously into the external works of the apostolate.

34. Religious priests are consecrated for the office of the   718
presbyterate so that they may be the prudent cooperators of
the episcopal order. Today they can be of even greater help
to bishops in view of the mounting needs of souls. Therefore,
in a certain genuine sense they must be said to belong to the
clergy of the diocese inasmuch as they share in the care of
souls and in carrying out works of the apostolate under the
authority of the sacred prelates.

Other members of religious communities, both men and   719
women, also belong in a special way to the diocesan family
and offer great assistance to the sacred hierarchy. With the
increasing demands of the apostolate, they can and should
offer that assistance more every day.

35. In order that the works of the apostolate be carried   720
out harmoniously in individual dioceses and that the unity of
diocesan discipline be preserved intact, these principles are
established as fundamental.

1.) Religious should always attend upon bishops, as upon   721
successors of the apostles, with devoted deference and
reverence. Whenever they are legitimately called upon to
undertake works of the apostolate, they are obliged to discharge their duties in such a way that they may be available
and docile helpers to bishops.[36] Indeed, religious should
comply promptly and faithfully to the requests and desires of
the bishops in order that they may thereby assume an even
more extensive role in the ministry of human salvation. They
should act thus with due respect for the character of their
institute and in keeping with their constitutions which, if
need be, should be adapted to this goal in accord with the
principles of this conciliar Decree.

Especially in view of the urgent need of souls and the   722
scarcity of diocesan clergy, religious communities which are
not dedicated exclusively to the contemplative life can be
called upon by the bishops to assist in various pastoral ministries. The particular character of each community should,
however, be kept in mind. Superiors should encourage this

work to the utmost, even by accepting parishes on a temporary basis.

723   2.) Religious engaged in the active apostolate, however, should be imbued with the spirit of their religious community, and remain faithful to the observance of their rule and to submissiveness toward their own superiors. Bishops should not neglect to impress this obligation upon them.

724   3.) The privilege of exemption, by which religious are called to the service of the Supreme Pontiff or other ecclesiastical authority and are withdrawn from the jurisdiction of bishops, applies chiefly to the internal order of their communities so that in them all things may be more aptly coordinated and the growth and depth of religious life better served.[37] These communities are also exempt in order that the Supreme Pontiff may make use of them for the good of the universal Church[38] or that any other competent authority may do so for the good of the churches under its own jurisdiction.

725   This exemption, however, does not exclude religious in individual dioceses from the jurisdiction of bishop in accordance with the norm of law, insofar as the performance of his pastoral office and the right ordering of the care of souls require.[39]

726   4.) All religious, exempt and non-exempt, are subject to the authority of the local Ordinaries in those things which pertain to the public exercise of divine worship (except where differences in rites are concerned), the care of souls, sacred preaching intended for the people, the religious and moral education of the Christian faithful, especially of children, catechetical instruction, and liturgical formation. Religious are subject to the local Ordinary also in matters of proper clerical decorum as well as in the various works which concern the exercise of the sacred apostolate. Catholic schools conducted by religious are also subject to the authority of the local Ordinaries as regards general policy and supervision, but the right of religious to direct them remains intact. Religious also are bound to observe all those things which episcopal councils or conferences legitimately prescribe for universal observance.

5.) A well-ordered cooperation is to be encouraged be-   727
tween various religious communities, and between them and
the diocesan clergy. There should also be a very close coordination of all apostolic works and activities. This depends
especially on a supernatural attitude of hearts and minds, an
attitude rooted in and founded upon charity. The Apostolic
See is competent to supervise this coordination for the universal Church; bishops are competent in their own respective
dioceses: and patriarchal synods and episcopal conferences in
their own territory.

With respect to those works of the apostolate which reli-   728
gious are to undertake, bishops or episcopal conferences, religious superiors or conferences of major religious superiors
should take action only after mutual consultations.

6.) In order to foster harmonious and fruitful relations   729
between bishops and religious, at stated times and as often as
it is deemed opportune, bishops and religious superiors should
be willing to meet for discussion of those affairs which pertain generally to the apostolate in their territory.

CHAPTER III

Concerning the Cooperation of Bishops for the Common Good of Many Churches

I. Synods, Councils, and Especially Episcopal Conferences

36. From the very first centuries of the Church the bishops   730
who were placed over individual churches were deeply influenced by the fellowship of fraternal charity and by zeal
for the universal mission entrusted to the apostles. And so
they pooled their resources and unified their plans for the
common good and for that of the individual churches. Thus
there were established synods, provincial councils, and plenary councils in which bishops legislated for various churches
a common pattern to be followed in teaching the truths of
faith and ordering ecclesiastical discipline.

This sacred Ecumenical Synod earnestly desires that the   731
venerable institution of synods and councils flourish with

new vigor. Thus, faith will be spread and discipline preserved more fittingly and effectively in the various churches, as the circumstances of the times require.

732   37. Nowadays especially, bishops are frequently unable to fulfill their office suitably and fruitfully unless they work more harmoniously and closely every day with other bishops. Episcopal conferences, already established in many nations, have furnished outstanding proofs of a more fruitful apostolate. Therefore, this most sacred Synod considers it supremely opportune everywhere that bishops belonging to the same nation or region form an association and meet together at fixed times. Thus, when the insights of prudence and experience have been shared and views exchanged, there will emerge a holy union of energies in the service of the common good of the churches.

733   Wherefore, this sacred Synod issues the following decrees concerning episcopal conferences:

734   38. 1.) An episcopal conference is a kind of council in which the bishops of a given nation or territory jointly exercise their pastoral office by way of promoting that greater good which the Church offers mankind, especially through forms and programs of the apostolate which are fittingly adapted to the circumstances of the age.

735   2.) Members of the episcopal conference are all local Ordinaries of every rite, coadjutors, auxiliaries, and other titular bishops who perform a special work entrusted to them by the Apostolic See or the episcopal conferences. Vicars general are not members. *De jure* membership belongs neither to other titular bishops nor, in view of their particular assignment in the area, to legates of the Roman Pontiff.

736   Local Ordinaries and coadjutors hold a deliberative vote. Auxiliaries and other bishops who have a right to attend the conference will exercise either a deliberative or a consultative vote, as the statutes of the conference determine.

737   3.) Each episcopal conference is to draft its own statutes, to be reviewed by the Apostolic See. In these statutes, among other agencies, offices should be established which will aid in achieving the conference's purpose more efficaciously: for

example, a permanent board of bishops, episcopal commissions, and a general secretariat.

4.) Decisions of the episcopal conference, provided they   738
have been made lawfully and by the choice of at least two-
thirds of the prelates who have a deliberative vote in the
conference, and have been reviewed by the Apostolic See, are
to have juridically binding force in those cases and in those
only which are prescribed by common law or determined by
special mandate of the Apostolic See, given spontaneously or
in response to a petition from the conference itself.

5.) Wherever special circumstances require and the Apos-   739
tolic See approves, bishops of many nations can establish a
single conference.

Moreover, contacts between episcopal conferences of dif-   740
ferent nations should be encouraged in order to promote and
safeguard their higher welfare.

6.) It is highly recommended that when prelates of the   741
Oriental Churches promote in synod the discipline of their
own churches and more efficaciously foster works for the
good of religion, they take into account also the common
good of the whole territory where many churches of different rites exist. They should exchange views on this point
at interritual meetings held in accord with the norms to be
given by the competent authority.

II. The Boundaries of Ecclesiastical Provinces and the Establishment of Ecclesiastical Regions

39. The welfare of souls requires appropriate boundaries   742
not only for dioceses but also for ecclesiastical provinces; indeed, it sometimes counsels the establishment of even wider
ecclesiastical units. Thus the needs of the apostolate will be
better provided for according to social and local circumstances. Thus, too, relations can be made more smooth and
productive between individual bishops, or between bishops
and their metropolitans or other bishops of the same country,
or between bishops and civil authorities.

40. Therefore, in order to accomplish these aims, this most   743
sacred Synod decrees as follows:

1.) The boundaries of ecclesiastical provinces are to be submitted to an early review, and the rights and privileges of metropolitans are to be defined according to new and suitable norms.

2.) As a general rule all dioceses and other territorial divisions which are by law equivalent to dioceses should be attached to an ecclesiastical province. Therefore dioceses which are now directly subject to the Apostolic See and not united to any other are either to be brought together to form a new ecclesiastical province, it that be possible, or else attached to that province which is nearer or more convenient. They are to be made subject to the metropolitan jurisdiction of the archbishop, in keeping with the norms of common law.

3.) Wherever advantageous, ecclesiastical provinces should be grouped into ecclesiastical regions, for the organization of which provision is to be made by law.

744   41. It is fitting that the competent episcopal conferences examine the question of the boundaries of such provinces or the establishment of such regions, in keeping with the norms given with respect to diocesan boundaries in Articles 23 and 24. They are then to submit their suggestions and wishes to the Apostolic See.

III. Bishops with an Interdiocesan Office

745   42. Since pastoral needs increasingly require that some pastoral undertakings be directed and carried forward as joint projects, it is fitting that certain offices be created for the service of all or many dioceses of a determined region or nation. These offices can even be filled by bishops.

746   This sacred Synod recommends that between the prelates or bishops serving in these offices on the one hand and the diocesan bishops and the episcopal conferences on the other, there always exist fraternal association and harmonious cooperation in matters of pastoral concern. These relationships should also be defined by common law.

747   43. Because of the special conditions of the way of life of military personnel, their spiritual care requires extraordinary

consideration. Hence, there should be established in every nation, if possible, a military vicariate. Both the military vicar and the chaplains should devote themselves unsparingly to this difficult work in harmonious cooperation with the diocesan bishops.[40]

Diocesan bishops should release to the military vicar a sufficient number of priests who are qualified for this serious work. At the same time they should promote all enterprises on behalf of improving the spiritual welfare of military personnel.[41]

748

General Directive

44. This most sacred Synod prescribes that in the revision of the Code of Canon Law suitable laws be drawn up in keeping with the principles stated in this Decree. Due consideration should also be given to observations made by individual commissions or Fathers of this Council.

749

This sacred Synod also prescribes that general directories be drawn up concerning the care of souls, for the use of both bishops and pastors. In this way, shepherds can be provided with sure methods designed to help them discharge their particular pastoral office with greater facility and success.

750

There should also be prepared individual directories concerning the pastoral care of special groups of the faithful, as the different circumstances of particular nations or regions require. Another directory should be composed with respect to the catechetical instruction of the Christian people, and should deal with the fundamental principles of such instruction, its arrangements, and the composition of books on the subject. In the preparation of these directories, too, special attention is to be given to the views which have been expressed by individual commissions and Fathers of the Council.

751

In the name of the most holy and undivided Trinity, the Father and the Son and the Holy Spirit.

752

The Decree on the Bishops' Pastoral Office in the Church has won the consent of the Fathers in this most sacred and

753

universal Second Vatican Synod that has been legitimately convoked.

754   We too, by the apostolic authority conferred on us by Christ, join with the Venerable Fathers in approving, decreeing, and establishing these things in the Holy Spirit, and we direct that what has thus been enacted in synod be published to God's glory.

755   Rome, at St. Peter's, October 28, 1965.

756   I, Paul, Bishop of the Catholic Church.

Vatican II
OPTATAM TOTIUS ECCLESIA
Decree on Training for the Priesthood
October 28, 1965

This Council is well aware that the renewal of the whole Church that is so ardently desired depends in no small measure on having the priestly ministry animated by the spirit of Christ.[1] Accordingly it reaffirms the vital importance of training for the priesthood, and it lays down certain basic principles from this that will strengthen the laws that many centuries' experience has shown to be sound and introduce into them new elements corresponding to the Constitutions and Decrees of this Council and the changing conditions of the times. The unity of the Catholic priesthood makes this priestly formation necessary for all priests of all rites, whether diocesan or religious; and so these regulations which directly have do with the diocesan clergy should be applied to all of the clergy, with the necessary adjustments being made.

I. Program of Training for the Priesthood to be Undertaken in Each Country

1. Because of the great differences to be found in various nations and regions, only general rules can be laid down. Hence a special "Program for Training for the Priesthood" is to be initiated in each individual country or rite by the Episcopal Conferences;[2] from time to time it is to be revised and approved by the Apostolic See. In it, universal laws are to be

758

adapted to special local circumstances, so that training for the priesthood will always be in tune with the pastoral needs of the particular area in which the ministry is to be carried on.

II. More Intense Fostering of Vocations to the Priesthood

759   2. The whole Christian community has the duty of fostering Christian vocations,[3] and the living of a fully Christian life is of very special help in this regard. A great contribution is made in this direction by families that are animated by a spirit of faith, love, and devotion, and thus turn into a kind of first seminary, and by parishes with a fruitful life in which teenagers take part. Teachers and all those who are in any way in charge of the training of boys and young men—the Catholic Societies in particular—should make every effort to guide the teenagers entrusted to them in such a way that they will be able to recognize God's call and be glad to respond to it. All priests should show a very special apostolic zeal for fostering vocations, and they should attract teenagers to the priesthood by the humility, hard work and cheerfulness of their own lives, by their priestly charity toward each other and by their fraternal cooperation.

760   It is up to bishops to stir their flocks to foster vocations and to coordinate all the efforts being made in this direction; and they should help those whom they feel have been called to the service of the Lord, without any counting of the cost.

761   These active efforts of the whole people of God in fostering vocations are a response to the action of God's Providence, which bestows upon the human beings who have been divinely called to share in the hierarchical Priesthood of Christ the endowments they need and the help of His grace, and which entrusts to the legitimate ministers of the Church the role of approving and calling those candidates whose fitness has been checked and who have sought this lofty office with a right intention and complete liberty, and the role of consecrating them with the sign of the Holy Spirit to the worship of God and the service of the Church.[4]

The Council wants first of all to commend the traditional 762 means of carrying on this effort in common—constant prayer, Christian penance, and a steadily improving instruction of the faithful, through preaching and catechesis and through the various media of communication, to recognize the necessity, the nature and the dignity of a vocation to the priesthood. It also commands the Organizations for vocations that have already been set up or that will be set up in individual dioceses, regions, or nations, in accordance with the papal documents dealing with this matter, to draw up systematic and coherent plans for organizing all the pastoral activity being devoted to fostering vocations, making full use of any information supplied by modern advances in psychology or sociology, and to promote this activity with prudence and zeal.[5]

The work of fostering vocations should come from an 763 open heart and should transcend the boundaries of individual dioceses, nations, religious communities or rites; it should look first to the needs of the universal Church and to help those regions where there is a more urgent demand for workers in the vineyard of the Lord.

3. In minor seminaries, which are built to nurture the seeds 764 of a vocation, the students should be given a special religious formation and, especially, suitable spiritual direction to help them follow Christ the Redeemer with a pure heart and a generous spirit. Under the fatherly direction of the superiors, and with timely cooperation from parents, they should lead a life that is in accord with the age, spirit, and development of teenagers and completely in keeping with the norms of sound psychology. And there should be no failure to provide them with the human experience they ought to have and with close contact with their own families.[6] All that is said about major seminaries later in this document is to be applied to them too, to the extent that it fits in with the nature and purpose of a minor seminary. The studies carried on by the students should be so arranged that they will be able to carry them on elsewhere without difficulty if they should decide to embrace another state in life.

The same kind of care should be shown for fostering the 765 seeds of a vocation in teenagers and young people who are studying in special institutes which serve the same purpose as minor seminaries as far as local circumstances are concerned, as well as in those who are in other schools and those who are being educated in other ways. Great care is to be taken to further institutions and other undertakings established to help those who answer the call to a divine vocation later in life.

III. Arrangements on Major Seminaries

766   4. Major seminaries are necessary for training for the priesthood. The whole training given to students in them ought to be directed toward making them real pastors of souls modeled on Our Lord Jesus Christ, who was Teacher, Priest and Pastor.[7] And so they should be gotten ready to carry out the ministry of the word, which means they should be brought to an ever better understanding of the revealed word of God, to a possession of it through their meditations, to an ability to express it in word and deed. They should be gotten ready for the ministry of worship and of sanctification, so that through prayer and through the performance of the sacred liturgical ceremonies they may carry out the work of salvation in the Eucharistic Sacrifice and in the Sacraments. They should be gotten ready for the ministry of a Pastor, so that they will know how to represent to men the Christ who did not "come to be ministered to, but to minister and to offer his soul as a redemption for man" (*Mk.* 10, 45; cf. *Jn.* 13, 12-17), and how to win many by becoming the servants of all (cf. *Cor.* 9, 19).

767   And so all aspects of the training—spiritual, intellectual, disciplinary—are to be directed toward this pastoral end by a concerted effort; all superiors and teachers are to work devotedly and harmoniously to achieve it, with fidelity to and respect for the authority of the bishops.

768   5. Since the training of the students depends on wise laws and even more on qualified people imparting the training, the directors and teachers in Seminaries are to be selected from among the best men[8] and they are to be carefully prepared in sound doctrine, suitable pastoral experience, and special spiritual and pedagogical training. Institutes with this aim in

mind, or at least well-laid out courses and regular meetings of
seminary rectors, ought to be promoted.

Directors and teachers should be keenly aware of just how   769
much their own way of thinking and acting influences the
outcome of the student's training. Under the leadership of the
rector, they should blend together to form a very closely-knit
community in spirit and action; they should, together with
the students, make up a family that will live up to the Lord's
prayer "That they may be one" (cf. *Jn.* 17, 11) and that will
foster among the students a joy in their vocations. The bishop
should show constant and loving care and concern for those
working in the seminary and offer them encouragement, and
he should prove a true father in Christ to the students. Finally,
all priests should look upon the seminary as the heart of the
diocese and they should be glad to offer it any help of their
own.[9]

6. In the case of each candidate, a careful inquiry taking   770
into consideration his age and stage of development should be
made into whether or not he has the proper intention and is
making a free choice, into his spiritual, moral and intellectual
suitability, and into his physical and mental health, with
proper attention being paid to traits he may have inherited
from his family. Some thought should also be given to the
candidate's ability to put up with the burdens that go with
the priesthood and to his ability to do the work of the pastoral ministry.[10]

In the whole process of choosing and testing students, a   771
due firmness should always be displayed, even if it results
in the lamentable situation of a shortage of priests,[11] for God
will not allow His Church to want for ministers if the worthy
are promoted and those not suited are directed in time in a
paternal way toward taking on some other role, if they are
helped to enter upon the lay apostolate eagerly, with a deep
awareness of their vocation as Christians.

7. Wherever individual dioceses are not up to properly   772
equipping a seminary of their own, then general seminaries
covering a number of dioceses or a whole area or nation ought
to be erected and fostered, so that students may be effectively
provided with sound training, which has to be regarded as the

supreme norm in this matter. If these seminaries are regional
or national, they are to be governed by the regulations set
down by the bishops concerned[12] and approved by the Apostolic See.

773   In seminaries with large numbers of students, unity is to be
maintained in the overall direction and in scholastic training,
but the students should also be suitably divided into smaller
groups so that better provisions can be made for the personal
formation of each individual.

IV. Careful Development of Spiritual Training

774   8. Spiritual training should be closely connected with doctrinal and pastoral training, and should be imparted in such
a way, especially through the help of the spiritual director,[13]
that the students will learn to live in close and constant union
with the Father through His Son Jesus Christ in the Holy Spirit. Since through sacred ordination they are to be modelled
upon Christ the Priest, they should get used to staying close
to Him as friends in an intimate sharing of their whole lives.[14]
They should live His Paschal Mystery in such a way that they
will know how to initiate into it the people who will be committed to them. They should be taught to look for Christ in
faithful meditation upon the word of God; in active communication with the sacred mysteries of the Church, especially
in the Eucharist and in the divine office;[15] in the bishop who
sends them and in the men to whom they are sent, especially
the poor, the little ones, the sick, the sinners, and the unbelievers. They should show a filial trust toward the Most Blessed
Virgin Mary whom Christ Jesus, as He hung dying upon the
Cross, gave to His disciples as a mother, and they should love
her and show devotion to her.

775   The devotional practices commended by long and venerable
use in the Church should be carefully fostered; but care must
be taken to see to it that spiritual training does not consist of
them alone and that it does more than develop religious feeling. The students should learn to live according to the pattern
of the Gospel, to be strengthened in faith, hope and charity,
so that they may, through the practice of these virtues, acquire

a spirit of prayer,[16] succeed in strengthening and safeguarding their vocation, obtain an increase of other virtues, and grow in zeal to see all men won for Christ.

9. The students should be so thoroughly imbued with the mystery of the Church, especially as it has been proposed by this Ecumenical Council, that they will be bound to the Vicar of Christ by a humble and filial love, and will, after ordination, stick by their own bishop as loyal helpers who work together with their brothers, thus giving testimony of the kind of unity that attracts men to Christ.[17] With their hearts opened wide, they should learn to take part in the life of the whole Church, in keeping with the words of St. Augustine: "The more someone loves the Church of Christ, the more he has the Holy Spirit."[18] Students should clearly understand that they are not destined to lord it over others nor to enjoy honors but rather they are totally bound to the service of God and to the pastoral ministry. Special care should be devoted to training them in priestly obedience and in a poor man's way of life and a spirit of self-denial,[19] so that they will get in the habit of very readily giving up even those things that are licit but not advisable, and of modelling themselves on Christ crucified.   776

Students should be informed about the burdens they will have to take upon themselves, and none of the difficulties of life in the priesthood should be hidden from them. But their attention should not be centered almost completely on the dangerous aspects of their future work; instead they should be trained for a spiritual life that will draw its greatest strength and support from their pastoral activity.   777

10. Students who, in keeping with the fixed and holy laws of their own rite, follow the venerable tradition of celibacy in the priesthood are to be carefully trained for this state in which they will be renouncing marriage for the sake of the kingdom of heaven (cf. *Mt.* 19, 12), cleaving to the Lord with the undivided love[20] that is so profoundly well suited to the New Covenant, offering testimony to the resurrection in the next world (cf. *Lk.* 20, 36),[21] and obtaining a help especially well suited to the constant exercise of the perfect charity that will enable them to become all things to all men in the priestly ministry.[22] They should have a profound appreciation   778

of the fact that this state ought to be taken up gratefully, not just as a precept of church law but rather as a precious gift to be humbly sought from God and to which they are to hasten to respond freely and generously, through the inspiration and aid of the grace of the Holy Spirit.

779   Students should have a proper knowledge of the duties and the dignity of Christian marriage, which represents the love that exists between Christ and the Church (cf. *Eph.* 5, 32 ff.); but they should also see virginity consecrated to Christ as something higher,[23] so that they may devote themselves to the Lord with complete dedication of soul and body through a mature, carefully-thought-out and generous choice.

780   They should be warned about the dangers that lie in the way of their chastity, especially in present-day society.[24] With the help of suitable divine and human safeguards, they should learn to integrate renunciation of marriage into their lives and activity in such a way that they not only will suffer no detriment but rather will gain a deeper mastery over soul and body and a fuller perception of the happiness of the Gospel.

781   11. The precepts of Christian education should be religiously observed and should be rounded out by the recent findings of sound psychology and pedagogy. Training should be carefully planned to develop in the students the natural maturity they should have; this will show itself in stability of mind, an ability to make carefully considered decisions and sound judgments on events and people. The students should get to know their own characteristics and how to handle them; they should be helped to develop strength of character, and they should, in general, learn to appreciate the virtues that count for a great deal with men and serve as a recommendation for a minister of Christ[25]—virtues such as sincerity, a constant concern for justice, fidelity to promises, refined manners, modesty and charity in conversation.

782   The discipline that goes with seminary life should be regarded not merely as an effective safeguard for community life and charity, but also as a necessary part of the whole training process, geared to the acquisition of self-control, the development of a solid personal maturity and the formation

of other attitudes that will be of greatest help to the orderly and fruitful activity of the Church. But it should be carried out in such a way that the students develop an internal attitude of accepting the authority of superiors because of personal conviction, that is, on the basis of conscience (cf. *Rom.* 13, 5) and for supernatural reasons. The disciplinary rules should be adapted to the age of the students so that, as they gradually learn to govern themselves, they get in the habit of using their freedom wisely, of acting energetically on their own[26] and of cooperating with their fellows and the laity.

The whole pattern of seminary life ought to be permeated   783
with an interest in piety and in silence and in helping each other, and it ought to be laid out in such a way as to serve as a kind of introduction into the life the student will be leading in the future as a priest.

12. In order to put spiritual training on a more solid basis   784
and to enable the students to make a more mature and deliberate choice in embracing their vocation, it will be fitting for bishops to establish a certain period of time for a more intensive apprenticeship in the spiritual life. It will also be up to them to give some thought to the advisability of setting up some kind of interruption of studies or providing for some suitable pastoral apprenticeship in order to make more adequate provision for testing candidates for the priesthood. Again, depending on local circumstances, it will be up to the bishops to decide about raising the age now required by common law for the reception of sacred orders and to give some thought to the advisability of establishing a rule that students who have completed their course in theology should exercise the order of diaconate for a suitable time before being promoted to the priesthood.

V. The Reorganization of Studies for the Priesthood

13. Before entering upon specifically ecclesiastical studies,   785
students should have acquired whatever training in the sciences and humanities qualifies young people in their own country to enter upon higher studies; in additon, they are to acquire a knowledge of Latin that will enable them to understand and

use the source-works in many fields and the documents of the church.[27] Study of the liturgical language of one's own rite should be regarded as necessary, and a suitable knowledge of the languages of Sacred Scripture and of Tradition should be very much encouraged.

786   14. In revising ecclesiastical studies, special care should be taken to fit philosophy and theology together better and to make them contribute harmoniously toward opening up the minds of the students more and more to the Mystery of Christ, which affects the whole history of mankind, constantly influences the Church and works especially through the priestly ministry.[28]

787   In order to communicate this vision to the students from the very beginning of their training, ecclesiastical studies should begin with an introductory course lasting for a suitable time. This initiation should propose the mystery of salvation in such a way that the students grasp the meaning, arrangement, and pastoral purpose of ecclesiastical studies, at the same time that they are being helped to base their whole lives on faith and to look upon them in the light of faith, and being strengthened in their determination to embrace their vocation cheerfully and in a spirit of personal dedication.

788   15. Philosophy should be taught in such a way that the students are in particular led to acquire a solid and coherent knowledge of man, the world, and God that rests on a permanently valid philosophical heritage,[29] with due attention being paid to the philosophical studies of succeeding periods, especially those which have exerted greater influence on the student's own country, and to recent scientific advances, so that the students will have a correct idea of the characteristics of the present age and will be properly prepared to carry on a dialogue with the men of their own time.[30]

789   History of philosophy should be taught in such a way that the students will get to know the basic principles of the various systems and will hold fast to whatever proves true in them and be able to detect the roots of their errors and refute them.

790   The way in which the subject is taught should stir up the students' desire to carry on a rigorous search for truth and to

hold fast to it and to demonstrate it, and along with this an honest recognition of the limitations of human knowledge. Very careful attention should be paid to the connection between philosophy and the real problems of life and also the questions that are stirring the minds of the students. They should also be helped to see the connections that exist between philosophical matters and the mysteries of salvation which theology looks at under the higher light of faith.

16. The theological disciplines are taught in the light of faith, under the direction of the magisterium of the Church,[31] in such a way that students will accurately draw Catholic doctrine out of divine revelation, will go into it profoundly, will make it the nourishment of their own spiritual lives,[32] and will be capable of proclaiming it, explaining it, and defending it in their priestly ministry.　　　　　　　　　791

Students should be trained with special care in the study of Sacred Scripture, which ought to be like the soul of all theology.[33] After a fitting introduction, they should be given a correct initiation into the method of exegesis, they should look into the great themes of divine Revelation, and they should receive encouragement and nourishment from a daily reading of and meditation on the Sacred Books.[34]　　　　792

Dogmatic theology should be so arranged that biblical themes are proposed first of all. The contribution made by the Fathers of the Eastern and Western Church to the faithful transmission and development of individual truths of Revelation should be shown to the students, along with the later history of dogma, with due attention being paid to its relationship to the general history of the Church.[35] Next, in order to cast light as completely as possible upon the mysteries of salvation, the students should learn to go into them more deeply and to perceive the connection between them through the use of speculation, with St. Thomas as their master.[36] They should be taught to recognize these mysteries as present and at work in the liturgy[37] and in the whole life of the Church; and they should learn to seek solutions to human problems under the light of Revelation, to apply its eternal truths to the changing circumstances of human affairs, and　　793 to communicate these truths in a way suited to the people of their own time.[38]

794   Again, let the other theological disciplines experience a renewal from a more vital contact with the mystery of Christ and the history of salvation. Special attention should be paid to the improvement of moral theology; the scientific treatment of it should be nourished more by the teachings of Sacred Scripture so that it will point up the loftiness of the vocation that the faithful have in Christ and their obligation to bear fruit in charity for the life of the world. In the same way, the explanation of canon law and the treatment of church history should take into account the mystery of the Church as it has been described in the Dogmatic Constitution on the Church promulgated by this Sacred Council. Sacred Liturgy, which ought to be regarded as a first and necessary source of a truly Christian spirit is to be taught according to the intention of articles 15 and 16 of the Constitution on the Sacred Liturgy.[39]

795   With due allowance being made for the varied circumstances in different regions, the students should be led to a fuller knowledge of the Churches and Ecclesial Communities separated from the Apostolic Roman See, so that they may be able to contribute to the restoration of unity among all Christians in accoardance with the prescriptions of this Holy Council.[40]

796   They should also be introduced into a knowledge of other religions which are more widespread in individual areas, so that they will be better able to acknowledge whatever good and truth these religions possess through God's disposition, and so that they will learn to refute their errors and be able to communicate the full light of truth to those who do not have it.

797   17. But since doctrinal training ought to aim not at a mere communication of ideas but at a genuine and profound formation of the students, teaching methods should be revised both with regard to lectures, discussions and seminars, and with regard to the encouragement of study on the part of students, either by themselves or in small groups. Great attention should be paid to the unity and solidity of the whole

course, with care being taken to avoid an excess of subjects or classes and to eliminate those questions that retain hardly any importance or ought to be put off to higher studies.

18. It will be up to the bishops to see to it that young   798
men with suitable temperament, virtue and ability are sent to special institutes or faculties or universities so that priests may receive the kind of advanced scientific training in the sacred sciences and in other fields judged to be useful that will enable them to meet the various needs and demands of the apostolate. However, their spiritual and pastoral training is by no means to be neglected, especially if they are not yet priests.

VI. The Promotion of Strictly Pastoral Training

19. The pastoral concern that ought to permeate the whole   799
training of the students[41] also calls for their careful instruction in matters having a special relationship to the sacred ministry, especially catechesis and preaching, liturgical worship and administration of the sacraments, works of charity, the duty of going out in search of the erring and the unbelievers, and other pastoral activities. They should be correctly trained in the art of directing souls so that they may be able to bring all the sons of the Church to live a fully conscious and apostolic life and to carry out the duties of their own state. Equal care should be devoted to their learning how to help Sisters and Brothers to perservere in the grace of their own vocation and to make progress in accordance with the spirit of their various Institutes.[42]

In general, students should develop the kind of capabilities   800
that will help them to carry on a dialogue with men, such as a capacity for listening to others and for opening their hearts and minds to various human situations and circumstances in a spirit of charity.[43]

20. They should also be taught to use the aids that peda-   801
gogy, psychology or sociology can offer,[44] following correct methods and the norms laid down by ecclesiastical authority. They should also be properly instructed in how to inspire and foster the apostolic activity of lay people,[45] and in how to

promote varied and more effective forms of the apostolate. They should be imbued with that truly catholic spirit that will get them in the habit of going beyond the boundaries of their own diocese, nation or rite to help meet the needs of the whole Church, with a readiness to preach the Gospel everywhere.[46]

802   21. Since there is a need for students to learn the art of carrying on the apostolate from a practical as well as a theoretical point of view and to become able to act on their own responsibility and cooperate with others, they should be initiated into pastoral practice during the course of studies and in vacation time as well, through timely projects. This should be done systematically under the direction of men who are experts in pastoral matters, in accordance with the prudent judgment of the bishops and in keeping with the age of the students and local circumstances; in the course of this, the preponderant importance of supernatural aids should never be forgotten.[47]

VII. Training to be Completed after the Course of Studies

803   22. Since conditions of present-day society in particular make it necessary for priestly training to be carried on and perfected even after the course of studies in the seminary has been completed,[48] it will be up to the episcopal conference in each nation to use the most suitable means for this, such as pastoral institutes carried on in cooperation with specially selected parishes, conferences convened at specified times, and projects geared to gradually introducing the younger clergy into the spiritual, intellectual and pastoral aspects of priestly life and apostolic activity and to enabling them to renew and foster that life and work more and more each day.

Conclusion

804   The Fathers of this holy Council, in carrying on the work begun by the Council of Trent, entrust to seminary directors and teachers the task of training Christ's future priests in the

spirit of the renewal that has been fostered by this Council, and they do so with confidence. At the same time, they earnestly encourage those preparing for the priestly ministry to realize that the hope of the Church and the salvation of souls is being entrusted to them; they are urged to willingly accept the rules laid down in this Decree, so that they may bear rich fruits that will last forever.

Each and every thing said in this Decree has met with the approval of the Fathers of the Sacred Council. And We, by the Apostolic power handed on to Us by Christ, together with the Venerable Fathers, approve them, declare them, and establish them in the Holy Spirit; and We command that what has thus been decreed by the Council be promulgated for the glory of God. 805

Rome, at St. Peter's, October 28, 1965. 806

Vatican II
APOSTOLICAM ACTUOSITATEM
Decree on the Apostolate of the Laity
November 18, 1965

This Holy Synod wishes to encourage a more intense apostolic activity by the whole people of God.[1] Therefore it begins now to consider with deep concern the role of those Christian faithful who are lay people. In previous constitutions,[2] the Synod has already declared that the place of lay Christians in the mission of the Church is an integral and altogether essential one. Their apostolate flows from the very calling to be followers of Christ and must always be present in the Church. Sacred Scripture itself clearly points out that in the earliest days of the Church the witness of lay people was quite spontaneous and markedly effective (cf. *Acts* 11, 19-21; 18, 26; *Rom* 16, 1-16; *Phil* 4, 3).

808   Our own age requires a similar zeal of lay people. Indeed, the modern situation demands of lay people an even more intense apostolate, and one broader in scope. The accelerating population increase, the rapid advances of science and technology, the more intimate and complex relationships between peoples, all these have immensely broadened the range of the lay person's apostolate (in which there is generally no substitute for the lay person). Further, the factors mentioned have generated entirely new areas of concern which require expert attention and investigation by lay people. This kind of apostolate becomes all the more urgent because so many areas of human life have inevitably become extremely specialized. This specialization, in some instances, is accompanied by an alien-

ation from moral and religious values, and consequent serious dangers to Christian living. In addition, without lay energies the Church could scarcely exercise its presence and ministry in the numerous places where priests are too few, or, as is sometimes the case, where priests are denied the freedom to minister.

This complex and pressing need for a vigorous lay aposto-   809
late is clearly signaled by the obvious action of the Holy Spirit today. More and more He awakens lay people to an awareness of their particular responsibilities in the Church and inspires them to dedicate themselves to Christ and His Church in every kind of service.[3]

In this decree, the Fathers of the Council will attempt to   810
clarify the characteristics of the lay person's apostolate, its range and particular properties. They will also try to outline its basic principles and offer some pastoral suggestions for its more effective realization. Whatever is thus suggested should be looked on as proper legislation in the revision of canon law concerning the apostolate of lay people.

Chapter I

The Calling of the Laity to the Apostolate

2. The destiny of the Church is to spread the kingdom of   811
Christ over the whole planet and to enable all men to be saved and redeemed to the glory of God our Father.[4] Through men, the Church is to bring about a genuine harmony between the whole created order of the world and Christ. All the energies of the Mystical Body toward this goal are included in the term "apostolate." The Church carries out this apostolate through all her members, but in many different manners. The invitation to be a Christian is of its very nature a summons also to the apostolic mission of the Church. Just as in biological structures each individual cell shares its own vitality with the life of the whole body, rather than being a passive component, so too in the body of Christ: this body is the Church, and the whole body "grows and builds itself up in proportion to the balanced activities of each one of the members" (*Eph* 4, 16). Indeed, the joint action and inter-

relation of the members in this body is so intimate that any single member who does not act to build up the Church according to his abilities must be said to do a disservice both to the Church and to himself (cf. *Eph* 4, 16).

812   In the Church itself there is a unity of mission but many kinds of ministry. Christ gave to the Apostles and their successors the task of teaching, sanctifying and governing in His own name and with His power. Lay people have also been made sharers in the priestly, prophetic and royal office of Christ, and thus they exercise their proper role in the mission of the whole people of God, both within the Church, and in the secular order.[5] They genuinely exercise the apostolate by their efforts to bring the news of the Gospel and the ways of holiness to mankind; they likewise exercise it by their efforts to permeate and perfect the secular order of things with the spirit of the Gospel. Thus their actions in this order will clearly witness Christ and work toward the salvation of mankind. It is the particular calling of lay people to be immersed in the secular world and its activities; and so they have a God-given vocation to cultivate a fervent Christian spirit and to act as a yeast in the secular order.

813   3. Lay people have a right and duty to exercise the apostolate which stems from their very union with Christ the Head. By Baptism they are joined to the Mystical Body of Christ; they are strengthened by the power of the Holy Spirit in Confirmation; and they are thus commissioned to the apostolate by the Lord Himself. They are consecrated into the holy people of God and His royal priesthood in order that, through all their activities, they will be offering spiritual sacrifices and thus witness Christ through all the world. Through the sacraments, and especially through the Holy Eucharist, there is given and nourished within them that love which is the driving force of the whole apostolate.[6]

814   The apostolate should be carried out in that faith, hope and charity which the Holy Spirit makes richly available to all members of the Church. Indeed it is by the precept of charity, the most important commandment of the Lord, that all followers of Christ are bound to work for the salvation of all men and to labor for the glory of God through the

coming of His kingdom: so that they may know the only true God and His ambassador Jesus Christ (cf. *Jn* 17, 3).

Therefore the foremost task of every faithful Christian is 815 to pour out his energies so that the divine message of redemption may be heard and welcomed by all men everywhere.

The Holy Spirit works for the holiness of God's people 816 through the sacraments and the service of ministry. To help them carry out their apostolate He also imparts to the faithful particular gifts which "he distributes among them just as he wishes" (1 *Cor* 12, 11), in order that "each may use whatever endowments he has received in the service of others," and thus become himself "a good steward of the manifold bounty of God" (1 *Pt* 4, 10), for the building up of the whole body through love (cf. *Eph* 4, 16). By possessing these charisms, even the ordinary ones, there arise for each of the faithful both the right and duty to use them in the Church and in the secular order for the well-being of mankind and the growth of the Church. They are to be used in the freedom of the Holy Spirit who "breathes wherever he will" (*Jn* 3, 8). They are to be used in mutual cooperation with all Christ's brothers, especially in cooperation with their pastors, whose duty it is to make judgment about the genuinity of these gifts and the disciplined use of them, not indeed "to extinguish the Spirit" (1 *Thes* 4, 19), but "to test all things and to hold on to that which is good" (1 *Thes* 5, 21).[7]

4. Christ, the ambassador of the Father, is the source and 817 well-spring of the whole apostolate. Clearly then the effectiveness of the lay people's apostolate depends on their living in union with Christ, as the Lord Himself said: "One bears abundant fruit only when he and I are mutually united; severed from me you can do nothing" (*Jn* 15, 5). This life of intimate union with Christ is sustained within the Church by many kinds of spiritual assistance which are equally offered to all the faithful, the chief of which is active participation in the sacred liturgy.[8] These spiritual aids should be used so that lay people, by fulfilling their obligations to the secular order in their everyday lives, deepen their union with Chirst through their secular work. That is the will of God for them. Certainly their union with Christ is not to be put into a sepa-

rate compartment. With such an attitude lay people should have a prompt and cheerful spirit in their search for holiness of life, working to overcome obstacles in patience and wisdom.[9] Neither family responsibilities nor any other concerns of secular life should be extraneous to the conduct of their spiritual lives, as the Apostle Paul said: "Whatever you do or say, let it always be in the name of the Lord Jesus, while you give thanks to God the Father through him" (*Col* 3, 17).

818   Such a life will demand a persevering exercise of faith, hope, and love.

819   Only by the guidance of faith and reflection on the word of God can any man come to recognize in every moment and every place the God "in whom we live and move and have our being" (*Acts* 17, 28). Only through faith and God's word can we seek out His will in our every decision, see Christ in every man, whether friend or stranger, and judge accurately the true meaning and value of secular realities both in themselves and in their relation to the final goal of man's life.

820   Those who possess such faith will live as sons of God, sure of the fulfillment of His Revelation, and mindful always of the death and resurrection of the Lord.

821   In this life's pilgrimage men of faith keep themselves from being enslaved to material affluence and, hidden with Christ in God, they turn their energies to enduring values; with a full and generous spirit they dedicate themselves to spreading the kingdom of God; they work to improve the secular order and to permeate it with a Christian spirit. Faced with the inevitable difficulties of life, they discover strength in Christian hope, counting "the sufferings of the present time as not worthy to be compared with the glory to come" (*Rom* 8, 18).

822   Inspired by that love which has its sources in God, Christians do good to all men, especially to those who are of the household of the faith (cf. *Gal* 6, 19); they put aside "all malice, all deceit, hypocrisy and envy, and all slander" (1 *Pt* 2, 1) and thus attract men to Christ. God's love is "poured forth in our hearts by the Holy Spirit who has been given to us" (*Rom* 5, 5) and enables lay people truly to express in their own lives the spirit of the Beatitudes. Because they follow Christ who was poor they are neither discouraged by poverty

nor carried away by affluence; because they imitate the humble Christ they are not desirous of empty glories (cf. *Gal* 5, 26); they seek earnestly to please God rather than man, and they are always ready to abandon everything else for the sake of Christ (cf. *Lk* 14, 26), and to suffer persecution for the sake of conscience (cf. *Mt* 5, 10), mindful of the word of the Lord: "If anyone wants to become my follower, he must renounce himself and shoulder his cross; then he may be a follower of mine" (*Mt* 16, 24). They cherish a Christian friendship with one another, and no matter what hardship they face, they offer help to each other.

The spiritual life of lay people, described above in outline, ought to take its distinctive qualities from their marriage and family life, their single or widowed state, their conditions of health, and from their involvement in their own professional and social lives. They should be earnest then in cultivating the qualities and talents that fit these states in life, and they should make use of the gifts which they themselves have received from the Holy Spirit.   823

Beyond this, those lay people who, while following their lay calling, have joined one of the associations or institutes encouraged by the Church, should try faithfully to incorporate into their own spirituality the distinctive qualities proper to each association.   824

They should also have high respect for professional competence, for a civic and familial sense of responsibility, and for the virtues particularly oriented to the social order; honesty, the spirit of justice, integrity of life, courage, and a gentle regard for all men; the genuinely Christian life cannot be lived without these.   825

The ideal model of this apostolic spirituality is the most blessed Virgin Mary, Queen of the Apostles. While on earth she lived a most ordinary life, busily working and caring for a family. Yet she was always united intimately with her Son and cooperated in an altogether unique manner in the work of the Redeemer. Now she has been assumed into heaven and with her maternal love concerns herself for the brothers of her Son who are still in pilgrimage, and involved in danger and difficulty until they arrive in their blessed fatherland.[10] All   826 should venerate her with devotion and commend their lives and apostolates to her maternal care.

Chapter II

The Goals to be Achieved

827   5. Christ's work of redemption is directed both toward the salvation of men as individuals, and at the renewal of the whole secular order. Hence the Church's mission is not only to preach Christ and His grace to men, but also to bring the secular order to perfection by permeating it with the spirit of the Gospels. Therefore lay people in carrying out this mission of the Church will exercise their apostolate both in the life of the world and within the Church, in both the sacred and secular orders. These two orders, though they are quite distinct from one another, are so bound together in God's one Providence, that God Himself clearly seeks in the work of Christ to gather up all the created universe in a new creative act, which is begun in time and brought to fulfillment in eternity.

828   6. The Church's mission is concerned with man's salvation, which is to be achieved through faith in Christ and by His grace. Therefore the apostolate of the Church and of all its members is principally directed toward witnessing Christ to the world by word and action, and by serving as a channel of His grace. This is done primarily through the ministry of word and sacrament which has been entrusted in a special way to the clergy. However, lay people have their own important part to play in this ministry too, so that they may become "fellow-workers for the truth" (3 *Jn* 8). On this level particularly, the apostolate of lay people and the pastoral ministry mutually complement each other.

829   Lay people have innumerable opportunities for the apostolate of evangelizing and sanctifying. The very witness of a Christian life and good works done for a supernatural motive powerfully attracts men to faith in God, as the Lord says: "Let your light shine before your fellowmen, that they may see your good example and praise your Father who is in heaven" (*Mt* 5, 16).

However, this kind of apostolate is something more than   830
just good example; the true apostle seeks out opportunities
of preaching Christ, sometimes by leading non-believers toward faith, sometimes by instructing the faithful themselves,
strengthening them, and stimulating them to a more dedicated
life; "love for Christ drives us on" (2 *Cor* 5, 14); the hearts of
all believers should echo with those words of the Apostle Paul:
"Woe betide me if I do not go on preaching the gospel" (1 *Cor*
9, 16).[11]

Further, our times witness the rise of new doubts. We are   831
threatened by quite dangerous errors which are working to
overturn religion, the moral order, and human society itself.
Because of them, this holy Synod heartily exhorts lay people
to be even more earnest in the explanation, defense and application of Christian principles to the problems of our day.
Naturally, they will do this, each in the light of his own talents and understanding, and in accord with the mind of the
Church.

7. God's plan for the universe calls for men, working har-   832
moniously together, to renew the secular order and continuously improve it.

All that makes up the secular order, goods and property,   833
family values, the economic order, the arts and professions,
political institutions, international relations and other similar
realities, together with their development and advancement,
are not merely meant to assist man toward his final goal.
They have a validity of their own. That validity is established
in them by God, and holds whether you look just at each one
in itself or see them as components of the whole secular order: "And God looked at all which he had created, and they
were indeed good things" (*Gn* 1, 31). To this natural goodness
of the created order is added a certain special dignity because
of its relation to the human person, for whose service it was
created. Finally, it pleased God to bring together in one person, Jesus Christ, all realities, both natural and supernatural,
"so that he may have pre-eminence over every creature" (*Col*
1, 18). This ordering of things, however, does not strip the
secular order of its own independence, its own goals, laws,

tools and importance for human welfare. Rather the secular order is thus perfected in its natural excellence and brought into harmony with the whole vocation of man here on earth.

834   In the course of history the handling of things in the secular order has been attended by serious abuses. That is because men, under the influence of original sin, have frequently fallen into a host of errors about the true God, the nature of man, and the principles of the moral law; thus morality and human institutions were corrupted, and frequently the human personality itself was held in contempt. Indeed many men of our own times, because they are overly impressed by advances in science and technology, tend to a sort of worship of the material order, thus making themselves slaves rather than masters of it.

835   It is the task of the whole Church to help enable mankind to harmonize the entire order of secular realities, and direct it toward God through Christ. It is the duty of pastors to explain clearly the principles concerning the purpose of creation and the use of material things, and to offer the spiritual and moral supports needed to renew the secular order in Christ.

836   But lay people must take the renewal of the secular order as their own proper task. They must immerse themselves directly and decisively in it, guided by the light of the Gospel and the mind of the Church, and motivated by Christian love. They must work as citizens together with other citizens, each person with his own specific competence, and his own proper responsibility; and their goal must be to seek always and in all matters the justice of the kingdom of God. The secular order must be so renewed that, without violence to the integrity of its own laws, it is brought into harmony with the deepest principles of Christian living, and made to conform to the human needs of our varying localities, times, and peoples. Principal among the tasks of this apostolate is the social action of Christians, which this holy Synod today desires to see extended to the whole range of temporal realities, and especially to the advancement of the intellectual order.[12]

837   8. Every work of the apostolate should be founded in charity and from charity draw its strength. Yet some particular

works are by their very nature capable of giving a more striking witness of love. Christ our Lord wished such works to be
the signs of His messianic mission (cf. *Mt* 11, 4-5).

The greatest commandment of the law is to love God with   838
our whole hearts, and to love our neighbor as ourselves (cf.
Mt 22, 37-40). Christ made this command of love for neighbor
His own, and enriched it with a new dimension when He
identified Himself with all His brothers as the object of our
charity, teaching us: "As long as you did it for one of these
least brothers of mine, you did it for me" (*Mt* 25, 40). For He,
by taking on a human nature, gathered all mankind into a
kind of supernatural and familial solidarity with Himself and
established love as the mark of His followers when He said:
"By this token all the world must know that you are my
disciples, that you have love one for another" (*Jn* 13, 35).

By coming together at the *agape* of the Eucharistic banquet,   839
the holy Church in her early days demonstrated that her
members were united around Christ in the bond of charity.
In the same way she is recognizable in every era by this outward sign of love. Thus, while she rejoices in the charitable
undertakings of others, she does claim the works of charity as
her own duty and right which cannot be taken from her. For
this reason our Church gives a special place of honor to
mercy for the sick and needy, to the works of charity, and to
mutual aid for the relief of every type of human need.[13]

In our time these activities and works are universally more   840
urgent, for geographical distances have been shrunken, communications between men made more instantaneous, and the
inhabitants of the whole planet have become, as it were, simply the members of a single family. Our charitable activity
today can and ought to include every single member of the
human family, and all his needs. Wherever people are poorly
fed, clothed, housed, lack medical care, employment, education and the facilities for living a genuinely human life, where-
ever they are tormented by hardship or illness, wherever they
suffer exile and imprisonment, there precisely should Christian
charity be present, seeking them out and finding them in order to comfort them with its deep concern and support them

with the help it offers. This obligation rests primarily on those individuals, and nations, who are themselves prosperous.[14]

841   So that no one may be excluded from this kind of love, and that its universality be sharply evident, let us see in our neighbor the likeness of God, to whose image he has been created, and the person of Christ the Lord, to whom in reality is offered whatever is given to the needy; let us respect with the greatest gentleness the personal dignity and freedom of those we help; let the purity of our intention be unsoiled by any seeking for our own advantage, or any search for power;[15] let us first satisfy the demands of justice and not offer as the outpouring of charity what is already owned under the claim of justice; let us eliminate the causes of distress, not merely its symptoms; and let us so manage our assistance that those who receive it will gradually be freed from dependence on others and become capable of helping themselves.

842   Lay people then must greatly respect the works of charity and devote their energies to them. They should cooperate with all men of good will in supporting the undertakings of "social welfare" both public and private and also international aid, by which effective assistance is made available to individuals and to nations.[16]

Chapter III

On the Various Areas of the Apostolate

843   9. Lay people exercise their diversified apostolate in the Church and in the secular order. On both levels there are a variety of areas for apostolic action, of which we wish to mention here the more important. They are: Church communities, the family, youth, the social environment, the nation and the international community. Further, in our times women have an increasingly larger role in the life of society; it is then quite important that they participate more intensively also in the various areas of the apostolate.

844   10. Because they are partners in the priestly, prophetic and regal role of Christ, lay people share actively in the life and action of His Church. Within the communities of the Church,

their cooperation is so much needed that without it the apostolate of the pastors would be largely ineffectual. Like the men and women who assisted Paul in spreading the Gospel (cf. *Acts* 18, 18-26; *Rom* 16, 23), lay people with a genuinely apostolic attitude make up for what their brothers lack, and refresh the spirit of pastors and fellow faithful alike (cf. 1 *Cor* 16, 17-18). They themselves are strengthened by sharing actively in the liturgical life of their own community, and are prompt to take part in its apostolic efforts; they attract back to the Church those who have fallen away; they cooperate earnestly in presenting the teaching of God, particularly by catechetical instruction; by offering their own competences they lend added efficiency to the care of souls and even to the management of Church properties.

The most obvious example of the community apostolate is   845
the parish. Here a wide variety of people are gathered together in one assembly and united with the Church universal.[17] We desire that lay people in the parish work in close cooperation with their priests,[18] that they bring to this assembly of the Church their own problems and the questions of the world relating to salvation, for common study and resolution; and finally, we hope that they will lend their energetic assistance to every apostolic and missionary program of this, their ecclesial family.

At the same time they should have an appreciation of the   846
diocese, of which the parish is a cell, as it were. They should readily lend their energies to diocesan programs too, at the invitation of their bishop. Indeed the needs of both urban and rural areas today[19] require that lay collaboration be extended outside the parish and diocesan territory to embrace the interparochial, interdiocesan, national and international levels. This is all the more needed because the increasing mobility of people, and the parallel speed of communication and growing closeness between segments of society no longer allow any one segment to be self-contained. And so they should be concerned for the needs of God's people over the whole range of the planet. Missionary works, then, through the contribution of material and even personal assistance, are of special importance. For it is the Christian's duty and

privilege to return to God a portion of the bounty received
from Him.

847   11. The conjugal and familial apostolate has special importance both for the Church and for civil society. For the
Creator of all things established the conjugal partnership as
the beginning and basis of human society and by His grace
has made it a great sacrament in Christ and in the Church (cf.
Eph 5, 32).

848   Christian couples are cooperators in grace and witnesses of
faith to each other, their children, and other members of the
household. To their children they give the first introduction
and instruction in the faith; by word and example they form
them for a Christian and apostolic life, counsel them wisely
in selecting their own vocation, and carefully nourish a sacred
vocation should they detect its presence.

849   It has always been the duty of married couples to give
witness and proof by their lives to the indissolubility and
sanctity of marriage, to insist vigorously on the right and
obligation of parents and teachers to give their children a
Christian education, and to uphold the dignity and lawful
autonomy of the family. Today these constitute the most
important part of their apostolate. They and other members
of the faithful should work together with men of good will to
see that these rights are upheld in civil legislation. They should
see that in social planning there is due concern for family
needs related to housing, education of children, working conditions, social security and tax structures. Further, the unity
of the family should be carefully protected in arrangements
for the movement of large groups of people.[20]

850   The family was established by God as the vital and fundamental cell of society. To fulfill its divine purpose it should,
by the mutual devotion of its members and by their prayer
made in common to God, become, as it were, a domestic
extension of the Church's sanctuary; the whole family should
involve itself in the liturgical worship of the Church; finally,
the family should show itself hospitable, just, and generous
of its resources in the service of all its brethren who are in
need. Among the various tasks of the family apostolate, these
may be mentioned: the adoption of abandoned children,

offering hospitality to the stranger, assistance in the operation of schools, counselling and material assistance for adolescents, the preparation of engaged couples for marriage, catechetical work, support for couples and families involved in financial or moral difficulty, help to the aging by securing for them not only the necessities of life but also an equitable share in the profits of an expanding economy.

In every case the most treasured witness of Christ to the world is given by Christian families who cling to the Gospel and radiate an example of Christian marriage by their whole style of life. This is especially true in lands where the seeds of the Gospel are just being sown, or where the Church is still in its infancy, or where it is racked by some critical difficulty.[21]   851

The organization of families into certain kinds of associations can lend itself to the more effective achievement of the goals of this apostolate.[22]   852

12. In modern society young people exert a most significant influence.[23] Their life situation, mental outlook, and even their relationship to their own families, have considerably changed. Frequently, their transition to a new social and economic status is too rapid. Moreover, while their social and even political impact steadily increases, they seem almost unequal to the task of adequately fulfilling these new responsibilities.   853

The increased influence they wield in society requires of them a proportionate apostolic activity. And the natural endowments of youth equip them for such an apostolate. As the awareness of their own personality grows, their enthusiasm for life and their youthful energies make them want to take on their own responsibilities and become involved in social and cultural life. If this enthusiasm be touched with the spirit of Christ, and enlivened with an obedient love for the Church, it can produce very fruitful results. Young persons themselves, then, should become the first and immediate apostles to other youth, exercising an apostolate of their own among themselves, with some consideration for the social environment of the place where they live.[24]   854

Adults should carefully establish friendly channels of communication with young people which will allow both to over-   855 come the chasm of age difference. They will then be able to understand each other and share with one another the insights which both possess. By example first, and, when occasion offers, by wise counsel and strong supportive assistance, adults should encourage young people to engage in the apostolate. On their part, young people should cultivate respect and trust toward adults and, granting their natural attraction for what is new, they should hold a proper esteem for the worthwhile traditions of the past.

856   Children too should have their own apostolic activities. According to their abilities, they also are true and living witnesses of Christ to their peers.

857   13. By this apostolate is meant the effort to touch with the Christian spirit the attitudes, morals, laws, and community structures in which one lives. This apostolate is so much the province and function of lay people that it should scarcely ever be attempted by anyone else. In this area lay people can carry out the apostolate of "like to like." Here they complement the witness of their example by the witness of their speech.[25] Here they are the ones best able to assist their brothers, whether the apostolate be one related to work, professional or academic life, the neighborhood, recreation or community activities.

858   Lay people carry out this mission of the Church to the secular order first and foremost by that inner consistency of works with faith, by which they become the light of the world, and by a constant integrity of life with attracts others to love what is true and good, and eventually brings them to Christ and the Church. Equally important is that fraternal love which makes them share in the life, labors, sorrows and aspirations of their fellowmen and thus gently but surely disposes their hearts for the workings of grace. They fulfill this mission finally by that mature awareness of their role in building up society which motivates them to carry out their domestic, social and professional functions with such Christian generosity that their very manner of acting gradually penetrates the environment in which they live and work.

859   This apostolate should be extended toward all persons, no matter where they be encountered, and should include every

spiritual and material benefit which can be offered. But true apostles will not be satisfied with this alone; they will seek to announce Christ to their neighbor by their words also. For many people will be able to hear the Gospel and acknowledge Christ only through the lay people who are close to them.

14. The nation and the international order constitute a vast   860 area for the apostolate. Here lay people especially are the bearers of Christian wisdom. For motives of patriotism and the faithful execution of their civic duty, Catholics should feel themselves obliged to promote what is genuinely the common good. They should see that the weight of their opinion favors the just exercise of civil power and the conformity of civil law to the precepts of morality and the common good. Catholics with political abilities who are also, as they should be, strong in faith and in Christian understanding, should not avoid public office, where by filling the office in a worthy manner they can at once work for the common good and prepare the way for the Gospel.

Catholics should welcome cooperation with all men of good   861 will to encourage whatever is true, whatever is just, whatever is holy, whatever is lovable (cf. *Phil* 4, 8). They should meet with them, rival them in prudence and regard for mankind, and study how our social and public institutions can be improved according to the spirit of the Gospel.

Among the phenomena of our times worthy of special   862 mention is the growing and inevitable sense of the solidarity of all peoples. Lay people in their apostolate should earnestly promote this sense of solidarity and transform it into a sincere and genuine fraternal love. Beyond this, lay people should be aware of international developments, and of the problems and solutions, both pratical and theoretical, relating to this field, particularly those concerning the developing nations.[26]

All who work in or give assistance to foreign nations should   863 bear in mind that relations between people should be a truly fraternal exchange, in which both giving and receiving is mutual. Lastly, let all who travel, whether for reasons of state, business or pleasure, remember that wherever they go they are messengers of Christ and that they should conduct themselves as such.

Chapter IV

On Various Types of the Apostolate

864   15. Lay people can exercise the apostolate either as individuals or in a variety of groups and associations.

865   16. The apostolate of the individual is a witness that springs up abundantly from the well-spring of a truly Christian life (cf. *Jn* 4, 14). It is the source and condition on which all other apostolates, including those of organizations, are founded. Nothing else can be a substitute for it.

866   Some lay people may lack the opportunity or ability to work together in apostolic associations. But all, whatever their situation, are invited and obliged to carry out the apostolate of the individual, which is in every instance a valuable apostolate, and in some situations the only one that can achieve results.

867   This apostolate has many forms by which lay people can build up the Church, sanctify the secular order and breathe the spirit of Christ into it.

868   One form of the individual apostolate is most appropriate for our times because it manifests Christ living in His believing followers. That is the witness of an entire lay life which is rooted in faith, hope and charity. Beyond this, the apostolate of the spoken word, which in certain situations is the required one, enables lay people to announce Christ, to explain His teaching, to spread it in a measure fitted to each one's ability and circumstances, and to profess it faithfully.

869   Further, while they work together as citizens to maintain and extend the secular order, lay people should search for still higher motivations in the light of faith for the conduct of family, professional, cultural and social affairs. Whenever the occasion offers they should make these motivations clear to others, conscious that by so doing they are cooperating with and offering praise to God the Creator, Redeemer and Sanctifier.

870   Finally, lay people should quicken their lives with charity and wherever they can, express that charity in works.

Let all remember that they can reach others and contribute   871
to the redemption of the world by prayer and public worship,
and by penance and the willing acceptance of life's toils and
hardships, by which they are conformed to the suffering
Christ (cf. 2 *Cor* 4, 10; *Col* 1, 24).

17. The individual apostolate is urgently needed in areas   872
where the Church's liberty of action is seriously curtailed.
Under these difficult circumstances lay people take the place
of their priests as far as possible, even at the risk of their own
liberty and lives. They instruct those around them in Christian
doctrine, encourage them to a religious life and Catholic outlook, and lead them to frequent reception of the sacraments
and especially to cultivating a devotion to the Eucharist.[27]
While heartily thanking God for continuing even in our day
to inspire lay people to heroic courage in the midst of persecution, this holy Synod with fatherly affection and grateful
heart embraces these lay people.

The individual apostolate has particular significance in areas   873
where Catholics are scattered and few in number. For the reasons cited or for special reasons arising from their professional
occupations, some lay people work in the apostolate only as
individuals. Such persons may well gather for serious inter-
changes in small groups without any more formal kind of
organization, provided they always evidence to others, as a
witness of their true charity, the clear indication that they
are a community of the Church.

18. All the Christian faithful as individuals are summoned   874
to exercise the apostolate in the various situations of their
lives. Yet we must remember that by his nature man is a social
being. It has pleased God to gather those who believe in Christ
into the people of God (1 *Pt* 2, 5-10) and unite them in one
body (cf. 1 *Cor* 12, 12). The organized apostolate of the faithful thus happily answers both a human and a Christian need.
At the same time it symbolizes the unity and community of
the Church in Christ, who said: "Wherever two or three are
assembled in my name, there I am in the midst of them" (*Mt*
18, 20).

For that reason the faithful should exercise their apostolate   875
by uniting their efforts with one another.[28] They should be

apostles in the community of the home, in their parishes and dioceses, which themselves express the community character of the apostolate, and in freely chosen societies which they decide to form among themselves.

876   Another reason for the importance of the organized apostolate is that, both in church communities and in various secular environments, the apostolate can only be effective through the concerted action of many. The organizations established to provide concerted action in the apostolate act as a support for their members, form them for the apostolate, organize and supervise their apostolic work. More effective results can thus be expected than if each one were acting independently.

877   In our present situation, as far as the work of lay people is concerned, we very much need to strengthen the organized and federative form of the apostolate. Only the close coordination of our resources will enable us to protect apostolic values adequately and achieve all the goals of the modern apostolate.[29] Here it is particularly important to note that the apostolate should reach out to the ordinary mentality and social situation of those to whom it is directed. Otherwise they will often falter under the pressure of public opinion or of other institutions in society.

878   19. There is a great variety among apostolic organizations.[30] Some have as their purpose the general apostolic goals of the Church; others specifically direct their efforts to sanctification and evangelization; still others work for the Christian enrichment of the secular order; some give their witness of Christ specifically through the works of charity and mercy.

879   Among these organizations we should prize highly those which advocate and foster a more intimate relationship between the faith of their members and their everyday lives. Organizations are not an end in themselves; they are rather instruments for service to the Church's mission in the world. Their apostolic value is rooted in the Christian witness and evangelical spirit of the whole organization, as well as the measure in which its goals coincide with the goals of the Church.

Looking both at the proliferation of institutions and the   880
rapid pace of modern society, the universality of the Church's
mission demands that the apostolic undertakings of Catholics
should more and more be brought together in coordinating
structures at the international level. International Catholic
organizations will more readily achieve their goals when the
organizations which unite to comprise them, and their mem-
berships, are more closely related to the international entity
itself.

Lay people have a right to form organizations,[31] manage   881
them, and join them, provided they maintain the proper
relationship to ecclesiastic authority.[32] However, they should
beware of spreading their resources too thinly, and that is
what happens when new organizations and operations are
needlessly brought into existence. We also waste our resources
when we keep in existence organizations and ways of doing
things which are obsolete. Nor is it always best to transfer
indiscriminately to other countries, the structures established
in one place.[33]

20. The lay people of numerous countries, out of increasing   882
zeal for the apostolate, have organized themselves over many
decades into a variety of associations and action groups which,
while pursuing directly apostolic goals, also maintain a rather
close relation to the hierarchy. Among these and similar
institutions, those known as "Catholic Action" are worthy of
special recognition. They have commonly been described as
"the cooperation of lay people in the apostolate of the
hierarchy." Deservedly, they have been recommended and
promoted by the Popes and numerous bishops, and they have
achieved excellent results for the kingdom of Christ.[34]

These forms of the apostolate, whether under the title   883
"Catholic Action" or some other, have an important value
for our times. They are characterized by the following com-
binations of values:

a) The immediate goal of these organizations is the apostolic goal of the Church, that is, the evangelization and
sanctification of men, and the formation in them of a Christian
conscience, so that the spirit of the Gospel will be brought
through them to their own environment and community.

b) While working with the hierarchy in the established way, the people contribute their own experience and take responsibility for directing the organizations, determining the circumstances in which the pastoral action of the Church is to be exerted, and designing and executing the plan of action.

c) There is an organic unity to this kind of lay action, which makes their apostolate more effective and more pointedly portrays the community nature of the Church.

d) Whether acting on their own initiative or at the invitation of the hierarchy to cooperate in their apostolate, these lay people are ultimately under the guidance of the hierarchy itself. The hierarchy may also expressly approve this type of cooperation by mandate.

884   Organizations which in the hierarchy's judgment exhibit this combination of characteristics are to be recognized as Catholic Action, no matter what structures or titles they may have in various countries.

885   This holy Council strongly recommends these organizations, which certainly answer the needs of the Church's apostolate in many lands. It invites priests and lay people working in them to seek an increasing verification in their groups of the characteristics outlined above, and commends to them a constant and brotherly cooperation with all other forms of the apostolate.

886   21. All apostolic organizations are to be properaly appreciated. Those which the hierarchy has at various times and places praised or recommended, or whose establishment they have decreed to be more needed, should all be very highly esteemed by priests, religious and lay people, and they should promote them to the extent of their abilities. Among them, international organizations and associations of Catholics are of particular importance today.

887   22. Worthy of special commendation and honor are those single and married lay persons who, either permanently or for a period of time, contribute their professional talents to Church institutions and their programs. We are equally pleased by the growing number of lay people who offer their assistance to apostolic organizations and programs at home,

in the international field and in Catholic missionary communities and newly established Churches.

The pastors of the Church should gladly and gratefully welcome these lay people. They should see that treatment of them is fully in keeping with the demands of justice, equity and charity, with special attention to proper support for them and their families. They should also enjoy all necessary instruction, spiritual assistance and incentive.   888

Chapter V
Maintaining Proper Relations

23. The apostolate of lay people, whether individual or in organizations, should be properly coordinated and fitted into the apostolate of the whole Church. In fact, an essential element of the Christian apostolate is its coordination under those designated by the Holy Spirit to rule the Church of God (cf. *Acts* 20, 28). Equally necessary is cooperation between various undertakings of the apostolate, which likewise should be coordinated by the hierarchy.   889

A mutual appreciation for all forms of the apostolate, and a coordination of them that leaves intact the particular qualities of each, is needed to secure a spirit of unity, so that destructive rivalries may be avoided, common goals achieved, and a spirit of fraternal charity radiated by the whole apostolate.[35]   890

And this is certainly most appropriate in a Church the nature of whose mission requires apostolic harmony and cooperation among clergy, religious and lay people.   891

24. The hierarchy should promote the apostolate of lay people, provide the principles and spiritual aids, direct its use to the Church's common good, and see that doctrine and due order are preserved.   892

The apostolate of lay people has many purposes and structures, and it may have many kinds of relation to the hierarchy.   893

There are in the Church numerous apostolic programs undertaken at the free choice of lay people and wisely managed by them. In certain circumstances the Church's mission is better implemented by such programs, and thus the hierarchy frequently recommends and praises them.[36] However,   894 dialogue with lay people they should carefully find out what structures make for a more productive apostolic effort; they should encourage a spirit of unity both within the organization and with other groups.

895   Finally, religious nuns and brothers should respect the apostolic works of lay people, and willingly lend themselves to promote their programs, in keeping with the statues and spirit of their own institutes,[40] and they should seek to complement, support and assist the function of priests in this work.

896   26. Wherever it is possible there should be diocesan councils which, through the cooperation of clergy and religious with lay people, can assist the apostolic work of the Church both in evangelizing and sanctifying, and in charitable, social and other endeavors. Such councils will be helpful to the mutual coordination of various lay enterprises and organizations without threatening the autonomy and special character of each group.[41]

897   Such councils should also be established, as far as possible, in the parish, and on the interparish, interdiocesan, national and international levels.[42]

898   There should also be established at the Holy See some special secretariat to promote and serve the apostolate of lay people. It should be a center for facilitating communications relating to the various apostolic programs of lay people, for research on modern problems in this field, and for consultation that will help both hierarchy and lay people in their apostolic works.

899   27. The common heritage of the Scriptures, and the common duty to give Christian witness that flows from this, recommends and often demands the cooperation of Catholics with other Christians on the national and international levels, this by Church communities as well as individuals, and in permanent organizations as well as on particular projects.[43]

900   Common human values also frequently call for a similar cooperation between Christians, who are pursuing apostolic goals, and others who do not profess Christianity but acknowledge the same values.

901   This dynamic and prudent cooperation[44] is of great importance in secular activities. Through it lay people give witness

both to Christ the Redeemer of the world, and to the solidarity of the human family.

Chapter VI

Formation for the Apostolate

28. The apostolate can be fully effective only if there is a   902
multi-faceted and integrated preparation for it. The steady
spiritual and doctrinal progress of lay people themselves, and
the variety of persons, tasks and environments to which their
efforts must be adapted, both require such preparation. This
formation should be based on the principles expressed in
other conciliar declarations and statements.[45] Beyond the
formation common to all Christians, many forms of apostolate
require special and specific training, due to the variety of
persons and circumstances involved.

29. Lay people have their own role in the Church's mission.   903
Therefore their apostolic formation takes on a distinctive
quality from the specific and peculiar character of lay life
and the spirituality proper to it.

Apostolic formation presupposes an integrated human   904
formation in keeping with the talents and situation of each
person. For the lay person should thoroughly understand the
modern secular world. He ought to be involved in his own
society and capable of adjusting himself to its specific character
and culture.

But first of all the lay person must have a living faith in the   905
divine mystery of creation and redemption; he must be moved
by the Holy Spirit, who enlivens the people of God and urges
all men to love God the Father and in Him the secular order
and its citizens. That is essential in learning how to carry out
the mission of Christ and His Church. Such a formation should
be considered the necessary basis for any effective apostolate.

Beyond this spiritual formation, the lay person needs a   906
thorough understanding of doctrine and even a knowledge of
philosophy, ethics and theology suited to each one's talents,
age and circumstances. The importance of general culture,
too, as well as practical and technical training, cannot be overlooked.

907   To further good relations with all men, lay people should respect truly human values, especially those related to living and working in brotherhood with others and establishing dialogue with them.

908   However, apostolic formation cannot be limited to purely theoretical instruction. Slowly indeed, and carefully, but from the very beginning of his formation, the lay person must learn to look at reality with the eyes of faith, make judgments about it, and act on them. By active involvement he forms and perfects himself in the company of others, and thus embarks on active service to the Church.[46] Moreover, the increasing maturity of the human personality and the complexity of modern problems require that this formation be a continuing one, leading to constantly higher levels of knowledge and corresponding action. In meeting the requirements of such a formation the integrity and unity of the human personality must be respected and pains taken to preserve and increase its balance and harmony.

909   With such a formation the lay person can involve himself vigorously and completely in the reality of the secular order and effectively undertake his role in its affairs. At the same time he is a living member and witness of the Church, and makes her actively present to the secular order.[47]

910   30. Apostolic formation should begin with the earliest instruction of childhood. However, special emphasis should be placed on orienting adolescents and young people to the apostolate and filling them with its spirit. As new responsibilities are assumed, this formation should be continued through the whole life-span. It is therefore obvious that those who supervise Christian education are also bound to offer training for the apostolate.

911   In the family, parents should orient their children to recognize God's love for all men. Gradually, and by example especially, they must teach them to be concerned about the material and spiritual needs of their neighbor. The whole family and its habits of life thus become a sort of novitiate for the apostolate.

912   Children should be educated, too, to see beyond the confines of the family and open their minds to the community,

both of the Church and of the secular world. They should be so assimilated into the community life of their local parish that they thereby acquire an awareness of themselves as living, active members of the people of God. Further, priests in their work as catechists, preachers, spiritual directors, and in other pastoral functions, should pay attention to the apostolic formation of their people.

Schools, colleges and other Catholic educational institutions should encourage in young people a genuinely Catholic attitude toward apostolic activity. Where this formation is for any reason lacking, as in the case of children who do not attend such schools, it is all the more important for parents, pastors and apostolic organizations to remedy the defect. On the other hand, teachers and educators who, by their very state in life are involved in an outstanding form of the lay apostolate, should have such competence in doctrinal content and pedagogical techniques that they can transmit this training effectively.   **913**

Lay associations and organizations, whether directed to the apostolate or other supernatural purposes, should likewise give earnest and diligent encouragement to formation for the apostolate, as their resources and objectives permit.[48] Often they are the normal means for a realistic apostolic formation, since they can offer a training in doctrine at once spiritual and practical. Their members can meet in small groups with associates and friends to assess the techniques and results of their apostolic work and to relate the context of their daily lives to the teachings of the Gospel.   **914**

Apostolic formation should be so directed that account is taken of the entire range of the lay person's apostolate. This apostolate is not limited to the activity of associations and organizations but is to be exercised in all the situations and contexts of life, with emphasis on professional and social life. Each person should be energetically devoted to his own apostolic formation, particularly so in his adult years. For with maturity the mind becomes more open and a person can more accurately measure his own God-given talents; this makes possible a more effective use of the charisms which the   **915**

Holy Spirit has imparted to each one for the advantage of his brothers.

916   31. The various forms of the apostolate require specific and comparable kinds of formation:

a) Regarding the apostolate of evangelizing and sanctifying men, lay people should be specially trained to initiate dialogue with others, both believers and non-believers, in order to witness Christ's message to all.[49]

917   Since we are currently witnessing a new kind of materialism which is generally pervasive, even among Catholics, lay people should be even more earnest in understanding Christian teaching, especially on controversial matters. And more important, they should oppose every form of materialism by the witness of a life lived according to the Gospels.

b) Regarding the Christian renewal of the secular order, lay people should be thoroughly instructed about the genuine meaning and value of secular things, both as self-contained realities and as they relate to the final goals of human life. They should be knowledgeable about the organizing of institutions and the intelligent use of secular things, with unremitting concern for the public welfare in accordance with the Church's moral and social teachings. The principles of her social doctrine, and the conclusions to which they lead, are to be so thoroughly assimilated by lay people that they become competent not only to apply that teaching intelligently to specific situations, but further, to take their own share in the further development of that doctrine.[50]

c) Since the most vivid witness of Christian life is afforded by the works of mercy and charity, the faithful should be taught from childhood to share the sufferings of their brothers and to assist them generously when in need.[51]

918   32. Numerous resources are already available, such as seminars, conventions, retreats, days of recollection, conferences, books and lectures; all these can help the lay person dedicated to the apostolate to arrive at a deeper knowledge of Scripture and Christian teaching. They will help him also to improve his spiritual life, to understand the secular situation, and to discover and develop effective techniques for the apostolate.[52]

These resources should take account of the various forms   919
of the apostolate and the environments in which it must be
exercised.

For the same end, centers of study and higher institutes   920
have also been founded, and already produce excellent results.

This holy Synod is delighted by undertakings of this nature,   921
which are already successful in some countries, and desires
their establishment in other places where they are needed.

Moreover, we urge the establishment of centers for research   922
and study, not only in theology, but also in anthropology,
psychology, sociology and methodology, so that for all the
areas of the apostolate the talents of lay people, men and
women, youth and adults, may be better developed.

33. This holy Council earnestly exhorts in the Lord all lay   923
people to give a glad, generous and prompt response to the
inspiration of the Holy Spirit and to the voice of Christ who,
at this hour, invites them even more insistently. Let our young
people feel that this summons is directed in a special way to
them. May they accept the summons with eagerness and
generosity. For through this holy Synod the Lord Himself
over and over agin invites all lay people to an increasingly
intimate union with Himself. He invites them to recognize
that what is His is also theirs (cf. *Phil* 2, 5) and wishes them
to associate themselves with Him in His mission of redemption.
He is sending them forth again to go ahead of Him to every
town and place where He intends to visit personally (cf. *Lk*
10, 1) so that in the many forms and expressions of the one
apostolate of the Church, which is constantly to be renewed
to meet modern needs, they may show themselves to be His
fellow-workers, devoting themselves fully at all times to the
Lord's work, realizing that their toil in the Lord can never be
in vain (cf. 1 *Cor* 15, 58).

Each and every thing said in this Decree has met with the   924
approval of the Fathers of the Sacred Council. And We, by
the Apostolic power handed on to Us by Christ, together
with the Venerable Fathers, approve them, declare them, and
establish them in the Holy Spirit; and We command that
what has thus been decreed by the Council be promulgated
for the glory of God.

925   Rome, at St. Peter's, November 18, 1965.

Suspension of Law

926   The Holy Father has established that there be a suspension of the new laws contained in the decree that has just been promulgated, until June 29, 1966, the feast of the Holy Apostles Peter and Paul in this coming year.

927   In the meantime the Supreme Pontiff will issue rules for the implementation of the aforesaid laws.

928   Rome, November 18, 1965.

Vatican II
PRESBYTERORUM ORDINIS
Decree on the Ministry and Life of Priests
December 7, 1965

PREFACE

The excellence of the order of priests in the Church has already been recalled several times to the minds of all by this most sacred Synod.[1] Since, however, in the renewal of Christ's Church tasks of the greatest importance and of ever-increasing difficulty are being assigned to this order, it has seemed eminently useful to treat of the subject of priests at greater length and depth. What is said here applies to all priests, especially those devoted to the care of souls, though suitable adaptations are to be made for priests who are religious.

By sacred ordination and by the mission they receive from their bishops, priests are promoted to the service of Christ, the Teacher, the Priest, and the King. They share in His ministry of unceasingly building up the Church on earth into the People of God, the Body of Christ, and the Temple of the Holy Spirit. 930

Now, the pastoral and human circumstances of the priesthood have in very many instances been thoroughly changed. Therefore, in order that the ministry of priests may be carried on more effectively and their lives better provided for, this most sacred Synod declares and decrees as follows. 931

CHAPTER I

The Priesthood in the Mission of the Church

932   2. The Lord Jesus, "whom the Father has made holy and sent into the world" (*Jn.* 10:36), has made His whole Mystical Body share in the anointing by the Spirit with which He Himself has been anointed.[2] For in Him all the faithful are made a holy and royal priesthood. They offer spiritual sacrifices to God through Jesus Christ, and they proclaim the perfections of Him who has called them out of darkness into His marvelous light. [3] Hence, there is no member who does not have a part in the mission of the whole Body. Rather, each one ought to hallow Jesus in his heart[4] and bear witness to Jesus in the spirit of prophecy.[5]

933   Now, the same Lord has established certain ministers among the faithful in order to join them together in one body where "all the members have not the same function" (*Rom.* 12:4). These ministers in the society of the faithful would be able by the sacred power of their order to offer sacrifice and to remit sins.[6] They would perform their priestly office publicly for men in the name of Christ.

934   So it was that Christ sent the apostles just as He Himself had been sent by the Father.[7] Through these same apostles He made their successors, the bishops,[8] sharers in His consecration and mission. Their ministerial role has been handed down[9] to priests in a limited degree. Thus established in the order of the priesthood, they are co-workers of the episcopal order[10] in the proper fulfillment of the apostolic mission entrusted to the latter order by Christ.

935   Inasmuch as it is connected with the episcopal order, the priestly office shares in the authority by which Christ Himself builds up, sanctifies, and rules His Body. Therefore, while it indeed presupposes the sacraments of Christian initiation, the sacerdotal office of priests is conferred by that special sacrament through which priests, by the anointing of the Holy Spirit, are marked with a special character and are so con-

figured to Christ the Priest that they can act in the person of Christ the Head.[11]

Since in their own measure priests participate in the office   936
of the apostles, God gives them the grace to be ministers of Christ Jesus among the people. They shoulder the sacred task of the gospel, so that the offering of the people can be made acceptable through the sanctifying power of the Holy Spirit.[12] For, through the apostolic proclamation of the gospel, the People of God is called together and assembled so that when all who belong to this People have been sanctified by the Holy Spirit, they can offer themselves as "a sacrifice, living, holy, pleasing to God" (*Rom.* 12:1). Through the ministry of priests, the spiritual sacrifice of the faithful is made perfect in union with the sacrifice of Christ, the sole Mediator. Through the hands of priests and in the name of the whole Church, the Lord's sacrifice is offered in the Eucharist in an unbloody and sacramental manner until He Himself returns.[13]

The ministry of priests is directed toward this work and is   937
perfected in it. For their ministry, which takes its start from the gospel message, derives its power and force from the sacrifice of Christ. Its aim is that "the entire commonwealth of the redeemed, that is, the community and society of the saints, be offered as a universal sacrifice to God through the High Priest who in His Passion offered His very Self for us that we might be the body of so exalted a Head."[14]

The purpose, therefore, which priests pursue by their minis-   938
try and life is the glory of God the Father as it is to be achieved in Christ. That glory consists in this: that men knowingly, freely, and gratefully accept what God has achieved perfectly through Christ, and manifest it in their whole lives. Hence, whether engaged in prayer and adoration, preaching the Word, offering the Eucharistic sacrifice, ministering the other sacraments, or performing any of the works of the ministry for men, priests are contributing to the extension of God's glory as well as to the development of divine life in men. Since all of these activities result from Christ's Passover, they will be crowned in the glorious return of the same Lord when He Himself hands over the kingdom to His God and Father.[15]

939   3. Priests are taken from among men and appointed for men in the things which pertain to God, in order to offer gifts and sacrifices for sins.[16] Hence they deal with other men as with brothers. This was the way that the Lord Jesus, the Son of God, a man sent by the Father to men, dwelt among us and willed to become like His brothers in all things except sin.[17] The holy apostles imitated Him; and blessed Paul, the teacher of the Gentiles, who was "set apart from the gospel of God" (*Rom*. 1:1), declares that he became all things to all men that he might save all.[18]

940   By their vocation and ordination, priests of the New Testament are indeed set apart in a certain sense within the midst of God's people. But this is so, not that they may be separated from this people or from any man, but that they may be totally dedicated to the work for which the Lord has raised them up.[19] They cannot be ministers of Christ unless they are witnesses and dispensers of a life other than this earthly one. But they cannot be of service to men if they remain strangers to the life and conditions of men.[20] Their ministry itself by a special title forbids them to be conformed to this world.[21] Yet at the same time this ministry requires that they live in this world among men, and that as good shepherds they know their sheep. It requires that they seek to lead those who are not of this sheepfold so that they too may hear the voice of Christ and that there may be one fold and one Shepherd.[22]

941   In the achievement of these goals, priests will find great help in the possession of those virtues which are deservedly esteemed in human affairs, such as goodness of heart, sincerity, strength and constancy of character, zealous pursuit of justice, civility, and those other traits which the Apostle Paul commends, saying: "Whatever things are true, whatever honorable, whatever just, whatever holy, whatever lovable, whatever of good repute, if there be any virtue, if anything worthy of praise, think upon these things" (*Phil.* 4:8).[23]

CHAPTER II

The Ministry of Priests

I. Priestly Functions

4. The People of God finds its unity first of all through the   942
Word of the living God,[24] which is quite properly sought from
the lips of priests.[25] Since no one can be saved who has not
first believed,[26] priests, as co-workers with their bishops,
have as their primary duty the proclamation[27] of the gospel
of God to all. In this way they fulfill the Lord's command:
"Go into the whole world and preach the gospel to every
creature" (*Mk.* 16:15).[28] Thus they establish and build up
the People of God.

For through the saving Word the spark of faith is struck in   943
the hearts of unbelievers, and fed in the hearts of the faithful.
By this faith the community of the faithful begins and grows.
As the Apostle says: "Faith depends on hearing and hearing
on the word of Christ" (*Rom.* 10:17).

Toward all men, therefore, priests have the duty of sharing   944
the gospel truth[29] in which they themselves rejoice in the
Lord. And so, whether by honorable behavior among the
nations they lead them to glorify God,[30] whether by openly
preaching they proclaim the mystery of Christ to unbelievers,
whether they hand on the Christian faith or explain the
Church's teaching, or whether in the light of Christ they
strive to deal with contemporary problems, the task of priests
is not to teach their own wisdom but God's Word, and to
summon all men urgently to conversion and to holiness.[31]

No doubt, priestly preaching is often very difficult in the   945
circumstances of the modern world. If it is to influence the
mind of the listener more fruitfully, such preaching must not
present God's Word in a general and abstract fashion only,
but it must apply the perennial truth of the gospel to the concrete circumstances of life.

946   Thus the ministry of the Word is carried out in many ways, according to the various needs of those who hear and the special gifts of those who preach. In areas or communities which are non-Christian, the gospel message draws men to faith and the sacraments of salvation.[32] In the Christian community itself, especially among those who seem to understand or believe little of what they practice, the preaching of the Word is needed for the very administration of the sacraments. For these are sacraments of faith, and faith is born of the Word and nourished by it.[33]

947   Such is especially true of the Liturgy of the Word during the celebration of Mass. In this celebration, the proclamation of the death and resurrection of the Lord is inseparably joined to the response of the people who hear, and to the very offering whereby Christ ratified the New Testament in His blood. The faithful share in this offering both by their prayers and by their recognition of the sacrament for what it is.[34]

948   5. God, who alone is holy and bestows holiness, willed to raise up for Himself as companions and helpers men who would humbly dedicate themselves to the work of sanctification. Hence, through the ministry of the bishop, God consecrates priests so that they can share by a special title in the priesthood of Christ. Thus, in performing sacred functions they can act as the ministers of Him who in the liturgy continually exercises his priestly office on our behalf by the action of His Spirit.[35]

949   By baptism men are brought into the People of God. By the sacrament of penance sinners are reconciled to God and the Church. By the oil of the sick the ailing find relief. And, especially by the celebration of Mass, men offer sacramentally the sacrifice of Christ. In administering all the sacraments, as St. Ignatius Martyr already bore witness in the days of the primitive Church,[36] priests by various titles are bound together hierarchically with the bishop. Thus in a certain way they make him present in every gathering of the faithful.[37]

950   The other sacraments, as well as every ministry of the Church and every work of the apostolate, are linked with the holy Eucharist and are directed toward it.[38] For the most blessed Eucharist contains the Church's entire spiritual wealth,

that is, Christ Himself, our Passover and living bread. Through His very flesh, made vital and vitalizing by the Holy Spirit, He offers life to men. They are thereby invited and led to offer themselves, their labors, and all created things together with Him.

Hence the Eucharist shows itself to be the source and the apex of the whole work of preaching the gospel. Those under instruction are introduced by stages to a sharing in the Eucharist. The faithful, already marked with the sacred seal of baptism and confirmation, are through the reception of the Eucharist fully joined to the Body of Christ.   951

Thus the Eucharistic Action is the very heartbeat of the congregation of the faithful over which the priest presides. So priests must instruct them to offer to God the Father the divine Victim in the sacrifice of the Mass, and to join to it the offering of their own lives. In the spirit of Christ the Shepherd, priests should train them to submit their sins with a contrite heart to the Church in the sacrament of penance. Thus, mindful of the Lord's words: "Repent, for the kingdom of God is at hand" (*Mt.* 4:17), the people will be drawn ever closer to Him each day.   952

Priests should likewise teach them to participate in the celebrations of the sacred liturgy in such a way that they can rise to sincere prayer during them. They must lead the faithful along to an ever-improved spirit of prayer offered throughout the whole of life according to the graces and needs of each. They must persuade everyone to the discharge of the duties of his proper state in life, and bring the saintlier ones to an appropriate exercise of the evangelical counsels. They must show the faithful how to sing to the Lord hymns and spiritual songs in their hearts, always giving thanks to God the Father for all things in the name of our Lord, Jesus Christ.[39]   953

Priests themselves extend to the different hours of the day the praise and thanksgiving of the Eucharistic celebration by reciting the Divine Office. Through it they pray to God in the name of the Church on behalf of the whole people entrusted to them and indeed for the whole world.   954

In the house of prayer the most Holy Eucharist is celebrated and preserved. There the faithful gather, and find help and   955 comfort through venerating the presence of the Son of God our Savior, offered for us on the sacrificial altar. This house must be well kept and suitable for prayer and sacred functions.[40] There, pastors and the faithful are called to respond with grateful hearts to the gift of Him who through His humanity constantly pours divine life into the members of His Body.[41]

956   Let priests take care to cultivate an appropriate knowledge and facility in the liturgy, so that by their own liturgical ministry, the Christian communities entrusted to them may ever more adequately give praise to God, the Father and the Son and the Holy Spirit.

957   6. To the degree of their authority and in the name of their bishop, priests exercise the office of Christ the Head and the Shepherd. Thus they gather God's family together as a brotherhood of living unity, and lead it through Christ and in the Spirit to God the Father.[42] For the exercise of this ministry, as for other priestly duties, spiritual power is conferred upon them for the upbuilding of the Church.[43]

958   In achieving this goal, priests must treat all with outstanding humanity, in imitation of the Lord. They should act toward men, not as seeking to win their favor[44] but in accord with the demands of Christian doctrine and life. They should teach and admonish men as dearly beloved sons,[45] according to the words of the Apostle: "Be urgent in season, out of season; reprove, entreat, rebuke with all patience and teaching." (2 *Tim.* 4:2).[46]

959   Therefore, as educators in the faith, priests must see to it, either by themselves or through others, that the faithful are led individually in the Holy Spirit to a development of their own vocation as required by the gospel, to a sincere and active charity, and to that freedom with which Christ has made us free.[47] Ceremonies however beautiful, or associations however flourishing, will be of little value if they are not directed toward educating men in the attainment of Christian maturity.[48]

960   To further this goal, priests should help men see what is required and what is God's will in the great and small events of life. Christians should also be taught that they do not live

for themselves alone, but, according to the demands of the new law of charity, every man must administer to others the grace he has received.[49] In this way all will discharge in a Christian manner their duties within the community of men.

Although he has obligations toward all men, a priest has the poor and the lowly entrusted to him in a special way. The Lord Himself showed that He was united to them,[50] and the fact that the gospel was preached to them is mentioned as a sign of Messianic activity.[51] With special diligence, priests should look after youth, as well as married people and parents. It is desirable that each of these groups join together in friendly associations and thereby help one another act more easily and adequately as Christians in a condition of life which is often demanding.

961

Priests should remember that all religious, both men and women,who have a distinguished place indeed in the house of the Lord, deserve special care in their pursuit of spiritual progress for the good of the whole Church. Finally and above all, priests must be solicitous for the sick and the dying, visiting them and strengthening them in the Lord.

962

The office of pastor is not confined to the care of the faithful as individuals, but is also properly extended to the formation of a genuine Christian community. If community spirit is to be duly fostered, it must embrace not only the local Church but the universal Church. The local community should not only promote the care of its own faithful, but filled with a missionary zeal, it should also prepare the way to Christ for all men. To this community in a special way are entrusted catechumens and the newly baptized, who must be gradually educated to recognize and lead a Christian life.

963

No Christian community, however, can be built up unless it has its basis and center in the celebration of the most Holy Eucharist. Here, therefore, all education in the spirit of community must originate.[52] If this celebration is to be sincere and thorough, it must lead to various works of charity and mutual help, as well as to missionary activity and to different forms of Christian witness.

964

Moreover, by charity, prayer, example, and works of penance, the Church community exercises a true motherhood

965

toward souls who are to be led to Christ. For this community
constitutes an effective instrument by which the path to
Christ and to His Church is pointed out and made smooth for
unbelievers, and by which the faithful are aroused, nourished,
and strengthened for spiritual combat.

966   In building the Christian community, priests are never to
put themselves at the service of any ideology or human faction. Rather, as heralds of the gospel and shepherds of the
Church, they must devote themselves to the spiritual growth
of the Body of Christ.

II. Priests as Related to Others

967   7. All priests, together with bishops, so share in one and
the same priesthood and ministry of Christ that the very unity
of their consecration and mission requires their hierarchical
communion with the order of bishops.[53] At times they express this communion in a most excellent manner by liturgical
concelebration. At every Mass, however, they openly acknowledge that they celebrate the Eucharistic Action in union with
the episcopate.[54] Therefore, by reason of the gift of the Holy
Spirit which is given to priests in sacred ordination, bishops
should regard them as necessary helpers and counselors in the
ministry and in the task of teaching, sanctifying, and nourishing the People of God.[55]

968   Already in the ancient days of the Church we find liturgical texts proclaiming this relationship with insistence, as when
they solemnyly called upon God to pour out upon the candidate for priestly ordination "the spirit of grace and counsel
so that with a pure heart he may help and govern the People
[of God], just as in the desert the spirit of Moses was extended
to the minds of seventy prudent men,[56] "and using them as
helpers, he easily governed countless multitudes among the
people."[57]

969   Therefore, on account of this communion in the same
priesthood and ministry, the bishop should regard priests as
his brothers and friends.[58] As far as in him lies, he should
have at heart the material and especially spiritual welfare of
his priests. For above all, upon the bishop rests the heavy re-

sponsibility for the sanctity of his priests.[59] Hence, he should exercise the greatest care on behalf of the continual formation of his priests.[60] He should gladly listen to them, indeed, consult them, and have discussions with them about those matters which concern the necessities of pastoral work and the welfare of the diocese.

In order to put these ideals into effect, a group or senate[61] of priests representing the presbytery should be established. It is to operate in a manner adapted to modern circumstances and needs and have a form and norms to be determined by law. By its counsel, this body will be able to give effective assistance to the bishop in his government of the diocese.   **970**

Keeping in mind the fullness of the sacrament of orders which the bishop enjoys, priests must respect in him the authority of Christ, the chief Shepherd. They must therefore stand by their own bishop in sincere charity and obedience.[62] This priestly obedience animated with a spirit of cooperation is based on the very sharing in the episcopal ministry which is conferred on priests both through the sacrament of orders and the canonical mission.[63]   **971**

This union of priests with their bishops is all the more necessary today since in our present age for various reasons apostolic activities are required not only to take on many forms, but to extend beyond the boundaries or one parish of diocese. Hence no priest can in isolation or singlehandedly accomplish his mission in a satisfactory way. He can do so only by joining forces with other priests under the direction of Church authorities.   **972**

8. Established in the priestly order by ordination, all priests are united among themselves in an intimate sacramental brotherhood. In a special way they form one presbytery in a diocese to whose service they are committed under their own bishop. For even though priests are assigned to different duties they still carry on one priestly ministry on behalf of men.   **973**

All priests are sent forth as co-workers in the same undertaking, whether they are engaged in a parochial or supraparochial ministry, whether they devote their efforts to scientific research or teaching, whether by manual labor they share in the lot of the workers themselves—if there seems to   **974** be need for this and competent authority approves—or whether they fulfill any other apostolic tasks or labors related to the apostolate. All indeed are united in the single goal of building up Christ's Body, a work requiring manifold roles and new adjustments, especially nowadays.

975   Hence it is very important that all priests, whether diocesan or religious, always help one another to be fellow workers on behalf of truth.[64] Each one therefore is united by special bonds of apostolic charity, ministry, and brotherhood and the other members of this presbytery.

976   This fact has been manifested from ancient times in the liturgy, when the priests present at an ordination are invited to join with the ordaining bishop in imposing hands on the new candidate, and when priests concelebrate the sacred Eucharist in unity of heart. Each and every priest, therefore, is joined to his brother priests by a bond of charity, prayer, and every kind of cooperation. In this manner, they manifest that unity with which Christ willed His own to be perfectly one, so that the world might know that the Son has been sent by the Father.[65]

977   Consequently, older priests should receive younger priests as true brothers and give them a hand with their first undertakings and assignments in the ministry. They should likewise try to understand the mentality of younger priests, even though it be different from their own, and should follow their projects with good will. For his part, a young priest should respect the age and experience of his seniors. He should discuss plans with them, and willingly cooperate with them in matters which pertain to the care of souls.

978   Inspired by a fraternal spirit, priests will not neglect hospitality,[66] but cultivate kindliness and share their goods in common.[67] They will be particularly solicitous for priests who are sick, afflicted, overburdened with work, lonely, exiled from their homeland, or suffering persecution.[68] They will readily and joyfully gather together for recreation, remembering the Lord's own invitation to the weary apostles: "Come apart into a desert place and rest a while" (*Mk.* 6:31).

979   Furthermore, in order that priests may find mutual assistance in the development of their spiritual and intellectual lives, that they may be able to cooperate more effectively in their ministry and be saved from the dangers which may arise from loneliness, let there be fostered among them some kind or other of community life. Such a life can take on several forms according to various personal or pastoral needs: for instance, a shared roof where this is feasible, or a common table, or at least frequent and regular gatherings.

Worthy too of high regard and zealous promotion are those   980
associations whose rules have been examined by competent Church authority, and which foster priestly holiness in the exercise of the ministry through an apt and properly approved rule of life and through brotherly assistance. Thus these associations aim to be of service to the whole priestly order.

Finally, by reason of the same communion in the priest-   981
hood, priests should realize that they have special obligations toward priests who labor under certain difficulties. They should give them timely help and also, if necessary, admonish them prudently. Moreover, they should always treat with fraternal charity and magnanimity those who have failed in some way, offering urgent prayers to God for them and continually showing themselves to be true brothers and friends.

9. In virtue of the sacrament of orders, priests of the New   982
Testament exercise the most excellent and necessary office of father and teacher among the People of God and for them. They are nevertheless, together with all of Christ's faithful, disciples of the Lord, made sharers in His kingdom by the grace of God who calls them.[69] For priests are brothers among brothers with all those who have been reborn at the baptismal font.[70] They are all members of one and the same body of Christ, whose upbuilding is entrusted to all.[71]

Priests therefore should preside in such a way that they seek   983
the things of Jesus Christ,[72] not the things which are their own. They must work together with the lay faithful and conduct themselves in their midst after the example of their Master, who among men "has not come to be served but to serve, and to give his life as a ransom for many" (*Mt.* 20:28).

Priests must sincerely acknowledge and promote the   984
dignity of the laity and the role which is proper to them in

the mission of the Church. They should scrupulously honor that just freedom which is due to everyone in this earthly city. They should listen to the laity willingly, consider their wishes in a fraternal spirit, and recognize their experience and competence in the different areas of human activity, so that together with them they will be able to read the signs of the times.

985   While testing spirits to see if they be of God[73] priests should discover with the instinct of faith, acknowledge with joy, and foster with diligence the various humble and exalted charisms of the laity. Among the other gifts of God which are found in abundance among the faithful, those are worthy of special attention which are drawing many to a deeper spiritual life. Priests should also confidently entrust to the laity duties in the service of the Church, allowing them freedom and room for action. In fact, on suitable occasions, they should invite them to undertake works on their own initiative.[74]

986   Finally, priests have been placed in the midst of the laity to lead them to the unity of charity, that they may "love one another with fraternal charity, anticipating one another with honor" (*Rom.* 12:10). It is their task, therefore, to reconcile differences of mentality in such a way that no one will feel himself a stranger in the community of the faithful. Priests are defenders of the common good, with which they are charged in the name of the bishop. At the same time, they are strenuous defenders of the truth, lest the faithful be tossed about by every wind of opinion.[75] To their special concern are committed those who have fallen away from the use of the sacraments, or perhaps even from the faith. As good shepherds, they should not cease from going after them.

987   Mindful of this Council's directives on ecumenism,[76] let them not forget their brothers who do not enjoy full ecclesiastical communion with us.

988   Finally, to them are commended all those who do not recognize Christ as their Savior.

989   The Christian faithful, for their part, should realize their obligations toward their priests and with filial love they should follow them as their shepherds and fathers. Likewise sharing their cares, they should help their priests by prayer and work

to the extent possible, so that their priests can more readily overcome difficulties and be able to fulfill their duties more fruitfully.[77]

The Distribution of Priests and Priestly Vocations

10. The spiritual gift which priests received at their ordination prepares them not for any limited and narrow mission but for the widest scope of the universal mission of salvation "even to the very ends of the earth" (*Acts* 1:8). For every priestly ministry shares in the universality of the mission entrusted by Christ to His apostles. The priesthood of Christ, in which all priests truly share, is necessarily intended for all peoples and all times. It is bound by no limits of blood, nationality, or time, a fact already mysteriously prefigured in the person of Melchisedech.[78]   990

Let priests remember then, that they must have at heart the care of all the churches. Hence priests belonging to dioceses which are rich in vocations should show themselves willing and ready, with the permission or at the urging of their own bishop, to exercise their ministry in other regions, missions, or activities which suffer from a shortage of clergy.   991

In addition, the norms of incardination and excardination should be so revised that while this ancient practice remains intact it will better correspond to today's pastoral needs. Where an apostolic consideration truly requires it, easier procedures should be devised, not only for the appropriate distribution of priests, but for special pastoral objectives on behalf of diverse social groups, whether these goals are to be achieved in a given area, a nation, or anywhere on earth.   992

To these ends, therefore, there can be usefully established certain international seminaries, special dioceses, or personal prelatures and other agencies of this sort. In a manner to be decreed for each individual undertaking, and without prejudice to the rights of local Ordinaries, priests can thereby be assigned or incardinated for the general good of the whole Church.   993

As far as possible, priests should not be sent singly to a new field of labor, especially to one in whose language and   994 customs they are not yet well versed. Rather, after the example of the disciples of Christ,[79] they should be sent in at least twos or threes so that they may be mutually helpful to one another. Likewise, thoughtful care should be given to their spiritual life as well as their mental and bodily strength. As far as possible the locale and circumstances of work should be adapted to the personal situation of each priest assigned.

995   At the same time it will be highly advantageous if those priests who seek to work in a nation new to them take care not only to know well the language of that place but also the psychological and social characteristics peculiar to the people they wish to serve in humility. Thus they will be able to communicate with them as successfully as possible and thereby imitate St. Paul, who could say of himself: "For, free though I was as to all, unto all I have made myself a slave that I might gain the more converts. And I have become to the Jews a Jew that I might gain the Jews" (1 *Cor.* 9:19-20).

996   11. The Shepherd and Bishop of our souls[80] so constituted His Church that the people whom He chose and purchased by His blood[81] would be due to have its priests always and to the end of time, lest Christians should ever be like sheep without a shepherd.[82] acknowledging Christ's desire and inspired by the Holy Spirit, the apostles considered it their duty to select ministers "who shall be competent in turn to teach others" (2 *Tim.* 2:2). This duty then is a part of the priestly mission by which every priest is made a partaker in the care of the whole Church, so that workers may never be lacking for the People of God on earth.

997   Since, however, "a common concern unites the captain of a ship with its passengers,"[83] the whole Christian people should be taught that it is their duty to cooperate in one way or another, by constant prayer and other means at their disposal,[84] so that the Chruch may always have the necessary number of priests to carry out her divine mission. In the first place, therefore, by the ministry of the Word and by the personal testimony of a life radiant with the spirit of service and true paschal joy, priests should have it dearly at heart to demonstrate to the faithful the excellence and necessity of the priesthood.

Sparing neither care nor inconvenience, let priests assist   998
those young men or adults whom they prudently judge to be
fit for so great a ministry, that they may prepare themselves
properly and then at last with full external and internal freedom be able to be called by the bishop. In this effort, careful
and prudent spiritual direction is of the greatest value.

Parents and teachers and all who are in any way engaged in   999
the education of boys and young men should so prepare them
that, recognizing the Lord's concern for His flock and considering the needs of the Church, they will be ready to respond
generously to our Lord if He should call, and will say with
the prophet: "Lo, here am I, send me" (*Is.* 6:8).

This voice of the Lord in summons, however, is never to be   1000
looked for as something which will be heard by the ears of
future priests in any extraordinary manner. It is rather to be
detected and weighed in the signs by which the will of God is
customarily made known to prudent Christians. These indications should be carefully noted by priests.

Vocational projects, therefore, whether diocesan or nation-   1001
al, are warmly recommended to priests.[85] In sermons, in
catechetical instructions, and in written articles, priests should
eloquently set forth the needs of the Church both local and
universal, putting into vivid light the nature and excellence of
the priestly ministry. In this ministry, weighty responsibilities
are mixed with profound joys. In it especially, as the Fathers
of the Church teach, a supreme testimony of love can be given
to Christ.

CHAPTER III

The Life of Priests

I. The Priestly Call to Perfection

12. By the sacrament of orders priests are configured to   1002
Christ the Priest so that as ministers of the Head and co-
workers of the episcopal order they can build up and establish His whole Body which is the Church. Already indeed, in
the consecration of baptism, like all Christians, they received

the sign and the gift of so lofty a vocation and a grace that even despite human weakness[86] they can and must puruse perfection according to the Lord's words: "You therefore are to be perfect, even as your heavenly Father is perfect" (*Mt.* 5:48).

1003   To the acquisition of this perfection priests are bound by a special claim, since they have been consecrated to God in a new way by the reception of orders. They have become living instruments of Christ the eternal priest, so that through the ages they can accomplish His wonderful work of reuniting the whole society of men with heavenly power.[87] Therefore, since every priest in his own way represents the person of Christ Himself, he is also enriched with special grace. Thus, serving the people committed to him and the entire People of God, he can more properly imitate the perfection of Him whose part he takes. Thus, too, the weakness of human flesh can be healed by the holiness of Him who has become for our sake a high priest "holy, innocent, undefiled, set apart from sinners" (*Heb.* 7:26).

1004   Christ, whom the Father sanctified and consecrated, and sent into the world,[88] "gave himself for us that he might redeem us from all iniquity and cleanse for himself an acceptable people, pursuing good works" (*Tit.* 2:14). And so He entered into His glory through His Passion.[89] Likewise, consecrated by the anointing of the Holy Spirit and sent by Christ, priests mortify in themselves the deeds of the flesh and devote themselves the sanctity with which they are endowed in Christ, to the point of perfect manhood.[90]

1005   And so it is that they are grounded in the life of the Spirit while they exercise the ministry of the Spirit and of justice,[91] as long as they are docile to Christ's Spirit, who vivifies and leads them. For by their everyday sacred actions themselves, as by the entire ministry which they exercise in union with the bishop and their fellow priests, they are being directed toward perfection of life.

1006   Priestly holiness itself contributes very greatly to a fruitful fulfillment of the priestly ministry. True, the grace of God can complete the work of salvation even through unworthy ministers. Yet ordinarily God desires to manifest His wonders through those who have been made particularly docile to the impulse and guidance of the Holy Spirit. Because of their intimate union with Christ and their holiness of life, these men can say with the Apostle: "It is now no longer I that live, but Christ lives in me" (*Gal.* 2:20).

This most holy Synod desires to achieve its pastoral goals   1007
of renewal within the Church, of the spread of the gospel throughout the world, and of dialogue with the modern world. Therefore it fervently exhorts all priests to use the appropriate means endorsed by the Church as they ever strive for that greater sanctity which will make them increasingly useful instruments in the service of all of God's People.

13. Priests will attain sanctity in a manner proper to them   1008
if they exercise their offices sincerely and tirelessly in the Spirit of Christ.

Since they are ministers of God's Word, they should every   1009
day read and listen to that Word which they are required to teach to others. If they are at the same time preoccupied with welcoming this message into their own hearts, they will become ever more perfect disciples of the Lord. For as the Apostle Paul wrote to Timothy: "Meditate on these things, give thyself entirely to them, that thy progress may be manifest to all. Take heed to thyself and to thy teaching, be earnest in them. For in so doing thou wilt save both thyself and those who hear thee" (1 *Tim.* 4:15-16).

As priests search for a better way to share with others the   1010
fruits of their own contemplation,[92] they will win a deeper understanding of the "unfathomable riches of Christ" (*Eph.* 3:8) as well as the manifold wisdom of God.[93] Remembering that it is the Lord who opens hearts[94] and that sublime utterance comes not from themselves but from God's power,[95] in the very act of preaching His word they will be united more closely with Christ the Teacher and be led by His Spirit. Thus joined to Christ, they will share in God's love, whose mystery, hidden for ages,[96] has been revealed in Christ.

As ministers of sacred realities, especially in the Sacrifice   1011
of the Mass, priests represent the person of Christ in a special way. He gave Himself as a victim to make men holy. Hence priests are invited to imitate the realities they deal with. Since

they celebrate the mystery of the Lord's death, they should see to it that every part of their being is dead to evil habits and desires.[97]

1012 Priests fulfill their chief duty in the mystery of the Eucharistic Sacrifice. In it the work of our redemption continues to be carried out.[98] For this reason, priests are strongly urged to celebrate Mass every day, for even if the faithful are unable to be present, it is an act of Christ and the Church.

1013 So it is that while priest are uniting themselves with the act of Christ the Priest, they are offering their whole selves every day to God. While being nourished by the Body of Christ, their hearts are sharing in the love of Him who gives Himself as food for His faithful ones.

1014 In a similar way, they are joined with the intention and love of Christ when they administer the sacraments. Such is especially the case when they show themselves entirely and always ready to perform the office of the sacrament of penance as often as the faithful reasonably request it. By reciting the Divine Office, they lend their voice to the Church as in the name of all humanity she perseveres in prayer along with Christ, who "lives always to make intercession for us" (*Heb.* 7:25).

1015 Guiding and nourishing God's People, they are inspired by the love of the Good Shepherd to give their lives for their sheep.[99] They are ready to make the supreme sacrifice, following the example of those priests who even in our time have not refused to lay down their lives.

1016 Since they are teachers in the faith, they themselves "are free to enter the Holies in virtue of the blood of Christ" (*Heb.* 10:19) and approach God "with a true heart in fullness of faith" (*Heb.* 10:22). They can build up a firm hope concerning their people.[100] Those who are in any distress they can console with the encouragement by which God encourages them.[101]

1017 As rulers of the community, they ideally cultivate the asceticism proper to a pastor of souls, renouncing their own conveniences, seeking what is profitable for the many and not for themselves, so that the many may be saved.[102] They are always going to greater lengths to fulfill their pastoral duties

more adequately. Where there is need, they are ready to undertake new pastoral approaches under the lead of the loving
Spirit who breathes where He will.[103]

14. In today's world men have so many obligations to ful-   1018
fill. There is, too, such a great diversity of problems vexing
them, and often enough, they have to attend to them hastily.
As a result they are sometimes in danger of scattering their
energies in many directions.

For their part, priests, who are already involved in and   1019
distracted by the very numerous duties of their office, cannot
without anxiety seek for a way which will enable them to
unify their interior lives with their program of external activities. No merely external arrangement of the works of the
ministry, no mere practice of religious exercises can bring
about this unity of life, however much these things can help
foster it. But priests can truly build up this unity by imitating
Christ the Lord in the fulfillment of their ministry, His food
was to do the will of Him who sent Him to accomplish His
work.[104]

In very fact Christ works through His ministers to achieve   1020
unceasingly in the world that same will of the Father by
means of the Church. Hence Christ forever remains the source
and origin of their unity of life. Therefore priests attain to
the unity of their lives by uniting themselves with Christ in
acknowledging the Father's will and in the gift of themselves
on behalf of the flock committed to them.[105]

Thus, by assuming the role of the Good Shepherd, they will   1021
find in the very exercise of pastoral love the bond of priestly
perfection which will unify their lives and activities. This
pastoral love flows mainly from the Eucharistic Sacrifice,
which is therefore the center and root of the whole priestly
life. The priestly soul strives thereby to apply to itself the
action which takes place on the altar of sacrifice. But this
goal cannot be achieved unless priests themselves penetrate
ever more deeply through prayer into the mystery of Christ.

That they may be able to verify the unity of their lives in   1022
concrete situations too, they should subject all their undertakings to the test of God's will,[106] which requires that projects should conform to the laws of the Church's evangelical

mission. For loyalty toward Christ can never be divorced from loyalty toward His Church.

1023   Hence pastoral love requires that a priest always work in the bond of communion with the bishop and with his brother priests, lest his efforts be in vain.[107] If he acts in this way, a priest will find the unity of his own life in the very unity of the Church's mission. Thus he will be joined with the Lord, and through Him with the Father in the Holy Spirit. Thus he will be able to be full of consolation and to overflow with joy.[108]

II. Special Spiritual Needs of the Priestly Life

1024   15. Among the virtues most necessary for the priestly ministry must be named that disposition of soul by which priests are always ready to seek not their own will, but the will of Him who sent them.[109] For the divine work which the Holy Spirit has raised them up[110] to fulfill transcends all human energies and human wisdom: ". . . the foolish things of the world has God chosen to put to shame the 'wise' " (1 *Cor.* 1:27).

1025   Therefore, conscious of his own weakness, the true minister of Christ labors in humility, testing what is God's will.[111] In a kind of captivity to the Spirit[112] he is led in all things by the will of Him who wishes all men to be saved. He can detect and pursue this will in the circumstances of daily life by humbly serving all those who are entrusted to him by God through the office assigned to him and through the various happenings of his life.

1026   Since the priestly ministry is the ministry of the Church herself, it can be discharged only by hierarchical communion with the whole body. Therefore pastoral love demands that acting in this communion, priests dedicate their own wills through obedience to the service of God and their brothers. This love requires that they accept and carry out in a spirit of faith whatever is commanded or recommended by the Sovereign Pontiff, their own bishop, or other superiors.

1027   Let them very gladly spend themselves and be spent[113] in any task assigned to them, even the more lowly and poor ones.

For in this way they will preserve and strengthen the necessary unity with their brothers in the ministry, most of all with those whom the Lord has appointed the visible rulers of His Church. Thus too they will work to build up Christ's Body, which grows "through every joint of the system."[114]

This obedience leads to the more mature freedom of God's sons. Of its nature it demands that in the fulfillment of their duty priests lovingly and prudently look for new avenues for the greater good of the Church. At the same time, it demands that they confidently propose their plans and urgently expose the needs of the flock committed to them, while remaining ready to submit to the judgment of those who exercise the chief responsibility for governing the Church of God. 1028

By such responsible and voluntary humility and obedience, priests make themselves like Christ, having in themselves the attitude which was in Christ Jesus, who "emptied himself, taking the nature of a slave . . . becoming obedient to death" (*Phil.* 2:7-9). By such obedience Christ overcame and redeemed the disobedience of Adam. For as the Apostle gave witness: "By the disobedience of the one man the many were constituted sinners, so also by the obedience of the one the many will be constituted just" (*Rom.* 5:19). 1029

16. With respect to the priestly life, the Church has always held in especially high regard perfect and perpetual continence on behalf of the kingdom of heaven. Such continence on behalf of the kingdom of heaven. Such continence was recommended by Christ the Lord[115] and has been the years and in our day too by many Christians. For it simultaneously signifies and stimulates pastoral charity and is a special fountain of spiritual fruitfulness on earth.[116] It is not, indeed, demanded by the very nature of the priesthood, as is evident from the practice of the primitive Church[117] and from the tradition of the Eastern Churches. In these Churches, in addition to all bishops and those others who by a gift of grace choose to observe celibacy, there also exist married priests of outstanding merit. 1030

While this most sacred Synod recommends ecclesiastical celibacy, it in no way intends to change that different discipline which lawfully prevails in Eastern Churches. It lovingly 1031 exhorts all those who have received the priesthood after marriage to persevere in their sacred vocation, and to continue to spend their lives fully and generously for the flock committed to them.[118]

1032   Celibacy accords with the priesthood on many scores. For the whole priestly mission is dedicated to that new humanity which Christ, the conqueror of death, raises up in the world through His Spirit. This humanity takes its origin "not of blood, nor of the will of the flesh, nor of the will of man, but of God" (*Jn.* 1:13). Through virginity or celibacy observed for the sake of the kingdom of heaven,[119] priests are consecrated to Christ in a new and distinguished way. They more easily hold fast to Him with undivided heart.[120] They more freely devote themselves in Him and through Him to the service of God and men. They more readily minister to His kingdom and to the work of heavenly regeneration, and thus become more apt to exercise paternity in Christ, and do so to a greater extent.

1033   Hence in this way they profess before men that they desire to dedicate themselves in an undivided way to the task assigned to them, namely, to betroth the faithful to one man, and present them as a pure virgin to Christ.[121] They thereby evoke that mysterious marriage which was established by God and will be fully manifested in the future, and by which the Church has Christ as her only spouse.[122] Moreover, they become a vivid sign of that future world which is already present through faith and charity, and in which the children of the resurrection will neither marry nor take wives.[123]

1034   For these reasons, which are based on the mystery of the Church and her mission, celibacy was at first recommended to priests. Then, in the Latin Church, it was imposed by law on all who were to be promoted to sacred orders. This legislation, to the extent that it concerns those who are destined for the priesthood, this most holy Synod again approves and confirms. It trusts in the Spirit that the gift of celibacy, which so befits the priesthood of the New Testament, will be generously bestowed by the Father, as long as those who share in Christ's priesthood through the sacrament of orders, and indeed the whole Church, humbly and earnestly pray for it.

This holy Synod likewise exhorts all priests who, trusting   1035
in God's grace, have freely undertaken sacred celibacy in
imitation of Christ to hold fast to it magnanimously and
wholeheartedly. May they persevere faithfully in this state,
and recognize this surpassing gift which the Father has given
them, and which the Lord praised so openly.[124] Let them
keep in mind the great mysteries which are signified and fulfilled in it.

Many men today call perfect continence impossible. The   1036
more they do so, the more humbly and perseveringly priests
should join with the Church in praying for the grace of fidelity.
It is never denied to those who ask. At the same time let priests
make use of all the supernatural and natural helps which are
available to all. Let them not neglect to follow the norms,
especially the ascetical ones, which have been tested by the
experience of the Church and which are by no means less
necessary in today's world. And so this most holy Synod be-
seeches not only priests, but all the faithful to have at heart
this precious gift of priestly celibacy. Let all beg of God that
He may always lavish this gift on His Church abundantly.

17. By friendly and fraternal dealings among themselves   1037
and with other men, priests can learn to cultivate human values and to esteem created goods as gifts of God. Still as they
go about in this world they should always realize that according to the word of our Lord and Master they are not of this
world.[125] Therefore, using the world as though they used it
not,[126] they will attain to that liberty which will free them
from all excessive concern and make them docile to the
divine voice which makes itself heard in everyday life.

From this freedom and docility will grow a spiritual dis-   1038
cernment through which a proper relationship to the world
and its goods will be worked out. Such a relationship is highly
important for priests, since the Church's mission is fulfilled in
the midst of the world and since created goods are altogether
necessary for the personal development of a man. Let them
therefore be grateful for everything which the heavenly Father
gives them for leading their lives properly. Nevertheless they
ought to evaluate in the light of faith everything which comes
their way. Thus they can be led to a right use of goods corre-

sponding to God's will, and can reject whatever would be harmful to their mission.

1039   The Lord is "the portion and the inheritance" (*Num.* 18: 20) of priests. Hence they should use temporal goods only for those purposes to which it is permissible to direct them according to the teaching of Christ the Lord and the regulations of the Church.

1040   With all possible help from experienced laymen, priests should manage those goods which are, strictly speaking, ecclesiastical as the norms of Church law and the nature of the goods require. They should always direct them toward the goals in pursuit of which it is lawful for the Church to possess temporal goods. Such are: the arrangement of divine worship, the procuring of an honest living for the clergy, and the exercise of works of the sacred apostolate or of charity, especially toward the needy.[127]

1041   Without prejudice to particular law, priests and bishops should devote primarily to their decent livelihood and to the fulfillment of the duties of their proper state the benefits which they receive when they exercise some church office. What remains beyond that they should devote to the good of the Church or to works of charity. Therefore they should not regard an ecclesiastical office as a source of profit, nor should they spend the revenue accruing to it for the advantage of their own families.[128] Hence by never attaching their hearts to riches,[129] priests will always avoid any greediness and carefully abstain from any appearance of merchandising.

1042   Indeed, they are invited to embrace voluntary poverty. By it they will be more clearly likened to Christ and will become more devoted to the sacred ministry. For Christ became poor for our sakes, whereas He had been rich, so that we might be enriched by His poverty.[130] By their own example the apostles gave witness that God's free gift must be freely given.[131] They knew how to abound and how to suffer want.[132]

1043   After the example of that communion of goods which was praised in the history of the primitive Church,[133] some common use of things can pave the way to pastoral charity in an excellent manner. Through this form of living, priests can laudably reduce to practice the spirit of poverty recommended by Christ.

Led, therefore, by the Lord's Spirit, who anointed the Sav-   1044
ior and sent Him to preach the gospel to the poor,[134] priests
as well as bishops will avoid all those things which can offend
the poor in any way. More than the other followers of Christ,
priests and bishops should spurn any type of vanity in their
affairs. Finally, let them have the kind of dwelling which will
appear closed to no one and which no one will fear to visit,
even the humblest.

III. The Means of Support for Priestly Life

18. That priests may be able to foster union with Christ in   1045
all the circumstances of life, they enjoy, in addition to the
conscious exercise of their ministry, those means, common
and particular, new and old, which the Spirit of God never
ceases to stir up in the People of God and which the Church
commends and indeed at times commands for the sanctification of her members.[135] Of all spiritual helps, those acts are
outstanding by which the faithful receive nourishment from
God's Word at the twofold table of sacred Scripture and the
Eucharist.[136] It is obvious how important for the proper
sanctification of priests is the energetic and frequent exercise
of such acts.

To Christ the Savior and Shepherd, ministers of sacramen-   1046
tal grace are intimately united through the fruitful reception
of the sacraments, especially the repeated sacramental act of
penance. For this sacrament, prepared for by a daily examination of conscience, greatly fosters the necessary turning of
the heart toward the love of the Father of mercies. With the
light of a faith nourished by spiritual reading, priests can carefully detect the signs of God's will and the impulses of His
grace in the various happenings of life, and thus can become
more docile day by day to the mission they have undertaken
in the Holy Spirit.

They can always find a wondrous model of such docility in   1047
the Blessed Virgin Mary. Led by the Holy Spirit, she devoted

herself entirely to the mystery of man's redemption.[137] With the devotion and veneration of sons, priests should lovingly honor this mother of the supreme and eternal Priest, this Queen of the Apostles and protectress of their ministry.

1048   That they may discharge their ministry with fidelity, they should prize daily conversation with Christ the Lord in visits of personal devotion to the most Holy Eucharist. They should gladly undertake spiritual retreats and highly esteem spiritual direction. In manifold ways, especially through approved methods of mental prayer and various voluntary forms of prayer, priests should search for and earnestly beg of God that Spirit of genuine adoration by which they themselves, along with the people entrusted to them, can unite themselves intimately with Christ the Mediator of the New Testament. Thus, as sons of adoption, they will be able to cry out: "Abba, Father" (*Rom.* 8:15).

1049   19. In the sacred rite of ordination the bishop admonishes priests to be "mature in knowledge," and to make their doctrine "a spiritual medicine for God's People."[138] The knowledge of a sacred minister should be sacred, since it is drawn from a sacred fountain and is directed to a sacred goal. Hence that knowledge should be drawn primarily from reading and meditating on the sacred Scriptures.[139] But it should also be fruitfully nourished by a study of the Holy Fathers and Doctors and other annals of tradition.

1050   In addition, that they may be able to provide proper answers to the questions discussed by the men of this age, priests should be well acquainted with the documents of the Church's teaching authority and especially of Councils and the Roman Pontiffs. They should consult, too, the best, approved writers in theological science.

1051   Since in our times human culture and the sacred sciences are making new advances, priests are urged to develop their knowledge of divine and human affairs aptly and uninterruptedly. In this way they will prepare themselves more appropriately to undertake discussions with their contemporaries.

1052   That priests may more easily pursue their studies and learn methods of evangelization and of the apostolate to better effect, every care should be taken to provide them with opportune aids. Such would be the instituting of courses or of congresses, according to the conditions of each region, the establishment of centers dedicated to pastoral studies, the setting up of libraries, and appropriate programs of study conducted by suitable persons.

Bishops, moreover, as individuals or jointly, should consider   1053
working out some easier way for their priests to attend courses giving them the opportunity to acquire a better grasp of pastoral methods and theological science, to strengthen their spiritual lives, and to share their apostolic experiences with their brothers.[140] Such courses should be held at set times, especially a few years after ordination. By these and other appropriate helps newly appointed pastors and those who are assigned to a new pastoral activity can be assisted with special care. The same is true of those who are sent to another diocese or country.

Finally, bishops must be concerned that some persons dedi-   1054
cate themselves to a more profound knowledge of theological matters. Thus there will never be any lack of suitable teachers to train clerics, and the rest of the clergy as well as the faithful can be assisted in providing themselves with the needed teaching. Thus, too, will be fostered that wholesome advancement in the sacred disciplines which is altogether necessary for the Church.

20. Dedicated to serving God through the discharge of the   1055
task assigned to them, priests are worthy of receiving a just recompense. For, "the laborer deserves his wages" (*Lk.* 10: 7),[141] and "the Lord directed that those who preach the gospel should have their living from the gospel" (1 *Cor.* 9:14). Hence, where a fitting recompense of priests is not otherwise provided for, the faithful themselves are bound by a genuine obligation to see that the needed means can be procured for them to lead a respectable and worthy life. For it is in behalf of the welfare of the faithful that priests labor.

Bishops are obliged to remind the faithful of their duty.   1056
They should see to it either individually for their own dioceses or, better, through several bishops acting simultaneously for a common territory, that norms are set up by which a decent

upkeep can be duly provided for those who perform some function in the service of God's People, or have done so.

1057   Depending on the nature of the office itself and the conditions of place and time, the recompense should be fundamentally the same for all those operating in the same circumstances. It should be adjusted to their situation and should also allow them to make a suitable return to those who dedicate themselves to the service of priests. It should also enable them to give some kind of personal assistance to the needy. From her earliest beginnings the Church has always held this ministry toward the poor in high regard.

1058   Moreover, this recompense should be such as to allow priests a requisite and sufficient vacation each year. Bishops should see to it that priests can have a vacation of this sort.

1059   The chief emphasis should be given to the office which sacred ministers fulfill. Hence the so-called benefice system should be abandoned or at least it should be reformed in such a way that the beneficiary aspect, that is, the right to revenues accruing to an endowed office, will be treated as secondary, and the main consideration in law will be accorded to the ecclesiastical office itself. From now on such an office should be understood as any function which has been permanently assigned and is to be exercised for a spiritual purpose.

1060   21. The example should never be overlooked of the believers in the primitive Church at Jerusalem. There "they had all things in common" (*Acts* 4:32) and "distribution was made to each, according as anyone had need" (*Acts* 4:35). Accordingly it is supremely appropriate that at least in areas where clerical support depends entirely or largely on the offerings of the faithful, some kind of diocesan agency should collect the offerings made for this purpose. The bishop is to administer it with the help of delegated priests and, where it may be useful, laymen skilled in economic affairs.

1061   It is also desirable, to the extent possible, that in individual dioceses or regions a common fund be established out of which bishops can satisfy different obligations to persons serving the Church, and to meet various diocesan needs. Through it, also, wealthier dioceses can help poorer ones, providing for the wants of the latter out of their abundance.[142] This common fund should be drawn primarily from the offerings of the faithful, but can derive from other sources too, as determined by law.

In some nations social security is not yet properly organized toward the support of the clergy. In such places Episcopal Conferences should see to it that under the vigilance of the hierarchy sufficient provision is made for an appropriate program of preventive medicine and so-called health benefits, and for the necessary support of priests burdened by infirmity, ill health, or old age. To this end there can be set up diocesan programs—and these can be amalgamated—or programs simultaneously instituted for various dioceses, or associations initiated for a whole territory. In any case, pertinent ecclesiastical and civil laws should always be taken into account.   **1062**

Motivated by a spirit of solidarity with their brothers and sharing in their trials,[143] priests should support these arrangements after they have been established. At the same time they should consider that they can thereby give themselves over entirely to the welfare of souls and practice poverty in a readier evangelical sense without anxiety about their future. Let those concerned be preoccupied that such associations in various nations be interrelated. In this way they can gain strength more surely and be more widely established.   **1063**

CONCLUSION AND EXHORTATION

22. While contemplating the joys of priestly life, this most holy Synod cannot overlook the difficulties which priests experience in the circumstances of contemporary life. For it realizes how deeply economic and social conditions and even the customs of men are being transformed, and how profoundly scales of value are being changed in the estimation of man.   **1064**

As a result, the ministers of the Church and even, at times, the faithful themselves feel like strangers in this world, anxiously looking for appropriate ways and words with which to communicate with it. For the modern obstacles blocking faith, the seeming sterility of their past labors, and also the bitter   **1065** loneliness they experience can lead them to the danger of becoming depressed in spirit.

1066   The world which is entrusted today to the loving ministry of the pastors of the Church is that world which God so loved that He gave His only Son for it.[144] The truth is that though entangled indeed in many sins this world is also endowed with great talents and provides the Church with the living stones[145] to be built up into the dwelling place of God in the Spirit.[146] Impelling the Church to open new avenues of approach to the world of today, this same Holy Spirit is suggesting and fostering fitting adaptations in the ministry of priests.

1067   Priests should remember that in performing their tasks they are never alone. Relying on the power of Almighty God and believing in Christ Who called them to share in His priesthood, they should devote themselves to their ministry with complete trust, knowing that God can intensify in them the ability to love.[147]

1068   Let them be mindful too that they have as partners their brothers in the priesthood and indeed the faithful of the entire world. For all priests cooperate in carrying out the saving plan of God. This plan is the mystery of Christ, the sacrament hidden from the ages in God.[148] It is brought to fulfillment only by degrees, through the collaboration of many ministries in the upbuilding of Christ's Body until the full measure of His manhood is achieved.

1069   Since all of these realities are hidden with Christ in God[149] they can be best grasped by faith. For the leaders of the People of God must walk by faith, following the example of the faithful Abraham, who in faith "obeyed by going out into a place which he was to receive for an inheritance; and he went out, not knowing where he was going" (*Heb.* 11:8). The dispenser of the mysteries of God can be truly compared to the man who sowed his field and of whom the Lord said: "Then he slept and rose, night and day. And the seed sprouted and grew without his knowing it" (*Mk.* 4:27).

1070   As for the rest, the Lord Jesus Who said: "Take courage, I have overcome the world" (*Jn.* 16:33), did not by these words promise His Church a perfect victory in this world.

This most holy Synod truly rejoices that the earth has been   1071
sown with the seed of the Gospel and now bears fruit in many
places under the influence of the Lord's Spirit. He it is who
fills the whole earth and has stirred up a true missionary spirit
in the hearts of many priests and faithful. For all of these
blessings, this most holy Synod gives most loving thanks to
all the priests of the world.

"Now to him who is able to accomplish all things in a   1072
measure far beyond what we ask or conceive, in keeping with
the power that is at work in us—to him be glory in the Church
and in Christ Jesus" (*Eph.* 3:20-21).

Each and every one of the things set forth in this Decree   1073
has won the consent of the Fathers of this most sacred Council. We too, by the Apostolic authoirty conferred on Us by
Christ, join with the Venerable Fathers in approving, decreeing
and establishing these things in the Holy Spirit, and we direct
that what has thus been enacted in synod be published to
God's glory.

Rome, at St. Peter's, December 7, 1965.   1074

SACRUM DIACONATUS ORDINEM
Motu Proprio of Pope Paul VI
on Restoring the Permanent Diaconate
June 18, 1967

The Catholic Church has held the sacred order of the diaconate in highest honor since the time of the Apostles; the Doctor of the Gentiles himself gives evidence of this when he addresses his greeting to the deacons as well as to the bishops[1] and when he instructs Timothy on the virtues and qualities of soul that should be expected of them if they are to carry out their ministry worthily.[2]

1076   The Second Vatican Ecumenical Council has carried on this ancient custom by praising the diaconate in the Dogmatic Constitution on the Church. After considering bishops and priests in that document, it also paid tribute to the third rank of sacred orders by explaining its dignity and listing its functions. But since the Council understood very well that "these duties which are very necessary for the life of the Church can be fulfilled only with difficulty in many regions, because of the discipline of the Latin Church prevailing today," and since it wanted to make better provision for something as desirable as this, it wisely decreed that "in time to come, the diaconate could be reinstated as a distinct and permanent rank of the hierarchy."[3]

1077   For even though some of the functions of deacons are usually committed to laymen, especially in missionary lands, still "it is helpful to strengthen, by the imposition of hands—which goes back to apostolic tradition—and to link more closely with the altar, men who are to perform truly diaconal functions . . . so that through the sacramental grace of the diaconate they will be enabled to fulfill their ministry more effectively."[4] This will be ideal to highlight the special nature of this order, which should not be regarded as just a step toward the priesthoood, but rather as enriched with an indelible character and a special grace of its own so that those who are called to it can "serve the mysteries of Christ and of the Church"[5] in a stable fashion.

But since the restoration of the permanent diaconate in   1078
the Latin Church is not something that has to be put into effect, but rather "it is up to competent territorial conferences of bishops . . . to decide, with the approval of the Supreme Pontiff, whether and where it would be opportune to appoint deacons of this type for the care of souls,"[6] We have decided that it is not only desirable but necessary that some well-defined rules be published adapting existing discipline to the new precepts of the Ecumenical Council, and to prescribe the right conditions for the proper exercise of the diaconal ministry and for a training of candidates which will be properly suited to their varying states of life, their common offices and their sacred dignity.

To begin with, We want to confirm all that is said in the   1079
Code of Canon Law about the rights and duties of deacons, either those rgihts and duties which they have in common with all clerics or those proper to themselves, except where We here state otherwise, and We decree that these rules are to apply to those who are to be permanent deacons as well. In addition We make the following provisions concerning them.

I

1. It is the function of legitimate episcopal conferences to   1080
decide, with the consent of the Roman Pontiff, whether and where the diaconate is to be established as a permanent rank in the hierarchy for the good of souls.

2. In submitting requests for the approval of the Apostolic   1081
See, the reasons should be given which make this new discipline advisable in a given area, and those special aspects

stated which afford genuine hope for success. Likewise, indications should be given of the kind of discipline involved, namely, whether it will be a case of conferring the diaconate "on suitable young men . . . for whom the law of celibacy must remain in force" or "on older man, including those living in the married state," or on candidates of both categories.

1082   3. Once the approval of the Apostolic See has been obtained, it will be up to each ordinary to approve and ordain candidates in his own territory, unless exceptions have been made in granting the faculty.

1083   In making his report on the state of his diocese, the ordinary should also recount the establishment of this discipline.

II

1084   4. On the basis of Church law, with the approval of the Ecumenical Council, young men called to the diaconate are bound by the law of celibacy.

1085   5. The permanent diaconate is not to be conferred before the age of 25; the episcopal conferences can require a greater age if they so choose.

1086   6. Young men who are to be trained for the office of deacon should go to a special college where they can be tested, trained to live a truly evangelical life, and instructed on how to perform their duties usefully.

1087   7. The bishops of a region—or where it would be useful, those of several regions in the same country—should join in establishing a college of this kind, depending on local circumstances. They should choose particularly well-fitted men to be in charge of it and should make clear rules regarding discipline and studies, in accordance with the norms that follow.

1088   8. Only those young men should be enrolled to train for the diaconate who have shown a natural inclination for service to the hierarchy and the Christian community, and who have received what is, by local standards, a good deal of doctrinal instruction.

1089   9. The period of preparation for the diaconate should run at least three years. The course of studies should be arranged in such a way that the candidates make orderly and gradual progress toward gaining an understanding of the various duties of the diaconate and toward being able to carry them out effectively. The whole course of studies might well be so planned that in the last year special training will be given in the principal functions to be carried out by the deacon.

10. In addition, there should be practice in teaching the 1090 fundamentals of the Christian religion to children and others of the faithful, in teaching people to sing sacred music and in leading them, in reading the books of Scripture at gatherings of the faithful, in giving talks to the people, in administering those sacraments which deacons may administer, in visiting the sick and, in general, in carrying out the ministries which may be required of them.

III

11. Men of more mature age, whether celibate or married, 1091 can be called to the diaconate; but married men should not be accepted unless there is clear evidence that their wives not only consent but also have the Christian moral character and attributes which will neither hinder their husbands' ministry nor be out of keeping with it.

12. "More mature age" means 35 years; but this is to be 1092 understood as meaning that no one can be called to the diaconate unless he has won the respect of the clergy and the faithful by having lived a truly Christian life for a long time, by his upright character, and by showing that his nature and disposition are inclined toward the ministry.

13. In the case of married men, care should be taken that 1093 only those are promoted to the diaconate who have lived as married men for a number of years and have shown themselves to be good heads of their own homes, and whose wives and children lead a truly Christian life and have good reputations.[7]

14. It is desirable for these deacons, too, to acquire a good 1094 deal of doctrine, as was said in nos. 8, 9 and 10 above, or at least for them to have the knowledge which the episcopal conference may judge they will need to fulfill their functions properly. They should therefore be admitted to a special col-

lege for a certain length of time in order to learn all they will have to know to carry out worthily the office of deacon.

1095   15. But if for some reason this cannot be done, then the candidate should be entrusted to some priest of excellent judgment who will take a special interest in him and teach him and who will be able to testify to his maturity and prudence. Great care must always be taken that only those who have enough learning in the sacred order.

1096   16. Those who have received the order of deacon, even those who are older, may not, in accordance with traditional Church discipline, enter into marriage.

1097   17. Care should be taken that deacons do not carry on a profession or trade which the local ordinary considers unsuitable or which will interfere with the fruitful exercise of their sacred office.

IV

1098   18. Any deacon who is not a professed member of a religious community should be duly enrolled in some diocese.

1099   19. Any rules now in force on the proper support of priests and on providing social security for them are to be applied also to permanent deacons, with due consideration being given to the families of married deacons and keeping in mind no. 21 of this document.

1100   20. It will be up to the episcopal conference to make specific rules on the decent support of a deacon and of his family if he is married, in accordance with local circumstances.

1101   21. Deacons who are practicing a secular profession should take care of their own needs and those of their family from this income insofar as possible.

V

1102   22. In accordance with the conciliar Constitution mentioned above, it is the function of the deacon—to the extent that he has been authorized by the local ordinary—to do the following:

1) To carry out, with bishop and priest, all the roles in liturgical rites which the ritual books attribute to him;

2) To administer Baptism solemnly and to supply the ceremonies that have been omitted at Baptism in the case of an infant or adult;

3) To have custody of the Eucharist, to distribute it to himself and to others, and to impart Benediction of the Blessed Sacrament to the people with the pyx;

4) To assist at and bless marriages in the name of the Church when there is no priest present, with delegation from the bishop or the pastor, so long as everything else commanded in the Code of Canon Law is observed,[8] and with no infringement on Canon 1098, in which case what is said of a priest is to be understood of a deacon as well;

5) To administer sacramentals, and to preside at funeral and burial rites;

6) To read the Scriptures to the faithful and to teach and preach to the people;

7) To preside over the offices of religious worship and prayer services when there is no priest present;

8) To direct Bible services when there is no priest present;

9) To do charitable, administrative and welfare work in the name of the hierarchy;

10) To legitimately guide outlying communities of Christians in the name of the pastor and the bishop;

11) To foster and aid the lay apostolate.

23. All these offices are to be carried out in complete com-   1103
munion with the bishop and his presbyterium, which means under the authority of the bishop and the priests who preside over the care of souls in that place.

24. Deacons should have a part in pastoral councils inso-   1104
far as this is possible.

VI

25. Deacons are serving the mysteries of Christ and the   1105
Church, and must abstain from any vice, strive to please God, and be "ready for any good work"[9] for the salvation

of men. Therefore, because of their reception of this order, they should far excel others in their liturgical lives, in devotion to prayer, in the divine ministry, in obedience, charity and chastity.

1106   26. It will be up to the episcopal conference to establish more effective rules for fostering the spiritual lives of deacons, both celibates and those who are married. But the local ordinaries should see to it that all deacons:

1) Apply themselves to carefully reading and attentively meditating on the word of God;

2) Attend Mass frequently—even daily if possible—receive the Blessed Sacrament of the Eucharist and visit it out of devotion;

3) Purify their souls frequently through the Sacrament of Penance, having prepared for it worthily through a daily examination of conscience;

4) Show a deep love and veneration for the Virgin Mary, the Mother of God.

1107   27. It is very fitting for permanent deacons to recite daily at least some part of the Divine Office—to be specified by the episcopal conference.

1108   28. Diocesan deacons must make a retreat at least once every three years in some pious or religious house designated by the ordinary.

1109   29. Deacons should not slacken in their studies, particularly of sacred doctrine; they should carefully read the Scriptures; they should devote themselves to ecclesiastical studies in such a way that they can correctly explain Catholic doctrine to others and day by day become better fitted to train and strengthen the souls of the faithful. With this in mind, deacons should be called to regular meetings at which matters concerning their life and sacred ministry will be treated.

1110   30. Deacons are obliged to profess reverence and obedience for the bishop in a special way because of the ministry committed to them; but bishops should have a high regard for these ministers of the People of God and show them paternal charity. If a deacon is going to remain outside his own diocese for a good reason for a length of time, he should willingly submit to the authority and supervision of the local ordinary in matters concerning the offices and duties of the diaconal state.[10]

31. As far as clothing is concerned, local custom is to be observed in accordance with the rules laid down by the episcopal conference.   1111

VII

32. Institution of the permanent diaconate among religious is a right reserved to the Holy See, which alone is competent to examine and approve the votes of general chapters in the matter.   1112

33. Deacons who belong to religious communities are to exercise their ministry under the authority of the bishop and of their own superiors, in accordance with the norms applicable to priests who are religious. They are also bound by the same laws as other members of their religious order.   1113

34. When a deacon who is a relgious is staying either permanently or for a while in an area that does not have a permanent diaconate, he is not to exercise his functions as a deacon without the consent of the ordinary.   1114

35. Whatever is said about religious in nos. 32-34 is to be understood as well about the members of other institutes professing the life of the evangelical counsels.   1115

VIII

36. As for the rite to be used in conferring the sacred order of diaconate and the orders that come before it, the present discipline is to continue in force until revised by the Holy See.   1116

Lastly, after laying down these rules, We find a wish springing up in Our heart that deacons, in carrying out their difficult office in the circumstances of this age of ours, may follow the shining examples which We propose to them of the protomartyr St. Stephen who was, as St. Irenaeus says, the "first to be chosen by the Apostles for the diaconate,"[11] and of St. Lawrence of Rome, "who was outstanding not only in administering the sacraments, but in managing the goods of the Church as well."[12]   1117

1118   We command that everything decreed in this letter that We have issued on Our own initiative be regarded as established and ratified, anything to the contrary notwithstanding.

1119   Given at Rome, at St. Peter's, on June 18th, the feast of the deacon St. Ephraem of Syria, in the year 1967, the fourth of Our pontificate.

Selection from Homily of Pope Paul VI
to the Third World Congress of Lay Apostolate
on the Layman's Sphere of Action
October 15, 1967

They are not new things, but they are true and important things. For you who listen to them and meditate on them here, they are fruitful and rich with an immense vitality. The first is this: the Church has given solemn recognition to the layman as a member of a society that is at one and the same time visible and mysterious. There you have what you might call an age-old novelty. The Church has reflected on her nature, her origin, her history, her functionalism, and has given the worthiest and richest definition of the layman who belongs to her. She has recognized that he is incorporated into Christ and that he shares in the priestly, prophetic and royal role of Christ Himself, without failing to recognize what is characteristic of him: that he is living a secular life as a citizen of this world, that he is occupied with earthly matters, that he practices a secular profession, that he has a family, that in all areas he devotes himself to temporal studies and interests.

The Church has proclaimed the dignity of the layman, not only because he is a man but also because he is a Christian. She has declared him worthy to be associated in the responsibilities of the life of the Church, to the extent and in the form appropriate to him. She has judged him capable of giving witness to his faith. She has recognized the full rights of the laity, both men and women: the right to equality in the hierarchy of grace; the right of liberty within the framework of moral law and Church law; the right to holiness in accord with the particular state of each individual.

1122   One might say that the Church took a certain satisfaction in making known this doctrine on the laity, since there are so many expressions of it to be read in a number of the Council documents—expressions that are repeated and interwoven. And while it might be said that in substance the Church has always thought this way, still it must be agreed that she has never expressed it so insistently and on such a broad scale.

1123   This recognition of the citizenship of the layman in the Church of God is something We want to repeat here now, for We are happy to confirm the words of the Council; happy to see in it the full flowering of a theological, canonical and sociological process that has long been desired by many penetrating minds. We are happy to base on this recognition the hopes of an authentic, rejuvenated Church, one better fitted to accomplish her mission for the Christian salvation of the world.

1124   But even when We have recognized and proclaimed what you are in the Church of God, dear sons and daughters, We still haven't said all We should. We must also recognize and proclaim what you can and must do there; what you, as Catholics who have freely dedicated yourselves to the apostolate, are effectively doing there. And here We have come to the heart of the matter, to the very definition of your ideal and your efforts, to what the whole world can read in the title of your congress: the apostolate of the laity.

1125   Here We find Ourself a little embarrassed, for We can only repeat to you in a different form what the Council has proclaimed with unparalleled authority and in carefully chosen formulas that are remarkable for their precision and for their wealth of content.

1126   The principle is laid down in the Dogmatic Constitution on the Church. That in itself is enough to tell you how important it is. "The laity," we read there, "are gathered together in the People of God and established in the one body of Christ under one head. Whoever they may be, they are called, as living members, to expend for the growth of the Church and its continual sanctification all the energy they have received. . . .

Thus upon all the laity falls the noble task of working to bring the divine plan of salvation ever closer to men of every epoch and every land."[1]

Thus the Church, as you can see, recognizes the layman not just as one of the faithful, but as an apostle. And in opening up an almost unlimited field before him, she confidently addresses to him the invitation of the Gospel parable: "Go you also into my vineyard."[2] This work will be many-sided and diversified. The Council's Decree on the Apostolate of the Laity, after having firmly set forth, in its turn, the principle that "the Christian calling is of its very nature a call to the apostolate," devotes two whole chapters to detailing the "various fields" and the "various types" of this apostolate. You are certainly well-acquainted with these texts. May this mention of them, dear sons and daughters, suffice to strengthen in your minds and hearts the unshakable conviction that the appeal addressed to you by the Church in the environment of the 20th century is a real one; that the trust she places in you is real, and so is the vast scope of the responsibilities she invites you to take upon yourselves in order to advance the kingdom of Christ among your brethren and to be more fully what the theme of your congress invites you to be—"the People of God on the journey of mankind." **1127**

At this point, an objection arises. In fact, one may say, if the tasks entrusted to lay people in the apostolate are so vast, should it not be admitted that henceforth there are, in the Church, two parallel hierarchies, as it were—two organizations existing side by side, the better to ensure the great work of the sanctification and salvation of the world? **1128**

This, however, would be to forget the structure of the Church, as Christ wished it to be, by means of the diversity of ministries. Certainly the People of God, filled with graces and gifts, marching toward salvation, presents a magnificent spectacle. But does it follow that the People of God are their own interpreters of God's word and ministers of His grace? That they can evolve religious teachings and directives, making abstraction of the faith which the Church professes with authority? Or that they can boldly turn aside from tradition and emancipate themselves from the magisterium? **1129**

1130   The absurdity of these suppositions suffices to show the lack of foundation of such an objection. The Decree on the Apostolate of the Laity was careful to recall that "Christ conferred on the apostles and their successors the duty of teaching, sanctifying and ruling in His name and power" (No. 2).

1131   Indeed, no one can take it amiss that the normal instrumental cause of the divine designs is the hierarchy, or that, in the Church, efficacity is proportional to one's adherence to those whom Christ "has made guardians, to feed the Church of the Lord."[3] Anyone who attempts to act without the hierarchy, or against it, in the field of the Father of the family, could be compared to the branch which atrophies because it is no longer connected with the stem which provides its sap. As history has shown, such a one would be only a trickle of water, cutting itself off from the great mainstream, and ending miserably by sinking into the sands.

1132   Do not think, beloved sons and daughters, that for this reason the Church desires to bridle your generous inspirations. Quite simply, she is faithful to herself, and to the will of her divine Founder. For the greatest service she can do for you is to define your exact place and role in that organism which is intended to bring to the world the good news of salvation. "In the Church there is diversity of service, but unity of purpose."[4]

1133   What does the Church expect of her laity, who are well-organized and wholeheartedly loyal to the Church authorities? First of all, she expects substantial help in the successful continuation of Church activities.

1134   The theological progress of which We often speak has clarified the areas of responsibility that belong to clergy and laity respectively. In view of the great shortage of clergy, both priests and deacons, in many parts of the world, the laity—both within Catholic Action and outside it—must take on more and more those tasks that do not necessarily require ordination to the priesthood.

1135   Even if it be a question of more modest tasks, like teaching catechism to children or doing the many works of charity, the spiritual and corporal works of mercy, you should keep it in mind that these tasks are fundamental, and undertake them with a joyful heart. In doing so, you will be giving witness to the spirit of service to which the Council called priest and layman alike.

Another task ought to be mentioned, since it expresses   1136
something that has become a cherished idea these last few years: the *consecratio mundi*, the sanctification of the world.

The world is your field of activity, to which you have been   1137
called. The natural course of events in this world—which depends on a thousand factors that We cannot mention individually here now—is pushing you in the direction of a development that contemporary thinkers, in the course of hailing it or regretting it, describe as secularization, laicization, or desacralization. We say it with sorrow, but those are even Catholic writers who oppose the Church's two-thousand-year tradition and loudly hail the progressive weakening and even the complete collapse of the sacred character of places, times and persons.

Beloved sons and daughters, your apostolate must counter-   1138
act these currents. The Council has reminded you of it again and again: the laity are supposed "to consecrate the world to God." You are supposed to be working for the "sanctification of the world," to give it "Christian inspiration," for the "improvement of living conditions and institutions in the world." This is what the Council documents say.

And what else can this mean if not the complete sanctifi-   1139
cation of the world once again through having it penetrated by the powerful spirit of faith in God and in Christ, which alone can lead it to salvation and true happiness?

The late Cardinal Cardijn often expressed this in moving   1140
words, and We also said it recently: "Lay people must consider it their task to improve the temporal order. . . . They have the duty . . . to infuse a Christian spirit into people's mental outlook and daily behavior, into the laws and structures of the civil community."[5]

We want to implant this deeply in your hearts once again: 1141
Bring to the world of our day every talent that can help you to advance along the road to progress and freedom, and that

can help solve its great problems—hunger, international justice and peace.

1142   Let Us conclude, beloved sons and daughters, with a few words on the spirituality that should characterize your activity. You are not hermits who have withdrawn from the world in order to devote yourselves to God. It is in the world and in its activity that you must sanctify yourselves. The spirituality that should inspire you will, as a result, have its own characteristics, and the Council has pointed them out in a long paragraph of the Decree on the Apostolate of the Laity (no. 4). It will suffice to put it in a few words for you: only your profound, personal union with Christ will assure the fruitfulness of whatever apostolate you may undertake. You will meet Christ in the Scriptures, in active participation in the Liturgy of the Word as well as in the Eucharistic Liturgy. You will meet Him in your silent, personal prayer, which is indispensable to ensure the contact of the soul with the living God, the source of all grace.

1143   The involvement of your apostolate in the midst of the world does not do away with any of these fundamental conditions for all spirituality; instead, it presupposes them and even demands them. Who was more involved than the great St. Teresa, whose feast we celebrate each year on this day, October 15th? And who was better able than she to find the strength and fruitfulness of her action in prayer and in union with God at every moment? We intend one day to accord her and St. Catherine of Siena the title of Doctor of the Church.

1144   We will add something else: may the grace of this congress, the grace of this meeting with the Vicar of Christ, the grace of Rome go with you and sustain you. When We were called upon to address some words to your Second World Congress in 1957, under Our predecessor Pius XII, We thought We could say to you: "Have confidence! Rome is going forward and the Pope is guiding her." Allow Us to repeat it to you now, with humble awareness of Our own limitations, but at the same time with a joyful assurance that has been reinforced by the shining experience the Church has been living during these last ten years.

May all the ardent faith of St. Peter and the fervent love   1145
of St. Paul re-echo in Our voice. With their authority, We
impart Our apostolic blessing to all of you with all Our heart,
and We extend it to your families, your countries, and the
Catholic laity of the whole world.

Address of Pope Paul VI
to a General Audience
on the Layman's Task
April 23, 1969

Let Us speak again of the Council. We will have to speak of it for a long time still. Our age is marked by this event. Do not be bored by Our frequent recourse to it, for it is pervading the life of the Church. Take, for example, the new language it has brought into honor in the teaching of Christian doctrine. New expressions, even if their existence is prior to the Council and if they can be found in the traditional literature, have entered into everyday use and have taken on characteristic meanings, important both for theological thought and for ordinary conversation between us believers.

1147 One of these expressions is *consecratio mundi*, the consecration of the world. These words have distant roots, but the credit for having made them particularly expressive in connection with the apostolate of the laity rests with Pius XII of honored memory. We find them in the address which that great Pope delivered on the occasion of the Second World Congress of the Lay Apostolate,[1] but he had referred to them also on other occasions;[2] more explicitly, then, on October 5, 1957, he affirmed that the *"consecratio mundi* is essentially the work of laymen . . . who are intimately a part of economic and social life."

1148 We Ourselves used this expression in Our 1962 pastoral to the archdiocese of Milan.[3] And the expression passed (another proof of the coherent continuity of ecclesiastical teaching) into the documents of the Council: ". . . The laity consecrate the world itself to God," the Dogmatic Constitution on the Church says.[4]

To evaluate this expression, we should analyze the meaning   1149
of three terms: consecration, world, the laity. These terms are rich in content, and are not always used in a univocal sense. Let it suffice here to recall that by consecration We do not mean the separation of a thing from what is profane in order to reserve it exclusively or particularly for the Divinity, but, in a wider sense, the reestablishment of a things's relationship to God according to its own order, according to the exigency of the nature of the thing itself, in the plan willed by God.[5]

By world We mean the set of natural, positive values which   1150
in the temporal order, or, as the Council says in this sense: "the whole human family along with the sum of those realities in the midst of which it lives."[6]

And what do We mean by the term "the laity"? There have   1151
been great discussions to specify the ecclesial meaning of this word, arriving at this descriptive definition: A layman is one of the faithful, belonging to the People of God, distinct from the hierarchy, which is separated from temporal activities[7] and presides over the community dispensing "God's mysteries" to it;[8] the layman, on the contrary, has a given temporal relationship with the secular world.[9]

A difficulty may seem to arise from the mere consideration   1152
of these terms. How is it possible to think of a *consecratio mundi* today, when the Church has recognized the autonomy of the temporal order, that is, the world as independent, with its own purposes, its own laws, its own means?[10] Everyone knows now the new position taken up by the Church with regard to earthly realities. The latter have a nature with an order and purpose of their own in the framework of creation, even though this order remains subordinate to the plan of redemption. The world is in itself secular. It has broken away from the unitarian conception of medieval Christianity. It is supreme in its own field, a field that covers the whole human world. How is it possible to think of its consecration? Isn't this a return to a sacral, clerical conception of the world?

Here is the answer; and here is the new concept, which is   1153
of great importance in the practical field. The Church agrees

to recognize the world as such—that is, free, autonomous, sovereign, and in a certain sense, self-sufficient. She does not try to make it an instrument for her religious purposes, far less for power of the temporal order. The Church also admits a certain emancipation for her faithful of the Catholic laity, when they act in the domain of temporal reality. She attributes to them freedom of action and a responsibility of their own, and she trusts them.

1154   Pius XII also spoke of a "legitimate secularity of the State."[11] The Council recommends that pastors recognize and promote "the dignity and responsibility of the laity,"[12] but adds, precisely when speaking of laymen and to laymen, that "by its very nature the Christian vocation is also a vocation to the apostolate."[13] And while the Council permits them—in fact, urges them—to act in the secular world with perfect observance of the duties it entails, it charges them to bring three things into this world (We are speaking very empirically). These are: the order corresponding to the natural values, characteristic of the secular world (cultural, professional, technical, political values, etc.), honesty and skill, we might say, competence and devotion, the art of duly developing and implementing these same values.

1155   Even in this connection alone, the Catholic layman should be a perfect citizen of the world, a positive and constructive element, a man worthy of esteem and trust, a person who loves society and his country. We hope that it will always be possible to hold this opinion of him; and We trust that he will not give in to the conformism of so many disturbing movements that are passing through the modern world, in various ways, today. The many who claim to be active by virtue of their membership in the Catholic laity would do well to meditate deeply upon the first Epistle of the Apostle Peter, and certain pages of the epistles of St. Paul, for example, *Romans*[13].

1156   The other influence that the Church, and not only the laity, can exert in the secular world, leaving it such and at the same time honoring it with a "consecration" such as the Council teaches us, is the inspiration[14] of Christian principle. In their vertical meaning, which refers to mankind's supreme and ultimate end, these principles are religious and supernatural; but in their efficiency, which today is said to be horizontal—that is, earthly—they are supremely human. They are the interpretation, the inexhaustible vitality, the sublimation of human life as such. The Council says, in this connection, that "the earthly and the heavenly city penetrate each other . . . (in order to) contribute greatly toward making the family of man and its history more truly human."[15] It reminds laymen "that they have an active part to play in the whole life of the Church," that they "are not only bound to penetrate the world with a Christian spirit, but are also called in the midst of the human community to be witnesses to Christ in all things."[16].

And it is in this sense that the Church, especially the Catholic laity, confers a new degree of consecration upon the world, not by bringing it specifically sacred and religious signs (although in certain forms and circumstances the latter are also desirable), but by coordinating it to the kingdom of God "in the exercise of the apostolate through faith, hope and charity."[17] *"Qui sic ministrat, Christo ministrat"*; he who serves his neighbor in this way, serves Christ, St. Augustine says in one of his noble pages.[18] It is holiness that spreads its light over the world and in the world. This is—or rather, may this be—the vocation of our times, of all of us, beloved sons, with Our apostolic blessing.

1157

Sacred Congregation for the Clergy
Letter to the Presidents of Episcopal Conferences
on Priests' Councils
April 11, 1970

Introduction

By sacred ordination and the mission they receive from the bishops, priests "are ordained to serve Christ, their Master, Priest and King, and to share His ministry. Thus the Church on earth is constantly built up into the People of God, the Body of Christ and Temple of the Holy Spirit."[1] Since the priestly ministry can be fulfilled only in the hierarchical communion of the whole Church,[2] "no priest can accomplish his mission satisfactorily in isolation or single-handedly. He can do so only by joining forces with other priests under the direction of those who preside over the Church."[3]

1159   Bishops, upon reception of their canonical mission, "govern the particular Churches entrusted to them as the vicars and legates of Christ."[4] For the proper fulfillment of their office of feeding a portion of the People of God, they take priests as their necessary helpers,[5] and in the exercise of the ministry the latter depend upon the bishops, with whom they are united in priestly dignity.[6]

1160   Priests who are called to serve the people constitute *one presbyterium* with their bishop, although that presbyterium is comprised of different offices.[7] In every diocese, therefore, there is a hierarchical communion between the bishop and all the priests.[8] This communion joins them closely to-

gether and forms them into a single family whose father is
the bishop.[9]

2. The Second Vatican Council has explained and illus-   1161
trated this close communion and thus interpreted the signs
of the times. For at present, when in fact apostolic undertakings of all the Christian faithful demand total and united
effort, when so many hardships press upon the Church,
everyone can see the great need for unity among sacred ministers. From this union, with its sacramental basis, there
must arise a union of hearts resting upon mutual charity.[10]
Only in this way can a common pastoral activity be born
which embraces the entire diocese and all its problems. To
the extent that this is put into practice, there is hope that
priests will join their will to the will of the bishop and make
their activity more fruitful and effective.

The Bishop's New Consultative Body

3. Canonical legislation for the government of particular   1162
Churches has always assigned to bishops some kind of consultative body, chiefly composed of priests, which the bishops themselves are obliged to hear and whose consent they
must obtain in some matters of major significance. In the
present Code of Canon Law, there are several bodies to assist
the bishop in the various needs of diocesan government—for
example, the diocesan synod, the synodal examiners, the
parish priest consultors, the cathedral chapter or board of
consultors, the diocesan council of administration, and so
forth.

In earlier periods such things were seen as the simple de-   1163
mands or needs of correct and prudent government, but they
were theologically explained by the Second Vatican Council
in its more profound inquiry into the nature of the Church.
We are taught by the Council that in the particular Church a
hierarchical communion exists between the bishop and his
priests, in virtue of which bishop and priests share in one and
the same priesthood and one and the same ministry, but in a
different grade[11] determined by the reception of Orders and
the canonical mission. In view of this, the Council, because of

its pastoral character, desired that this unity of mission should be directed to the good of the diocese by means of a new consultative body: "In a way suited to modern conditions and according to rules yet to be laid down, a committee or senate of priests, representative of the body of the clergy, will be set up to advise and help the bishop in diocesan administration."[12]

1164 Following this desire of the Second Vatican Council, the Supreme Pontiff Pope Paul VI directed in the apostolic letter *Ecclesiae Sanctae* that this body, which is called a priests' council, should be established in every diocese.[13] This enabling law, enacted experimentally, determined only a few things concerning the composition of the council, its competence and its function, with the intention that a necessary period of time be left for the development of the new consultative body.

Plenary Session of the Congregation

1165 4. In the third year after the promulgation of the above mentioned law, the Sacred Congregation for the Clergy, which has responsibility for the priests' councils,[14] sent a circular letter on January 15, 1969, to the presidents of episcopal conferences.[15] In accord with the intention of this law, the letter asked that the bishops present to the Congregation information and opinions concerning experiments with this new body. When responses, as well as the statutes of these councils, had reached the Congregation from almost all the ecclesiastical provinces governed by the common law, this Congregation, having heard the opinion of its consultants, held a plenary session on October 10, 1969, to discuss the principal questions concerning this consultative body.

Obligation of Establishing a Priests' Council

1166 5. The scope and function of the priests' council necessarily flows from the hierarchical communion which exists between bishop and priests, and in some fashion manifests this institutionally. Therefore, the establishment of this body

in every diocese, in harmony with the principles already explained by the 'motu proprio' *Ecclesiae Sanctae,* is prescribed
as of obligation.

This obligation, moreover, is appropriate at the present   1167
time, for it is most opportune and useful today that a body
for common consultation or exchange be set up between
bishops and priests. Its usefulness is already clear from the
very many responses sent by bishops to the Congregation:
contact with priests is made easier; their intentions and desires are better known; information on the state of the diocese can be more accurately determined; common experiences can be suitably communicated; the needs of pastors
and of God's flock are more apparent; apostolic undertakings
suited to today's circumstances are better conceived; by
common effort difficulties are adequately solved or at
least better understood.

Composition of the Priests' Council

6. The priests' council should express the whole presby-   1168
terium of the diocese. In the judgment of the bishops and
Fathers at the plenary session, this requisite is better achieved
the more completely the opinions and experience of the
priests are consulted. The representative character of the
council is achieved if the following are represented within it,
insofar as possible: a) different ministries (parish priests,
associate pastors, chaplains, etc.); b) the regions or pastoral
areas of the diocese; c) the various age groups of priests. If
any difficulty arises in this makeup of the council, it seems
that a representation in proportion to the principal ministries
of priests is to be preferred.

Religious who exercise the care of souls in the diocese or   1169
are dedicated to apostolic works under the jurisdiction of the
bishop may also be included among the members of the
council.[16]

7. The manner of designating the members of the council   1170
has been entrusted to the bishops.[17] As is clear from their
responses, however, they have decreed by almost unanimous
consent that a large part of the members should be chosen by

free vote of the priests. The Fathers at the plenary session approved the resolution that the majority of the members be selected by vote of all the priests.[18]

1171 Other members are designated directly by the bishop or declared to be members *ipso facto,* so that they may represent in the council the office they hold (for example, vicar general, rector of the seminary, and so forth).

1172 This composition of members—some elected by the priests, others named by the bishop, others designated by reason of their office—on the one hand increases the confidence of the priests, who feel they are represented in the council, and on the other hand gives the bishop an assurance of maintaining a balance. And sometimes it makes it possible to express better the representative character of the council.

Competence of the Priests' Council

1173 8. The competence of the priests' council is to assist the bishop in the government of the diocese by means of its counsel. Therefore, questions of major significance pertaining to the sanctification of the faithful, doctrinal teaching and diocesan government are considered by the council if the bishop proposes them or at least allows their consideration. In proposing or admitting a question, the bishop will take into account the observance of the universal laws of the Church.

1174 The council, to the extent that it represents the entire presbyterium of the diocese, has been instituted to promote the good of the diocese itself. All questions properly admitted, therefore, and not only those which concern the life of priests, may be dealt with by the council as matters pertinent to the priestly ministry which they exercise for the benefit of the ecclesiastical community.

1175 In general it is for the council to urge norms which may be established and to propose questions of principle, but not to deal with questions which of their nature demand a more discreet procedure—for example, the conferral of offices.

Consultative Character of the Priests' Council

9. The priests' council is a special consultative organ. It   **1176**
is called consultative because it does not have a deliberative
vote. Therefore, it is not competent to make decisions
which bind the bishop unless the universal law of the Church
provides otherwise or the bishop in individual cases gives a
deliberative vote to the council. It is called a special consultative body because by its nature and its procedure it is
preeminent among other bodies of the same character.

The nature of this council, as a sign of hierarchical com-   **1177**
munion, demands that consultation be entered into for the
good of the diocese, in union with the bishop and never without him—that is to say, with a devotion that is common to
the bishop and the members. This manner of acting is required by the Second Vatican Council and is enjoined by the
words of the 'motu proprio' *Ecclesiae Sanctae:* "In this council the bishop should listen to his priests, consult them and
talk to them about things pertaining to pastoral needs and
the good of the diocese."[19]

This common effort—of exchanging opinions and infor-   **1178**
mation on issues, bringing up pastoral needs, weighing arguments and submitting proposals—demands that both bishop
and priests be properly prepared, open to profound change,
and marked by humility and patience.

When the common effort has been completed, the decision   **1179**
belongs to the bishop, who is bound by a personal responsibility toward the portion of the People of God entrusted to
him;[20] and therefore the bishop's responsibility should be
helped, but in no way replaced, by the work of the council.

10. The Fathers of the plenary congregation were influ-   **1180**
enced by these considerations and expressed their judgment
that the title and name "senate of the bishop in the government of the diocese" belongs exclusively to the priests
council.[21]

With regard to the older senate of the bishop, namely, the   **1181**
cathedral chapter, where this exists, and the board of con-

sultors elsewhere, the Fathers agreed with the disposition of the 'motu proprio' *Ecclesiae Sanctae,* which prescribes that these institutes should retain their proper function and proper competence until they are reformed.[22]

1182   Since the circumstances which affect the historical evolution of cathedral chapters vary in different regions of the Church, the individual episcopal conferences will prepare recommendations for the revision of the cathedral chapter and the reform or confirmation of the board of consultors.

1183   Meanwhile, until the Code of Canon Law is revised, the priests' council ceases during the vacancy of the episcopal see.[23] Therefore, unless the Holy See provides otherwise, the cathedral chapter or the board of consultors designates the vicar capitular according to the norm given in canons 429-444 and 427 of the Code of Canon Law, which remain in effect.

Conclusions

1184   I. In view of all these principles, this Sacred Congregation for the Clergy strongly requests and urges:

a) Where it is lacking, the priests' council should be established as quickly as possible and be given the title and function of the senate of the bishop;

b) Every priests' council should prepare its own statutes, to be approved by the bishop, taking into account the indications given in this circular letter.

1185   II. Since it is desirable that the bishops assembled in their conferences should consider in common questions affecting the priests' council,[24] the Sacred Congregation asks the following:

a) Questions of major importance which are to be considered in the priests' council should be indicated by the episcopal conference;

b) Likewise, norms concerning the procedure in priests' councils, frequency of meetings, cooperation with other consultative bodies, relationship of the council with all the priests of the diocese, may suitably be proposed by the episcopal conference.

III. Finally, this Sacred Congregation asks that each   1186
episcopal conference present its recommendations to the
Congregation before December 31, 1970, concerning the
cathedral chapter and the board of consultors, as mentioned
above in no. 10.

In this letter the Sacred Congregation intends to indicate   1187
the principles and general criteria which have developed from
consultation with the episcopal conferences and the discussion of the Fathers. These may help the bishops in fulfilling
their serious duty in relation to the constitution and mode of
action of the priests' councils. The Congregation therefore
trusts that the episcopal conferences will keep it informed of
their experience in these matters, for consideration in another plenary session which may perhaps be held before the
new Code of Canon Law is published.

Rome, April 11, 1970, the Feast of St. Leo the Great,   1188
Pope and Doctor of the Church.

Address of Pope Paul VI
to 21st Italian National Week of Pastoral Renewal
on Local Church Structures
September 9, 1971

In spite of the pressure of Our unending occupations, We very readily granted the request to receive in audience the participants in the 21st National Week of Pastoral Renewal. We thank you for the opportunity thus offered Us to meet a numerous and qualified group of pastoral workers, and to express to you, who have gathered from all over Italy, Our cordial and respectful greeting, as well as the assurances of the interest and esteem with which We follow your work.

1190 The 21st meeting of this National Week of Pastoral Renewal is in itself a sign of the good and wise effectiveness of the initiative, which has for some time now become a point of reference for the Italian clergy, religious and laity in the field of the apostolate. But this year it is even more so, owing to the participation of numerous organizations operating in various sectors of the apostolate. We express Our deep satisfaction to the Pastoral Orientation Center and to the Institute of Applied Research, Documentation and Studies, which promoted the Week, and particularly to the beloved and esteemed Msgr. Grazioso Ceriani, whom We are glad to see here, and to whose zeal goes the credit not only for having started these providential meetings, but also for having stimulated their continual growth.

1191 You have been called to discuss together the subject: "Diocese, parish and grass-roots community." This is a very important topic—especially at this moment, which is so full of tensions and problems, but also rich in promise and hope for the Church in general and the Italian Church in particular. The importance of the subject proposed, as well as the gravity and complexity of the problems relating to it, would call for a long talk on Our part that would go to the heart of the matter. This is not Our intention, also because time would not permit it. We will merely call your attention briefly to the fundamental points with which your discussions will deal.

The Local Church, or Diocese

As clearly indicated by the subject of the meeting, your work rightly starts from a thorough examination of the conception of a particular or local Church, with which the concept of the diocese concretely coincides, namely: "that portion of God's people which is entrusted to a bishop to be shepherded by him with the cooperation of the presbytery. Adhering thus to its pastor and gathered together by him in the Holy Spirit through the Gospel and the Eucharist, this portion constitutes a particular Church in which the one, holy, catholic and apostolic Church of Christ is truly present and operative."[1]   1192

In the face of innovative and questionable trends regarding the meaning of the term "local Church"—which has been so popularized since the Council—We consider it more necessary than ever not to depart from the definition given by the Council itself. From it we can deduce that the local or particular Church is *locally* a portion of the one universal Church, and a local (or particular) manifestation of the universal communion proper to the Church.   1193

We should speak of a local Church, therefore, not as a "fraction of a Church" which is added to other "fractions" to form the universal Church, almost in the manner of an arithmetic sum; nor as an autonomous, self-sufficient Church, juridically closed within itself or, worse, contrasted to the universal Church, with prerogatives that are proper to the latter; but as an authentic expression (even if often with original characteristics) of the one Catholic Church, authorized   1194 and guaranteed by the relationship with the organic and hierarchical structure, and with the animation of the Holy Spirit through which the whole Church lives. It is clear that all discussion of a valid apostolate should start from this genuine concept, and it is here that a solution should be found to problems concerning authentic renewals of structure and action.

1195   But the *pastoral* aspect of the local Church is more directly important for the purpose of your Week. In this connection, since there is so much talk of changing the "structures" of the Church in order to adapt them better to the new attainments of ecclesial life and of society, We believe that it is not superfluous to assure you that the structures of the diocese as a community of salvation headed by the bishop, the successor of the Apostles, will remain in canon law in their traditional pattern.

1196   Then what pastoral significance should be attributed to these structures? What valuable aspect should be developed to make them more effective? And what deformation or decline, if any, should be removed? Certainly you have already studied this renewal of the diocese. It will be enough for Us now to refer only to some particular aspects.

1197   In the first place, there is the *territorial dimension*. It is true that the concept of diocese in itself fails to consider this aspect. But it is a fact that in the vast majority of cases the diocese is contained within precise territorial limits which have a considerable effect on fulfillment of the aims of the diocese itself. For this reason, in obedience to the Council's precise directions, a study is being made in Italy to revise the territorial districts. Thus geography and apostolate are realities that must be studied together; and by geography We mean a set of ethnical, historical, social and economic elements, as well as statistical and population data. But it is clear that this analysis, in the framework of pastoral action, has no other value than in terms of facilitating the exercise of the ministry, better identification of specific responsibilities for the care of souls, and contribution to better formation of the "feeling for the Church" in a given territory. This is how other important experiments going on should be understood, such as the tendency to group together dioceses that are too small, often of feudal or communal origin, and the tendency to subdivide large urban concentrations into suffragan dioceses or vicariates.

Now from these experiments that are under way, some guidelines emerge that must be kept well in mind: in the first place, the necessity of giving full value to the person, function and authority of the bishop—not in his exterior aspect, which would offend modern sensibilities, but in his spiritual and moral significance, having the first charism of apostolicity. Without this full appreciation of the ministerial authority of the Church, it will not be possible to speak of an effective pastoral life. "In a certain sense it is from the bishop that the faithful who are under his care derive and maintain their life in Christ."[2] He is the steward of the grace of the supreme priesthood;[3] he is the authentic teacher who proclaims with authority God's word on faith and morals.[4]

The other guideline that must be kept in mind is the necessity for close, organic and personal collaboration by all members of the diocese with their own bishop. The latter's pastoral function, though preeminent, is neither solitary nor separated in its concrete exercise, but needs the contribution of all the members. Priests must make this contribution not only from a functional or practical motive, but also and especially from a theological one, which the Council expresses as follows: "By reason of Orders and ministry, all priests— both diocesan and religious—are connected with the body of bishops and serve the welfare of the whole Church according to their vocation and grace."[5] And so we have the priests' council, and the ancient but admirable chapter; so, too, we have the pastoral council, by means of which light is thrown on the ecclesial function of laymen, not only as recipients of the pastoral ministry but also as active agents of it—not just by concession of the hierarchy, but on account of the inborn vocation of the laity themselves and the intrinsic requirement of the Church.

1198

1199

The Parish

1200   What has been said so far leads as a natural consequence to the subject of the *parish*, which is, as it were, the living cell of the diocese[6] because it is the community organized locally under the guidance of a pastor representing the bishop. Today there is talk of a crisis of the parish, and some people go so far as to contemplate abolition of this institution. In spite of the real or alleged crises affecting the parish, it certainly cannot be supposed that it is now an obsolete institution. Even in very densely populated cities, territorial limits must not be disregarded.

1201   From very thorough analyses carried out by the Sacred Congregation for the Clergy on the revision of this canonical institution, the conclusion has been reached that the parish must be maintained, or rather improved, especially by encouraging life in common for the clergy, and by putting into effect different forms of community assistance among the various social groups and on behalf of those joined by common interests—particularly young people, workers, various professions, the sick, prisoners and the unemployed. The parish should also be improved by integrating its pastoral care with that of neighboring parishes and of non-territorial parishes, such as the military, the faithful of different rites, refugees and tourists.

Grass-Roots Communities

1202   Discussion of the organic pastoral action of the local Church and of the parish cannot fail to include examination of a phenomenon that is developing more and more today, even in Italy: the phenomenon of ecclesial groups, known by various names, which you have explicitly grouped under the heading and in the study sessions of the Week as "grass-roots communities."

1203   We are aware of the dangers to which these new community forms are easily exposed, particularly the tendency to break away from the institutional Church in opposition to its external structures, in the name of simplicity and authenticity of life lived according to the Gospel.

But We are of the opinion that it is necessary to make an effort to assist these groups, to understand their dynamic tensions and the positive values they can have, in order to insert them in the ecclesial communion of the local Church. Thus integrated, these groups will be able to help reanimate the sense of community, which today seems to have lost the attraction it had in past years—and above all, to rediscover and reconstruct the sense of ecclesial communion, as desired by the Council. In this way it will render an effective service to the local Church's apostolate. **1204**

The household church also—the original and primitive form of the congregation of the faithful—can have its function in certain situations, for example, where the Church's public life is hindered, or occasionally where a special circumstance summons relatives and friends to a moment of prayer, instruction and study. This splintering of the ecclesial community must not be encouraged, however, without good reason or due authorization, nor should personal interpretations of religious life be supported. Rather it is necessary for those with spiritual and religious sensibilities to be infused with the taste for a personal spiritual life and for contact with God, as well as for outward charity and for celebrating together the mysteries of faith and the liturgy. **1205**

We have wished to entrust to your attention, beloved sons, the points We thought it useful to touch upon, confident that your zeal, wisdom and spirit of service to the Church will find the most suitable ways and means to ensure every desired increase and progress for the religious life of the Italian nation. And while We accompany the work of your congress with Our fervent prayer for this purpose, We warmly impart to all Our affectionate apostolic blessing. **1206**

Address of Pope Paul VI
to the International Catechetical Congress
on Catechetics and Contemporary Problems
September 25, 1971

We cannot keep silent about Our satisfaction and emotion at seeing you gathered round Us here for the first International Catechetical Congress. The number of participants, the contemporary appeal of the subjects discussed, and the high level of preparation of the *rapporteurs* make this congress not only a really important event for the Church, but also an extremely significant and consoling expression of her own post-conciliar work.

1208   We are happy, therefore, to extend Our affectionate greeting to the cardinals, the presidents of episcopal conferences and the bishops here present, and to all those who have come with them from all over the world to share at this congress the fruit of their catechetical experience and competence.

1209   We warmly thank all of you without distinction for this incomparable service to the Church; and in particular We express Our gratitude to Cardinal Wright who, with the help of his collaborators in the Sacred Congregation for the Clergy, has prepared this congress with foresight and wisdom.

1210   In welcoming you, honored brothers and beloved sons, Our thought turns to all those who are working to serve the Word of God in the midst of the world, both in young Churches and within Christian communities where the Gospel penetrated centuries ago: bishops and priest, religious men and women, Christian laity and parents from all walks of life. We are all servants of the Gospel.

Some of you are carrying out a fruitful joint experience;   1211
others know solitude, and many are so painfully aware of
their limitations that they are driven to groan like the prophet: "Ah, Lord God! Behold, I cannot speak, for I am a child."[1]
Yet, as the Council's missionary decree reminds us, the task
of spreading the faith and of spending one's energies on evangelization devolves upon every disciple of Christ, according to
his own possibilities.[2]

Your International Catechetical Congress clearly reveals   1212
the place occupied in the Church by the care of proclaiming
the Word of God in its fullness and in a manner adapted to
the men of our times, as We said not long ago to all Our
brother bishops: "That means trying to use a language easily
accessible to them, answering their questions, arousing their
interest and helping them to discover, through poor human
speech, the whole message of salvation brought to us by
Jesus."[3]

Today an immense work is being carried out in this direc-   1213
tion in the Church, amid diverse cultures and in many forms.
We wished to encourage this work with the General Catechetical Directory prepared and published by the Congregation
for the Clergy last Easter.

The preparation of this text has shown, moreover, the fruit-   1214
ful collaboration between the episcopal conferences and the
Holy See, as well as the beneficial exchange between those
engaged in various ways in the transmission of the faith, and
those studying the present crisis of language and thought and
the many demands of human knowledge. We are also delighted
to know that more and more persons are collaborating in
catechetical work, bringing to it the living testimony of their
life of faith and their multiform Christian commitment—
those generous laymen, that is, whose apostolate "is so much
their province and function that it should scarcely ever be
attempted by anyone else."[4]

The ministry of the Word is thus placed at the very center   1215
of the whole Church's daily apostolic action. Consequently,
catechesis is reflected in the whole of life, whether it be in
the way in which the People of God, gathered together,
celebrate the Eucharist, or sing God's praises or live their

faith in daily life. Isn't the Church a mystery that makes us always discover more "in an experimental and existential manner" ". . . in the secret vitality which is characteristic of her, which makes her past a source of her perennial rebirth and of her future, through living and active fidelity to her tradition"?[5] Catechesis cannot be isolated—for it would be a fatal isolation—from the life of prayer, nor from the Christian commitment of communities united by the same faith in Christ the Savior.

1216   In a world in process of secularization, the Church rediscovers her prophetic mission as messenger of the good news of salvation. Thus the sharp edge of the sword of the Word will never be blunted.[6] Far from remaining neutral, the Church judges all personal and collective realities that men experience and in which Christians agree to let themselves be guided by her, listening to Him whose personal question echoes unceasingly from generation to generation: "But who do you say that I am?"[7]

1217   Catechesis, therefore, cannot ignore "the questions which today confront a believer who is rightly anxious to acquire a more profound understanding of his faith. We must lend an ear to these questions, not in order to cast suspicion on what is well founded, nor to deny their postulates, but so that we may do justice to their legitimate demands within our own proper field, which is that of faith. . . . (They are) modern man's great questions concerning his origins, the meaning of life, the happiness to which he aspires and the destiny of the human family."[8]

1218   This means that a twofold movement will always be necessary to announce the Word of God to the men of our time "in its entirety and purity so that they may understand it and accept it freely."[9] It is the Word of God that we must transmit, not a human word, and this Word is offered to us by the Church, whose magisterium guarantees its authenticity, and whose life as the People of God shows us its fruitfulness, while we ourselves have personal experience of it in meditation and prayer. Just as the message of salvation cannot be reduced to our worldly conformisms, so also it cannot be identified with given social or historical cultural forms.

The magisterium's first concern is that the strength of the   1219
Word of God should unceasingly be freed of all the obstacles
that hold it in check, and that its dynamism should penetrate
the lives of all men, revealing to them the mystery of the good
news of the love that saves. At the same time, this revelation
reveals men to themselves, giving their existence that ultimate
significance which they are often desperately seeking. "In this
way the ministry of the Word not only recalls the revelation
of divine wonders which took place in time and was brought
to perfection by Christ, but at the same time interprets—in
the light of this revelation—modern life, the signs of the times
and the realities of this world, since God's plan for men's
salvation is unfolded in these."[10]

Similarly, the discovery of the complete mystery of our   1220
salvation in faith cannot take place except through the testimony of a real life of faith on the part of the ecclesial community. "In fact, catechesis speaks with greater efficacy of
what really appears in the external life of the community.
The catechist is, so to speak, the interpreter of the Church to
those who are catechized by him. He reads and teaches them
to read the signs of faith, the principal one of which is the
Church herself."[11] Even more, he teaches them to discern
spiritual connections, already present in men's lives, according
to the fruitful method of the dialogue of salvation, which We
proposed in Our first encyclical: "Before speaking, we must
take great care to listen not only to what men say, but more
especially to what they have it in their heart to say. . . . Dialogue thrives on friendship."[12]

As we declared on the day of Our coronation: "Superficial-   1221
ly the man of today may seem to be more and more a stranger
to all that is spiritual and religious. . . . But behind this gran-
diose facade (that of spectacular technical successes), it is easy
to find the profound voices of this modern world, which is
also stirred by the Spirit and by grace. It aspires to justice; to
progress . . . to peace . . . We say it without any hesitation: all
this is Ours. . . , We are listening to these profound voices of
the world. . . . We will continue to offer unremittingly to
mankind today . . . the answer to its appeals: Christ and His
unfathomable riches. Will Our voice be heard?"[13]

1222   It is therefore the task of catechesis—a task that is incessantly reborn and incessantly renewed—to understand these
problems that rise from man's heart, in order to lead them
back to their hidden source: the gift of love that creates and
saves, revealed through events and the words of God to His
people. Prayerful meditation of Holy Scripture, faithful study
of the "wonders of God" throughout the whole span of the
history of salvation, the living Tradition of the Church and
attention to man's history, are thus harmoniously united to
help men discover this God, who is already at work in the
depths of their hearts and minds in order to draw them to
Himself and fill them with His love, which invites them to
enter into communion with the Word.

1223   In this way the entire history of mankind acquires its significance in direct reference to the history of salvation, which
makes it a sacred history. "God, who through the Word creates
all things (see *Jn.* 1, 3) and keeps them in existence, gives
men an enduring witness to Himself in created realities (see
Rom. 1, 19-20). Planning to make known the way of heavenly
salvation, He went further and manifested Himself from the
beginning. . . . Then . . . He sent His Son, the eternal Word . . .
so that He might tell them of the innermost being of God
(see *Jn.* 1, 1-18) . . . and He completes the work of salvation."[14]

1224   Today as yesterday, therefore, catechesis must listen to
man, on whom God's splendor is reflected,[15] so as to reveal
to him the true light that enlightens him[16] and gives the utmost meaning to his demands and aspirations to have greater
fulfillment, to live in brotherhood, to work for justice and
peace, while it gives him something infinitely higher: "Things
beyond the mind of man, all that God has prepared for those
who love him."[17] Precisely because He is transcendent, God
is within man and his ways—deeper within him than man is
within himself, according to St. Augustine's profound intui-
tion. Echoing God's Word, the catechist enables it to "run
and be glorified"[18] in men's hearts, which he has stirred by
his own life and his poor words.

1225   Following a Council that wished to purify her countenance,
the Church feels more than ever impelled to work that the

light of God's Word may shine ever brighter. She must divest herself of some contingent forms that have weighed her down, in order to become again, and ever more manifestly, the "sign raised in the midst of the nations," as is the nature of her vocation. Isn't this ever reflourishing youth of the People of God revealed in the ardor of neophytes, in the fervor of new-born communities, in the fruitful search of so many catechu-mens?

Yes, the Spirit is always at work in His Church, and we are in admiration before the strength which He imparts to those who announce His Word, as well as to those "who hear the word, and welcome it, and yield fruit, one thirty, another sixty, and another a hundred-fold."[19] In them and through them the Acts of the Apostles continue, and the People of God, through the pains and joys of labor, write the new pages of their sacred history.   1226

Honored brothers and beloved sons, may this congress af-firm the fruitful collaboration of the priestly ministry, reli-gious life and lay apostolate for a renewed announcement of the Word of salvation, which constitutes the essential mission of the Church and, at the same time, the perennial source of her joy in giving birth to new children. With one heart, we must all attend tirelessly to this fundamental task which Christ has entrusted to His Church: to bring to the world the Word it is awaiting, to free it from sin and cause it to shine with all the virtues and capacities of a son of God, since this Word is spirit, light and life!   1227

With these sentiments We invoke upon you the abundance of divine graces and wholeheartedly impart Our apostolic blessing.   1228

1971 Synod of Bishops
The Ministerial Priesthood
December 9, 1971

INTRODUCTION

In recent times, especially since the close of the Second
Vatican Council, the Church has been experiencing a
profound renewal movement, which all Christians
should follow with great joy and fidelity to the Gospel. The
power of the Holy Spirit is present to illumine, strengthen
and perfect our mission.

1230   Every true renewal certainly brings the Church benefits of
great value. We well know that through the recent Council
priests have been fired with new zeal and that by their daily
solicitude they have contributed much to fostering this renewal. We have in mind our many heroic brothers who, in
fidelity to their ministry, lead lives joyfully dedicated to God,
either among peoples where the Church is subjected to a harsh
yoke or in mission lands. At the same time, however, this
renewal also entails difficulties which are felt in a particular
way by all in the priesthood, whether bishops or priests.

1231   We should all scrutinize the signs of the times in this age
of change, and interpret them in the light of the Gospel,[1] in
order that we may work together in distinguishing spirits to
see if they come from God, lest ambiguity cloud the unity of
the Church's mission or excessive uniformity hinder needed
adaptation. Thus, by testing everything and holding fast to

what is good, the present crisis can offer the occasion for an increase of faith.

In accordance with its importance, the Holy Father pro-   1232
posed the ministerial priesthood for discussion by this year's Synod. Before the Synod many episcopal conferences examined this theme together with priests and quite frequently with lay people. Some priests were also invited to the Synod as auditors to assist the bishops in dealing with important questions.

We intend to fulfill the mandate entrusted to us with the   1233
evangelical simplicity befitting pastors who are serving the Church. Considering our responsibility before the fraternal community of the Church, we desire to strengthen the faith, rekindle the hope and stimulate the love of our brothers in the ministerial priesthood and of all the faithful. May our words bring solace and renewed joy to the People of God and the priests dedicated to their service!

The Present Situation

1. The extent of the Church's mission was amply illustrated   1234
by the Second Vatican Council. Indeed, the Church's relationship with the world was the specific subject of the Pastoral Constitution on the Church in the World of Today. Many good results followed from a closer consideration of this matter: it is more clearly understood that salvation is not, as it were, an abstract category outside of history and time, but that it comes from God and hence ought to permeate the whole of man and of his history, and lead men freely to the kingdom of God, so that finally "God may be all in all."[2]

However, as is understandable, difficulties have also arisen.   1235
Some priests feel themselves estranged in the face of various popular movements and incapable of solving the problems that vitally concern mankind. Often the problems and troubles of priests derive from the fact that in their pastoral and missionary care they must deal with the modern mentality while using methods which are now perhaps obsolete. Serious problems and numerous questions then arise, above all because

of the real difficulties which priests experience in exercising their ministry and not—although this is sometimes the case—from a harsh spirit of protest or from selfish personal concerns. Is it possible to exhort the laity from the outside, so to speak? Is the Church sufficiently present in certain groups without the active presence of the priest? If a priest's typical situation consists in segregation from secular life, isn't the layman's situation preferable? What is to be thought of the celibacy of Latin rite priests in present-day circumstances, and of the personal spiritual life of the priest immersed in the world?

1236   2. Many priests, experiencing within themselves the questionings that have arisen with the secularization of the world, feel the need to sanctify worldly activities by performing them personally, and to bring the leaven of the Gospel into the very midst of events. Similarly, there is a developing desire for cooperation with men's joint efforts to construct a more just and fraternal society. In a world in which almost all problems have political aspects, participation in politics and even in revolutionary activity is considered by some as indispensable.

1237   3. The Council emphasized the preeminence of the proclamation of the Gospel, which should lead through faith to the fullness of the celebration of the sacraments. But current thinking about the religious phenomenon fosters doubts in many minds concerning the sense of a sacramental, cultic ministry. Many priests who are by no means suffering from a personal identity crisis ask themselves another question: What methods should be used so that sacramental practice may be an expression of faith really affecting the whole of personal and social life, so that Christian worship is not wrongly reduced to a mere external ritualism?

1238   Priests are very concerned with the self-image that the Church seems to present to the world, and are at the same time deeply conscious of the singular dignity of the human person. Hence, they desire to bring about, within the Church herself, a change in relationships among persons, between them and institutions, and in the very structures of authority.

4. Relationships between bishops and priests, and among   1239
priests themselves, are also becoming more difficult as the
exercise of the ministry becomes more diversifed. Present-day
society is dvided into many groups with different disciplines,
which call for a variety of skills and forms of apostolate. This
gives rise to problems concerning brotherhood, union and
consistency in the priestly ministry.

Happily, the recent Council has recalled the traditional and   1240
fruitful teaching on the common priesthood of the faithful.[3]
But from this, as by a swing of the pendulum, certain questions have arisen which seem to obscure the position of the
priestly ministry in the Church and which deeply trouble the
minds of some priests and faithful. Many activities once
reserved to priests—for instance, catechetical work, administrative activity in the communities, and even liturgical activities—are today quite frequently carried out by lay people,
while at the same time many priests, for reasons already
mentioned, are trying to involve themselves in the circumstances of lay life.

Hence a number of questions are being asked: Does the   1241
priestly ministry have any specific nature? Is this ministry
necessary? Is it true that the priesthood, of its very nature,
cannot be lost? What does being a priest mean today? Would
not Christian communities be sufficiently served by presidents
designated for the preservation of the common good, without
sacramental ordination, and exercising their office for a fixed
period?

5. Still more serious questions are posed, some of them as   1242
a result of exegetical and historical research, which reveal a
crisis of confidence in the Church: Is the present-day Church
too far removed from its origins to be able to proclaim the
ancient Gospel to modern man in a credible way? Is it still
possible to reach the reality of Christ after so many critical
investigations? Are the essential structures of the early Church
well enough known to us that they can and must be considered an invariable plan for every age, including our own?

6. The above-mentioned questions—some of them new,   1243
others already long familiar but appearing in new forms to-

day—cannot be understood outside of the whole context of modern culture, which has strong doubts about its own meaning and value. New technological discoveries have aroused an excessively enthusiastic hope and a profound anxiety at the same time. It is rightly asked whether man will be capable of controlling his work and of directing it toward progress.

1244   Some, especially the young, have a pessimistic conception of this world's meaning and seek salvation in purely meditative systems or in artificial, remote paradises, abandoning the common striving of mankind.

1245   Others dedicate themselves, with ardent utopian hope devoid of reference to God, to the attainment of a state of total liberation, and transfer the meaning of their whole personal existence from the present to the future.

1246   There is therefore a profound cleavage between action and contemplation, work and recreation, culture and religion, and between immanent and transcendent aspects of human life.

1247   Thus the world itself is obscurely awaiting a solution to this dilemma, and is paving a way along which the Church may go forward proclaiming the Gospel. Certainly, the only complete salvation offered to men is Christ Himself, Son of God and Son of Man, who makes Himself present in history through the Church. He joins inseparably love for God, God's unfailing love for men as they seek life amid the shadows, and the value of human love through which a man gives his life for his friends. In Christ, and only in Him, all of these elements become one whole, and in this synthesis the meaning of human life, both individual and social, is clearly revealed.

1248   Consequently, far from being obsolete, the mission of the Church, Christ's Body, is rather of the highest relevance for the present and the future; the whole Church is the witness and effective sign of this union, especially through the priestly ministry. The minister's proper task in the Church's midst is to render present God's love in Christ for us through the word and sacrament, and at the same time to promote men's fellowship with God and with each other. All of this, of course, demands that all of us, especially those who perform the sacred office, should strive to renew ourselves daily in accordance with the Gospel.

7. We know that there are some parts of the world in which   1249
this profound cultural change has hitherto been less felt, and
that the questions raised above are not being asked everywhere,
nor by all priests, nor in the same way. But since communications between men and peoples have today become more
frequent and more rapid, we deem it proper and opportune
to examine these questions in the light of faith, and to propose—humbly, but in the strength of the Holy Spirit—some
principles for finding more concrete answers to them.

Although this response must be applied differently accord-   1250
ing to the circumstances of each region, it will have the force
of truth for all those faithful and priests who live in situations
of greater tranquility. Therefore, ardently desiring to strength-
en the witness of faith, we fraternally urge all the faithful to
strive to contemplate the Lord Jesus living in His Church, and
to realize that He wants to work in a special way through His
ministers. They will thus be convinced that the Christian community cannot fully accomplish its mission without the ministerial priesthood. Let priests be aware that the bishops truly
share their anxieties and desire to share them still more.

PART ONE

Doctrinal Principles

1. Christ, Alpha and Omega

Jesus Christ, the Son of God and the Word, "whom the   1251
Father has made holy and sent into the world,"[4] and who
was marked with the seal of the fullness of the Holy Spirit,[5]
proclaimed to the world the Good News of reconciliation
between God and men. His prophetic preaching, confirmed
by miracles, reaches its summit in the Paschal mystery, the
supreme word of the divine love with which the Father spoke
to us. On the Cross Jesus showed Himself to the greatest extent as the Good Shepherd, who gave His life for His sheep in
order to gather them into that unity which has its foundation
on Him.[6] Exercising a supreme and unique priesthood by the
offering of Himself, He surpassed, by fulfilling them, all the

ritual priesthoods and holocausts of the Old Testament and, indeed, of the pagans. In His sacrifice He took upon Himself the troubles and sacrifices of men of every age, and also the efforts of those who suffer for the cause of justice or who are daily oppressed by misfortune. He took upon Himself the endeavors of those who abandon the world and seek to reach God by ascetisicm and contemplation, as well as the labors of those who sincerely devote their lives to a better present and future society. He bore the sins of us all on the Cross; rising from the dead and being made Lord, He reconciled us with God by asceticism and contemplation, as well as the labors of those who sincerely devote their lives to a better present and

1252 He is the one Mediator between God and men, the man Christ Jesus,[7] "for in him were created all things,"[8] and everything is brought together under Him, as head.[9] Since He is the image of the Father and manifestation of the unseen God,[10] by emptying Himself and by being raised up He brought us into the fellowship of the Holy Spirit where He Himself lives with the Father. When we speak of the priesthood of Christ, therefore, we should have in mind a unique, incomparable reality, which includes the prophetic and royal office of the Incarnate Word of God.

1253 Thus Jesus Christ signifies and manifests in many ways the presence and effectiveness of the prevenient love of God. The Lord Himself, constantly influencing the Church by His Spirit, stirs up and fosters the response of all those who offer themselves to this freely given love.

2. Drawing Near to Christ in the Church

1254 Contact with the person and mystery of Christ always takes place in the Holy Spirit through the Scriptures, which are part of the living Tradition of the Church. All the Scriptures, especially those of the New Testament, must be interpreted as intimately interlinked and interrelated by their single inspiration. The books of the New Testament are not of such differing value that some of them can be reduced to mere inventions of a much later date.

A personal, immediate relationship with Christ, in the   1255
Church should provide even today's faithful with sustenance
for their entire spiritual life.

3. The Church from Christ

Christ announced that He would build His Church on Peter,   1256
and He founded it upon the Apostles,[11] in whom two aspects
of the Church were already manifested. In the group of 12
Apostles there were already present both fellowship in the
Spirit and the origin of the hierarchical ministry.[12] For this
reason, the New Testament writings speak of the Church as
founded on the Apostles.[13] This reality was concisely expressed by ancient tradition: "The Church from the Apostles,
the Apostles from Christ, Christ from God."[14]

The Church, founded on the Apostles and sent into the   1257
world, where she is a pilgrim, was established to be a sacrament of the salvation which came to us from God in Christ.
In her, Christ is present and operative in the world as a Savior,
so that the love offered by God to men, and their response,
harmonize with each other. In and through the Church the
Holy Spirit stirs up impulses of generous free will, by which
man participates in the very work of Creation and Redemption.

4. Origin and Nature of Hierarchical Ministry

The Church, endowed by the gift of the Spirit with an or-   1258
ganic structure, participates in diverse ways in Christ's functions as Priest, Prophet and King, in order to carry out her
mission of salvation in His name and by His power, as a
priestly people.[15]

It is clear from the New Testament writings that an apostle   1259
and a community of faithful, united with one another by a
mutual link under Christ the Head and the influence of His
Spirit, are the proper elements of the Church's original inalienable structure. In fact, the 12 Apostles exercised their mission
and functions, and they not only had "various helpers in their
ministry,[16] but, in order that the ministry entrusted to them

might be carried on after their death, they also bequeathed a legacy to their immediate co-workers—the task of consolidating and completing the work they themselves had begun.[17] The Apostles gave them the task of attending to the whole flock, in which the Holy Spirit had placed them to nourish God's Church.[18] Thus the Apostles appointed such men and then gave them the order that, on their decease, other approved men should take up their ministry.[19]"[20]

1260   St. Paul's letters show that he was conscious of acting by Christ's mission and mandate.[21] The powers entrusted to the Apostle for the good of the Churches were handed on to others insofar as they were communicable,[22] and these others in their turn were also obliged to hand them on.[23]

1261   This essential structure of the Church—consisting of a flock and of pastors appointed for this purpose[24]—was always and remains the norm, according to the Tradition of the Church herself. Precisely as a result of this structure, the Church can never remain closed in on herself, and is always subject to Christ as her origin and head.

1262   Among the various charisms and services, only the priestly ministry of the New Testament—which continues Christ's function as mediator, and which is distinct in essence and not merely in degree from the common priesthood of all the faithful[25]—perpetuates the essential work of the Apostles: by effectively proclaiming the Gospel, by gathering together and leading the community, by remitting sins, and especially by celebrating the Eucharist, it makes Christ, the head of the community, present in the exercise of His work of redeeming mankind and glorifying God perfectly.

1263   Indeed, bishops and, on a subordinate level, priests, by virtue of the Sacrament of Orders, which confers an anointing of the Holy Spirit and configures them to Chirst,[26] become sharers in the functions of sanctifying, teaching and governing, and the exercise of these functions is more precisely determined by hierarchical communion.[27]

1264   The priestly ministry reaches its summit in the celebration of the Eucharist, which is the source and center of the Church's unity. Only a priest is able to act in the person of Christ in presiding over and effecting the sacrificial banquet wherein the People of God are associated with Christ's offering.[28]

The priest is a sign of the divine prevenient plan which is   1265
today proclaimed and effective in the Church. He makes
Christ, the Savior of all men, sacramentally present among his
brothers and sisters in both their personal and social lives. He
is a guarantor of the first proclamation of the Gospel for the
assembling together of the Church, and also of the ceaseless
renewal of the Church which has already been assembled. If
the Church lacks the presence and activity of the ministry
that is received by the laying on of hands with prayer, she
cannot have full certainty of her fidelity and of her visible
continuity.

5. Permanence of the Priesthood

By the laying on of hands a gift of the Holy Spirit is com-   1266
municated which cannot be lost.[29] This reality configures
the ordained minister to Christ the Priest, consecrates him,[30]
and makes him a sharer in Christ's mission under its two aspects of authority and service.

This authority does not belong to the minister as his own: 1267
it is a manifestation of the Lord's *exousia*, or power, by which
the priest is an ambassador of Christ in the eschatological
work of reconciliation.[31] He also assists in directing human
freedom toward God for the building up of the Christian
community.

The lifelong permanence of this reality which imprints a   1268
sign—and this is a doctrine of faith referred to in Church
tradition as the priestly character—expresses the fact that
Christ irrevocably associated the Church with Himself for the
salvation of the world, and that the Church herself is consecrated to Christ in a definitive way for the fulfillment of His
work. The minister, whose life bears the seal of the gift received
through the Sacrament of Orders, reminds the Church that
God's gift is irrevocable. In the midst of the Christian community which lives by the Spirit, he is a pledge, despite his
defects, of the salvific presence of Christ.

1269   This special participation in Christ's priesthood is in no way lost, even if a priest, for ecclesial or personal reasons, is dispensed or removed from the exercise of his ministry.

6. In the Service of Community

1270   Even if he exercises his ministry in a particular community, the priest nevertheless cannot be exclusively devoted to a single group of the faithful. His ministry always tends toward the unity of the whole Church and to the gathering together in her of all men. Each individual community of faithful needs communion with the bishop and the universal Church. In this way the priestly ministry also is essentially communitarian within the presbyterium and with the bishop who, preserving communion with the successor of Peter, is a part of the body of bishops. This holds also for priests who are not in the immediate service of a community or who work in remote and isolated territories. Religious priests also, within the context of the special purpose and structure of their institute, are indissolubly part of a mission which is ecclesially ordered.

1271   Let the whole life and activity of the priest be imbued with a spirit of catholicity, that is, with a sense of the Church's universal mission, so that he will willingly recognize all the gifts of the Spirit, give them freedom and direct them toward the common good.

1272   Following Christ's example, let priests cultivate with the bishop and with each other that brotherhood which is founded on their odination and the oneness of their mission, so that priestly witness may be more credible.

7. The Priest and Temporal Matters

1273   All truly Christian undertakings are related to the salvation of mankind which, while it is of an eschatological nature, also embraces temporal matters. Every reality of this world must be subjected to the lordship of Christ. This does not mean, however, that the Church claims technical competence in the secular order, with disregard for the latter's autonomy.

The proper mission entrusted by Christ to the priest, as to   1274
the Church, is not of the political, economic or social order,
but of the religious order;[32] nevertheless, in the pursuit of
his ministry, the priest can contribute greatly to the establishment of a more just secular order, especially in places where
the human problems of injustice and oppression are more
serious. He must always preserve ecclesial communion, however, and must reject violence in words or deeds as not conforming to the Gospel.

In fact, the Gospel Word which he proclaims in the name   1275
of Christ and the Church, and the effective grace of sacramental life which he administers, should free man from his personal and social egoism and foster among men those conditions of justice that are a sign of the love of Christ present
among us.[33]

PART TWO

Guidelines for the Priestly Life and Ministry

Considering the priestly mission in the light of the ministry   1276
of Christ and the communion of the Church, the Fathers of
this Synod, united with the Roman Pontiff and conscious of
the anxieties which bishops and priests are experiencing today in the exercise of the common role, present the following
guidelines to clarify certain questions and to give encouragement.

I. Priests in the Mission of Christ and the Church

1. Mission: Evangelization and Sacramental Life

a) "The priests of the New Law are by their calling and   1277
ordination set apart, to a certain extent, in the midst of the
People of God. But the purpose of this is not to separate
them from the rest of the People of God nor, indeed, from
the rest of men but only to ensure that they are completely
dedicated to the work to which God calls them."[34] Thus

priests find their identity to the extent that they fully live the Church's mission and exercise it in various ways in communion with the entire People of God, as pastors and ministers of the Lord in the Spirit, in order to fulfill by their work the plan of salvation in history.

1278   "Through their own ministry—which is concerned chiefly with the Eucharist, which brings the Church to perfection—priests are in communion with Christ the Head and lead others to this communion. Consequently, they cannot help realizing how much is still lacking to the fullness of that Body, and hence how much remains to be done that it may grow from day to day."[35]

1279   b) Priests are sent to all men, and their mission must begin with the preaching of God's Word. "The first duty of priests is to preach the Gospel to all men. . . . It is through the saving Word that faith is aroused in the hearts of unbelievers and nourished in the hearts of the faithful."[36] The goal of evangelization is "that all who are made sons of God by faith and Baptism should come together to praise God in the midst of His Church, to take part in the Sacrifice, and to eat the Lord's supper."[37] The ministry of the Word, if rightly understood, leads to the sacraments and to the Christian life as it is practiced in the Church's visible community and in the world.

1280   The sacraments are celebrated in conjunction with the proclamation of the Word of God, and thus they develop faith by strengthening it with grace. They cannot be underestimated, because through them the Word is brought to fuller effect, namely, communion in the mystery of Christ. Priests, then, should perform their ministry in such a way that the faithful will "frequent with great eagerness those sacraments
1281 which were instituted to nourish the Christian life."[38]

    But lasting evangelization and the well ordered sacramental life of the community demand, by their nature, a *diaconia* of authority—that is, service to unity and leadership over the community in charity. Thus the mutual relationship between evangelization and the celebration of the sacraments is clearly seen in the Church's mission. A separation between the two would divide the heart of the Church to the point of endangering the faith, and the priest, who is dedicated to the service of unity in the community, would be gravely distorting his ministry.

The unity between evangelization and sacramental life is   1282
always characteristic of the ministerial priesthood and must
be carefully kept in mind by every priest. But the application
of this principle to the life and ministry of individual priests
must be made with discretion, for the exercise of the priestly
ministry must often take different forms in practice, so as to
better meet special or new situations in which the Gospel
needs to be proclaimed.

c) Although the pedagogy of faith demands that man be   1283
gradually initiated into the Christian life, the Church must
nevertheless always proclaim to the world the Gospel in its
entirety. Each priest shares in the special responsibility of
preaching the whole of the Word of God and of interpreting
it according to the faith of the Church.

The proclamation of the Word of God—the announcement   1284
in the power of the Spirit of the wonders performed by God
and the calling of men to share the Paschal mystery and to
introduce it as a leaven into concrete human history—is the
action of God, in which the power of the Holy Spirit brings
the Church together internally and externally. The minister
of the Word prepares the ways of the Lord by evangelization
with great patience and faith, adapting himself to the various life circumstances of individuals and nations, which are
evolving more or less rapidly.

Impelled by the need to keep in view both the personal   1285
and social aspects of the announcement of the Gospel, so
that in it an answer may be given to men's most fundamental
questions,[39] the Church not only preaches conversion to
God to individuals, but also, almost as society's conscience,
she speaks as best she can to society itself and performs a
prophetic function in this regard, always taking pains to
effect her own renewal.

As regards the experiences of life—whether of men in gen-   1286
eral or of priests—which must be kept in mind and always
interpreted in the light of the Gospel, these experiences cannot be either the sole or the principal norm of preaching.

1287 d) Salvation, which is effected through the sacraments, does not come from us but from God; this demonstrates the primacy of action of Christ, the one Priest and Mediator, in His Body, which is the Church.

1288 Since the sacraments are truly sacraments of faith,[40] they require conscious and free participation by every Christian who has the use of reason. This makes clear the great importance of preparation and of a disposition of faith on the part of the person receiving the sacraments; it also makes clear the necessity for a witness of faith on the part of the minister in his entire life, but above all in the way he values and celebrates the sacraments themselves.

1289 To bishops and—in cases provided for by law—to episcopal conferences, is entrusted the task of authentically promoting, according to norms established by the Holy See, pastoral activity and liturgical renewal that are better adapted to each region, and also of determining the criteria for admission to the sacraments. These criteria, which priests have the obligation to apply, are likewise to be explained to the faithful, so that a person who requests a sacrament may be more aware of his own responsibility.

1290 Let priests, conscious of their office of reconciling all men in the love of Christ, and with attention to the dangers of divisions, strive with great prudence and pastoral charity to form communities which are imbued with apostolic zeal and which will make the Church's missionary spirit present everywhere. Small communities that are not opposed to the parish or diocesan structure ought to be inserted into the parochial or diocesan community in such a way that they may serve it as a leaven of missionary spirit. The need to find apt forms for effectively bringing the Gospel message to all men according to their various circumstances offers a place for the multiple exercise of ministeries lower than the priesthood.

2. Secular Political Activity

1291 a) The priestly ministry, even if compared with other activities, is to be considered not only as a fully valid human activity, but indeed as more excellent than others, though this great value can be fully understood only in the light of faith. Thus, as a general rule, the priestly minstry ought to be a full-time occupation. Sharing in men's secular activities is by no means to be considered the principal aim, nor can such participation suffice to give expression to the specific responsibility of priests. Without being of the world and without taking it as their model, priests must nevertheless live in the world[41] as witnesses and stewards of another life.[42]

In order to determine in concrete circumstances whether secular activity is in accord with the priestly ministry, it should be asked whether and in what way those duties and activities serve the mission of the Church, those who have not yet received the Gospel message and, finally, the Christian community. This is to be judged by the local bishop with his presbyterium, in consultation, if necessary, with the episcopal conference.   1292

When activities of this sort, which ordinarily pertain to the laity, are demanded by the priest's very mission to evangelize, they must be harmonized with his other ministerial activities, since in those circumstances they can be considered as necessary forms of true ministry.[43]   1293

b) Together with the entire Church, priests are obliged, to the utmost of their ability, to select a definite pattern of action when there is question of defending fundamental human rights and of promoting full development of persons and pursuit of the cause of peace and justice; the means must indeed always be consonant with the Gospel. These principles are all valid not only in the individual sphere, but also in the social field; consequently, priests should assist the laity in the task of forming a right conscience.   1294

In circumstances where different political, social and economic options legitimately exist, priests—like all citizens— have a right to make their own choice. But since political options are by nature contingent and never interpret the Gospel in a completely adequate and lasting way, the priest, who is the witness of things to come, must keep a certain distance from any political office or involvement.   1295

In order to remain a valid sign of unity and be able to preach the Gospel in its entirety, the priest may sometimes   1296 be obliged to abstain from the exercise of his own right in this field. Moreover, care must be taken lest his option appear to Christians to be the only legitimate one or become a cause of division among the faithful. Let priests be mindful of the laity's maturity, which is to be valued highly when their specific role is involved.

1297   Leadership or active militancy on behalf of any political party is to be excluded by every priest unless, in concrete and exceptional circumstances, this is truly required by the good of the community and receives the consent of the bishop after consultation with the priest's council and, if circumstances call for it, with the episcopal conference.

1298   The priority of the specific mission which absorbs the entire priestly existence must therefore always be kept in mind so that, with great confidence, and having renewed experience in the things of God, priests may be able to announce these things effectively and joyfully to those who await them.

3. Spiritual Life of Priests

1299   Every priest will find in his very vocation and ministry the deep motivation for living his entire life in oneness and strength of spirit. Called like the rest of the baptized to become a true image of Christ,[44] the priest, like the Apostles, shares, moreover, in a special way in companionship with Christ and in His mission of supreme Pastor: "And he appointed twelve that they might be with him and that he might send them forth to preach."[45] In priestly life, therefore, there can be no dichotomy between love for Christ and zeal for souls.

1300   Just as Christ, anointed by the Holy Spirit, was impelled by His deep love for His father to give His life for men, so the priest, consecrated by the Holy Spirit and made like to Christ the Priest in a special way, dedicates himself to the work of the Father performed through the Son. Thus the whole rule for the priest's life is summed up in Jesus's words: "And for them I sanctify myself, that they also may be sanctified in truth."[46]

1301   Following the example of Christ, who was continually in prayer, and led by the Holy Spirit in whom we cry "Abba,

Father," priests should give themselves to the contemplation of the Word of God and daily take the opportunity to examine life's events in the light of the Gospel, so that, having become faithful and attentive hearers of the Word, they may become true ministers of the Word. Let them be assiduous in personal prayer, in the Liturgy of the Hours, in frequent reception of the Sacrament of Penance, and especially in devotion to the mystery of the Eucharist. Even if the Eucharist is celebrated without participation by the faithful, it nevertheless remains the center of life of the entire Church and the heart of priestly existence.

With his mind raised to heaven and sharing in the communion of saints, the priest should very often turn to Mary the Mother of God, who received the Word of God with perfect faith; and he should daily ask her for the grace of conforming himself to her Son.   1302

Apostolic activities furnish an indispensable nourishment for fostering the priest's spiritual life: "By playing the part of the Good Shepherd in carrying out work of pastoral charity, they will discover the bond of priestly perfection which unites their life and action."[47] The priest is enlightened and strengthened by the exercise of his ministry by the action of the Church and the example of the faithful. The renunciations imposed by pastoral life itself help him acquire an ever greater sharing in Christ's Cross, and hence a purer pastoral charity.   1303

This same charity will also cause priests to adapt their spiritual lives to modes and forms of sanctification more suitable and fitting for the men of their own times and culture. Desiring to be all things to all men in order to save all,[48] the priest should be attentive to the inspiration of the Holy Spirit. Thus he will not only announce the Word of God by human means but he will be taken as a valid instrument by the Word Himself, whose message is "living and efficient and keener than any two-edged sword."[49]   1304

4. Celibacy

a) The Basis for Celibacy

1305   Celibacy for priests is in full harmony with the vocation to the apostolic following of Christ, and also with the unconditional response of the person who is called and who undertakes pastoral service. The priest, following his Lord, more fully shows his availability through celibacy, and embarking upon the Way of the Cross with paschal joy, he ardently desires to be consumed in an offering comparable to that of the Eucharist.

1306   If celibacy is lived in the evangelical spirit, in prayer and vigilance, with poverty, joy, contempt of honors, and brotherly love, it is a sign which cannot long be hidden, but which effectively proclaims Christ to modern men also. For today words are scarcely heeded, but the witness of a life that displays the radical character of the Gospel has a strong attraction.

b) Convergence of Motives

1307   Celibacy, as a personal option for some more important good, even a merely natural one, can promote the full maturity and integration of the human personality. This is all the more true of celibacy undertaken for the kingdom of heaven, as is evident in the lives of so many saints and faithful who, living the celibate life, dedicated themselves totally to promoting human and Christian progress for the sake of God and men.

1308   In modern culture, where spiritual values are to a great extent obscured, the celibate priest indicates the presence of the Absolute God, who invites us to be renewed in His image. Where the value of sexuality is so exaggerated that genuine love is forgotten, celibacy for the sake of Christ's kingdom calls men back to the sublimity of faithful love and reveals the ultimate meaning of life.

1309   Furthermore, one rightly speaks of celibacy's value as an eschatological sign. By transcending every contingent human value, the celibate priest associates himself in a special way with Christ as the final, absolute good, and shows forth in advance the freedom of God's children. While the value of the sign and holiness of Christian marriage is fully recognized, celibacy for the sake of the kingdom nevertheless more clearly displays that spiritual fruitfulness or generative power of the New Law by which the apostle knows that in Christ he is the father and mother of his communities.

From this special way of following Christ, the priest draws greater strength and power for the building up of the Church; and this power can be preserved and increased only by an intimate and pemanent union with Christ's Spirit. The faithful People of God wished to recognize this union with Christ in their pastors, and they are able to discern it.   1310

Through celibacy, priests can more easily serve God with undivided heart and spend themselves for their sheep; as a result they are able more fully to promote evangelization and the Church's unity. For this reason, even if priests are fewer, with the help of this outstanding, resplendent witness of life they will enjoy greater apostolic fruitfulness.   1311

Priestly celibacy, furthermore, is not just the witness of one person alone, but also takes on a social character, by reason of the special fellowship linking members of the presbyterium as the witness of the whole priestly order, intended for the enrichment of the People of God.   1312

c) Necessity of Retaining Celibacy in the Latin Church

The traditions of the Eastern Churches, as they are presently in force in various territories, will remain unchanged.   1313

The Church has the right and duty to determine the concrete form of the priestly ministry and therefore to select more suitable candidates, endowed with certain human and supernatural qualities. When the Latin Church demands celibacy as a necessary condition for the priesthood,[50] she does not do so out of a belief that this way of life is the only path to attaining sanctification, but she does so while carefully considering the concrete form of exercising the ministry in the community, for the building up of the Church.   1314

Because of the intimate, many-sided coherence between the pastoral function and a celibate life, the existing law is upheld: one who freely wills total availability, which is the distinctive characteristic of this function, also freely under-   1315 takes a celibate life. The candidate should understand this form of living not as having been imposed from outside, but rather as the manifestation of his free self-giving, which is accepted and ratified by the Church through the bishop. In this way the law becomes a protection and safeguard of the freedom wherewith the priest gives himself to Christ, and proves to be "an easy yoke."

d) Conditions Favoring Celibacy

1316   We well know that in today's world particular difficulties threaten celibacy from all sides; indeed, priests have already repeatedly experienced them in the course of the centuries. But they can overcome these difficulties if suitable conditions are fostered, namely: growth of the interior life through prayer, renunciation, fervent love for God and one's neighbor, and other aids to the spiritual life; human balance through well ordered integration into the fabric of social relationships; fraternal association and companionship with other priests and with the bishop through more suitable pastoral structures and also with the assistance of the community of the faithful.

1317   It must be admitted that celibacy, as a gift of God, cannot be preserved unless the candidate is adequately prepared for it. From the beginning, candidates should give attention to the positive reasons for choosing celibacy, without letting themselves be disturbed by objections whose accumulation and continual pressure are rather a sign that the primary value of celibacy itself has been called in question. Let them also remember that the power with which God strengthens us is always available for those who strive to serve Him faithfully and entirely.

1318   A priest who leaves the ministry should receive just and fraternal treatment; but even though he can assist in the service of the Church, he is not to be admitted to the exercise of priestly activities.

e) The Law of Celibacy

1319   The law of priestly celibacy existing in the Latin Church is to be kept in its entirety.[51]

f) The Ordination of Married Men

Two formulas were proposed to the Fathers for their   1320
vote:[52]
Formula A: Always excepting the right of the Supreme
Pontiff, priestly ordination of married men is not permitted,
even in particular cases.
Formula B: It belongs solely to the Supreme Pontiff, in particular cases, by reason of pastoral needs and the good of the
universal Church, to allow priestly ordination of married men
of mature age and proven integrity.

II. Priests in the Communion of the Church

I. Relations Between Priests and Bishops

Priests will adhere more faithfully to their mission the   1321
more they know and prove themselves faithful to ecclesial
communion. Thus the pastoral ministry, which is exercised
by bishops, priests and deacons, becomes an eminent sign of
this ecclesial communion, in that they have received a special
mandate to serve this communion. But in order for this ministry to really become a sign of communion, the actual conditions in which it is exercised must be considered supremely
important.

The guiding principle expressed by the Second Vatican   1322
Council in the Decree on the Priestly Ministry and Life—
namely, that the very unity of consecration and mission requires the hierarchical communion of priests with the order
of bishops—is considered fundamental to a practical restoration or renewal, with full confidence, of the mutual
relationship between the bishop and the presbyterium over
which he presides. This principle, however, ought to be more
concretely put into practice, especially as a result of action
by the bishops.

The service of authority on the one hand, and the exercise   1323
of not merely passive obedience on the other, should be carried out in a spirit of faith, mutual charity, filial and friendly
confidence, and constant, patient dialogue. Thus the collabo-

ration and responsible cooperation of priests with the bishop will be sincere, human and at the same time supernatural.[53]

1324   Personal freedom, which responds to the individual vocation and to the charism received from God, and also the ordered solidarity of all for the service of the community and the good of the mission to be fulfilled, are two conditions which should shape the Church's proper mode of pastoral action.[54] The guarantee of these conditions is the bishop's authority, to be exercised in a spirit of service.

1325   The priests' council, which is diocesan by nature, is an institutional manifestation of the brotherhood among priests which has its basis in the Sacrament of Orders. This council's activity cannot be fully shaped by law. Its effectiveness depends chiefly on the repeated effort to listen to the opinions of all in order to reach a consensus with the bishop, to whom it belongs to make the final decision. If all this is done with the greatest sincerity and humility, and if all onesidedness is overcome, it will be easier to provide properly for the common good.

1326   The priests' council is an institution in which priests recognize, at a time when variety in the exercise of their ministry increases every day, that they are mutually complementary in serving one and the same mission of the Church. It is the task of this council, among other things, to seek out clear and distinctly defined aims, to suggest priorities, to indicate methods of acting, to assist whatever the Spirit frequently stirs up through individuals or groups, and to foster the spiritual life from which the necessary unity may more easily be attained.

1327   New forms of hierarchical communion between bishops and priests must be found[55] in order to facilitate contacts between local Churches. A search must be made for ways whereby priests may collaborate with bishops in bodies and enterprises which go beyond diocesan boundaries.

1328   Collaboration of religious priests with the bishop in the presbyterium is necessary, even though their work provides substantial assistance to the universal Church.

2. Relations of Priests with Each Other

Since priests are bound together by an intimate sacramental   1329
brotherhood and by their mission, and since they work and
plan together for the same tasks, some community of life or
some type of life in common should be encouraged among
them and can take various forms, including non-institutional
ones. This should be provided for by law with appropriate
norms, and by renewed or newly discovered pastoral structures.

Priestly associations should also be fostered which, in a   1330
spirit of ecclesial communion and with recognition by the
competent ecclesiastical authority, "through an apt and
properly approved rule of life and through brotherly assistance,"[56] seek to advance the aims which belong to their
function and "sanctity in pastoral work."[57]

It is desirable that every effort be made to seek means—   1331
even if these prove rather difficult—whereby associations
which can serve to divide the clergy into factions may be
brought back to communion and to the ecclesial structure.

There should be a greater communication between religious   1332
and diocesan priests so that true priestly fraternity may exist
among them and they may provide one another with mutual
help, particularly in spiritual matters.

3. Relations Between Priests and Laity

Let priests remember that "The laity must be trusted to   1333
share the work of the Church and left free to do things in a
layman's way. They should be encouraged to show initiative
and not wait to be asked before undertaking apostolic
work."[58] The laity, "likewise sharing their anxieties, ought
to help the clergy with their prayers and personal service,
enabling them more easily to overcome their difficulties and
conduct a more fruitful ministry."[59]

It is necessary always to keep in mind the special character   1334
of the Church's communion in order that personal freedom,

in accordance with the recognized duties and charisms of each person, and the unity of life and action of the People of God, may be fittingly harmonized.

1335   The pastoral council, in which specially chosen clergy, religious and lay people take part,[60] furnishes by its study and reflection the necessary elements enabling the diocesan community to plan its pastoral program systematically and to fulfill it effectively.

1336   The more the co-responsibility of bishops and priests increases—especially through priests' councils—the more desirable it becomes that a pastoral council be established in each diocese.

4. Economic Affairs

1337   The Church's economic problems cannot be adequately solved unless they are carefully examined within the context of the communion and mission of the People of God. All the faithful have the duty of assisting the Church's needs.

1338   In treating these questions, account must be taken not only of solidarity within the local Church, diocese or religious institute, but also of the condition of dioceses in the same region or nation—indeed, of the whole world—especially of Churches in so-called mission territories, and of other poor regions.

1339   The remuneration of priests—which should certainly be determined in a spirit of evangelical poverty, but which should be as equitable and sufficient as possible—is a duty of justice and ought to include social security. Excessive inequalities in this matter must be removed, especially among priests of the same diocese or jurisdiction, account also being taken of the general condition of the people of the region.

It seems very desirable for the Christian people to be gradually instructed in such a way that priests' incomes may be separated from the acts of their ministry, especially sacramental ones.

1340   New ways are open to priests—who exercise the ministry of the Spirit[61] in the midst of the communion of the entire Church—for giving a profound renewed witness in today's world. It is therefore necessary to look to the future with Christian confidence and to implore the Holy Spirit that by His guidance and inspiration doors may be opened to the Gospel, in spite of dangers which the Church cannot overcome by merely human means.

Always looking upon the Apostles, especially Peter and Paul, as examples for priestly renewal, we must give thanks to God the Father, because He has given us all the opportunity to manifest more faithfully the countenance of Christ.   **1341**

Already there are true signs of a rebirth of spiritual life, while men everywhere, amid the uncertainties of the present, look forward to fullness of life. This great renewal certainly cannot take place without a sharing in the Lord's Cross, for the servant is not greater than his master.[62] Forgetting the past, let us strive for what is still to come.[63]   **1342**

With real daring we must show the world the fullness of the mystery hidden through all ages in God, so that through their sharing in it, men may be able to enter into the fullness of God.[64]   **1343**

"We announce to you, the Life Eternal which was with the Father, and has appeared to us. What we have seen and have heard we announce to you, in order that you also may have fellowship with us, and that our fellowship may be with the Father, and with his Son Jesus Christ."[65]   **1344**

MINISTERIA QUAEDAM
Motu Proprio of Pope Paul VI
on the Ministries of Lector and Acolyte
August 15, 1972

Even in the earliest times certain ministries were established by the Church for the purpose of suitably giving worship to God and for offering service to the People of God according to their needs. By these ministries the performance of duties of a liturgical and charitable nature appropriate to varying circumstances was entrusted to the faithful. Conferral of these functions often took place in a special rite in which, after God's blessing had been implored, the individual was appointed to a special class or rank for the fulfillment of some ecclesiastical duty.

1346   Some of these functions, which were more closely connected with the liturgical action, slowly came to be considered as preparatory institutions for the reception of sacred orders, so that the offices of porter, lector, exorcist and acolyte were called minor orders in the Latin Church in relation to the subdiaconate, diaconate and priesthood, which were called major orders. Generally, though not everywhere, these minor orders were reserved to those who received them on their way to the priesthood.

1347   Nevertheless, since the minor orders have not always been the same, and many tasks connected with them have also been performed by the laity, as at present, it seems fitting to reexamine this practice and to adapt it to contemporary needs, so that what is obsolete in these offices may be removed, what is useful may be retained, what is necessary may be defined, and at the same time what is required of candidates for Holy Orders may be determined.

While the Second Vatican Council was in preparation,   1348
many pastors of the Church requested that the minor orders
and subdiaconate be reexamined. Although the Council decreed nothing about this for the Latin Church, it did enunciate
certain principles for resolving the question. There is no doubt
that the norms laid down by the Council regarding the general
and orderly renewal of the liturgy[1] also include those areas
which concern ministries in the liturgical assembly, so that
from the very arrangement of the celebration the Church
clearly appears structured in different orders and ministries.[2]
Thus the Second Vatican Council decreed that "in liturgical
celebrations each person, minister or layman, who has an
office to perform, should do all of, but only, those parts
which pertain to his office by the nature of the rite and the
norms of liturgy."[3]

There is a close connection between this statement and an   1349
earlier one in the same constitution: "Mother church earnestly desires that all the faithful should be led to that full, conscious, and active participation in liturgical celebrations
which is demanded by the very nature of the liturgy. Such
participation by the Christian people as 'a chosen race, a
royal priesthood, a holy nation, a purchased people' (*1 Pt* 2, 9;
see 2, 4-5) is their right and duty by reason of their baptism.
In the restoration and promotion of the sacred liturgy, this
full and active participation by all the people is the aim to be
considered before all else; for it is the primary and indispensable source from which the faithful are to derive the true
Christian spirit; and therefore pastors of souls must zealously
strive to achieve it, by means of the necessary instruction, in
all their pastoral work."[4]

Among the specific functions to be preserved and adapted   1350
to contemporary needs, there are some which are especially
connected with the ministries of the Word and of the Altar
and which, in the Latin Church, are called the offices of
lector, acolyte and subdeacon. It is fitting that these be preserved and adapted in such a way that from now on the two

offices of lector and acolyte should include the functions of the subdiaconate.

1351   There is nothing to prevent episcopal conferences from requesting the Apostolic See to permit other offices besides those common to the Latin Church, if they judge the establishment of such offices in their region to be necessary or very useful because of special reasons. These include, for example, the offices of porter, exorcist and catechist,[5] as well as others conferred upon those dedicated to works of charity, where this service has not been given to deacons.

1352   In accordance with the real situation and with the contemporary outlook, the above-mentioned ministries shall no longer be called minor orders; their conferral will not be called "ordination," but "installation"; moreover, only those who have received the diaconate will be properly known as clerics. Thus the distinction will be more apparent between clergy and laity, between what is proper and reserved to the clergy and what can be entrusted to the laity; thus their mutual relationship will appear more clearly, insofar as "the common priesthood of the faithful and the ministerial or hierarchical priesthood, while they differ in essence and not only in degree, are nevertheless interrelated. Each of them shares in its own special way in the one priesthood of Christ."[6]

1353   Having weighed well every aspect of the question, having sought the opinion of experts, having consulted with the episcopal conferences and taken their views into account, and having taken counsel together with Our esteemed brothers who are members of the Sacred Congregations competent in this matter, by Our apostolic authority We enact the following norms, derogating—if and insofar as necessary—from provisions of the Code of Canon Law presently in force, and We promulgate them with this letter.

The New Norms

1354   I. First tonsure is no longer conferred; entrance into the clerical state is joined to the diaconate.

1355   II. Those orders hitherto called minor orders are henceforth to be called "ministries."

III. Ministries may be committed to lay Christians; hence   1356
they are no longer to be considered as reserved to candidates
for the Sacrament of Orders.

IV. Two ministries adapted to present-day needs are to be   1357
preserved in the whole Latin Church, namely, those of lector
and acolyte. The functions heretofore committed to the subdeacon are entrusted to the lector and the acolyte; consequently, the major order of the subdiaconate no longer exists
in the Latin Church. There is nothing, however, to prevent
the acolyte being also called a subdeacon in some places, if
the episcopal conference so decides.

V. The lector is appointed for his own special function,   1358
that of reading the Word of God in the liturgical assembly.
Accordingly, he is to read the lessons from Sacred Scripture,
except for the Gospel, in the Mass and other sacred celebrations; he is to recite the psalm between the readings when
there is no psalmist; in the absence of a deacon or cantor, he
is to present the intentions for the Prayer of the Faithful; he
is to direct the singing and the participation of the faithful;
he is to prepare the faithful for the worthy reception of the
sacraments. He can also, insofar as necessary, attend to preparing other members of the faithful who are temporarily
appointed to read the Sacred Scripture in liturgical celebrations. In order that he may more fittingly and perfectly fulfill
these functions, he should meditate assiduously on Sacred
Scripture.

The lector should be familiar with the office he has under-   1359
taken and should make every effort and employ suitable
means to acquire that increasingly warm, vital love[7] and
knowledge of the Scriptures that will make him a more
perfect disciple of the Lord.

VI. The acolyte is appointed to aid the deacon and to   1360
minister to the priest. It is therefore his duty to serve at the
altar and to assist the deacon and priest in liturgical celebrations, especially in the celebration of Mass. He is also to distribute Holy Communion as an extraordinary minister when
the ministers referred to in canon 845 of the Code of Canon
Law are not available or are prevented by ill health, age or
another pastoral ministry from performing this function, or

when the number of those approaching the Sacred Table is so great that the celebration of Mass would be unduly prolonged.

1361   In the same extraordinary circumstances the acolyte can be entrusted with exposing the Blessed Sacrament for public adoration by the faithful and he can replace it afterwards, but he cannot bless the people. He can also, as necessary, take care of instructing other faithful who are temporarily appointed to assist the priest or deacon in liturgical celebrations by carrying the missal, cross, candles, and so forth, or by performing other such duties. He will carry out these functions more worthily if he participates in the Holy Eucharist with increasingly fervent piety, receives nourishment from it and deepens his knowledge of it.

1362   Especially destined as he is for the service of the altar, the acolyte should learn about all matters concerning public divine worship and strive to grasp their inner spiritual meaning; in that way he will be able daily to offer himself entirely to God, to be an example to all by his seriousness and reverence in the sacred precincts, and to have a sincere love for the Mystical Body of Christ, that is, the People of God, and especially for the weak and the sick.

1363   VII. In accordance with the venerable tradition of the Church, installation in the ministries of lector and acolyte is reserved to men.

1364   VIII. The following are requirements for admission to the ministries:

a) presentation of a petition freely made out and signed by the aspirant to the ordinary (the bishop and, in clerical institutes of perfection, the major superior), who has the power to decide on its acceptance;

b) a suitable age and specific qualities to be determined by the episcopal conference;

c) a firm desire to give faithful service to God and the Christian people.

1365   IX. The ministries are conferred by the ordinary (the bishop and, in clerical institutes of perfection, the major superior) according to the liturgical rite *"De Institutione Lectoris"* and *"De Institutione Acolythi,"* being revised by the Apostolic See.

X. Intervals determined by the Holy See or the episcopal   1366
conferences shall be observed between the conferral of the
ministry of lector and that of acolyte whenever more than
one of these is conferred on the same person.

XI. Candidates for the diaconate and priesthood are to   1367
receive the ministries of lector and Acolyte, unless they have
already done so, and are to exercise them for a suitable
period, in order to be better disposed for the future service
of the Word and of the Altar. Dispensation of such candidates from undertaking these ministries is reserved to the
Holy See.

XII. The conferral of ministries does not imply the right   1368
to maintenance or salary from the Church.

XIII. The installation rite for lectors and acolytes is to be   1369
published soon by the competent department of the Roman
Curia.

These norms shall come into effect on January 1, 1973.   1370

We order that what We have decreed in this letter that is   1371
issued on Our own initiative, be established and ratified, notwithstanding anything to the contrary.

Given at Rome, at St. Peter's, August 15, the Solemnity   1372
of the Assumption of the Blessed Virgin Mary, in the year
1972, the tenth of Our pontificate.

AD PASCENDUM
Selection from Motu Proprio of Pope Paul VI
on the Role of Deacons
August 15, 1972

Permanent diaconate established

On June 18, 1967, We issued on Our own initiative the apostolic letter *Sacrum Diaconatus Ordinem*, establishing suitable canonical norms for the permanent diaconate.[22] On June 17 of the following year, through the apostolic constitution *Pontificalis Romani Recognito*,[23] We authorized a new rite for conferring the sacred orders of diaconate, priesthood and episcopacy, and at the same time We defined the matter and the form of the ordination itself.

1374   Now that We are proceeding further and are today promulgating the apostolic letter *Ministeria Quaedam*, We deem it appropriate to issue certain norms concerning the diaconate. We also want candidates for the diaconate to know what ministries they are to exercise before sacred ordination, and when and how they are to assume the responsibilities of celibacy and liturgical prayer.

1375   Since entrance into the clerical state is deferred until the diaconate, the rite of first tonsure—by which a layman formerly became a cleric—no longer exists. But a new rite is introduced, by which one aspiring to the diaconate or priesthood publicly manifests his desire to offer himself to God and the Church, so that he may exercise a sacred order. The Church, accepting this offering, selects and calls him to prepare himself to receive a sacred order, and thus he is properly numbered among candidates for the diaconate or priesthood.

It is especially fitting that the ministries of lector and acolyte be entrusted to those who, as candidates for the order of diaconate or priesthood, desire to devote themselves to God and the Church in a special way. For the Church, which "does not cease to take the bread of life from the table of the Word of God and the Body of Christ and offer it to the faithful,"[24] considers it very opportune that both by study and by gradual exercise of the ministry of the Word and of the Altar candidates for sacred orders should, through intimate contact, understand and reflect upon the dual aspect of the priestly office. In this way the authenticity of the ministry shines forth most effectively. Indeed, the candidates come to sacred orders fully aware of their vocation, fervent in spirit, serving the Lord, constant in prayer and looking on the needs of the saints as their own.[25]

Having weighed well every aspect of the question, having sought the opinion of experts, having consulted with the episcopal conferences and taken their views into account, and having taken counsel with Our honored brothers who are members of the Sacred Congregations competent in this matter, by Our apostolic authority We enact the following norms, derogating—if and insofar as necessary—from provisions of the Code of Canon Law presently in force, and We promulgate these norms with this letter.

1376

1377

The New Norms

I. a) A rite is introduced for admission of candidates to the diaconate and to the priesthood. In order that this admission may be properly made, the free petition of the aspirant, made out and signed in his own hand, is required, as well as a written acceptance from the competent ecclesiastical superior, who is empowered to select for the Church.

Professed members of clerical congregations who seek the priesthood are not bound to this rite.

b) The competent superior for this acceptance is the ordinary (the bishop and, in clerical institutes of perfection, the

1378

1379

1380

major superior). Those can be accepted who give signs of an authentic vocation and, endowed with good moral qualities and free from mental and physical defects, wish to dedicate their lives to the Church's service for the glory of God and the good of souls. It is necessary for those aspiring to the transitional diaconate to have completed at least their 20th year and to have begun their course of theological studies.

1381   c) By virtue of his acceptance, the candidate must take special care with his vocation and foster it. He also acquires a right to the necessary spiritual assistance by which he can develop his vocation and submit unconditionally to the will of God.

1382   II. Candidates for the permanent or transitional diaconate and for the priesthood are to receive the ministries of lector and acolyte, unless they have already done so, and are to exercise them for a fitting time, in order to be better disposed for the future service of the Word and of the Altar.

1383   Dispensation from reception of these ministries by such candidates is reserved to the Holy See.

1384   III. The liturgical rites by which admission of candidates for the diaconate and the priesthood takes place and the above-mentioned ministries are conferred, should be performed by the ordinary of the aspirants (the bishop and, in clerical institutes of perfection, the major superior).

1385   IV. The interval established by the Holy See or by the episcopal conferences between conferral—during the course of theological studies—of the ministry of lector and that of acolyte, and between the ministry of acolyte and the order of deacon, must be observed.

1386   V. Before ordination, candidates for the diaconate shall give to the ordinary (the bishop and, in clerical institutes of perfection, the major superior) a declaration made out and signed in their own hand, testifying that they are about to receive the sacred order freely and of their own accord.

1387   VI. The special consecration of celibacy observed for the sake of the kingdom of heaven, and its obligation for candidates to the priesthood and for unmarried candidates to the priesthood and for unmarried candidates to the diaconate, are in fact linked with the diaconate. The public commitment to holy celibacy before God and the Church is to be celebrated in a particular rite, even by religious, and is to precede ordination to the diaconate. Celibacy accepted in this way is a diriment impediment to marriage.

In accordance with traditional Church discipline, a married deacon who has lost his wife cannot enter a new marriage.[26]   1388

VII. a) Deacons called to the priesthood are not to be or-   1389 dained until they have completed the course of studies prescribed by the norms of the Apostolic See.

b) With regard to the course of theological studies preced-   1390 ing the ordination of permanent deacons, the episcopal conferences, taking into consideration the local situation, will issue suitable norms and submit them to the Sacred Congregation for Catholic Education for approval.

VIII. In accordance with norms 29-30 of the General In-   1391 struction on the Liturgy of the Hours:

a) Deacons called to the priesthood are bound by their sacred ordination to the obligation of celebrating the Liturgy of the Hours.

b) It is most fitting that permanent deacons recite daily at least a part of the Liturgy of the Hours, to be determined by the episcopal conference.

IX. Entrance into the clerical state and incardination into   1392 a diocese are brought about by ordination to the diaconate.

X. The rite for admission of candidates to the diaconate   1393 and priesthood, and for the special consecration of holy celibacy, will soon be published by the competent department of the Roman Curia.

Transitional Norms

Candidates for the Sacrament of Orders who have already   1394 received first tonsure before the promulgation of this letter retain all the duties, rights and privileges of clerics. Those who have been promoted to the order of subdiaconate are held to the obligations they have taken on regarding both celibacy and the Liturgy of the Hours. But they must renew their public commitment to celibacy before God and the

Church by the new special rite preceding ordination to the diaconate.

1395   We order that what We have decreed in this letter that We have issued on Our own initiative, be regarded as established and ratified, notwithstanding any measure to the contrary, and is to take effect on January 1, 1973.

1396   Given at Rome, at St. Peter's, August 15th, the Solemnity of the Blessed Virgin Mary, in the 1972, the tenth of Our pontificate.

Sacred Congregation for the Doctrine of the Faith
Declaration in Defense of Church Doctrine
June 24, 1973

The mystery of the Church, upon which the Second Vatican Council shed fresh light, has been repeatedly dealt with in numerous writings of theologians. While not a few of these studies have served to make this mystery more understandable, others through the use of ambiguous or even erroneous language, have obscured Catholic doctrine and at times have gone so far as to be opposed to Catholic faith even in fundamental matters.

To meet this situation the bishops of several nations, conscious of their duty of "keeping pure and entire the deposit of faith," and of their task of "proclaiming the Gospel unceasingly,"[1] have sought through closely related declarations to protect the faithful entrusted to their care from the danger of error. In addition, the second general assembly of the Synod of Bishops, in dealing with the ministerial priesthood, expounded a number of important doctrinal points regarding the Church's constitution.

1398

Likewise, the Sacred Congregation for the Doctrine of the Faith, whose task it is "to safeguard the doctrine of faith and morals in the whole Catholic world,"[2] intends to gather together and explain a number of truths concerning the mystery of the Church which are at present being either denied or endangered. In this it will follow chiefly the lines laid down by the two Vatican Councils.

1399

I. The Oneness of Christ's Church

1400   The Church is one—which "our Savior, after His Resurrection, entrusted to Peter's pastoral care (*Jn* 21, 17); which He commissioned Peter and the other Apostles to spread and to rule (*Mt* 28, 18 ff.); which He erected in perpetuity as 'the pillar and the mainstay of the truth' (*1 Tm* 3, 15)." And this Church of Christ, "set up and structured as a society in this world, perdures in the Catholic Church under the government of Peter and the bishops in communion with him."[3] This declaration of Vatican II is illustrated by the same Council's statement that "it is only through the Catholic Church of Christ, which is the all-embracing aid to salvation, that the fullness of the means of salvation can be obtained,"[4] and that same Catholic Church "has been endowed with all the truth revealed by God and with all the means of grace"[5] with which Christ wished to enhance His messianic community.

1401   This is no obstacle to the fact that during its earthly pilgrimage the Church, "holy and yet always in need of purification, embraces sinners in its bosom and endlessly pursues the way of penance and renewal;"[6] nor to the fact that "outside its structure"—namely, in Churches and ecclesial communities which are joined to the Catholic Church by an imperfect communion—"many elements of sanctification and truth may be found, elements which are an impetus to universal unity insofar as they are gifts proper to the Church of Christ."[7]

1402   For these reasons, "Catholics ought to be glad to acknowledge and show esteem for the truly Christian endowments, deriving from our common heritage, that are to be found among our separated brethren;"[8] and they must strive for the reestablishment of unity among all Christians by making a common effort of purification and renewal,[9] so that the will of Christ may be fulfilled and the division of Christians may cease to be an obstacle to the proclamation of the Gospel throughout the world.[10] But at the same time Catholics are bound to profess that through the gift of God's mercy they belong to that Church which Christ founded and which is governed by the successors of Peter and the other Apostles, who are the depositaries of the original apostolic tradition, living and intact, which is the permanent heritage of doctrine and holiness of that same Church.[11]

The followers of Christ are therefore not permitted to imagine that Christ's Church is nothing more than a collection—divided, but still possessing a certain unity—of Churches and ecclesial communities. Nor are they free to hold that Christ's Church does not really exist anywhere today and that it is to be considered only as an end which all Churches and ecclesial communities must strive to reach.

1403

II. The Infallibility of the Universal Church

"In His gracious goodness, God has seen to it that what He had revealed for the salvation of all nations would abide perpetually in its full integrity."[12] For this reason He entrusted to the Church the treasury of God's Word, so that pastors and holy people might strive together to preserve and study it, and to apply it to life.[13]

1404

God, who is absolutely infallible, thus deigned to bestow upon His new people, which is the Church, a certain shared infallibility, which is restricted to matters of faith and morals; which is present when the whole People of God unhesitatingly holds a point of doctrine pertaining to these matters; and which finally always depends upon the wise providence and anointing of the grace of the Holy Spirit, who leads the Church into all truth until the glorious coming of her Lord.[14] Vatican II speaks about this infallibility of the People of God as follows: "The universal body of the faithful, who have the Holy One's anointing (*1 Jn* 2, 20, 27), cannot err in belief; and it manifests this distinctive property it enjoys when, through the whole body's supernatural understanding of the faith, it shows universal agreement on matters of faith and morals 'from the bishops to the last of the laity' (St. Augustine, *De Praed. Sanct.*, 14, 27)."[15]

1405

1406   The Holy Spirit enlightens and assists the People of God, inasmuch as it is the Body of Christ united in a hierarchical communion. Vatican II indicates this fact by adding to the words quoted above: "This discernment in matters of faith is aroused and sustained by the Spirit of truth. Through this discernment, and under the guidance of the sacred magisterium which it follows faithfully, the People of God truly receive the word of God—no longer just the word of men (*1 Thes* 2, 13); it adheres unwaveringly to the faith handed down once and for all to the saints (*Jude* 1, 3), with sound judgment penetrates deeper into this faith, and applies it more fully to actual life."[16]

1407   Certainly the faithful, who share in their own way in Christ's prophetic office,[17] contribute in many ways to increasing the understanding of faith in the Church. For as the Second Vatican Council says, "there is a growth in the understanding of the realities and words which have been handed down. This comes about through the contemplation and study made by believers, who treasure these things in their hearts (*Lk* 2, 19, 51); through a penetrating understanding of the spiritual realities which they experience; and through the preaching of those who have received the charism of truth through episcopal succession."[18] And Pope Paul VI observes that the witness which bishops offer is "rooted in Sacred Tradition and Holy Scripture, and nourished by the ecclesial life of the whole People of God."[19]

1408   But by divine institution it is the exclusive task of these bishops alone, the successors of Peter and the other Apostles, to teach the faithful authentically, that is, with the authority of Christ shared in different ways, so that the faithful, who may not simply listen to them as experts in Catholic doctrine, must accept their teaching given in Christ's name, with an assent that is proportionate to the authority that they possess and that they mean to exercise.[20] For this reason the Second Vatican Council, in harmony with the First Vatican Council, teaches that Christ made Peter "a perpetual, visible foundation and touchstone of unity in faith and communion;"[21] and Pope Paul VI has declared: "The teaching office of the bishops is for the believer the sign and channel which enable him to receive and recognize the Word of God."[22]

Thus, however much the sacred magisterium avails itself of the thought, life and study of the faithful, its office is not reduced to ratifying the assent already expressed by the latter; indeed, in interpreting and explaining the written or transmitted Word of God, the magisterium can anticipate or demand their assent.[23] Lest it lose the communion of the one faith in the one Body of the Lord (*Eph* 4, 4-5), the People of God has particular need of the magisterium's intervention and assistance when internal disagreements arise and spread concerning a doctrine that must be believed or held.

1409

III. The Infallibility of the Church's Magisterium

Jesus Christ wished the magisterium of the bishops, whom He entrusted with the task of teaching the Gospel to all His people and to the entire human family, to be endowed with a fitting charism of infallibility in matters regarding faith and morals. Since this charism does not come from new revelations enjoyed by the successor of Peter and the college of bishops,[24] it does not dispense them from studying with appropriate means the treasure of Divine Revelation contained in Sacred Scripture, which teaches us intact the truth that God willed to be written down for our salvation,[25] and in the living Tradition that comes from the Apostles.[26] In carrying out their task, the bishops of the Church enjoy the assistance of the Holy Spirit; this assistance reaches its highest point when they teach the People of God in such a way that, through the promises given by Christ to Peter and the other Apostles, the doctrine they propose is necessarily immune from error.

1410

This occurs when the bishops scattered throughout the world but teaching in communion with Peter's successor, are definitively in agreement in their thinking.[27] It occurs even more clearly when the bishops by a collegial act—as in ecumenical councils—together with their visible head define a doctrine to be held,[29] and when the Roman Pontiff "speaks

1411

ex cathedra, that is, when, exercising the office of pastor and teacher of all Christians, through his supreme apostolic authority he defines a doctrine concerning faith or morals to be held by the universal Church."[29]

1412   According to Catholic doctrine, the infallibility of the Church's magisterium extends not only to the deposit of faith but also to those matters without which that deposit cannot be rightly preserved and expounded.[30] In fact, the extension of this infallibility to the deposit of faith itself is a truth that the Church has held with certainty from the beginning as having been revealed in Christ's promises. The First Vatican Council, basing itself upon this truth, defined the matter of Catholic faith as follows: "All those things are to be believed by divine and Catholic faith which are contained in the written or transmitted Word of God and which are pointed out by the Church, either by a solemn judgment or by the ordinary, universal magisterium, as requiring belief because divinely revealed."[31] Therefore the objects of Catholic faith—which are called dogmas—necessarily are and always have been the unalterable norm both for faith and for theological science.

IV. The Church's Gift of Infallibility Not to be Diminished

1413   From what has been said about the extent of and conditions governing the infallibility of the People of God and of the Church's magisterium, it follows that the faithful are in no way permitted to see in the Church a merely fundamental permanence in truth, which some say could be reconciled with occasional errors in propositions that the Church's magisterium teaches to be held irrevocably, and in the People of God's unhesitating assent on matters of faith and morals.

1414   It is of course true that through the faith that leads to salvation men are converted to God,[32] who reveals Himself in His Son Jesus Christ; but it would be wrong to deduce from this that the Church's dogmas can be belittled or even denied. Indeed, the conversion to God which we should realize through faith is a form of obedience (*Rom* 16, 26), which should correspond to the nature of Divine Revelation and its demands. Now this Revelation, in the whole plan of salvation, reveals the mystery of God who sent His Son into the world (*1 Jn* 4, 14), and teaches its application to Christian conduct. Moreover, it demands that, in full obedience of the intellect and will to God who reveals,[33] we accept the proclamation of the good news of salvation as it is infallibly taught by the bishops of the Church. The faithful, therefore, are being converted to God through faith as is necessary; He reveals Himself in Christ when they adhere to Him in the integral doctrine of the Catholic faith.

It is true that there exists an order and, as it were, a hierarchy of the Church's dogmas, as a result of their varying relationships to the foundation of the faith.[34] This hierarchy means that some dogmas are founded on other dogmas, which are the principal ones, and are illuminated by these. But all dogmas, since they are revealed, must be believed with the same divine faith.[35]   1415

V. The Notion of the Church's Infallibility Not to be Falsified

The transmission of Divine Revelation by the Church encounters difficulties of various kinds. These arise from the fact that the hidden mysteries of God "by their nature so far transcend the human intellect that even if they are revealed to us and accepted by faith, they remain concealed by the veil of faith itself and are, as it were, wrapped in darkness."[36] Difficulties arise also from the historical condition that affects the expression of Revelation.   1416

With regard to this historical condition, it must first be observed that the meaning of the pronouncements of faith depends partly upon the expressive power of the language used at a given time and under given circumstances. Moreover, it sometimes happens that some dogmatic truth is first expressed incompletely (but not falsely), and at a later date, when considered in a broader context of faith or human knowledge, is expressed more fully and perfectly. In addition, when the Church makes new pronouncements she   1417 intends to confirm or clarify what is in some way contained in Sacred Scripture or in previous expressions of Tradition; but at the same time she usually intends to solve certain questions or remove certain errors.

1418   All these things have to be taken into account so that these pronouncements may be properly interpreted. Finally, even though the truths which the Church intends to teach through her dogmatic formulas are distinct from the changeable conceptions of a given epoch and can be expressed without them, nevertheless it can sometimes happen that these truths may be enunciated by the sacred magisterium in terms that bear traces of such conceptions.

1419   In view of the above, it must be stated that the dogmatic *formulas* of the Church's magisterium have suitably communicated revealed truth from the very beginning and that, remaining the same, these formulas will continue to communiate this truth forever to those who interpret them correctly.[37] It does not follow, however, that every one of these formulas has been or will be suitable for this purpose to the same extent. For this reason theologians seek to define exactly the intention of teaching proper to the various formulas, and in carrying out this work they are of considerable assistance to the living magisterium of the Church, to which they remain subordinate.

1420   For this reason also it often happens that ancient dogmatic formulas and others closely connected with them remain alive and fruitful in the habitual usage of the Church, but with suitable expository and explanatory additions that maintain and clarify their original meaning. In addition, it has sometimes happened that in this habitual usage certain of these formulas have given way to new expressions, proposed or at least approved by the sacred magisterium, which brought out that meaning more clearly or completely.

1421   As for the *meaning* of dogmatic formulas, this remains ever true and constant in the Church, even when it is expressed with greater clarity or fuller understanding. The faithful must therefore shun the opinion, first, that dogmatic formulas (or some category of them) cannot signify truth in a determinate way, but can only offer changeable approximations to it, which to a certain extent distort or alter it; secondly, that these formulas signify the truth only in an indeterminate way, this truth being like a goal that is constantly being sought by means of such approximations. Those who hold such opinions do not escape dogmatic relativism, and they are corrupting the concept of the Church's infallibility relative to the truth to be taught or held determinately.

Moreover, such opinions clearly are at variance with the declarations of the First Vatican Council which, while fully aware of the progress of the Church in her knowledge of revealed truth,[38] nevertheless taught as follows: "That meaning of sacred dogmas . . . which Holy Mother Church declared once and for all, must always be maintained, and must never be departed from under the guise or in the name of a more advanced understanding."[39] The Council moreover condemned the opinion that "dogmas once proposed by the Church must, with the progress of science, be given a meaning other than that which the Church has understood and still understands."[40] There is no doubt that, according to these conciliar texts, the meaning attributed to dogmas by the Church is determinate and unalterable.

These opinions likewise differ from what Pope John asserted regarding Christian doctrine as he opened the Second Vatican Council: "What is needed is that this certain and immutable doctrine, to which the faithful owe obedience, be studied afresh and reformulated in contemporary terms. For this deposit of faith, or truths which are contained in our time-honored teaching, is one thing; the manner in which these truths are set forth (with their meaning preserved intact) is something else."[41]

Since Peter's successor is speaking here about certain and immutable Christian doctrine, about the deposit of faith being the same as the truths contained in that doctrine and, finally, about the necessity to preserve the meaning of these truths intact, he is clearly acknowledging that we can know the true and unchanging meaning of dogmas. What is new and what he recommends in view of the needs of the times pertains only to the modes of studying, expounding and presenting that doctrine while keeping its permanent meaning. In a

1422

1423

1424

similar way Pope Paul VI exhorted the bishops of the Church in the following words: "Nowadays a serious effort is required of us to ensure that the teaching of the faith should keep the fullness of its meaning and scope while expressing itself in a form which allows it to reach the minds and hearts of those to whom it is addressed."[42]

VI. The Church Associated with Christ's Priesthood

1425   Christ the Lord, the High Priest of the new and everlasting covenant, wished to associate with His perfect priesthood and to form in its likeness the poeple He had bought with His own Blood (*Heb* 7, 20-22, 26-28; 10, 14 and 21). He therefore granted His Church a share in His priesthood, which consists of the common priesthood of the faithful and the ministerial or hierarchical priesthood. These differ from each other not only in degree but also in essence; yet they are mutually complementary within the communion of the Church.[43]

1426   The common priesthood of the laity—which is also rightly called a royal priesthood (*1 Pt* 2, 9; *Ap* 1, 6; 5, 9 ff.), since through it the faithful are united as members of the messianic people with their heavenly King—is conferred by the Sacrament of Baptism. "Incorporated into the Church through Baptism, the faithful are set aside for the cult of the Christian religion by virtue of the character they receive; reborn as sons of God, they must profess before men the faith which they have received from God through the Church."[44] Thus those who are reborn in Baptism "by virtue of their royal priesthood . . . join together in offering the Eucharist. And they exercise that priesthood by receiving the Sacraments, by prayer and thanksgiving, by the testimony of a holy life, by self-denial and active charity."[45]

1427   Moreover, Christ, the Head of the Church, which is His Mystical Body, appointed His apostles, and through them their successors the bishops, as ministers of His priesthood, that they might act in His person within the Church[46] and also in turn legitimately transmit to priests, in a subordinate degree, the sacred ministry which they had received.[47] Thus there arose in the Church the apostolic succession of the ministerial priesthood for the glory of God and for the service of His people and of the entire human family, which must be converted to God.

By means of this priesthood bishops and priests are "set apart, to a certain extent, in the midst of the People of God. But the purpose of this is not to separate them from the rest of the People of God nor, indeed, from the rest of men but only to ensure that they are completely dedicated to the work to which God calls them,"[48] namely, the work of sanctifying, teaching and ruling, the actual execution of which is more precisely specified by the hierarchical communion.[49] The continuous preaching of the Gospel serves as the basis and foundation of this many-sided work,[50] but the summit and source of the entire Christian life is the Eucharistic sacrifice.[51] Priests, acting in the person of Christ the Head, offer this sacrifice in the Holy Spirit to God the Father in the name of Christ and of the members of His Mystical Body.[52] This sacrifice is completed in the holy supper by which the faithful, partaking of the one Body of Christ, are all made into one body (*1 Cor* 10, 16 ff.).

1428

The Church has ever more closely examined the nature of the ministerial priesthood, which can be shown to have been invariably conferred from apostolic times by a sacred rite (*1 Tm* 4, 15; *2 Tm* 1, 6). By the assistance of the Holy Spirit, she recognized more clearly as time went on that God wished her to understand that this rite conferred upon priests not only an increase of grace for carrying out ecclesiastical duties in a holy way, but also a permanent designation by Christ, or character, by virtue of which they are equipped for their work and endowed with the necessary power that is derived from the supreme power of Christ. The permanent existence of this character, the nature of which is explained in different ways by theologians, was taught by the Council of Florence[53] and reaffirmed by two decrees of the Council of Trent.[54] In recent times Vatican II mentioned it more than once,[55] and the second general assembly of the Synod of Bishops rightly considered the enduring nature of the priestly

1429

character throughout life as pertaining to the teaching of faith.[56] This existence of a stable priestly character must be recognized by the faithful and has to be taken into account if correct judgments are to be made about the nature of the priestly ministry and the appropriate ways of exercising it.

1430   Faithful to Sacred Tradition and to many documents of the magisterium, Vatican II taught the following concerning the power belonging to the ministerial priesthood: "Even though all believers can baptize, it is the priest's role to complete the building-up of the body through the Eucharistic sacrifice."[57] And again: "To create unity in the Body 'whose members do not all have the same function' (*Rom* 12, 4), our Lord ordained that some must be appointed ministers. These were to be given the sacred power of Orders to offer sacrifice, forgive sin."[58]

1431   In much the same way the second general assembly of the Synod of Bishops rightly affirmed that only the priest can act in the person of Christ and preside over and perform the sacrificial banquet in which the People of God are united with Christ's oblation.[59]

1432   Letting pass questions regarding the ministers of the various sacraments, the evidence of Sacred Tradition and of the sacred magisterium makes it clear that the faithful who have not received priestly ordination and who take upon themselves the office of performing the Eucharist, attempt to do so not only in a completely illicit way but also invalidly. Such abuses, wherever they may occur, must clearly be eliminated by the pastors of the Church.

1433   This declaration has not attempted, nor was it intended, to prove by a study of the foundations of our faith that Divine Revelation was entrusted to the Church so that she might thereafter preserve it unaltered in the world. But this dogma, from which the Catholic faith takes its beginning, has been recalled, together with other truths related to the mystery of the Church, so that in the uncertainty of the present day the faith and doctrine which the faithful must hold might clearly emerge.

1434   The Sacred Congregation for the Doctrine of the Faith rejoices that theologians are exploring the mystery of the

Church with more and more zeal. It recognizes also that in their work they touch on many questions which can only be clarified by complementary studies and by various efforts and conjectures. However, the due freedom of theologians must always be limited by the Word of God as it is faithfully preserved and expounded in the Church and taught and explained by the living magisterium of the bishops, and especially of the shepherd of the entire People of God.[60]

The Sacred Congregation entrusts this declaration to the diligent attention of the bishops and of all those who in any way share the task of guarding the patrimony of truth which Christ and His Apostles committed to the Church. It also confidently addresses the declaration to the faithful and particularly to priests and theologians, in view of the important office which they hold in the Church, so that all may be of one mind in the faith and may be in sincere harmony with the Church.   1435

In an audience granted to the undersigned Prefect of the Sacred Congregation for the Doctrine of the Faith on May 11, 1973, Pope Paul VI, by Divine Providence Supreme Pontiff, ratified and confirmed this declaration in defense of the Catholic doctrine on the Church against certain errors of the present day, and ordered its publication.   1436

Given at Rome, from the offices of the Sacred Congregation for the Doctrine of the Faith, on June 24, 1973, the feast of St. John the Baptist.   1437

Franjo Cardinal Seper, *Prefect*

Jerome Hamer, Tit. Archbishop of Lorium, *Secretary*

Homily of Pope Paul VI
at a Concelebrated Mass
on the Meaning of Ecclesial Power
September 22, 1974

Greetings to you, Our brethren! We repeat the greeting with which this extraordinary celebration began: "The grace of our Lord Jesus Christ and the love of God and the fellowship of the Holy Spirit be with you all."[1]

1439   Greetings to you, who have come to Rome to find strength, in faith and hope and love, as pastors of the Church of God in a great and modern land. You give to Us, and certainly to yourselves as well, a moment of wonderful and truly Catholic experience. This experience is one of evangelical love. Through this love, as our Head and Teacher taught us at the Last Supper—and it is the memory and mysterious reality of this Last Supper which we are now celebrating and renewing—we give evidence of being disciples of the Lord, as He proclaimed with solemn simplicity: "This is how all will know you for my disciples: your love for one another."[2]

1440   And as we now seek to fulfill in ourselves this word of the Lord, we cannot escape the impression that we are giving witness, in a concrete, evident and persuasive manner, to an aspect of the Church which, yesterday and still today, is much challenged by many Christians who are unfortunately separated from us. We are speaking of the *visible nature* of the Church, her human and social reality, her body made up of real and living persons, living in this world and its actual history. And then there is another aspect of the Church that is affirmed by the celebration of this Mass, which itself is an identical and authentic reenactment of the Lord's Supper. This aspect is the *institutional* one, the organizational and hierarchical aspect of the Church. Here it is placed in a light that defends it from the tendencies of other brethren who challenge it, and who are opposed to the recognition of an institutional Church—as though it were possible to imagine a Church of charity freed from her organic and ministerial structures.

The real Church, the living Church, our Church and the Church of all her followers—those who are called Catholics, that is, universalists—is now being celebrated in this rite. It is a rite to which we are accustomed, but yet one that is new and original in this Mass, which moreover is rendered more radiant, more full and eloquent in significance, by your presence, my brothers, by our magnificent ecclesial communion. 1441

These are things both sublime and simple. But are they not perhaps worthy of being recalled here and now, as though to imbue our hearts with the study of theology and spirituality that you, pilgrims to this Apostolic See, are engaged upon? And is there not perhaps exalted at the same time the mystical and supernatural element of the Church precisely at this moment in which we, the humble heirs of the Apostles, are affirming her unequivocal physical, visible and hierarchical existence? The Church, as we well know, is the Mystical Body of Christ.[3] In her unbreakable and harmonious unity, she demands a complex system of complementary functions—a system which indeed concerns us directly because of that "work of service"[4] that has been specifically assigned to us as bishops of the Church of God. 1442

What is this ministry that has been assigned to us? We know it well. It is the ministry of authority, of *exousia,* of power, that the New Testament so often speaks to us about, not only with regard to Christ but also with regard to the Apostles, in relation, that is, to the mission on which they have been sent and to the work of instruction, sanctification and leadership to which they have been destined. 1443

We shall give the greatest amount of attention to this word "power," which means the capacity to act and to require the ecclesial—that is, loving—obedience of those to whom this 1444 word is directed. For this word expresses a divine thought, a precise concept in ecclesiology, which must recognize the two parts that make it up—pastors and flock. These are the two aspects that constitute it and define it: the hierarchical society and the community of grace. And we shall admire this reality, which divinely reflects the countenance of the Church in order, vitality, beauty and love. And for this we shall bless the Lord, with the resolution to recognize with fidelity and courage the consequences that flow from the divine plan of the Church.

1445   Yes, with fidelity and courage. For we know that in human language, and also in historical reality, this expression *exousia,* "power," is seen to be ambivalent in its twofold possible translation as "domination" or "service." And we know that our Lord has given a very clear solution to the possible misunderstanding as regards the disciples invested with authority: "Let the greater among you be as the junior, the leader as the servant."[5] Thus we have just heard His voice in the reading of the Gospel.

1446   Our power is not a power of domination; it is a power of service. It is a *diakonia;* it is a function destined to the ministry of the community. St. Augustine's motto referring to the ecclesial power is well known: "Let pleasure be taken not in commanding but in being of service."[6] This motto becomes, with St. Benedict and St. Gregory, a norm that often recurs in ecclesiastical speech—and it is reaffirmed by Our venerable predecessor Pius XII, in regard to this Apostolic See.[7]

1447   Confronted with the evangelical and ecclesial interpretation of our authority in the community of the faithful, our hearts could remain fearful and paralyzed. How shall we be able to exercise our function if its proper meaning is apparently turned upside down? Is the Church going to be governed by the faithful, to the service of whom the bishops are bound? No, we know it well: the bishops are constituted by the Holy Spirit to shepherd the Church of God. To shepherd, *poimainein*—this is a decisive word, a word that with the depth of its meaning links in a marvelous way the juridical charism of authority with the sovereign charism of love.

It gives the pastor his true Gospel figure, that of goodness—a
goodness that is provident and strong—and that of the disciple of Christ, set up to exercise the "care of souls" which demands a complete gift of self, an inexhaustible spirit of sacrifice.

This is love in its highest and fullest expression: the love of   1448
truth,[8] exercised through the "Teach all nations,"[9] and by
vigilance over the "deposit" of the faith to be preserved.[10]
It is the love that dispenses the mysteries of God,[11] the charity that pours out the supreme love owed to Christ in the
wise and untiring leadership of His flock.[12]

There is nothing new to you, venerable brothers, in Our   1449
drawing your attention to these teachings; but it is never a
useless thing to recall them, especially if it is done in circumstances like these present ones, when you are seeking to rekindle in your souls the light of the Holy Spirit which you received at the moment of your episcopal ordination,[13] and
when you are comparing your pastoral mission with your beloved local Churches and with the immense and trembling
world of our day.

Thus may Jesus Christ, the Pastor of pastors, assist and   1450
bless us all! And on Our part We take this joyful occasion
likewise to extend Our greetings in the Lord to all your beloved people. Through you We send Our apostolic blessing to
your local Churches. We thank your clergy, your religious
and your laity for their diligent ecclesial communion with
you and with Ourself, and for the shared solicitude they
show for their brothers and sisters in the other local Churches
throughout the world. As successor of Peter and in fulfillment of Our own role of service, We would confirm you all
in faith in the Lord Jesus.

Sacred Congregation for the Doctrine of the Faith
Declaration on the Question of the Admission of
Women to the Ministerial Priesthood
October 15, 1976

INTRODUCTION

The Role of Women in Modern Society and the Church

Among the characteristics that mark our present age, Pope John XXIII indicated, in his Encyclical *Pacem in Terris* of April 11, 1963, "the part that women are now taking in public life . . . This is a development that is perhaps of swifter growth among Christian nations, but it is also happening extensively, if more slowly, among nations that are heirs to different traditions and imbued with a different culture".[1] Along the same lines, the Second Vatican Council, enumerating in its Pastoral Constitution *Gaudium et Spes* the forms of discrimination touching upon the basic rights of the person which must be overcome and eliminated as being contrary to God's plan, gives first place to discrimination based upon sex.[2] The resulting equality will secure the building up of a world that is not levelled out and uniform but harmonious and unified, if men and women contribute to it their own resources and dynamism, as Pope Paul VI recently stated.[3]

1452   In the life of the Church herself, as history shows us, women have played a decisive role and accomplished tasks of outstanding value. One has only to think of the foundresses of the great religious families, such as Saint Clare and Saint Teresa of Avila. The latter, moreover, and Saint Catherine of Siena, have left writings so rich in spiritual doctrine that Pope Paul VI has included them among the Doctors of the Church. Nor could one forget the great number of women who have consecrated themselves to the Lord for the exercise of charity or for the missions, and the Christian wives who have had a profound influence on their families, particularly for the passing on of the faith to their children.

But our age gives rise to increased demands. "Since in our   1453
time women have an ever more active share in the whole life of society, it is very important that they participate more widely also in the various sectors of the Church's apostolate".[4] This charge of the Second Vatican Council has already set in motion the whole process of change now taking place: these various experiences of course need to come to maturity. But as Pope Paul VI also remarked,[5] a very large number of Christian communities are already benefitting from the apostolic commitment of women. Some of these women are called to take part in councils set up for pastoral reflection, at the diocesan or parish level; and the Apostolic See has brought women into some of its working bodies.

For some years now various Christian communities stem-   1454
ming from the sixteenth-century Reformation or of later origin have been admitting women to the pastoral office on a par with men. This initiative has led to petitions and writings by members of these communities and similar groups, directed towards making this admission a general thing: it has also led to contrary reactions. This therefore constitutes an ecumenical problem, and the Catholic Church must make her thinking known on it, all the more because in various sectors of opinion the question has been asked whether she too could not modify her discipline and admit women to priestly ordination. A number of Catholic theologians have even posed this question publicly, evoking studies not only in the sphere of exegesis, patrology and Church history but also in the field of the history of institutions and customs, of sociology and of psychology. The various arguments capable of clarifying this important problem have been submitted to a critical examination. As we are dealing with a

debate, which classical theology scarcely touched upon, the current argumentation runs the risk of neglecting essential elements.

1455   For these reasons, in execution of a mandate received from the Holy Father and echoing the declaration which he himself made in his letter of November 30, 1976,[6] the Sacred Congregation for the Doctrine of the Faith judges it necessary to recall that the Church, in fidelity to the example of the Lord, does not consider herself authorized to admit women to priestly ordination. The Sacred Congregation deems it opportune at the present juncture to explain this position of the Church. It is a position which will perhaps cause pain but whose positive value will become apparent in the long run, since it can be of help in deepening understanding of the respective roles of men and of women.

1

The Church's Constant Tradition

1456   The Catholic Church has never felt that priestly or episcopal ordination can be validly conferred on women. A few heretical sects in the first centuries, especially Gnostic ones, entrusted the exercise of the priestly ministry to women: this innovation was immediately noted and condemned by the Fathers, who considered it as unacceptable in the Church.[7] It is true that in the writings of the Fathers one will find the undeniable influence of prejudices unfavorable to women, but nevertheless, it should be noted that these prejudices had hardly any influence on their pastoral activity, and still less on their spiritual direction. But over and above considerations inspired by the spirit of the times, one finds expressed— especially in the canonical documents of the Antiochian and Egyptian traditions—this essential reason, namely, that by calling only men to the priestly Order and ministry in its true sense, the Church intends to remain faithful to the type of ordained ministry willed by the Lord Jesus Christ and carefully maintained by the Apostles.[8]

1457   The same conviction animates medieval theology,[9] even if the Scholastic doctors, in their desire to clarify by reason the data of faith, often present arguments on this point that modern thought would have difficulty in admitting or would even rightly reject. Since that period and up to our own time, it can be said that the question has not been raised again, for the practice has enjoyed peaceful and universal acceptance.

The Church's tradition in the matter has thus been so firm   1458
in the course of the centuries that the Magisterium has not felt the need to intervene in order to formulate a principle which was not attacked, or to defend a law which was not challenged. But each time that this tradition had the occasion to manifest itself, it witnessed to the Church's desire to conform to the model left to her by the Lord.

The same tradition has been faithfully safeguarded by the   1459
Churches of the East. Their unanimity on this point is all the more remarkable since in many other questions their discipline admits of a great diversity. At the present time these same Churches refuse to associate themselves with requests directed towards securing the accession of women to priestly ordination.

2

The Attitude of Christ

Jesus Christ did not call any woman to become part of   1460
the Twelve. If he acted in this way, it was not in order to conform to the customs of his time, for his attitude towards women was quite different from that of his milieu, and he deliberately and courageously broke with it.

For example, to the great astonishment of his own dis-   1461
ciples Jesus converses publicly with the Samaritan woman (cf. *Jn* 4:27); he takes no notice of the state of legal impurity of the woman who had suffered from haemorrhages (cf. *Mt* 9:20-22), he allows a sinful woman to approach him in the house of Simon the Pharisee (cf. *Lk* 7:37 ff.); and by pardoning the woman taken in adultery, he means to show that one must not be more severe towards the fault of a woman than towards that of a man (cf. *Jn* 8:11). He does not hesitate to depart from the Mosaic Law in order to affirm

the equality of the rights and duties of men and women with regard to the marriage bond (cf. *Mk* 10:2-11; *Mt* 19:3-9).

1462   In his itinerant ministry Jesus was accompanied not only by the Twelve but also by a group of women: "Mary, surnamed the Magdalene, from whom seven demons had gone out, Joanna the wife of Herod's steward Chuza, Susanna, and several others who provided for them out of their own resources" (*Lk* 8:2-3). Contrary to the Jewish mentality, which did not accord great value to the testimony of women, as Jewish law attests, it was nevertheless women who were the first to have the privilege of seeing the risen Lord, and it was they who were charged by Jesus to take the first paschal message to the Apostles themselves (cf. *Mt* 28:7-10; *Lk* 24:9-10; *Lk* 24:9-10; *Jn* 20:11-18), in order to prepare the latter to become the official witnesses to the Resurrection.

1463   It is true that these facts do not make the matter immediately obvious. This is no surprise, for the questions that the Word of God brings before us go beyond the obvious. In order to reach the ultimate meaning of the mission of Jesus and the ultimate meaning of Scripture, a purely historical exegesis of the texts cannot suffice. But it must be recognized that we have here a number of convergent indications that make all the more remarkable the fact that Jesus did not entrust the apostolic charge[10] to women. Even his Mother, who was so closely associated with the mystery of her Son, and whose incomparable role is emphasized by the Gospels of Luke and John, was not invested with the apostolic ministry. This fact was to lead the Fathers to present her as the example of Christ's will in this domain; as Pope Innocent III repeated later, at the beginning of the thirteenth century, "Although the Blessed Virgin Mary surpassed in dignity and in excellence all the Apostles, nevertheless it was not to her but to them that the Lord entrusted the keys of the Kingdom of Heaven".[11]

3

The Practice of the Apostles

1464   The apostolic community remained faithful to the attitude of Jesus towards women. Although Mary occupied a privileged place in the little circle of those gathered in the Upper Room after the Lord's Ascension (cf. *Acts* 1:14), it was not she who was called to enter the College of the Twelve at the time of the election that resulted in the choice of Matthias: those who were put forward were two disciples whom the Gospels do not even mention.

On the day of Pentecost, the Holy Spirit filled them all, men and women (cf. *Acts* 2:1; 1-14), yet the proclamation of the fulfillment of the prophecies in Jesus was made only by "Peter and the Eleven" (*Acts* 2:14).   1465

When they and Paul went beyond the confines of the Jewish world, the preaching of the Gospel and the Christian life in the Greco-Roman civilization impelled them to break with Mosaic practices, sometimes regretfully. They could therefore have envisaged conferring ordination on women, if they had not been convinced of their duty of fidelity to the Lord on this point. In the Hellenistic world, the cult of a number of pagan divinities was entrusted to priestesses. In fact the Greeks did not share the ideas of the Jews: although their philosophers taught the inferiority of women, historians nevertheless emphasize the existence of a certain movement for the advancement of women during the Imperial period. In fact we know from the book of the Acts and from the Letters of Saint Paul that certain women worked with the Apostle for the Gospel (cf. *Rom* 16:3-12; *Phil* 4:3). Saint Paul lists their names with gratitude in the final salutations of the Letters. Some of them often exercised an important influence on conversions: Priscilla, Lydia and others; especially Priscilla, who took it on herself to complete the instruction of Apollos (cf. *Acts* 18:26); Phoebe, in the service of the Church of Cenchreae (cf. *Rom* 16:1). All these facts manifest within the Apostolic Church a considerable evolution vis-a-vis the customs of Judaism. Nevertheless at no time was there a question of conferring ordination on these women.   1466

In the Pauline Letters, exegetes of authority have noted a difference between two formulas used by the Apostle: he writes indiscriminately "my fellow workers" (*Rom* 16:3; *Phil* 4:2-3) when referring to men and women helping him in   1467 his apostolate in one way or another; but he reserves the title "God's fellow workers" (*1 Cor* 3:9; cf. *1 Thess* 3:1) to Apollos, Timothy and himself, thus designated because they are directly set apart for the apostolic ministry and the preaching of the Word of God. In spite of the so important role played by women on the day of the Resurrection, their collaboration was not extended by Saint Paul to the official and public proclamation of the message, since this proclamation belongs exclusively to the apostolic mission.

4

Permanent Value of the Attitude of Jesus and the Apostles

1468   Could the Church today depart from this attitude of Jesus and the Apostles, which has been considered as normative by the whole of tradition up to our own day? Various arguments have been put forward in favor of a positive reply to this question, and these must now be examined.

1469   It has been claimed in particular that the attitude of Jesus and the Apostles is explained by the influence of their milieu and their times. It is said that, if Jesus did not entrust to women and not even to his Mother a ministry assimilating them to the Twelve, this was because historical circumstances did not permit him to do so. No one however has ever proved—and it is clearly impossible to prove—that this attitude is inspired only by social and cultural reasons. As we have seen, an examination of the Gospels shows on the contrary that Jesus broke with the prejudices of his time, by widely contravening the discriminations practiced with regard to women. One therefore cannot maintain that, by not calling women to enter the group of the Apostles, Jesus was simply letting himself be guided by reasons of expediency. For all the more reason, social and cultural conditioning did not hold back the Apostles working in the Greek milieu, where the same forms of discrimination did not exist.

1470   Another objection is based upon the transitory character that one claims to see today in some of the prescriptions of Saint Paul concerning women, and upon the difficulties that some aspects of his teaching raise in this regard. But it must be noted that these ordinances, probably inspired by the customs of the period, concern scarcely more than disciplinary practices of minor importance, such as the obligation imposed upon women to wear a veil on the head (*1 Cor* 11:2-16); such requirements no longer have a normative value. However, the Apostle's forbidding of women "to speak" in the assemblies (cf. *1 Cor* 14:34-35; *1 Tim* 2:12) is of a different nature, and exegetes define its meaning in this way: Paul in no way opposes the right, which he elsewhere recognizes as possessed by women, to prophesy in the assembly (cf. *1 Cor* 11:5); the prohibition solely concerns the official function of teaching in the Christian assembly. For Saint Paul this prescription is bound up with the divine plan of creation (cf. *1 Cor* 11:7; *Gen* 2:18-24): it would be difficult to see in it the expression of a cultural fact. Nor should it be forgotten that we owe to Saint Paul one of the most vigorous texts in the New Testament on the fundamental equality of men and women, as children of God in Christ (cf. *Gal* 3:28). Therefore there is no reason for accusing him of prejudices against women, when we note the trust that he shows towards them and the collaboration that he asks of them in his apostolate.

But over and above these objections taken from the history of apostolic times, those who support the legitimacy of change in the matter turn to the Church's practice in her sacramental discipline. It has been noted, in our day especially, to what extent the Church is conscious of possessing a certain power over the sacraments, even though they were instituted by Christ. She has used this power down the centuries in order to determine their signs and the conditions of their administration: recent decisions of Popes Pius XII and Paul VI are proof of this.[12] However, it must be emphasized that this power, which is a real one, has definite limits. As Pope Pius XII recalled: "The Church has no power over the substance of the sacraments, that is to say, over what Christ the Lord, as the sources of Revelation bear witness, determined should be maintained in the sacramental sign".[13] This was already the teaching of the Council of Trent, which declared: "In the Church there has always existed this power,

1471

that in the administration of the sacraments, provided that their substance remains unaltered, she can lay down or modify what she considers more fitting either for the benefit of those who receive them or for respect towards those same sacraments, according to varying circumstances, times or places".[14]

1472   Moreover, it must not be forgotten that the sacramental signs are not conventional ones. Not only is it true that, in many respects, they are natural signs because they respond to the deep symbolism of actions and things, but they are more than this: they are principally meant to link the person of every period to the supreme Event of the history of salvation, in order to enable that person to understand, through all the Bible's wealth of pedagogy and symbolism, what grace they signify and produce. For example, the sacrament of the Eucharist is not only a fraternal meal, but at the same time the memorial which makes present and actual Christ's sacrifice and his offering by the Church. Again, the priestly ministry is not just a pastoral service; it ensures the continuity of the functions entrusted by Christ to the Apostles and the continuity of the powers related to those functions. Adaptation to civilizations and times therefore cannot abolish, on essential points, the sacramental reference to constitutive events of Christianity and to Christ himself.

1473   In the final analysis it is the Church, through the voice of her Magisterium, that, in these various domains, decides what can change and what must remain immutable. When she judges that she cannot accept certain changes, it is because she knows that she is bound by Christ's manner of acting. Her attitude, despite appearances, is therefore not one of archaism but of fidelity: it can be truly understood only in this light. The Church makes pronouncements in virtue of the Lord's promise and the presence of the Holy Spirit, in order to proclaim better the mystery of Christ and to safeguard and manifest the whole of its rich content.

1474   This practice of the Church therefore has a normative character: in the fact of conferring priestly ordination only on men, it is a question of an unbroken tradition throughout the history of the Church, universal in the East and in the

West, and alert to repress abuses immediately. This norm, based on Christ's example, has been and is still observed because it is considered to conform to God's plan for his Church.

5

The Ministerial Priesthood in the Light of the Mystery of Christ

Having recalled the Church's norm and the basis thereof, it seems useful and opportune to illustrate this norm by showing the profound fittingness that theological reflection discovers between the proper nature of the sacrament of Order, with its specific reference to the mystery of Christ, and the fact that only men have been called to receive priestly ordination. It is not a question here of bringing forward a demonstrative argument, but of clarifying this teaching by the analogy of faith.

The Church's constant teaching, repeated and clarified by the Second Vatican Council and again recalled by the 1971 Synod of Bishops and by the Sacred Congregation for the Doctrine of the Faith in its Declaration of June 24, 1973, declares that the bishop or the priest, in the exercise of his ministry, does not act in his own name, *in persona propria:* he represents Christ, who acts through him: "the priest truly acts in the place of Christ", as Saint Cyprian already wrote in the third century.[15] It is this ability to represent Christ that Saint Paul considered as characteristic of his apostolic function (cf. *2 Cor* 5:20; *Gal* 4:14). The supreme expression of this representation is found in the altogether special form it assumes in the celebration of the Eucharist, which is the source and center of the Church's unity, the sacrificial meal in which the People of God are associated in the sacrifice of Christ: the priest, who alone has the power to perform it, then acts not only through the effective power conferred on him by Christ, but *in persona Christi,*[16] taking the role of Christ, to the point of being his very image, when he pronounces the words of consecration.[17]

1475

1476

1477   The Christian priesthood is therefore of a sacramental nature: the priest is a sign, the supernatural effectiveness of which comes from the ordination received, but a sign that must be perceptible[18] and which the faithful must be able to recognize with ease. The whole sacramental economy is in fact based upon natural signs, on symbols imprinted upon the human psychology: "Sacramental signs," says Saint Thomas, "represent what they signify by natural resemblance."[19] The same natural resemblance is required for persons as for things: when Christ's role in the Eucharist is to be expressed sacramentally, there would not be this "natural resemblance" which must exist between Christ and his minister if the role of Christ were not taken by a man: in such a case it would be difficult to see in the minister the image of Christ. For Christ himself was and remains a man.

1478   Christ is of course the firstborn of all humanity, of women as well as men: the unity which he re-established after sins is such that there are no more distinctions between Jew and Greek, slave and free, male and female, but all are one in Christ Jesus (cf. *Gal* 3:28). Nevertheless, the Incarnation of the Word took place according to the male sex: this is indeed a question of fact, and this fact, while not implying an alleged natural superiority of man over woman, cannot be disassociated from the economy of salvation: it is, indeed, in harmony with the entirety of God's plan as God himself has revealed it, and of which the mystery of the Covenant is the nucleus.

1479   For the salvation offered by God to men and women, the union with him to which they are called—in short, the Covenant—took on, from the Old Testament Prophets onwards, the privileged form of a nuptial mystery: for God the Chosen People is seen as his ardently loved spouse. Both Jewish and Christian tradition has discovered the depth of this intimacy of love by reading and rereading the Song of Songs; the divine Bridegroom will remain faithful even when the Bride betrays his love, when Israel is unfaithful to God (cf. *Hos* 1-3; *Jer* 2). When the "fullness of time" (*Gal* 4:4) comes, the Word, the Son of God, takes on flesh in order to establish and seal the new and eternal Covenant in his blood, which will be shed for many so that sins may be forgiven. His death will gather together again the scattered children of God; from his pierced side will be born the Church, as Eve was born from Adam's side. At that time there is fully and eternally accomplished the nuptial mystery proclaimed and hymned in the Old Testament: Christ is the Bridegroom; the Church is his Bride, whom he loves because he has gained her by his blood and made her glorious, holy and without blemish, and henceforth he is inseparable from her. This nuptial theme, which is developed from the Letters of Saint Paul onwards (cf. *2 Cor* 11:2; *Eph* 5:22-23) to the writings of Saint John (cf. especially *Jn* 3:29; *Rev* 19:7, 9), is present also in the Synoptic Gospels: the Bridegroom's friends must not fast as long as he is with them (cf. *Mk* 2:19); the Kingdom of Heaven is like a king who gave a feast for his son's wedding (cf. *Mt* 22:1-14). It is through this Scriptural language, all interwoven with symbols, and which expresses and affects man and woman in their profound identity, that there is revealed to us the mystery of God and Christ, a mystery which of itself is unfathomable.

That is why we can never ignore the fact that Christ is a man. And therefore, unless one is to disregard the importance of this symbolism for the economy of Revelation, it must be admitted that, in actions which demand the character of ordination and in which Christ himself, the author of the Covenant, the Bridegroom and Head of the Church, is represented, exercising his ministry of salvation—which is in the highest degree the case of the Eucharist—his role (this is the original sense of the word *persona*) must be taken by a man. This does not stem from any personal superiority of the latter in the order of values, but only from a difference of fact on the level of functions and service.   **1480**

Could one say that, since Christ is now in the heavenly condition, from now on it is a matter of indifference whether he be represented by a man or by a woman, since "at the resurrection men and women do not marry" (*Mt* 22:30)? But this text does not mean that the distinction between man and woman, insofar as it determines the identity proper to   **1481** the person, is suppressed in the glorified state; what holds for us holds also for Christ. It is indeed evident that in human beings the difference of sex exercises an important influence, much deeper than, for example, ethnic differences: the latter do not affect the human person as intimately as the difference of sex, which is directly ordained both for the communion of persons and for the generation of human beings. In Biblical Revelation this difference is the effect of God's will from the beginning: "male and female he created them" (*Gen* 1:27).

1482   However, it will perhaps be further objected that the priest, especially when he presides at the liturgical and sacramental functions, equally represents the Church: he acts in her name with "the intention of doing what she does." In this sense the theologians of the Middle Ages said that the minister also acts *in persona Ecclesiae,* that is to say, in the name of the whole Church and in order to represent her. And in fact, leaving aside the question of the participation of the faithful in a liturgical action, it is indeed in the name of the whole Church that the action is celebrated by the priest: he prays in the name of all, and in the Mass he offers the sacrifice of the whole Church. In the new Passover, the Church, under visible signs, immolates Christ through the ministry of the priest.[20] And so, it is asserted, since the priest also represents the Church, would it not be possible to think that this representation could be carried out by a woman, according to the symbolism already explained? It is true that the priest represents the Church, which is the Body of Christ. But if he does so, it is precisely because he first represents Christ himself, who is the Head and Shepherd of the Church. The Second Vatican Council[21] used this phrase to make more precise and to complete the expression *in persona Christi.* It is in this quality that the priest presides over the Christian assembly and celebrates the Eucharistic sacrifice "in which the whole Church offers and is herself wholly offered."[22]

1483   If one does justice to these reflections, one will better understand how well-founded is the basis of the Church's practice; and one will conclude that the controversies raised in our days over the ordination of women are for all Christians a pressing invitation to meditate on the mystery of the Church, to study in greater detail the meaning of the episcopate and the priesthood, and to rediscover the real and pre-eminent place of the priest in the community of the baptized, of which he indeed forms part but from which he is distinguished because, in the actions that call for the character of ordination, for the community he is—with all the effectiveness proper to the sacraments—the image and symbol of Christ himself who calls, forgives, and accomplishes the sacrifice of the Covenant.

6

The Ministerial Priesthood Illustrated by the Mystery of the Church

It is opportune to recall that problems of sacramental   1484
theology, especially when they concern the ministerial
priesthood, as is the case here, cannot be solved except in the
light of Revelation. The human sciences, however valuable
their contribution in their own domain, cannot suffice here,
for they cannot grasp the realities of faith: the properly
supernatural content of these realities is beyond their competence.

Thus one must note the extent to which the Church is a   1485
society different from other societies, original in her nature
and in her structures. The pastoral charge in the Church is
normally linked to the sacrament of Order: it is not a simple
government, comparable to the modes of authority found in
States. It is not granted by people's spontaneous choice:
even when it involves designation through election, it is the
laying on of hands and the prayer of the successors of the
Apostles which guarantee God's choice; and it is the Holy
Spirit, given by ordination, who grants participation in the
ruling power of the Supreme Pastor, Christ (cf. *Acts* 20:28).
It is a charge of service and love: "If you love me, feed my
sheep" (cf. *Jn* 21:15-17).

For this reason one cannot see how it is possible to pro-   1486
pose the admission of women to the priesthood in virtue of

the equality of rights of the human person, an equality which holds good also for Christians. To this end use is sometimes made of the text quoted above, from the Letter to the Galatians (3:28), which says that in Christ there is no longer any distinction between men and women. But this passage does not concern ministries: it only affirms the universal calling to divine filiation, which is the same for all. Moreover, and above all, to consider the ministerial priesthood as a human right would be to misjudge its nature completely: baptism does not confer any personal title to public ministry in the Church. The priesthood is not conferred for the honor or advantage of the recipient, but for the service of God and the Church; it is the object of a specific and totally gratuitous vocation: "You did not choose me, no, I chose you; and I commissioned you..." (*Jn* 15:16; cf. *Heb* 5:4).

1487   It is sometimes said and written in books and periodicals that some women feel that they have a vocation to the priesthood. Such an attraction, however noble and understandable, still does not suffice for a genuine vocation. In fact a vocation cannot be reduced to a mere personal attraction, which can remain purely subjective. Since the priesthood is a particular ministry of which the Church has received the charge and the control, authentication by the Church is indispensable here and is a constitutive part of the vocation: Christ chose "those he wanted" (*Mk* 3:13). On the other hand, there is a universal vocation of all the baptized to the exercise of the royal priesthood by offering their lives to God and by giving witness for his praise.

1488   Women who express a desire for the ministerial priesthood are doubtless motivated by the desire to serve Christ and the Church. And it is not surprising that, at a time when they are becoming more aware of the discriminations to which they have been subject, they should desire the ministerial priesthood itself. But it must not be forgotten that the priesthood does not form part of the rights of the individual, but stems from the economy of the mystery of Christ and the Church. The priestly office cannot become the goal of social advancement; no merely human progress of society or of the individual can of itself give access to it: it is of another order.

It therefore remains for us to meditate more deeply on the 1489 nature of the real equality of the baptized which is one of the great affirmations of Christianity: equality is in no way identity, for the Church is a differentiated body, in which each individual has his or her role. The roles are distinct, and must not be confused; they do not favor the superiority of some vis-a-vis the others, nor do they provide an excuse for jealousy; the only better gift, which can and must be desired, is love (cf. *1 Cor* 12:13). The greatest in the Kingdom of Heaven are not the ministers but the saints.

The Church desires that Christian women should become 1490 fully aware of the greatness of their mission: today their role is of capital importance, both for the renewal and humanization of society and for the rediscovery by believers of the true face of the Church.

His Holiness Pope Paul VI, during the audience granted to 1491 *the undersigned Prefect of the Sacred Congregation on October 15, 1976 approved this Declaration, confirmed it and ordered its publication.*

Given in Rome, at the Sacred Congregation for the Doc- 1492 trine of the Faith, on October 15, 1976, the feast of Saint Teresa of Avila.

Franjo Cardinal Seper, *Prefect*

Motu Proprio of Pope Paul VI
on the Council of the Laity
December 10, 1976

The various forms of apostolate or divisions of ministries[1] which help build up Christ's Mystical Body, the Church, are a proper concern of the laity. The Second Vatican Ecumenical Council has reminded our age of this truth and shed new light on the traditional teaching in this regard: lay people "live in the world, in each and all of the occupations and tasks of the world and in the day-to-day circumstances of social and family life. These are the strands out of which their life is woven. Here they are called by God to work for the salvation of the world from within, as it were, . . . revealing Christ to others, by the testimony of their lives primarily, as shining examples of faith, hope and charity."[2]

1494 The present age evidently requires that the laity exercise an even more vigorous and wide-ranging apostolate. "This complex and pressing need . . . is clearly signaled by the obvious action of the Holy Spirit today. More and more he awakens lay people to an awareness of their particular responsibilities in the Church and inspires them to dedicate themselves to Christ and his Church in every kind of service."[3]

1495 The new situation and the advice of the Ecumenical Council[4] led Us to establish within the Roman Curia a Council of the Laity. This We did in the Apostolic Letter *Catholicam Christi Ecclesiam* of January 6, 1967.[5] We may recall, however, that the council was established on a trial basis for five years, since practice and experience would surely suggest changes and improvements.[6]

We attest that the council has zealously carried out the functions entrusted to it, whether in promoting, integrating and ordering the apostolate of the laity among the peoples of the world and within the body of the Church or pursuing research in this area or engaging in new undertakings.   1496

Meanwhile, however, the reasons for which the council was established have become even more urgent and the problems to be tackled and solved in the area of the Catholic apostolate have become even more serious and comprehensive. In addition, the experience of the last few years has brought further useful knowledge. For all these reasons, We have thought it profitable to give this particular ministry of the Roman Curia—a ministry which is one of the outstanding results of the Second Vatican Council—a new, permanent and more excellent form.   1497

Therefore, after careful consideration and after having sought the advice of experts, We establish and decree the following: 1498

I. The Council of the Laity shall henceforth be called the Pontifical Council of the Laity.   1499

II. The head and moderator of the council will be a Cardinal President who will have a presidential commission consisting of three cardinals resident in Rome and a secretary of the council.   1500

The presidential commission will meet every other month and as often in addition as the Cardinal President may judge necessary for handling business of special importance.   1501

The Cardinal President shall be aided by a secretary and an under-secretary. All those here named shall, in accordance with law, deal with all matters which require the sacred power of orders and jurisdiction.   1502

III. The majority of the members of this Pontifical Council shall be lay people, chosen from the various parts of the world, active in various areas of the lay apostolate and with a due proportion of men and women. The lay people shall be joined by some bishops and priests.   1503

1504   The members shall meet once a year, unless special circumstances dictate otherwise; they shall meet together with the presidential commission, under the chairmanship of the Cardinal President, assisted by the secretary.

1505   IV. The council shall seek the help of consultors who are noted for their virtue, learning and prudence. The experts shall be chosen with lay people in the majority and with men and women in equal numbers. Additional experts, by reason of office, shall be the secretaries of the following Sacred Congregations: for Bishops, for the Oriental Churches, for the Clergy, for Religious and Secular Institutes and for the Evangelization of Peoples, as well as the secretary for the Pontifical Commission for Justice and Peace. It is desirable that among the consultors there be one or more religious women.

1506   V. The consultors shall form a commission or committee, the function of which is to study in depth all matters on which the members of the council must decide and to carry out faithfully the projects entrusted to them by those in charge.

1507   The consultors may be assembled as a body or in the form of smaller committees to deal with a particular problem or may be asked individually for their views on various matters.

1508   VI. The Pontifical Council for the Laity shall have for its area of competence the apostolate of the laity in the Church and the discipline of the laity as such.

1509   Specifically, the functions of this Pontifical Council shall be the following:

1510   1) To stimulate the laity to participation in the life and mission of the Church, whether as members of associations formed for apostolic purposes (this kind of participation is especially desirable) or as individual Christians.

1511   2) To consider, direct and, if need be, promote undertakings relating to the apostolate of the laity in the various areas of the life of society. The competence of the other agencies and ministries of the Roman Curia must, however, be respected.

1512   3) To handle all matters concerning:
—the lay commissions which deal with the apostolate at

the international and national levels without, however, infringing on the competence of the Secretariat of State (Papal Secretariat);

—Catholic associations which promote the apostolate, spiritual life and zeal of the laity, while respecting the right of the Sacred Congregation for the Evangelization of Peoples to oversee associations whose *exclusive* purpose is to promote cooperation with the missions;

—pious associations (archconfraternities, confraternities, pious unions, sodalities of any kind); the Council is to act in cooperation with the Congregation for Religious and Secular Institutes whenever there is question of associations founded by a religious family or secular institute;

—Third Orders of Seculars, but only in matters pertaining to their apostolic activities, and without infringing on the competence of the Sacred Congregation for Religious and Secular Institutes in all other matters;

—associations of which both clergy and laity are members but without infringing on the competence of the Sacred Congregation for the Clergy as far as the observance of the general laws of the Church is concerned (cf. the norms of the Apostolic Signatura).

4) To take the initiative in promoting the active participation of the laity in the areas of catechetics, liturgy, sacraments, education and others. In these various areas the council is to cooperate with the agencies of the Roman Curia which deal with the same matters.   1513

5) To see to it that the Church's laws regarding the laity are dutifully observed and to handle the administrative side of disputes involving the laity.   1514

6) In cooperation with the Sacred Congregation for the Clergy, to handle all matters pertaining to pastoral councils whether parochial or diocesan, so that the laity may be led to participate in pastoral work which is properly unified and seen in its global context.   1515

VII. The Council for the Family is subordinate to the Pontifical Council for the Laity but has its own proper form and divisions.   1516

1517   The Cardinal President of the Pontifical Council for the Laity is also head of the Council for the Family; here, too, he is assisted by the secretary of the Council for the Laity.

1518   One of the cardinals who is an official of the Council for the Laity shall have the task of handling the ordinary business of the Council for the Family.

1519   We hereby confirm and ratify everything We have decreed in this letter, which We have issued on Our own initiative *(motu proprio)*, anything to the contrary notwithstanding.

1520   Rome, at St. Peter's, December 10, 1976, the 14th year of Our pontificate.

References

EST SANE MOLESTUM, Letter of Pope Leo XIII on the Apostolate of the Laity, December 17, 1888.

1   Cf. *Mt.* 18:17.
2   *Heb.* 13:17.

SAPIENTIAE CHRISTIANAE, Selection from Encyclical Letter of Pope Leo XIII on the Chief Duties of Christian Citizens, January 10, 1890.

1   *Jn.* 16:33.
2   *Rom.* 10:14-17.
3   *Acts* 22:28.
4   Conc. Vatican., Const. *Dei Filius*, sub fine.
5   *Col.* 1:24.
6   *Rom.* 12:4-5.
7   *Cant.* 6:9.

IL FERMO PROPOSITO, Encyclical Letter of Pope Pius X on Catholic Action in Italy, June 11, 1905.

1   *Eph.* 4:16.

2   *Eph.* 4:12.

3   *Col.* 1:10.

4   1 *Col.* 1:23.

5   *Eph.* 1:10.

6   *Tim.* 4:8.

7   1 *Pet.* 2:15.

8   *Supra*, No. 173 ff.

9   Cf. *supra*, No. 316 ff.

10   *Lk.* 10:16.

11   *Ibid.*, 11:23.

12   2 *Cor.* 9:22.

13   *Mt.* 9:36.

14   *Phil.* 2:1-5.

15   *Col.* 3:17.

16   *Rom.* 11:36.

17   Sequence of Whit Sunday.

HAERENT ANIMO, Selection from Exhortation of Pope Pius X to the Catholic Clergy on Priestly Sanctity, August 4, 1908.

1   *Hebr.* 13: 17.

2   Encyclical *Supremi Apostolatus:* cf. *supra*, n. 24.

3   1 *Tim.* 6: 11.

4   *Ephes.* 4: 23-24.

5   *Dan.* 3: 39.

6   *Col.* 1: 10.

7   *Hebr.* 5: 1.

8   *Tit* 1: 16.

9   *Acts* 1: 1.

10   *Mt.* 5: 13.

11   *I Cor.* 4: 1.

12   *II Cor.* 5: 20.

13   *Jn.* 15: 15-16.

14   *Hebr.* 7: 26.

15   S. John Chrysostom, *Hom.* LXXXII *in Matth.*, n. 5: cf. *supra*, n. 68.

16   *Ps.* 15:5.

17   *Ep.* LII, *ad Nepotianum*, n. 5.

18   *Col.* 1:28.

19   Cf. *supra*, n. 70.

20   *Sess.* XXII, *de Reform.*, c. 1.

21   *Ps.* 92: 5.

22   Letter *Testem Benevolentiae* to the Archbishop of Baltimore (22 January 1899. *AAS* XXXI, p. 476) condemning "Americanism."

23   *Rom.* 8: 29.

24   *Hebr.* 13: 8.

25   *Mt.* 11: 29.

26   *Phil.* 2: 8.

27   *Gal.* 5: 24.

28   Leo XIII, *loc. cit.*

29   *AAS* II, (1910), p. 910.

30   *Mt.* 16: 24.

31   *Mt.* 20: 1.

32   *Acts.* 10: 38.

33   *I Cor.* 3: 7.

34   *I Cor.* 1: 27-28.

35   Cf. *supra*, n. 32.

36   *II Cor.* 6: 5-6.

Letter of Pope Pius XI to Cardinal Bertram on the Origins of Catholic Action, November 13, 1928.

1   *Phil.* 4:3.

2 "Catholic Action, being the participation of the laity in the apostolate of the hierarchy, is by its nature, as old as the Church herself; but in these latter times it has taken new forms suited to new needs." Let. of the Cardinal Secretary of State, to the President of Italian Catholic Action, March 30, 1930.

3 *Supra,* No. 446.

4 "It must constantly be remembered that Catholic Action, being by its very nature coordinated with, and subordinated to, the hierarchy, receives from it in return its mandate and directives, with a view to forming a whole army of souls consumed with the desire to participate in the apostolate of the Church and to cooperate under her orders in the extension of the kingdom of Jesus Christ in individuals, in families and in society as a whole."

MENTI NOSTRAE, Apostolic Exhortation of Pope Pius XII on the Development of Holiness in Priestly Life, September 23, 1950.

1 Cf. Ioann., XXI, 15 et 17.

2 I *Petr.,* V, 2 et 3.

3 Praef. Miss. in festo Iesu Christi Regis.

4 Cf. I *Cor.,* IV, 1.

5 Cf. I *Cor.,* III, 9.

6 Cf. II *Tim.,* III, 17.

7 Exhortatio *Haerent animo; Acta Pii X,* vol. IV, p. 237 sq.

8 Litt. Enc. *Ad catholici sacerdotii, A.A.S.,* XXVIII, 1936, p. 5 sq.

9 *A.A.S.,* XXXV, 1943, p. 193 sq.

10 *A.A.S.,* XXXIX, 1947, p. 521 sq.

11 Ioann., XX, 21.

12 Luc., X, 16.

13 *Hebr.,* V, 1.

14 I *Cor.,* III, 9.

15 II *Cor.,* II, 15.

16 *Pontificale Rom.,* De ord. presbyt.

17 Cf. *Col.,* III, 3.

18 Cf. *Matth.,* XXII, 37, 38, 39.

19 Cf. I *Cor.,* XIII, 4, 5, 6, 7.

20 *Col*, III, 14.

21 *C.I.C.*, can. 124.

22 *Act. Ap.*, X, 38.

23 Ioann., XIII, 15.

24 *Matth.*, XI, 29.

25 Ioann., XV, 5.

26 *Matth.*, XX, 28.

27 Cf. *Matth.*, XVI, 24.

28 II *Cor.*, XII, 5.

29 *Acta Ap.*, V, 41.

30 I *Cor.*, VIII, 32, 33.

31 *Missale Rom.*, can.

32 I *Petr.*, V, 8.

33 Marc., XIV, 38.

34 *Pontificale Rom.*, In ordin. Diacon.

35 II *Cor.*, XII, 14.

36 *De imit. Christi*, IV, c. 5, v. 13, 14.

37 S. Athanas., *De incarnatione*, n. 12: Minge, P.G., XXVI. 1003s.

38 Cf. S. Aug., *De civitate Dei*; 1. X, c. 6: Minte, P.L., XLI, 284.

39 Cf. *Matth.*, V, 6.

40 *Rom.*, XIII, 14.

41 *Sermo CVIIIs* Minge, P.L., LII, 500, 501.

42 *A.A.S.*, XXXIX, 1947, pp. 552, 553.

43 *Hebr.*, V, 1.

44 *Brev. Rom.*, Hymn. pro. off. Dedic. Eccl.

45 Luc., XVIII, 1.

46 *Hebr.*, XIII, 15.

47 *Ibid.*, V, 7.

48 S. Aug., *Ennar. in Ps. LXXXV*, n. 1: Minge, P.L., XXXVII, 1081.

49 Cf. Litt. Enc. *Mediator Dei: A.A.S.*, XXXIX, 1947, p. 574.

50 Cf. can. 125, 2^0.

51 Cf. *C.I.C.*, can. 125, 2.

52 *C.I.C.*, can. 125, 1^0.

53 Litt. Enc. *Mystici Corporis Christi: A.A.S.*, XXXV, 1943, p. 235.

54   Luc., I, 74, 75.

55   I *Cor.*, IV, 1.

56   Cf. I *Cor.*, X, 33.

57   I *Cor.*, III, 7.

58   I *Petr.*, IV, II.

59   I *Cor.*, IV, 16.

60   Cf. *A.A.S.*, XXXVI, 1944, p. 239; Epist. *Cum proxime exeat.*

61   Cf. *Orat. die* XII mensis sept. a. MCMXXXXVII habitam.

62   Cf. *Philipp.*, IV, 13.

63   II *Cor.*, XII, 15.

64   *Acta Ap.*, X, 38.

65   Ioann., IV, 37.

66   *Matth.*, XVIII, 22.

67   I *Tim.*, VI, 8.

68   Cf. *Matth.*, XIII, 52.

69   Luc., X, 2.

70   Ibidem.

71   Cf. can. 1353.

72   Litt. Enc. *Quod Multum*, ad Episcopos Hungariae, die 22 mensis Augusti a. 1886: *Acta Leonis*, vol. VI, p. 158.

73   Cf. Allocut. d. 25 Novembris a. 1948 habitam: *A.A.S.*, XL, 1948, p. 552.

74   Cf. Orationem die 24 mensis Iunii 1939 habitam: *A.A.S.*, XXXI, 1939, pp. 245-251.

75   Luc., XVI, 3.

76   Cf. *C.I.C.*, can. 1366, 2.

77   Cf. *Matth.*, V, 13, 14.

78   *Hebr.*, X, 7.

79   *Ad Smyranaeos*, VIII, I; Minge, P.G., VIII, 714.

80   *Ibid.*, IX, 714, 715.

81   *Ad Philadelphinses* VII, 2; Minge, P.G., V, 700.

82   Cf. *C.I.C.*, can. 132.

83   Cf. *A.A.S.*, XLI, 1949, pp. 165-167.

84   Cf. *C.I.C.*, can. 134.

85   Can. 129.

86   Can. 130, 1^0.

87   Can. 131, 1^0.

88   Cf. Epistulam Emi Card. Petri Gasparri, a publicis Ecclesiae negotiis, ad Italiae Episcopos datam die 15 mensis Aprilis anno 1923: in *Enchiridion Celicorum*, Typ. Pol. Vat., 1937, p. 613.

89   Luc., XIX, 8.

90   Ioann., XIII, 35.

91   Luc., X, 7.

92   I *Tim.*, IV, 14.

93   *Tit.*, II, 7, 8.

94   *Ephes.*, IV, 23, 24.

95   *Ibid.*, V, 1, 2.

96   *Ibid.*, V, 18, 19.

97   *Ibid.*, VI, 18.

Address of Pope Pius XII to the Cardinals and Bishops on the Role of the Laity, November 2, 1954.

1   Session XXII, chap. 2. *Denzinger*, no. 940.

2   Council of Trent, Session XXII cap. 2. *Denzinger*, no. 940.

3   1 *Pet.* 2:9.

4   1 *Pet.* 2:5.

5   *Mt.* 10:27.

6   *Gal.* 4:2.

7   1 *Cor.* 13:11.

8   *Eph.* 4:13.

9   Encycl. *Ad Beatissimi Apostolorum Principis*.

10   *John* 10:11 and 10.

11   *John* 21:15, 17.

12   Cf. *John* 10:12-13.

13   Cf. *Matt.* 23:1, 4.

14   *Matt.* 11:29-30.

ECCLESIAM SUAM, Selection from Encyclical Letter of Pope Paul VI on the Ways in which the Church Must Carry Out Its Mission in the Contemporary World, August 6, 1964.

36	*Rom.* 12, 2.
37	*Rom.* 6, 3-4.
38	*2 Cor.* 6, 14-15.
39	*Jn.* 17, 15-16.
40	*I Tim.* 6, 20.
41	*Mt.* 28, 19.
42	*Mt.* 13, 52.
43	*Jn.* 3, 17.
44	Cf. *Bar.* 3, 38.
45	*I Jn.* 4, 10.
46	*Jn.* 3, 16.
47	*Lk.* 5, 31.
48	Cf. *Mt.* 11, 21.
49	Cf. *Mt.* 12, 38 ff.
50	Cf. *Mt.* 13, 13 ff.
51	Cf. *Col.* 3, 11.
52	Cf. *Mt.* 13, 31.
53	Cf. *Eph.* 4, 16.
54	*Mt.* 11, 29.
55	Cf. *Mt.* 7, 6.
56	*I Cor.* 9, 22.
57	Cf. *Jn.* 13, 14-17.
58	Cf. *Jer.* 1, 6.
59	Cf. *Rom.* 10, 17.
60	Cf. *Ps.* 18, 5 and *Rom.* 10, 18.
61	*Mark* 1, 3.
62	Cf. N. 54.
63	*Dial. Contra Luciferianos*, N. 9.
64	*Phil.* 2, 8.
65	*I Cor.* 1, 10.

LUMEN GENTIUM, Selections from the Dogmatic Constitution on the Church, November 21, 1964.

1   *Cf. St. Cyprian. "Epist.," 69, 6: PL 3, 1142 B (Hartel, III B, p. 754): "inseparabile unitatis sacramentum" ["the unbreakable sacrament of unity"].*

2   *Cf. Pius XII, allocution "agnificate Dominum," Nov. 2, 1954: AAS 46 (1954), p. 669; Pius XII, encyclical "mediator Dei," Nov. 20, 1947: AAS 39 (1947), p. 555.*

3   *Cf. Pius XI, encyclical "Miserentissimus Redemptor," May 8, 1928: AAS 20 (1928), pp. 171 f.; Pius XII, allocution "Vous nous avez" Sept. 22, 1956: AAS 48 (1956) p. 714.*

4   *Cf. St. Thomas, "Summa Theol.," 3, q. 63, a. 2.*

5   *PG 33, 1009-12; Nic. Cabasilas, "De vita in Christo," bk. III, De utilate chrismatis: PG 150, 569-80; and St. Thomas, "Summa Theol.," 3, q. 65, a. 3 and q. 72, a. 1 and 5.*

6   *Cf. Fius XII, encyclical "Mediator Dei," Nov. 20, 1947: AAS 39 (1947), especially pp. 552 f.*

7   *1 Cor 7:7: "Everyone has his own particular gift ["idion charisma"] from God, some one thing and some another." Cf. St. Augustine, "De dono persev.," 14, 37: PL 45, 1015 f.: "It is not just continence that is a gift of God—so also is the chastity of the married."*

8   *Cf. St. Augustine, "De praed, sanct.," 14, 27: PL 44, 980.*

9   *Cf. St. John Chrysostom, "In Io.," Hom. 65, 1: PG 59, 361.*

10   *Cf. St. Irenaeus, "Adv. haer.," III, 16, 6; III, 22, 1-3: PG 7, 925 C-926 A and 955 C-958 A (Harvey, 2, 87 f. and 120-3; Sagnard, pp. 290-2 and 372 ff.).*

11   *Cf. St. Ignatius of Antioch, "Ad Rom.," Praef.: ed. Funk, I, p. 252.*

12   *Cf. St. Augustine, "Bapt. c. Donat.," V, 28, 39: PL 43, 197: "It is certainly clear that when we speak of 'within' and 'without' with regard to the Church, our consideration must be directed to what is in the heart, not to what is in the body." See also in the same work, III, 19, 26: PL 43, 152; V, 18, 24: PL 43, 189; and the same author's "In Jo.," tr. 61, 2; PL 35, 1800, as well as many texts in other of his works.*

13   *Cf. Lk. 12:48: "Much will be expected from the one who has been given much." Also, Mt. 5:19-20; 7:21-2; 25:41-6; Jas. 2:14.*

14   *Cf. Leo XIII, apostolic epistle "praeclara gratulationis," June 20, 1894: Acta Sanctae Sedis, 26 (1893-4), p. 707.*

15 *Cf. Leo XIII, encyclical "Satis Cognitum," June 29, 1896: Acta Sanctae Sedis, 28 (1895-6), p. 738; Leo XIII, encyclical "Caritatis studium," July 25, 1898; Acta Sanctae Sedis, 31 (1898-9), p. 11; and the radio message of Pius XII, "Nell'abla," Dec. 24, 1941: AAS 34 (1942), p. 21.*

16 *Cf. Pius XI, encyclical "Rerum Orientalium," Sept. 8, 1928: AAS 20 (1928), p. 287; Pius XII, encyclical "Orientalis Ecclesiae," Apr. 9. 1944: AAS 36 (1944), p. 137.*

17 *Cf. instruction of the Holy Office, Dec. 20, 1949: AAS 42 (1950), p. 142.*

18 *Cf. St. Thomas, "Summa Theol.," 3, q. 8, a. 3, ad 1.*

19 *Cf. letter of the holy Office to the Archbishop of Boston: Denz. 3869-72.*

20 *Cf. Eusebius of Caesarea, "Praeparatio evangelica," 1, 1: PG 21, 28 AB.*

21 *Cf. Benedict XV, apostolic epistle "maximum illud": AAS 11 (1919), p. 440 and especially pp. 451 ff.; Pius XI, encyclical "Rerum Ecclesiae": AAS 18 (1926), pp. 68-70; Pius XII, encyclical "fidei donum," Apr. 21, 1957: AAS 49 (1957), pp. 236-7.*

22 *Cf. the "Didache," 14: ed. Funk, I, p. 32; St. Justin, "Dial.," 41: PG 6, 564; St. Irenaeus, "Adv. haer.," IV, 17, 5: PG 7, 1023 (Harvey, 2, pp. 199f.); and the Council of Trent, Session 22, Chap. 1: Denz. 939 (1742).*

23 *Cf. Vatican Council I, Session 4, the dogmatic constitution "Pastor aeternus": Denz. 1821 (3050 f.).*

24 *Cf. the Council of Florence, "Decretum pro Graecis": Denz. 694 (1307); and Vatican Council I as cited in the preceding footnote: Denz. 1826 (3059).*

25 *Cf. St. Gregory, "Liber sacramentorum," Praef. in natali S. Matthiae et S. Thomae: PL 78, 51 and 152—compare Cod, Vat. lat. 3548, f. 18; St. Hilary, "In Ps.," 67, 10: PL 9, 450 (CSEL, 22, p. 286); St. Jerome, "Adv.Iovin.," 1, 26: PL 23, 247 A; St. Augustine, "In Ps.," 86, 4: PL 37, 1103; St. Gregory the Great, "Mor. in Iob," XXVIII, V: PL 76, 455-6; Primasius, "Comm. in Apoc.," V: PL 68, 924 BC; and Paschasius Radbertus, "In Matth.," Bk. VIII, c. 16: PL 120, 561 C. Also, Leo XIII, epistle "Et sane," Dec. 17, 1888: Acta Sanctae Sedis 21 (1888), 321.*

26 *Cf. Acts 6:2-6; 11:30; 13:1; 14:23; 20:17; 1 Th. 5:12; Phil. 1:1; Col. 4:11 and passim.*

27 *Cf. Acts 20:25-7; 2 Tim. 4:6 f., taken together with 1 Tim. 5:22; 2 Tim. 2:2; Tit. 1:5; and St. Clement of Rome, "Ad Cor.," 44, 3 ed. Funk, I p. 156.*

28   St. Clement of Rome, "Ad Cor.," 44, 2: ed. Funk, I, pp 154 f.

29   Tertullian, "Praescr. haer.," 32: PL 52 f.; and St. Ignatius of Antioch, passim.

30   Cf. Tertullian, "Praescr. haer.," 32: PL 2, 53.

31   Cf. St. Irenaeus, "adv. Haer.," III, 3,1; PG 7, 848 A (Harvey 2, 8; Sagnard, pp. 100 f.); "manifestatam" ["having been made manifest"].

32   Cf. Irenaeus, "Adv. Haer.," III, 2, 2: PG 7, 848 (Harvey, 2, 7; Sagnard, p. 100); "custoditur" ["is guarded"]. And see also St. Irenaeus, "Adv. haer.," IV, 26, 2: PG 7, 1053 (Harvey, 2, 236); IV, 33, 8: PG 7, 1077 (Harvey, 2, 262).

33   St. Ignatius of Antioch, "Ad Philad.," Praef.: ed. Funk, I, p. 264.

34   Funk, I, pp. 264 and 234.

35   St. Clement of Rome, "Ad Cor.," 43, 3-4; 57, 1-2: ed. Funk, I, 152, 156, 171 f.; St. Ignatius of Antioch, "Ad Philad.," 2; "Ad Smyrn.," 8: "Ad Magn.," 3; "Ad Trall.," 7: ed. Funk, I, pp. 265 f., 282, 232, 246 f. etc.; St. Justin, "apol.," 1, 65: PG 6, 428; and St. Cyprian, "Epist.," passim.

36   Cf. Leo XIII, encyclical "Satis Cognitum," June 29, 1896: Acta Sanctae Sedis 28 (1895-6), p. 732.

37   Cf. the Council of Trent, Session 23, the decree "De sacr. Ordinis," c. 4: Denz. 960 (1768); Vatican Council I, Session 4, the first dogmatic constitution "De Ecclesia Christi," c. 3: Denz. 1828 (3061); Pius XII, encyclical "Mystici Corporis," June 29, 1943: AAS 35 (1943), pp. 209 and 212; and the Code of Canon Law, c. 329, 1.

38   Cf. Leo XIII, epistle "Et sane," Dec. 17, 1888; Acta Sanctae Sedis 21 (1888), pp. 321 f.

39   Having completed its discussion of the relationship between bishops and the apostles, the Constitution turns to the nature of the episcopacy.

40   St. Leo the Great, "Serm.," 5, 3: PL 54, 154.

41   The Council of Trent, Session 23, c. 3, cites the words of 2 Tim. 1:6-7 to show that order is a true sacrament: Denz., 959 (1766).

42   In the "Apostolic Tradition," 3, ed. Botte, "Sources Chr.," pp. 27-30, there is attributed to the bishop "primatus sacerdotii" ["primacy of priesthood"]. See the "Sacramentarium Leonianum," ed. C. Mohlberg, "Sacramentarium Vernonense" (Rome, 1955), p. 119: ". . .ad summi sacerdotii ministerium. . . . Comple in sacerdotibus tuis mysterii tui summam . . ." [". . . to the ministry of the high priest . . . Fill up in Your priests the highest point of Your mystery . . ."]; and the same

editor's "Liber Sacramentorum Romanae Ecclesiae" (Rome, 1960), pp. 121-2: "Tribuas eis, Domine, cathedram episcopalem and regendam Ecclesiam tuam et plebem universam" people"]. See PL 78, 224.

43   "Apostolic Tradition," 2: ed. Botte, p. 27.

44   The Council of Trent, Session 23, c. 4, teaches that the sacrament of order imprints an indelible character: Denz. 960 (1767). See the allocution of John XXIII, "Jubilate Deo," May 8, 1960: AAS 52 (1960), p. 466; and the homily of Paul VI in St. Peter's Basilica, Oct. 20, 1963: AAS 55 (1963), p. 1014.

45   St. Cyprian, "Epist.," 63, 14: PL 4, 386 Hartel, IIIB, p. 713): "Sacerdos vice Christi vere fungitur" ["The priest truly acts in the place of Christi"]; St. John Chrysostom, "In 2 Tim.," Hom. 2, 4: PG 62, 612: The priest is the "symbolon" of Christ; St. Ambrose, "In Ps.," 38, 25-6: PL 14, 1051-2 (CSEL, 64, 203-4); Ambrosiaster, "In 1 Tim.," 5, 19: PL 17, 479 C and "In Eph.," 4, 11-2: PL 17, 387C; Theodore of Mopsuestia, "Hom. Catech.," XV, 21 and 24: ed. Tonneau, pp. 497 and 503; and Hesychius of Jerusalem, "In Lev.," 2, 9, 23: PG 93, 894 B.

46   Cf. Eusebius of Caesarea, "Hist. Eccl.," V, 24, 10: GCS 11, 1, p. 495 (ed. Bardy, "Sources chr.," II, p. 69); and Dionysius as given in Eusebius of Caesarea, "Hist. Eccl.," VII, 5, 2: GCS II, pp. 638 f. (ed. Bardy, II, pp. 168 f.).

47   For the ancient Councils, cf. Eusebius of Caesarea, "Hist. Eccl.," V, 23-4: GCS II, 1, pp. 488 ff. (ed. Bardy, II, p. 66 ff.) and passim, Council of Nicaea, can. 5: "Conc. Oec. Decr.," p. 7.

48   Tertullian, "De ieiunio," 13: PL 2, 972 B (CSEL, 20, p. 292, lines 13-6).

49   St. Cyprian, "Epist.," 56, 3: Hartel, III B. p. 650 (ed. Bayard, p. 154).

50   Cf. official "Relatio" of Zinelli during Vatican Council I: Mansi, 52, 1109 C.

51   Cf. Vatican Council I, schema for the second dogmatic constitution "De Ecclesia Christi," c. 4: Mansi, 53, 310. See also the "Relatio" of Kleutgen on the revised schema: Mansi, 53, 321 B-322 B; and the statement by Zinelli: Mansi, 52, 1110 A. And see, too, St. Leo the Great, "Serm.," 4, 3: PL 54, 151 A.

52   Cf. Code of Canon Law, c. 227.

53   Cf. Vatican Council 1, the dogmatic constitution "Pastor aeternus": Denz. 1821 (3050 f.).

54   Cf. St. Cyprian, "Epist.," 66, 8: Hartel, III B, p. 733: "Episcopus in Ecclesia et Ecclesia in episcopo" ["The bishop is in the Church and the Church in the bishop"].

55   *Cf. St. Cyprian, "Epist.," 55:24: Hartel, III B, p. 642, line 13: "Una Ecclesia per totum mundum in multa membra divisa" ["The one Church divided throughout the entire world into many members"]; and "Epist.," 36, 4: Hartel, III B, p. 575, lines 20-1.*

56   *Cf. Pius XII, encyclical "Fidei donum," Apr. 21, 1957: AAS 49 (1957) p. 237.*

57   *Cf. St. Hilary of Poitiers, "In Ps.," 14, 3 PL 9, 206 (CSEL 22, p. 86); St. Gregory the Great, "Moral," IV, 7, 12: PL 75, 643; and pseudo-Basil, "In Is.," 15, 296: PG 30, 637 C.*

58   *St. Celestine, "Epist.," 18, 1-2 to the Covncil of Ephesus: PL 50, 505 AB (Schwartz, "Acta Conc. Oec.," I, 1, 1, p. 22). Cf. Benedict XV, apostolic epistle "Maximum illud": AAS 11 (1919), p. 440; Pius IX, encyclical "Rerum Ecclesiae," Feb, 28, 1926: AAS 18, (1926), p. 69; Pius XII, encyclical "Fidei Donum," April 21, 1957: AAS 49 (1957), p. 237.*

59   *Cf. Leo XIII, encyclical "Grande Munus," Sept, 30, 1880: AAS 13 (1880), p. 145. Cf. Code of Canon Law, c. 1327; c. 1350, §2.*

60   *On the rights of patriarchal sees, see the Council of Nicaea, canon 6 on Alexandria and Antioch, canon 7 on Jerusalem: "Conc. Oec. Decr.," p. 8; Lateran Council IV in the year 1215, Constitution V: "De dignitate Patriarcharum": "Conc. Oec. Decr.," p. 212; and the Council of Ferrara-Florence: "Conc. Oec. Decr., "p. 504.*

61   *Cf. Code of Law for Eastern Churches cc. 216-314: on Patriarchs; cc. 324-39: on major archbishops; cc. 362-91: on other dignitaries; and in particular, cc. 238, §3; 216; 240; 251; 255: on the naming of bishops by a Patriarch.*

62   *Cf. Council of Trent, Decree on reform, Session 5, c. 2, n. 9; and Session 24, c. 4: "Conc. Oec. Decr.," pp. 645 and 739.*

63   *Cf. Vatican Council I, the dogmatic constitution "Dei Filius," 3: Denz. 1712 (3011). Cf. note (taken from St. Robert Bellarmine) adjoined to Schema second constitution "De Ecclesia Christi" with the commentary of Kleutgen: Mansi, 53, 313 AB. Cf. Pius IX, epistle, "Tuas libenter": Denz. 1683 (2879).*

64   *Cf. Code of Canon Law, cc. 1322-3.*

65   *Cf. Vatican Council I, the odgmatic constitution "Pastor aeternus": Denz. 1839 (3074).*

66   *Cf. explanation of Gasser at Vatican Council I: Mansi, 52, 1213 AC.*

67   *Gasser, Vatican Council I: Mansi, 52, 1214 A.*

68   *Gasser, Vatican Council I: Mansi, 52, 1215 CD, 1216-7 A.*

69   *Gasser, Vatican Council I, Mansi, 52, 1213.*

70   *Vatican Council I, the dogmatic constitution "Pastor aternus,"
4: Denz. 1836 (3070).*

71   *Prayer of episcopal consecration in the Byzantine rite: "Euchol-
ogion to mega" (Rome, 1873), p. 139.*

72   *Cf. St. Ignatius of Antioch, "Ad Smyrn.," 8, 1: ed. Funk, I,
p. 282.*

73   *Cf. Acts 8:1; 15:22-3; 20:17; and passim.*

74   *Mozarabic prayer: PL 96, 759 B.*

75   *Cf. St. Ignatius of Antioch, "Ad Smyrn.," 8, 1: ed. Funk, I,
p. 282.*

76   *Cf. St. Thomas, "Summa Theol.," 3, q. 73, a. 3.*

77   *Cf. St. Augustine, "C. Faustum," 12, 20: PL 42, 265; "Serm.,"
57, 7: PL 38, 389; and elsewhere.*

78   *St. Leo the Great, "Serm.," 63, 7: PL 54, 357 C.*

79   *The "Apostolic Tradition" of Hippolytus, 2-3: ed. Botte, pp. 26-
30.*

80   *Cf. text of the "Examen" at the beginning of the consecration
of a bishop and the Prayer at the end of the Mass of the same consecration after the Te Deum.*

81   *Benedict XIV, brief, "Romana Ecclesia," Oct. 5, 1752, §1:
"Bullarium Benedicti XIV," t. IV (Rome, 1758), 21: "Episcopus
Christi typum gerit, Eiusque munere fungitur" ["The bishop is an
image of Christ and performs His work"]; and Pius XII, encyclical
"Mystici Corporis," June 29, 1943: AAS 35 (1943), p. 211: "Assignatos
sibi greges singuli singulos Christi nomine pascunt et regunt" ["In the
name of Christ each one takes care of and rules the individudal flock assigned to him"].*

82   *Leo XII, encyclical "Satis cognitum," June 29, 1896: Acta
Sanctae Sedis 28 (1895-6), p. 732; the same Pontiff's epistle "Officio
sanctissimo," Dec. 22, 1887: Acta Sanctae Sedis 20 (1887), p. 264;
Pius IX, apostolic letter to the bishops of Germany, Mar. 12, 1875,
and his consistorial allocution of Mar. 15, 1875: Denz. 3112-7 (only
in the new edition).*

83   *Vatican Council I, the dogmatic constitution "Pastor aeternus,"
3: Denz. 1828 (3061), Cf. "Relatio" of Zinelli: Mansi, 52, 1114D.*

84   *Cf. St. Ignatius of Antioch, "Ad Ephes.," 5, 1: ed. Funk, 1, p.
216.*

85   *Cf. St. Ignatius of Antioch, "Ad Ephes.," 6, 1: ed. Funk, 1, p.
218.*

86 *Cf. Council of Trent, Session 23, "De sacr. Ordinis," c. 2: Denz. 958 (1765); and c. 6: Denz. 966 (1776).*

87 *Cf. Innocent I, "Epist. ad Decentium": PL 20, 554 A (Mansi, 3, 1029; Denz. 98 [215]: "Presbyteri, licet secundi sint sacerdotes, pontificatus tamen apicem non habent" ["The presbyters, though they are priests of the second grade, do not possess the crown of being pontiffs"]); and St. Cyprian, "Epist.," 61, 3: ed. Hartel, III B, p. 696.*

88 *Cf. Council of Trent as citied in footnote 86, Denz. 956a-968 (1763-78) and in particular c. 7: Denz. 967 (1777); and the apostolic constitution of Pius XII, "Sacramentum Ordinis": Denz. 2301 (3857-61).*

89 *Cf. Innocent I as cited in footnote 87; St. Gregory Nazianzen, "Apoi.," II, 22: PG 35, 432 B; and pseudo-Dionysius, "Eccl. Hier.," 1, 2: PG 3 372B.*

90 *Cf. Council of Trent, Session 22: Denz. 940 (1743) and Pius XII, encyclical "Mediator Dei," Nov. 20, 1947. AAS 39 (1947 p. 553 (Denz. 2300 [3850]).*

91 *Cf. Council of Trent, Session 22: Denz. 938 (1739-40); and Vatican Council II, "Constitution on the Sacred Liturgy," Art. 7 and 47.*

92 *Cf. Pius XII, encyclical "Mediator Dei," as cited in footnote 90.*

93 *Cf. St. Cyprian, "Epist.," 11, 3: PL 4, 242 B (Hartel, III B, p. 497).*

94 *Ceremony of priestly ordination, at the imposition of the vestments.*

95 *Ceremony of priestly ordination, the Preface.*

96 *Cf. St. Ignatius of Antioch, "Ad Philad.," 4: ed. Funk, 1, p. 266; and St. Cornelius I as given in St. Cyprian, "Epist.," 48, 2: Hartel, III B, p. 610.*

97 *"Constitutiones Ecclesiae aegyptiacae," III, 2: ed. Funk, "Didiascalia," II, p. 103; and "Statuta Ecclesiae antiquae," 37-41: Mansi, 3, 954.*

98 *St. Polycarp, "Ad Phil.," 5, 2: ed. Funk, I, p. 300: Christ is said "to have become the deacon of all." See "Didache," 15, 1: ed. Funk, I, p. 32; St. Ignatius of Antioch, "Ad Trall.," 2, 3: ed. Funk, I, p. 242; and "Constitutiones Apostolorum," 8, 28, 4: ed. Funk, "Didascalia," I, p. 530.*

99 *St. Augustine, "Serm.," 340, 1: PL 38, 1483.*

100   *Cf. Pius XI, encyclical "Quadragesimo anno," May 15, 1931: AAS 23 (1931), pp. 221 f.; and the allocution of Pius XII, "De quelle consolation," Oct. 14, 1951: AAS 43 (1951), pp. 790 f.*

101   *Cf. Pius XII, allocution "Six ans se sont ecoules," Oct. 5, 1957: AAS 49 (1957), p. 927.*

102   *From the Preface of the Feast of Christ the King.*

103   *Cf. Leo XIII, encyclical "Immortale Dei," Nov. 1, 1885: Acta Sanctae Sedis 18 (1885), pp. 166 ff.; the same Pontiff's encyclical "Sapientiae Christianae," Jan. 10, 1890: Acta Sanctae Sedis 22 (1889-90), pp. 397 ff.; and the allocution of Pius XII, "Alla vostra filiale," March 23, 1958: AAS 50 (1958), p. 220: "La legittima sana laicita dello Stato" ["the legitimate and healthy laicity of the State"].*

104   *Code of Canon Law, c. 682.*

105   *Cf. Pius XII, allocution "De quelle consolation": AAS 43 (1951), p. 789: "Dans les batailles decisives, c'est parfois du front que partent les plus heureuses initiatives . . ." ("In the case of decisive battles, it happens at times that the best initiatives come from the front-line"); and the same Pontiff's allocution "L'importance de la presse catholique," Feb. 17, 1950: AAS 42 (1950), p. 256.*

106   *Cf. 1 Th. 5:19 and 1 Jn 4:1.*

107   *"Epist. ad Diognetum," 6:ed. Funk, I, p. 400. Cf. St. John Chrsostom, "In Matth.," Hom. 46(47), 2: PG 58, 478, on the leaven in the dough.*

108   *Roman Missal, the Gloria in Excelsis. Cf. LK. 1:35; Mk. 1:24; Lk. 4:34; Jn. 6:69 (ho hagios tou theou [the holy one of God]), Acts 3:14, 4:27 and 30; Heb. 7:26; 1 Jn. 2:20; Apoc. 3:7.*

109   *"De oratione," 11: PG 34, 861 AB; and St. Thomas 'Summa Theol.," 2-2, q. 184, a. 3.*

110   *Cf. St. Augustine, "Retract.," II, 18: PL 32 637 f.; and the encyclical of Pius XII, "Mystici Corporis," June 29, 1943: AAS 35 (1943), p. 225.*

111   *Cf. Pius XI, encyclical "Rerum omnium," Jan. 26, 1923: AAS 15 (1923), pp. 50 and 59-60; Pius XI, encyclical "casti connubii," Dec. 31, 1930: AAS 22 (1930), p. 548; the apostolic constitution of Pius XII, "Provida Mater," Feb. 2, 1947: AAS 39 (1947), p. 177; the same Pontiff's allocution "Annus sacer," Dec. 8, 1950: AAS 43 (1951), pp. 27-8; and his allocation, "Nel darvi," July 2, 1956: AAS 48 (1956), pp. 574 f.*

112   *Cf. St. Thomas, "Summa Theol.," 2-2, q. 184, aa. 5 and 6; the same author's "De perf. vitae spir.," c. 18; and Origen, "In Is.," Hom 6, 1: PG 13, 239.*

113   *Cf. St. Ignatius of Antioch, "Ad Magn.," 13, 1: ed. Frank, 1, p. 241.*

114   *Cf. St. Pius X, exhortation "Haerent animo," Aug. 4, 1908: Acta Sanctae Sedis 41 (1908), pp. 560 f.; Code of Canon Law, c. 124; and Pius XI, encyclical "Ad catholici sacerdotii," Dec. 20, 1935: AAS 28 (1936), pp. 22 f.*

115   *Ceremony of priestly ordination, the initial exhortation.*

116   *Cf. St. Ignatius of Antioch, "Ad Trall.," 2, 3: ed. Funk I, p. 244.*

117   *Cf. Pius XII, allocution "Sous la maternelle protection," Dec. 9, 1957: AAS 50 (1958), p. 36.*

118   *Pius XI, encyclical "Casti connubii," Dec. 31, 1930: AAS 22 (130), pp. 548 f. Cf. St. John Chrysostom, "In Ephes.," Hom. 20, 2: PG 62, 136 ff.*

119   *Cf. St. Augustine, "Enchir.," 121, 32: PL 40, 288; St. Thomas, "Summa Theol.," 2-2, q. 184, a. 1; and the apostolic exhortation of Pius XII, "Menti nostrae," Sept. 23, 1950: AAS 42 (1950), p. 660.*

120   *On the counsels in general, see Origen, "Comm. in Rom.," X, 14: PG 14, 1275 B; St. Augustine, "De si virginitate," 15, 15: PL 40, 403; and St. Thomas, "Summa Theol.," 1-2, q. 100, a. 2 c at the end and 2-2, q. 44, a. 4, ad 3.*

121   *On the excellence of holy virginity, see Tertullian, "Exhort. cast.," 10: PL 2, 925 C; St. Cyprian, "Hab. virg.," 3 and 22: PL 4, 443 B and 461 A j.; St. Athanasius (?), "De virg.,"; PG 28, 252 ff.; and St. John Chrysostom, "De virg.," PG 48, 553 ff.*

122   *On spiritual poverty, Cf. Mt. 5:3 and 19-21; Mk. 10:21; Lk. 18: 22; with regard to obedience, the example of Christ is given: Jn. 4:34; 6:38; Phil. 2:8-10; Heb. 10:5-7. The Fathers and the founders of orders have much to say about these matters.*

123   *On the effective practice of the counsels which is not imposed on all, see St. John Chrysostom, "In Matth.," Hom. 7, 7: PG 57, 81 j.; and St. Ambrose, "De viduis," 4, 23: PL 16, 241 f.*

124   *Cf. H. Rosweyde, "Vitae patrum" (Antwerp, 1628); "Apophthegmata patrum": PG 65; Palladius, "Historia lausiaca": PG 34, 995 ff. (ed. C. Butler, Cambridge, 1898 [1904]); the apostolic constitution of Pius XI, "Umbratilem," July 8, 1924: AAS 16 (1924), pp. 386-7; and Pius XII, allocution "Nous sommes heureux," Apr. 11, 1958; AAS 50 (1958), p. 283.*

125   *Paul VI, allocution "Magno Gaudio," May 23, 1964: AAS 56 (1964), p. 566.*

126   *Cf. Code of Canon Law, cc. 487 and 488, 4; Pius XII, allocution apostolic constitution "Provida Mater," Feb. 2, 1947: AAS 39 (1947), pp. 120 ff.*

127   *Paul VI, as cited in footnote 210, p. 567.*

128   *Cf. St. Thomas, "Summa Theol.," 2-2, q. 184, a. 3 and q. 188, a. 2; and St. Bonaventure, Opusc. XI, "Apologia pauperum," c. 3, 3: ed. Opera, Quaracchi, t. 8, 1898, p. 245 a.*

129   *Cf. Vatican Council I, Schema "De Ecclesia Christi," c. XV and Annotation 48: Mansi, 51, 549 f. and 619 f.; Leo XIII, epistle "Au milieu des consolations," Dec. 23, 1900: Acta Sanctae Sedis 33 (1900-1), p. 361; and Pius XII, apostolic constitution "Provida Mater," as cited in footnote 211, pp. 114 f.*

130   *Cf. Leo XIII, constitution "Romanos Pontifices," May 8, 1881: Acta Sanctae Sedis 13 (1880-1), p. 483; and Pius XII, allocution "Annus Sacer," Dec. 8, 1950: AAS 43 (1951), pp. 28 f.*

131   *Pius XII, allocution "Annus Sacer," as cited in the preceding footnote, p. 28; the same Pontiff's apostolic constitution "Sedes Sapientiae," May 31, 1956: AAS 48 (1956), p. 355; and the allocution of Paul VI, as cited in footnote 125, pp. 570-1.*

132   *Cf. Pius XII, encyclical "Mystici Corporis," June 29, 1943: AAS 35 (1943), pp. 214 f.*

133   *Cf. Pius XII, allocution "Annus Sacer," as cited in footnote 130, p. 30;*

Vatican II, CHRISTUS DOMINUS, Decree on the Bishops' Pastoral Office in the Church, October 28, 1965

1   *Cf. Mt. 1:21.*

2   *Cf. Jn. 20:21.*

3   *Cf. First Vatican Council, fourth session, part 1 of Dogmatic Constitution on the Church of Christ, c. 3, Denz. 1828 (306).*

4   *First Vatican Council, fourth session, Introduction to Dogmatic Constitution on the Church of Christ, Denz. 1821 (3050).*

5   *Cf. Second Vatican Council, Dogmatic Constitution on the Church, Chap. 3, Art. 21, 24, and 25: AAS 57 (1965) pp. 24-25, 29-31.*

6   *Cf. Second Vatican Council, Dogmatic Constitution on the Church, Chap 3, Art. 21: AAS 57 (1965), pp. 24-25.*

7   *Cf. John XXIII, apostolic constitution "Humanae Salutis," Dec. 25, 1961: AAS 54 (1962), p. 6.*

8   *Cf. Second Vatican Council, Dogmatic Constitution on the Church, Chap. 3, Art. 22: AAS 57 (1965), pp. 25-27.*

9   *Ibid.*

10 *Ibid.*

11 *Ibid.*

12 *Cf. Paul VI, motu proprio "Apostolica Sollicitudo," Sept. 15, 1965.*

13 *Cf. Second Vatican Council, Dogmatic Constitution on the Church, Chap.3, Art. 23: AAS 57 (1965), pp. 27-28.*

14 *Cf. Pius XII, encyclical letter "Fidei Donum," Apr. 21, 1957; AAS 49 (1957), p. 27 ff.; also, cf. Benedict XV, apostolic letter "Maximum Illud," Nov. 30, 1919; AAS 11 (1919), p. 440; Pius XI, encyclical letter "Rerum Ecclesiae," Feb. 28, 1926; AAS 18 (1926), p. 68.*

15 *Cf. AAS 18 (1926); 49 (1957); 11 (1919).*

16 *Cf. Paul VI, allocution to the cardinals, prelates, and various officials of the Roman Curia, Sept. 21, 1963: AAS 55 (1963), p. 793 ff.*

17 *Cf. Second Vatican Council, Decree on Eastern Catholic Churches, Nov. 21, 1964, Art. 7-11: AAS 57 (1965), pp. 29 ff.*

18 *Cf. Council of Trent, fifth session, Decree "De Reform.," c. 2, Mansi 33, 30: 24th session, Decree "De Reform.," c. Mansi 33, 159 (cf. Second Vatican Council, Dogmatic Constitution on the Church, Chap. 3, Art. 25: AAS 57 (1965), p. 29 ff.*

19 *Cf. Second Vatican Council, Dogmatic Constitution on the Church, Chap. 3, Art. 25: AAS 57 (1965), pp. 29-31.*

20 *Cf. John XXIII, encyclical letter "Pacem in Terris," Apr. 11, 1963, passim: AAS 55 (1965), pp. 257-304.*

21 *Cf. Paul VI, encyclical letter "Ecclesiam Suam," Aug. 6, 1964: AAS 56 (1964), p. 639.*

22 *Cf. Paul VI, encyclical letter "Ecclesiam Suam," Aug. 6, 1964: AAS 56 (1964), pp. 644-645.*

23 *Cf. Second Vatican Council, Decree on the Instruments of Social Communication, Dec. 4, 1963: AAS 56 (1964), pp. 145-153.*

24 *Cf. Second Vatican Council, Constitution on the Sacred Liturgy, Dec. 4, 1963: AAS 56 (1964), p. 97 ff.; Paul VI, motu proprio "Sacram Liturgiam," Jan. 25, 1964: AAS 56 (1964), p. 139 ff.*

25 *Cf. Pius XII, encyclical letter "Mediator Dei," Nov. 20, 1947; AAS 39 (1947), p. 97 ff.: Paul VI, encyclical letter "Mysterium Fidei," Sept. 3, 1965.*

26 *Cf. Acts 1:14 and 2:46.*

27 *Cf. Second Vatican Council; Dogmatic Constitution on the Church, Chap. 6, Art. 44 and 45: AAS 57 (1965), pp. 50-52.*

28 *Cf. Lk. 22:26-27.*

29   *Cf. Jn. 15:15.*

30   *Cf. Second Vatican Council, Decree on Ecumenism, Nov. 21, 1964; AAS 57 (1965), pp. 90-107.*

31   *Cf. AAS 54 (1952); 50 (1958).*

32   *Cf. St. Pius X, motu proprio "Iampridem," Mar. 19, 1914; AAS 6 (1914), p. 174 ff.; Pius XII, apostolic constitution "Exsul Familia," Aug. 1, 1952: AAS 54 (1952), p. 652 ff.; "Leges Operis Apostolatus Maris," compiled under the authority of Pius XII, Nov. 21, 1957: AAS 50 (1958), p. 375 ff.*

33   *Cf. Second Vatican Council, Decree on Eastern Catholic Churches, Nov. 21, 1964, Art. 4: AAS 57 (1965), p. 77.*

34   *Cf. Jn. 13:35.*

35   *Cf. CIC, can. 459.*

36   *Cf. Pius XII, allocution of Dec. 8, 1950: AAS 43 (1951), p. 28; cf. also Paul VI, allocution of May 23, 1964: AAS 56 (1964), p. 571.*

37   *Cf. Leo XIII, apostolic constitution "Romanos Pontifices," May 8, 1881; Acta Leonis XIII, vol. 2, 1882, p. 234.*

38   *Cf. Paul VI, allocution of May 23, 1964: AAS 56 (1965), pp. 570-571.*

39   *Cf. Pius XII, allocution of Dec. 8, 1950, loc. cit.*

40   *Cf. Sacred Consistorial Congregation's Instruction to Military Ordinariates, Apr. 23, 1951: AAS 43 (1951), pp. 562-565; Formula Regarding the Conferring of the Status of Military Ordinariates, Oct. 20, 1956: AAS 49 (1957), pp. 150-163; Decree on Ad Limina Visits of Military Ordinariates, Feb. 28, 1959; AAS 51 (1959), pp. 272-274; Decree on the Granting of Faculties for Confessions to Military Chaplains, Nov. 27, 1960: AAS 53 (1961), pp. 49-50. Also cf. Congregation of Religious' Instruction on Religious Military Chaplains, Feb. 2, 1955: AAS 47 (1955), pp. 93-97.*

41   *Cf. Sacred Consistorial Congregation, letter to the cardinals, archbishops, and bishops of Spanish-speaking nations, June 27, 1951: AAS 43 (1951), p. 566.*

Vatican II, OPTATAM TOTIUS ECCLESIA, Decree on Training for the Priesthood, October 28, 1965.

1   The fact that progress among all the people of God depends primarily on the will of Christ Himself and the ministry of priests, is clear from the words by which the Lord constituted His Apostles and their successors and cooperators, as heralds of the Gospel, leaders of the

new chosen people and dispensers of the mysteries of God; it is likewise confirmed by the utterances of the Fathers and saints and repeatedly in documents of the Supreme Pontiffs. Cf. especially: St. Pius X, Exhortation to the clergy *Haerent Animo*, Aug. 4, 1908: *S. Pii X Acta IV*, pp. 237-264. Pius XI, Encycl. letter *Ad Catholici Sacerdotii*, Dec. 20, 1935: *AAS* 28 (1936), especially pp. 37-52. Pius XII, Apost. exhortation *Menti Nostrae*, Sept. 23, 1950: *AAS* 42 (1950), pp. 657-702. John XXIII, Encyc. letter *Sacerdotii Nostri Primordia*, Aug. 1, 1959: *AAS* 51 (1959), pp. 545-579. Paul VI, Apost. letter *Summi Dei Verbum*, Nov. 4, 1963: *AAS* 55 (1963), pp. 979-995.

2   The whole training for priesthood—that is, regulation of the seminary, spiritual training, the course of studies, the common life and discipline of the students, practical pastoral training—are all to be acommodated to local circumstances. This accommodation is, as far as main principles are concerned, to be carried out in accordance with common norms set down by the episcopal conferences as far as secular priests are concerned, and in a suitable way by competent superiors in the case of the Religious clergy (cf. General Statutes attached to the apostolic constitution *Sedes Sapientiae*, article 19).

3   Among the main afflictions troubling the Church today, the shortage of vocations stands out almost everywhere. Cf. Pius XII, Apost. exhortation *Menti Nostrae*: ". . . the number of priests both in Catholic regions and mission territories is in most cases insufficient to the growing needs" (*AAS* 42 (1950), p. 682). John XXIII: "The problem of vocations to the priesthood and the religious life is a daily preoccupation of the Pope. . . . It is the object of yearning in his prayer, the ardent desire of his soul" (from his allocution to the First International Congress on Vocations to the States of Perfection, Dec. 16, 1961: *L'Osservatore Romano*, Dec. 17, 1961).

4   Pius XII, Apost. constitution *Sedes Sapientiae*, May 31, 1956: *AAS* 48 (1956), p. 357; Paul VI, Apost. letter *Summi Dei Verbum*, Nov. 4, 1963: *AAS* 55 (1963), pp. 984 ff.

5   Cf. especially: Pius XII, Motu proprio *Cum Nobis* "Concerning the establishment of the Pontifical Society for Priestly Vocations under the direction of the Sacred Congregation of Seminaries and Universities," Nov. 4, 1941: *AAS* 33 (1941), p. 479; with the related norms and statutes promulgated Sept. 8, 1943, by the same Sacred Congregation; Motu proprio *Cum Supremae* "Concerning the Pontifical Society for Religious Vocations," Feb. 11, 1955: *AAS* 47 (1955), p. 266; with the related norms and statutes promulgated by the Sacred Congregation of Religious (*ibid.*, pp. 298-301). Second Vatican Council, *Decree on the Renovation of the Religious Life*, no. 24; *Decree on the Pastoral Duties of Bishops in the Church*, no. 15.

6   Cf. Pius XII, Apost. exhortation *Menti Nostrae*, Sept. 23, 1950: *AAS* 42 (1950), p. 685.

7   Cf. Second Vatican Council, *Dogmatic Constitution on the Church*, no. 28: *AAS* 57 (1965), p. 34.

8   Cf. Pius XI, Encyc. letter *Ad Catholici Sacerdotii*, Dec. 20, 1935: *AAS* 28 (1936), p. 37: "The selection of moderators and teachers should be especially careful. . . . Assign priests endowed with the highest virtue to sacred colleges of this kind; and do not be upset over taking them from other offices, for even those of great importance cannot be compared with this matter of capital importance, whose place no other can take." This principle of selecting the best is again inculcated by Pius XII in his apostolic letter to the Ordinaries of Brazil of April 23, 1947, *Discorsi e Radiomessaggi* IX, pp. 579-580.

9   Concerning the common duty of supporting zealously the work in seminaries, cf. Paul VI, Apost. letter *Summi Dei Verbum*, Nov. 4, 1963: *AAS* 53 (1963), p. 984.

10   Cf. Pius XII, Apost. exhortation *Menti Nostrae*, Sept. 23, 1950: *AAS* 42 (1950), p. 684; and cf. Sacred Congregation of the Sacraments, Circular letter *Magna Equidem* to local Ordinaries, Dec. 27, 1935, no.
10.   For Religious, cf. General Statutes attached to the apostolic constitution *Sedes Sapientiae* of May 31, 1956, art. 33. Paul VI, Apost. letter *Summi Dei Verbum*, Nov. 4, 1963: *AAS* 55 (1963), p. 987 ff.

11   Cf. Pius XI, Encyc. letter *Ad Catholici Sacerdotii*, Dec. 20, 1935: *AAS* 28 (1936), p. 41.

12   It is established by statute that in drawing up the regulation for regional or national seminaries all the bishops concerned are to take part, despite the prescription of Canon 1357, part 4 of the Code of Canon Law.

13   Cf. Pius XII, Apost. exhortation *Menti Nostrae*, Sept. 23, 1950: *AAS* 42 (1950), p. 674; Sacred Congregation of Seminaries and Universities, *The Spiritual Formation of the Candidate for the Priesthood*, Vatican City, 1965.

14   Cf. St. Pius X, Exhortation to the clergy *Haerent Animo*, Aug. 4, 1908: *S. Pii X Acta IV*, pp. 242-244; Pius XII Apost. exhortation *Menti Nostrae*, Sept. 23, 1950: *AAS* 42 (1950), pp. 659-661: John XXIII, Encyc. letter *Sacerdotii Nostri Primordia*, Aug. 1, 1959: *AAS* 51 (1959), p. 550 ff.

15   Cf. Pius XII, Encyc. letter *Mediator Dei*, Nov. 20, 1947: *AAS* 39 (1947), pp. 547 ff. and 572 ff.; John XXIII, Apost. exhortation *Sacrae Laudis*, Jan. 6, 1962: *AAS* 54 (1962), p. 69; Second Vatican Council, *Constitution on the Sacred Liturgy*, art. 16 and 17: *AAS* 56 (1964), p. 104 ff; Sacred Congregation of Rites, *Instruction for the*

Implementation of the Constitution on the Sacred Liturgy, Sept. 26, 1964, no. 14-17: *AAS* 56 (1964), p. 880 ff.

16   Cf. John XXIII, Encyc. letter *Sacerdotii Nostri Primordia: AAS* 51 (1959), p. 599 ff.

17   Cf. Second Vatican Council, *Dogmatic Constitution on the Church*, no. 28: *AAS* 57 (1965), p. 35 ff.

18   St. Augustine, *Tract on John*, 32, 8: *PL* 35, 1646.

19   Cf. Pius XII, Apost. exhortation *Menti Nostrae: AAS* 42 (1950), pp. 662 ff., 685, 690; John XXIII, Encyc. letter *Sacerdotii Nostri Primordia: AAS* 51 (1959), pp. 551-553, 556 ff; Paul VI, Encyc. letter *Ecclesiam Suam*, Aug. 6, 1964: *AAS* 56 (1964), p. 634 ff.; Second Vatican Council, *Dogmatic Constitution on the Church*, especially no. 8: *AAS* 57 (1965), p. 12.

20   Cf. Pius XII, Encyc. letter *Sacra Virginitas*, March 25, 1954: *AAS* 46 (1954), pp. 165 ff.

21   Cf. St. Cyprian, *De Habitu Virginum*, 22: *PL* 4, 475; St. Ambrose, *De Virginibus*, I, 8, 52: *PL* 16, 202 ff.

22   Cf. Pius XII, Apost. exhortation *Menti Nostrae: AAS* 42 (1950), p. 663.

23   Cf. Pius XII, Encyc. letter *Sacra Virginitas*, l.c., pp. 170-174.

24   Cf. Pius XII, Apost. exhortation *Menti Nostrae*, l.c., pp. 664 and 690.

25   Cf. Paul VI, Apost. letter *Summi Dei Verbum*, Nov. 4, 1963: *AAS* 55 (1963), p. 991.

26   Cf. Pius XII, Apost. exhortation *Menti Nostrae*, l.c., p. 686.

27   Cf. Paul VI, Apost. letter *Summi Dei Verbum*, l.c., p. 993.

28   Cf. Second Vatican Council, *Dogmatic Constitution on the Church*, no. 7 and 8: *AAS* 57 (1965), pp. 9-11, 33 ff.

29   Cf. Pius XII, Encyc. letter *Humani Generis*, Aug. 12, 1950: *AAS* 42 (1950), pp. 571-575.

30   Cf. Paul VI, Encyc. letter *Ecclesiam Suam*, Aug. 6, 1964: *AAS* 56 (1964), pp. 637 ff.

31   Cf. Pius XII, Encyc. letter *Humani Generis*, Aug. 12, 1950: *AAS* 42 (1950), pp. 567-569; Allocution *Si Diligis*, May 31, 1954: *AAS* 46 (1954), p. 314 ff.; Paul VI, Alloc. given at Pontifical Gregorian University, March 12, 1964: *AAS* 56 (1964), p. 364 ff.; Second Vatican Council, *Dogmatic Constitution on the Church*, no. 25: *AAS* 57 (1965), pp. 29-31.

32   Cf. St. Bonaventure, *Itinerarium Mentis in Deum*, Prol., no. 4: "Let no one believe that reading suffices of itself without unction,

speculation without devotion, investigation without wonder, circum-spection without exultation, conscientiousness without peity, knowl-edge without charity, intelligence without humility, zeal without divine grace, observation without divinely-inspired wisdom" (St. Bonaventure, *Complete Works*, V, Quaracchi 1891, p. 296).

33   Cf. Leo XIII, Encyc. letter *Providentissimus Deus*, Nov. 18, 1893: *AAS* 26 (1893-1894), p. 283.

34   Cf. Pontifical Biblical Commission, *Instruction on the Teaching of Sacred Scripture*, May 13, 1950: *AAS* 42 (1950), p. 502.

35   Cf. Pius XII, Encyc. letter *Humani Generis*, Aug. 12, 1950: *AAS* 42 (1950), p. 568 ff.: ". . . sacred studies always find rejuvenation in the study of the sacred fonts; while on the other hand speculation be-comes sterile when it neglects deeper inquiry into the sacred deposit, as we know from experience."

36   Cf. Pius XII, Talk to seminarians, June 24, 1939: *AAS* 31 (1939), p. 247: "Competition . . . in pursuing the truth and speading it is not suppressed by commending the doctrine of St. Thomas; instead it is stimulated and safely directed." Paul VI, Allocution given at the Pontifical Gregorian University, March 12, 1964: *AAS* 56 (1964), p. 365: "[Teachers] should reverently listen to the voice of the Church's Doctors, among whom the blessed Aquinas holds a main place; such is the power of the Angelic Doctor's genius and such his sincere love of truth, so great his wisdom in investigating the highest truths, in explain-ing them and tying them together with the most appropriate bonds of unity, that as a result his doctrine is a most effective instrument not only for safeguarding the foundations of the faith, but also for reaping the fruits of sound progress with assurance and great benefit." Cf. also the allocution addressed to the Sixth International Thomistic Congress, Sept. 10, 1965.

37   Cf. Second Vatican Council, *Constitution on the Sacred Liturgy*, no. 7 and 16: *AAS* 56 (1964), pp. 100 ff. and 104 ff.

38   Cf. Paul VI, Encyc. letter *Ecclesiam Suam*, Aug. 6, 1964: *AAS* 56 (1964), p. 640 ff.; Second Vatican Council, schema of the Pastoral Constitution on the Church in the Modern World (1965).

39   Second Vatican Council, *Constitution on the Sacred Liturgy*, no. 10, 14, 15, 16; Sacred Congregation of Rites, *Instruction for the Implementation of the Constitution on the Sacred Liturgy*, Sept. 26, 1964, no. 11 and 12: *AAS* 56 (1964), p. 879 ff.

40   Second Vatican Council, *Decree on Ecumenism*, no. 1, 9, 10, *AAS* 57 (1965), pp. 90 and 98 ff.

41   The ideal picture of a pastor can be gleaned from the documents of recent pontiffs that deal specifically with the life, endowments and

training of priests, especially: St. Pius X, Exhortation to the clergy *Haerent Animo, S. Pii X Acta IV*, pp. 237 ff. Pius XI, Encyc. letter *Ad Catholici Sacerdotii: AAS* 28 (1936), pp. 5 ff. John XXIII, Encyc. letter *Sacerdotii Nostri Primordia: AAS* 51 (1959), pp. 545 ff. Paul VI, Apost. letter *Summi Dei Verbum: AAS* 55 (1963), pp. 979 ff. Much concerning pastoral formation can be found also in the encyclicals *Mystici Corporis* (1943), *Mediator Dei* (1947), *Evangelii Praecones* (1951), *Sacra Virginitas* (1954), *Musicae Sacrae Disciplina* (1955), *Princeps Pastorum* (1955), and in the apostolic constitution *Sedes Sapientiae* (1956) for Religious. Pius XII, John XXIII and Paul VI have often illustrated the ideal of the good pastor in their allocutions to seminarians and priests as well.

42   Concerning the importance of the state constituted by the profession of the evangelical counsels, cf. Second Vatican Council, *Dogmatic Constitution on the Church*, Ch. VI: *AAS* 57 (1965), pp. 49-53; *Decree on the Renovation of the Religious Life*.

43   Cf. Paul VI, Encyc. letter *Ecclesiam Suam*, Aug. 6, 1964: *AAS* 56 (1964), throughout especially pp. 635 ff. and 640 ff.; Second Vatican Council, schema of the Pastoral Constitution on the Church in the Modern World (1965).

44   Cf. especially John XXIII, Encyc. letter *Mater et Magistra*, May 15 1961: *AAS* 53 (1961), pp. 401 ff.

45   Cf. in particular Second Vatican Council, schema of the Decree on the Lay Apostolate (1965), no. 25 and 30, pp. 54, 62.

46   Cf. Second Vatican Council, *Dogmatic Constitution on the Church*, no. 17: *AAS* 57 (1965), p. 20 ff.; schema of the Decree on the Church's Missionary Activity (1965), especially no. 36 and 37, p. 25 ff.

47   Several pontifical documents warn against the danger in pastoral action of neglecting the supernatural goal and considering supernatural aids of little importance at least in practice; cf. especially the documents cited in note 41.

48   More recent documents of the Holy See urge particular care and concern for newly ordained priests. Especially noteworthy are: Pius XII, Motu proprio *Quandoquidem*, April 2, 1949: *AAS* 41 (1949), pp. 165-167; Apost. exhortation *Menti Nostrae*, Sept. 23, 1950: *AAS* 42 (1950), Apost. constitution (for Religious) *Sedes Sapientiae*, May 31, 1956, and General Statutes attached; Alloc. to priests from the diocese of Barceloa, June 14, 1957, *Discorsi e Radiomesaggi* XIX, pp. 271-273. Paul VI, Alloc. to priests of the Gian Matteo Giberti Institute in the diocese of Verona, Italy, March 11, 1964.

Vatican II, APOSTOLICAM ACTUOSITATEM, Decree on the Apostolate of the Laity, November 18, 1965.

1 Cf. John XXIII, Apost. constitution *Humanae Salutis*, Dec. 25, 1961: *AAS* (1962), 7-10.

2 Cf. Second Vatican Council, *Dogmatic Constitution on the Church*, no. 33 ff.: *AAS* 57 (1965), 39 ff.; cf. also *Constitution on the Sacred Liturgy*, nos. 26-40: *AAS* 56 (1964), 107-111; cf. *Decree on Instruments of Social Communication: AAS* 56 (1964), 145-153; cf. *Decree on Ecumenism: AAS* 57 (1965), 90-107; cf. *Decree on Pastoral Duties of Bishops*, nos. 16, 17, 18; cf. *Declaration on Christian Education*, nos. 3, 5, 7.

3 Cf. Pius XII, Allocution to cardinals, Feb. 18, 1946: *AAS* 38 (1964), 101-102; idem, Sermon to Young Christian Workers, Aug. 25, 1957: *AAS* 49 (1957), 843.

4 Cf. Pius XI, Encyc. letter *Rerum Ecclesiae: AAS* 18 (1926), 65.

5 Cf. Second Vatican Council, *Dogmatic Constitution on the Church*, no. 31: *AAS* 57 (1965), 37.

6 Cf. *ibid.*, no. 33, p. 39; cf. also no. 10, *ibid.*, p. 14.

7 Cf. *ibid.*, no. 12, p. 16.

8 Cf. Second Vatican Council, *Constitution on the Sacred Liturgy*, chap. 1, no. 11: *AAS* 56 (1964), 102-103.

9 Cf. Second Vatican Council, *Dogmatic Constitution on the Church*, no. 32: *AAS* 57 (1965), 38; cf. also nos. 40-41: *ibid.*, pp. 45-47.

10 *Ibid.*, no. 62, p. 63; cf. also no. 65, *ibid.*, pp. 64-65.

11 Cf. Pius XI, Encyc. letter *Ubi Arcano*, Dec. 23, 1922: *AAS* 14, 659; Pius XII, Encyc. letter *Summi Pontificatus*, Oct. 20, 1939: *AAS* 31, 442-443.

12 Cf. Leo XIII, Encyc. letter *Rerum Novarum: AAS* 23(1890-91), 647; Pius XI, Encyc. letter *Quadragesimo Anno: AAS* 23 (1931), 190; Pius XII, Radio message of June 1, 1941: *AAS* 33 (1941), 207.

13 Cf. John XXIII, Encyc. letter *Mater ei Magistra: AAS* 53 (1961), 402.

14 Cf. *ibid.*, pp. 440-441.

15 Cf. *ibid.*, pp. 442-443.

16 Cf. Pius XII, Allocution to "Pax Romana," April 25, 1957: *AAS* 49 (1957), 298-299; and especially John XXIII, to representatives

of the Food and Agriculture Organization, Nov. 10, 1959: *AAS* 51, 865-866.

17   Cf. St. Pius X, Apost. letter *Creationis duarum novarum paroeciarum*, June 1, 1905: *AAS* 38 (1905), 65-67; Pius XII, Allocution to faithful of parish of St. Saba, Jan. 11, 1953: *Discorsi e Radiomessaggi di S.S. Pio XII* 14 (1952-53), 449-454; John XXIII, Allocution to clergy and faithful of Albano, Aug. 26, 1962: *AAS* 54 (1962), 656-660.

18   Cf. Leo XIII, Allocution of Jan. 28, 1894: *Acta* 14 (1894), 424-425.

19   Cf. Pius XII, Allocution to pastors and others, Feb. 6, 1951: *Discorsi e Radiomessaggi di S.S. Pio XII* 12 (1950-51), 437-443; March 8, 1952: *ibid.* 14 (1952-53), 5-10; March 27, 1953: *ibid.* 15 (1953-54), 27-35; Feb. 28, 1954: *ibid.*, pp. 585-590.

20   Cf. Pius XI, Encyc. letter *Casti Connubii: AAS* 22 (1930), 554; Pius XII, Radio message, Jan. 1, 1941: *AAS* 33 (1941), 203; idem, to members of the International Union to Protect the Rights of Families, Sept. 20, 1949: *AAS* 41 (1949), 552; idem, to heads of families on pilgrimage from France to Rome, Sept. 18, 1951: *AAS* 43 (1951), 731; idem, Christmas Radio Message of 1952: *AAS* 45 (1953), 41; John XXIII, Encyc. letter *Mater et Magistra*, May 15, 1961: *AAS* 53 (1961), 429, 439.

21   Cf. Pius XII, Encyc. letter *Evangelii Praecones*, June 2, 1951: *AAS* 43 (1951), 514.

22   Cf. Pius XII, to members of the International Union to Protect the Rights of Families, Sept. 20, 1941: *AAS* 41 (1949), 552.

23   Cf. Pius X, Allocution to Association of French Catholic Youth, Sept. 25, 1904: *AAS* 37 (1904-05), 296-300.

24   Cf. Pius XII, Letter *Dans quelques semaines* to Archbishop of Montreal, Canada, to be relayed to the Assemblies of Canadian Young Christtian Workers, May 24, 1947: *AAS* 39 (1947), 257: radio message to Young Christian Workers, Brussels, Sept. 3, 1950: *AAS* 42 (1950), 640-641.

25   Cf. Pius XI, Encyc. letter *Quadragesimo Anno*, May 15, 1931: *AAS* 23 (1931), 225-226.

26   Cf. John XXIII, Encyc. letter *Mater et Magistra*, May 15, 1961: *AAS* 53 (1961), 448-450.

27   Cf. Pius XIII, Allocution to the first convention of laymen representing all nations on the promotion of the apostolate, Oct. 15, 1951: *AAS* 43 (1951), 788.

28   *Ibid.*, pp. 787-788.

29   Cf. Pius XII, Encyc. letter *Le Pelerinage de Lourdes*, July 2, 1957: *AAS* 49 (1957), 615.

30   Cf. Pius XII, Allocution to the assembly of the International Federation of Catholic Men, Dec. 8, 1956: *AAS* 49 (1957), 26-27.

31   Cf. Sacred Congregation of the Council on the dissolution of the diocese of Corrientes, Argentina, Nov. 13, 1920: *AAS* 13 (1921), 139.

32   Cf. below, chap. 5, no. 24.

33   Cf. John XXIII, Encyc. letter *Princeps Pastorum*, Dec. 10, 1959: *AAS* 51 (1959), 856.

34   Cf. Pius XI, Letter *Quae nobis* to Cardinal Bertram, Nov. 13, 1928: *AAS* 20 (1928), 385. Cf. also Pius XII, Allocution to Italian Catholic Action, Sept. 4, 1940: *AAS* 32 (1940), 362.

35   Cf. Pius XI, Encyc. letter *Quamvis Nostra*, April 30, 1936: *AAS* 28 (1936), 160-161.

36   Cf. Sacred Congregation of the Council on the dissolution of the diocese of Corientes, Argentina, Nov. 13, 1920: *AAS* 13 (1921), 137-140.

37   Cf. Pius XII, Allocution to the second conventionof laymen representing all nations on the promotion of the apostolate, Oct. 5, 1957: *AAS* 49 (1957), 927.

38   Cf. Second Vatican Council, *Dogmatic Constitution on the Church*, no. 37: *AAS* 57 (1965), 42-43.

39   Cf. Pius XII, Apost. exhortation *Menti Nostrae*, Sept. 23, 1950: *AAS* 42 (1950), 660.

40   Cf. Second Vatican Council, *Decree on the Adaptation and Renewal of Religious Life*, no. 8.

41   Cf. Benedict XIV, *On the Diocesan Synod*, I, 3, chap. 9, no. 7.

42   Cf. Pius XI, Encyc. letter *Quamvis Nostra*, April 30, 1936: *AAS* 28 (1936), 160-161.

43   Cf. John XXIII, Encyc. letter *Mater et Magistra*, May 15, 1961: *AAS* 53 (1961), 456-457. Cf. Second Vatican Council, *Decree on Ecumenism*, no. 12: *AAS* 57 (1965), 99-100.

44   Cf. Second Vatican Council, *Decree on Ecumenism*, no. 12: *AAS* 57 (1965), 100. Cf. also *Dogmatic Constitution on the Church*, no. 15: *AAS* 57 (1965), 19-20.

45   Cf. Second Vatican Council, *Dogmatic Constitution on the Church*, chaps. 2, 4 and 5: *AAS* 57 (1965), 12-21, 37-49; also cf. *Decree on Ecumenism*, nos. 4, 6, 7 and 12: *AAS* 57 (1965), 94-100. Cf. also above, no. 4.

46   Cf. Pius XII, Allocution to the first international Boy Scouts congress, June 6, 1952: *AAS* 44 (1952), 579-590; John XXIII, Encyc. letter *Mater et Magistra*, May 15, 1961: *AAS* 53 (1961), 456.

47   Cf. Second Vatican Council, *Dogmatic Constitution on the Church*, no. 33: *AAS* 57 (1965), 39.

48   Cf. John XXIII, Encyc. letter *Mater et Magistra*, May 15, 1961: *AAS* 53 (1961), 455.

49   Cf. Pius XII, Encyc. letter *Sertum Laetitiae*, Nov. 1, 1939: *AAS* 31 (1939), 643-644; cf. idem, to graduates of Italian Catholic Action, May 24, 1953.

50   Cf. Pius XII, Allocution to the universal congress of the World Federation of Young Catholic Women, April 18, 1951: *AAS* 44 (1952), 414-419. Cf. idem, Allocution to Italian Christian Workers Association, May 1, 1955: *AAS* 47 (1955), 403-404.

51   Cf. Pius XII, to delegates of the Assembly of Charity Associations, April 27, 1952: pp. 470-471.

Vatican II, PRESBYTERORUM ORDINIS, Decree on the Ministry and Life of Priests, December 7, 1965.

1   *Second Vatican Council, Constitution on the Sacred Liturgy, Dec. 4, 1963: AAS 56 (1964), p. 97 ff.: dogmatic constitution "Lumen Gentium" Nov. 21, 1964: AAS 57 (1965), p. 5 ff.: decree "Christus Dominus" on the Bishops' Pastoral Office in the Church, Oct. 28, 1965; Decree on Priestly Formation, Oct. 28, 1965.*

2   *Cf. Mt. 3:16; Lk. 4:18; Acts 4:27; 10:38.*

3   *Cf. 1 Pet. 2:5, and 9.*

4   *Cf. 1 Pet. 3:15.*

5   *Cf. Apoc. 1910; Second Vatican Council, dogmatic constitution "Lumen Gentium." Nov. 21, 1964, Art. 35: AAS 57 (1965), pp. 40-41.*

6   *Council of Trent, 23rd session, Chap. 1, c. 1: Denz. 957 and 961 (1764 and 1771).*

7   *Cf. Jn. 20:21; Second Vatican Council, dogmatic constitution "Lumen Gentium," Nov. 21, 1964, Art. 18: AAS 57 (1965), pp. 21-22.*

8   *Cf. Second Vatican Council, dogmatic constitution "Lumen Gentium," Nov. 21, 1964, Art. 22: AAS 57 (1965), pp. 33-36.*

9   *Cf. ibid.*

10   *Cf. Roman Pontifical, "Ordination of Priests," preface.*

11   *Cf. Second Vatican Council, dogmatic constitution "Lumen Gentium," Nov. 21, 1964, Art. 10: AAS 57 (1965), pp. 14-15.*

12   *Cf. Rom. 15:16 (Greek).*

13   *Cf. 1 Cor. 11:26.*

14   *St. Augustine, "De Civitate Dei" 10, 6: PL 41, 284.*

15   *Cf. 1 Cor. 15:24.*

16   *Cf. Heb. 5:1.*

17   *Cf. Heb. 2:17; 4:15.*

18   *Cf. 1 Cor. 9:19-23 (Vg.).*

19   *Cf. Acts 13:2.*

20   *"Ecclesiam Suam," Aug. 6, 1964: AAS 56 (1964), pp. 627 and 638.*

21   *Cf. Rom. 12:2.*

22   *Cf. Jn. 10:14-16.*

23   *Cf. St. Polycarp, Epist. ad Phillippenses, 6, 1.*

24   *Cf. 1 Pet. 1:23; Acts 6:7; 12:24.*

25   *Cf. Mal. 2:7; 1 Tim. 4:11-13; 1 Tim. 1:9.*

26   *Cf. Mk. 16:16.*

27   *Cf. 2 Cor. 11:7; Cf. "Statuta Ecclesiae Antiqua," c. 3; "Decree of Gratian," c. 6, D. 88; Council of Trent, Decree "De Reform.," Session 5, c. 2, n. 9.*

28   *Cf. "Constitutiones Apostolorum" II, 26, 7.*

29   *Cf. Gal. 2:5.*

30   *Cf. 1 Pet. 2:12.*

31   Cf. Rite of priestly ordination in the Alexandrian Jacobite Church.

32   *Cf. Mt. 28:19; Mk. 16:16; Tertullian, "On Baptism," 14, 2; St. Athanasius, "Against the Arians," 2, 42; St. Jerome, "On Matthew," 28, 19; St. Thomas, "Exposition of the first decretal," Art. 1.*

33   *Cf. Second Vatican Council, Constitution on the Sacred Liturgy, Dec. 4, 1963, Art. 35, 2: AAS 56 (1964), p. 109.*

34   *Cf. ibid., Art. 33, 35, 48, 52, (pp. 108-109, 113, 114).*

35   *Cf. ibid., Art. 7 (pp. 100-101); Pius XII, encyclical letter "Mystici Corporis," June 29, 1943: AAS 35 (1943), p. 230.*

36   *St. Ignatius Martyr, "Smyrn.," 8, 1-2; "Constitutions of the Apostles," VIII, 12, 3; VIII, 29, 2 (p. 532).*

37   *Cf. Second Vatican Council, dogmatic constitution "Lumen Gentium," Nov. 21, 1954, Art. 28: AAS 57 (1965), pp. 33-36.*

38   *"The Eucharist indeed is a quasi consummation of the spiritual life, and the goal of all the sacraments" (St. Thomas, "Summa Theol.," III, q. 73, a. 3 c); cf. "Summa Theol.," III, q. 65, 1. 3.*

39   *Cf. Eph. 5:19-20.*

40   *Cf. St. Jerome, Epistles, 114, 2 (PL 22, 934). See Second Vatican Council, Constitution on the Sacred Liturgy, Dec. 4, 1963, Art. 122127: AAS 56 (1964), pp. 130-132.*

41   *Encyclical letter "Mysterium Fidei," Sept. 3, 1965: AAS 57 (1965), p. 771.*

42   *Cf. Second Vatican Council, dogmatic constitution "Lumen Gentium," Nov. 21, 1964, Art. 28: AAS 57 (1965), pp. 33-36.*

43   *Cf. 2 Cor. 10:8; 13:10.*

44   *Cf. Gal. 1:10.*

45   *Cf. 1 Cor. 4:14.*

46   *Cf. "Didascalia," II, 34, 3; II, 46, 6; II, 47, 1; "Constitutions of the Apostles," II, 47, 1.*

47   *Cf. Gal. 4:3; 5:1 and 13.*

48   *Cf. St. Jerome, Epistles, 58, 7.*

49   *Cf. 1 Pet. 4:10 ff.*

50   *Cf. Mt. 25:34-35.*

51   *Cf. Lk. 4:18.*

52   *Cf. "Didascalia," II, 59, 1-3.*

53   *Cf. Second Vatican Council, dogmatic constitution "Lumen Gentium," Nov. 21, 1964, Art. 28: AAS 57 (1965), p. 35.*

54   *Cf. cited "Ecclesiastical Constitution of the Apostles," XVIII.*

55   *Cf. "Didascalia," II, 28, 4; "Constitutions of the Apostles," II, 28, 4; II, 34, 3 (ibid., pp. 109 and 177).*

56   *Cf. Num. 11:16-25.*

57   *Roman Pontifical, "Ordination of Priests," preface.*

58   *Cf. Second Vatican Council, dogmatic constitution "Lumen Gentium," Nov. 21, 1964, Art. 28: AAS 57 (1965), p. 35.*

59   *Cf. John XXIII, encyclical letter "Sacerdotii Nostri Primorida," Aug. 1, 1959: AAS 51 (1959), p. 576; St. Pius X, exhortation to the clergy "Haerent Animo," August 4, 1908; Acts of St. Pius X, vol. IV (1908), pp. 237 ff.*

60   *Cf. Second Vatican Council, Decree on the Bishops' Pastoral Office in the Church, Oct. 28, 1956, Art. 15 and 16.*

61   *St. Ignatius Martyr, "Magn." 6, 1.*

62   *Cf. Paul VI, allocution to the family heads of Rome and Lenten speakers, Mar. 1, 1965, in the Sistine Hall: AAS 57 (1965), p. 326.*

63   *Cf. "Constitutions of the Apostles," VIII 47, 39.*

64   *Cf. 3 Jn. 8.*

65 · *Cf. Jn. 17:23.*

66   *Cf. Heb. 13:1-2.*

67   *Cf. Heb. 13:16.*

68   *Cf. Mt. 5:10.*

69   *Cf. 1 Th. 2:12; Col. 1:13.*

70   *Cf. Mt. 23:8. Also Paul VI, encyclical letter "Ecclesiam Suam," Aug. 6, 1964: AAS 58 (1964), p. 647.*

71   *Cf. Eph. 4:17 and 16; "Constitutions of the Apostles," VIII, 1, 20.*

72   *Cf. Phil. 2:21.*

73   *Cf. 1 Jn. 4:1.*

74   *Cf. Second Vatican Council, dogmatic constitution "Lumen Gentium," Nov. 21, 1964, Art. 37: AAS 57 (1965), pp. 42-43.*

75   *Cf. Eph. 4:14.*

76   *Second Vatican Council, Decree on Ecumenism, Nov. 21, 1964: AAS 57 (1965), pp. 90 ff.*

77   *Cf. Second Vatican Council, dogmatic constitution "Lumen Gentium," Nov. 21, 1964, Art. 37: AAS 57 (1965), pp. 42-43.*

78   *Cf. Heb. 7:3.*

79   *Cf. Lk. 10:1.*

80   *Cf. 1 Pet. 2:25.*

81   *Cf. Acts 20:28.*

82   *Cf. Mt. 9:36.*

83   *Roman Pontifical, "Ordination of Priests."*

84   *Cf. Second Vatican Council, Decree on Priestly Formation, Oct. 28, 1965, Art. 2.*

85   *Cf. Second Vatican Council, Decree on Priestly Formation, Oct. 28, 1965, Art. 2.*

86   *Cf. 2 Cor. 12:9.*

87   *Cf. Pius XI, encyclical letter "Ad Catholici Sacerdotii," Dec. 20,*
1935: AAS 28 (1936), p. 10.

88   *Cf. Jn. 10:36.*

89   *Lk. 24:26.*

90   *Cf. Eph. 4:13.*

91   *Cf. 2 Cor. 3:8-9.*

92   *Cf. St. Thomas "Summa Theol.," II-II, q. 188, a. 7.*

93   *Cf. Heb. 3:9-10.*

94   *Acts 16:14.*

95   *Cf. 2 Cor. 4:7.*

96   *Cf. Eph. 3:9.*

97   *Cf. Roman Pontifical, "Ordination of Priests."*

98   *Cf. Roman Missal, Prayer over the Offerings of the Ninth Sunday*
after Pentecost.

99   *Cf. Jn. 10:11.*

100   *Cf. 2 Cor. 1:7.*

101   *Cf. 2 Cor. 1:4.*

102   *Cf. 1 Cor. 10:33.*

103   *Cf. Jn. 3:8.*

104   *Cf. Jn. 4:34.*

105   *Cf. 1 Jn. 3:16.*

106   *Cf. Rom. 12:2.*

107   *Cf. Gal. 2:2.*

108   *Cf. 2 Cor. 7:4.*

109   *Cf. Jn. 4:34; 5:30; 6:38.*

110   *Cf. Acts 13:2.*

111   *Cf. Eph. 5:10.*

112   *Cf. Acts 20:22.*

113   *Cf. 2 Cor. 12:15.*

114   *Cf. Eph. 4:11-16.*

115   *Cf. Mt. 19:12.*

116   *Cf. Second Vatican Council, dogmatic constitution "Lumen*
Gentium," Nov. 21, 1964, Art. 42: AAS 57 (1965), pp. 47-49.

117   *Cf. 1 Tim. 3:2-5: Tit. 1:6.*

118   *Cf. Pius XI, encyclical letter "Ad Catholici Sacerdotii," Dec. 20, 1935: AAS 28 (1936), p. 28.*

119   *Cf. Mt. 19:12.*

120   *Cf. 1 Cor. 7:32-34.*

121   *Cf. 2 Cor. 11:2.*

122   *Cf. Second Vatican Council, dogmatic constitution "Lumen Gentium," on the Aporopriate Renewal of Religious Life, Oct. 28, 1965, Art. 12.*

123   *Cf. Luke 20:35-36; Pius XI, encyclical letter "Ad Catholici Sacerdotii," Dec. 20, 1935, AAS 28 (1936), pp. 24-28; Pius XII, encyclical letter "Sacra Virginitas," Mar. 25, 1954, AAS 46 (1954), pp. 169-172.*

124   *Cf. Mt. 19:11.*

125   *Cf. Jn. 17:14-16.*

126   *Cf. 1 Cor. 7:31.*

127   *Council of Antioch, can. 25: Mansi 2, 1328; "Decree of Gratian," c. 23, c. 12 q. 1.*

128   *Council of Paris a, 829, can. 15: M.G.H. Sect. III, "Concillia," t. 2, para. 6 622; Council of Trent, Session XXV, "De Reform.," Chap. I.*

129   *Ps. 62:11 (Vg. 61).*

130   *Cf. 2 Cor. 8:9.*

131   *Cf. Acts 8:18-25.*

132   *Cf. Phil. 4:12.*

133   *Cf. Acts 2:42-47.*

134   *Cf. Lk. 4:18.*

135   *Cf. Code of Canon Law, 125 ff.*

136   *Cf. Second Vatican Council, Decree on the Appropriate Renewal of Religious Life, Oct. 28, 1965, Art. 6; Dogmatic Constitution on Divine Revelation, Nov. 18, 1965, Art. 21.*

137   *Cf. Second Vatican Council, dogmatic constitution "Lumen Gentium," Nov. 21, 1964, Art. 65: AAS 57 (1965), pp. 64-65.*

138   *Roman Pontifical, "Ordination of Priests."*

139   *Cf. Second Vatican Council, Dogmatic Constitution on Divine Revelation, Nov. 18, 1965, Art. 25.*

140   *Second Vatican Council, Decree on the Bishops' Pastoral Office in the Church, Oct. 28, 1965, Art. 16.*

141   *Cf. Mt. 10:10; 1 Cor. 9:7; 1 Tim. 5:18.*

142   *Cf. 2 Cor. 8:14.*

143   *Cf. Phil. 4:14.*

144   *Cf. Jn. 3:16.*

145   *Cf. 1 Pet. 2:5.*

146   *Cf. Eph. 2:22.*

147   *Cf. Roman Pontifical, "Ordination of Priests."*

148   *Cf. Eph. 3:9.*

149   *Cf. Col. 3:3.*

SACRUM DIACONATUS ORDINEM, Motu Proprio of Pope Paul VI on Restoring the Permanent Diaconate, June 18, 1967.

1   See *Phil* 1, 1.

2   See *1 Tm* 3, 8-13.

3   See no. 29; *AAS* 57 (1965), 36.

4   Second Vatican council, *Decree on the Missionary Activity of the Church*, no. 16: *AAS* 58 (1966), 967.

5   See *Dogmatic Constitution on the Church*, no. 41: *AAS* 57 (1965), 46.

6   Ibid., no. 29: *AAS* 57 (1965), 36.

7   See *1 Tm* 3, 10-13.

8   See Canons 1095, §2; and 1096.

9   See *2 Tm* 2, 21.

10   Code of Oriental Law, *De Personis,* Canon 87: *AAS* 49 (1957), 462.

11   *Adversus Haereses,* IV, 15, 1: *PG* 7, 1013.

12   St. Leo the Great, Sermon 85: *PL* 54, 436.

Selection from Homily of Pope Paul VI to the Third World Congress of Lay Apostolate on the Layman's Sphere of Action, October 15, 1967.

1   *Dogmatic Constitution on the Church,* no. 33.

2   *Mt.* 20, 4.

3   See *Acts* 20, 28.

4   *Decree on the Apostolate of the Laity*, no. 2.

5   *Populorum Progressio*, no. 81.

Address of Pope Paul VI to a General Audience on the Layman's Task, April 23, 1969.

1   See *Discorsi* XIX, 459, and *AAS* 49 (1957), 927.

2   See *Discorsi* III, 460; XIII, 295; XV, 590, etc.

3   See *Rivista Dioc.*, 1962, p. 263.

4   *Dogmatic Constitution on the Church*, no. 34, no. 35, no. 36; *Decree on the Apostolate of the Laity*, no. 7.

5   See Lazzati, in *Studium*, 1959, pp. 791-805; Congar, *Jesus Christ*, p. 215 ff.

6   *Pastorial Constitution on the Church in the World of Today*, no. 2.

7   See *Acts* 6, 4.

8   See 1 *Cor.* 4, 1; 2 *Cor.* 6, 4.

9   See E. Schillebeeckx, *La Chiesa del* Vat. II, p. 960 ff.

10   *Decree on the Apostolate of the Laity*, no. 7; *Pastoral Constitution on the Church in the World of Today*, no. 42; etc.

11   *AAS* 50 (1958), 220.

12   *Dogmatic Constitution on the Church*, no. 37.

13   *Decree on the Apostolate of the Laity*, no. 2.

14   *Ibid.*, no. 7; *Pastoral Constitution on the Church in the World of Today*, no. 42.

15   *Pastoral Constitution on the Church in the World of Today*, no. 40.

16   *Ibid.*, no. 43; *Decree on the Apostolate of the Laity*, no. 2.

17   See *Decree on the Apostolate of the Laity*, no. 3.

18   In *Jo.* tract. 51, no. 12: *PL* 35, 1768.

Sacred Congregation for the Clergy, Letter to the Presidents of Episcopal Conferences on Priests' Councils, April 11, 1970.

1   Vat. Coun. II, *Decree on the Priestly Ministry and Life*, no. 1.

2   Ibid., no. 15.

3   Ibid., no. 7.

4   Vat. Coun. II, *Dogmatic Constitution on the Church*, no. 27.

5   *Decree on the Priestly Ministry and Life*, no. 7.

6   *Constitution on the Church*, no. 28.

7   *Constitution on the Church*, no. 28; *Decree on the Priestly Ministry and Life*, no. 8.

8   *Decree on the Priestly Ministry and Life*, no. 7.

9   Vat. Coun. II, *Decree on the Pastoral Office of Bishops in the Church*, no. 28.

10   *Decree on the Priestly Ministry and Life*, no. 8.

11   *Decree on the Pastoral Office of Bishops in the Church*, no. 28; *Decree on the Priestly Ministry and Life*, no. 7.

12   *Decree on the Priestly Ministry and Life*, no. 7.

13   *AAS* 58 (1966), 776 ff.

14   Apost. const. *Regimini Ecclesiae Universae*, no. 68: *AAS* 59 (1967), 68.

15   'Motu proprio' *Ecclesiae Sanctae*, Introduction.

16   *Ecclesiae Sanctae*, I, no. 15, §2.

17   Ibid., I, no. 15, §1.

18   The statues of the council, to be approved by the bishop, should prescribe the election procedure, by analogy with canon 160 and the following, as well as canon 2294 of the Code of Canon Law.

19   *Ecclesiae Sanctae*, I, no. 15, §1; *Decree on the Pastoral Office of Bishops in the Church*, no. 28.

20   See *Decree on the Pastoral Office of Bishops in the Church*, no. 11; *Constitution on the Church*, no. 23.

21   See *Decree on the Priestly Ministry and Life*, no. 7; *Ecclesiae Sanctae*, I, no. 15, §1.

22   *Ecclesiae Sanctae*, I, no. 17, §2.

23   *Ecclesiae Sanctae,* I, no. 15, §4; See also apost. const. *Regimini Ecclesiae Universae,* no. 68, §4.

24   *Ecclesiae Sanctae,* I, no. 17, §1.

Address of Pope Paul VI to 21st Italian National Week of Pastoral Renewal on Local Church Structures, September 9, 1971.

1   Vat. Coun. II, *Decree on the Pastoral Office of Bishops in the Church,* no. 11.

2   Vat. Coun. II, *Constitution on the Sacred Liturgy,* no. 41.

3   See Vat. Coun. II, *Dogmatic Constitution on the Church,* no. 26.

4   *Ibid.,* no. 25.

5   *Dogmatic Constitution on the Church,* no. 28.

6   See Vat. Coun. II, *Decree on the Apostolate of the Laity,* no. 10.

Address of Pope Paul VI to the International Catechetical Congress on Catechetics and Contemporary Problems, September 25, 1971.

1   *Jer.* 1, 6.

2   See *Decree on the Missionary Activity of the Church,* nos. 23 and 36.

3   Apost. exhortation *Quinque iam annos,* Dec. 8, 1970.

4   *Decree on the Apostolate of the Laity,* no. 13.

5   Address to General Audience, Nov. 18, 1970: *L'Osservatore Romano,* Nov. 19, 1970.

6   See *Heb.* 4, 12; *Ap.* 1, 16 and 2, 16.

7   *Mt.* 16, 15.

8   Apost. exhortation *Quinque iam annos.*

9   Message to Council to the world, Oct. 20, 1962: *AAS* 54 (1962), 822.

10   *Catechetical Directory,* no. 11.

11   *Ibid.,* no. 35.

12   *Ecclesiam Suam,* no. 87.

13   See *L'Osservatore Romano*, July 1-2, 1963.

14   *Dogmatic Constitution on Divine Revelation*, nos. 3-4.

15   See *Gn.* 1, 26.

16   See *Jn.* 1, 9.

17   I *Cor.* 2, 9.

18   2 *Thes.* 3, 1.

19   *Mk.* 4, 20.

1971 Synod of Bishops, The Ministerial Priesthood, December 9, 1971.

1   See *Pastoral Constitution on the Church in the World of Today*, no. 4.

2   1 *Cor.* 15, 28.

3   See *Dogmatic Constitution on the Church*, no. 10.

4   *Jn.* 10, 36.

5   See *Lk.* 4, 1, 18-21; *Acts* 10, 38.

6   See *Jn.* 10, 15 ff.; 11, 52.

7   1 *Tm.* 2, 5.

8   *Col.* 1, 16; see *Jn.* 1, 3 ff.

9   See *Eph.* 1, 10.

10   See *Col.* 1, 15.

11   See *Dogmatic Constitution on the Church*, no. 18.

12   See *Decree on the Missionary Activity of the Church*, no. 5.

13   See *Ap.* 21, 14; *Mt.* 16, 18.

14   Tertullian, *De Praescr. Haer.* XXI, 4; see also I Letter of St. Clement *Ad Cor.* XLII, 1-4; St. Ignatius of Antioch, *Ad Magn.* VI and passim; St. Irenaeus, *Adv. Haer.* 4, 21, 3; Origen, *De Princip.* IV, 2, 1; Serapion, Bishop of Antioch, in Eusebius, *Hist. Eccl.* VI, 12.

15   See *Dogmatic Constitution on the Church*, no. 10.

16   See *Acts* 6, 2-6; 11, 30; 13, 1; 14, 23; 20, 17; 1 *Thes.* 5, 12-13; *Phil.* 1, 1; *Col.* 4, 11 and passim.

17   See *Acts* 20, 25-27; 2 *Tm.* 4, 5 f. in conjunction with 1 *Tm.* 5, 22; 2 *Tm.* 2, 2; *Ti.* 1, 5; St. Clement of Rome, *Ad Cor.* 44, 3.

18   See *Acts* 20, 28.

19   See St. Clement of Rome, *Ad Cor.* 44, 2.

20   *Dogmatic Constitution on the Church*, no. 20.

21   See 2 *Cor.* 5, 18 ff.

22   See 2 *Tm.* 1, 6.

23   See *Ti.* 1, 5.

24   See 1 *Pt.* 5, 1-4.

25   See *Dogmatic Constitution on the Church*, no. 10.

26   See *Decree on the Priestly Ministry and Life*, no. 2.

27   See *Dogmatic Constitution on the Church*, nos. 24, 27 and 28.

28   See *ibid.*, no. 28.

29   See 2 *Tm.* 1, 6.

30   See *Decree on the Priestly Ministry and Life*, no. 2.

31   See 2 *Cor.* 5, 18-20.

32   See *Pastoral Constitution on the Church in the World of Today*, no. 42.

33   See *ibid.*, no. 58.

34   *Decree on the Priestly Ministry and Life*, no. 3.

35   *Decree on the Missionary Activity of the Church*, no. 39.

36   *Decree on the Priestly Ministry and Life*, no. 4.

37   *Constitution on the Sacred Liturgy*, no. 10.

38   *Ibid.*, no. 59.

39   See *Decree on the Pastoral Office of Bishops in the Church*, no. 13.

40   See *Constitution on the Sacred Liturgy*, no. 59.

41   See *Decree on the Priestly Ministry and Life*, nos. 3 and 17; *Jn.* 17, 14-16.

42   See *Decree on the Priestly Ministry and Life*, no. 3.

43   See *ibid.*, no. 8.

44   See *Rom.*, 8, 29.

45   *Mk.* 3, 14.

46   *Jn.* 17, 19.

47   *Decree on the Priestly Ministry and Life*, no. 14.

48   See 1 *Cor.* 9, 22.

49   *Heb.* 4, 12.

50   See *Decree on the Priestly Ministry and Life*, no. 16.

51   Result of the vote on this proposition: *Placet*, 168; *non placet*, 10; *placet iuxta modum*, 21; abstentions, 3.

52   According to the directives of the presidents, the vote was taken not by *Placet* or *Non placet*, but by the choice of the first or second formula. The first formula, *A*, obtained 107 votes; the second, *B*, obtained 87. There were 2 abstentions and also 2 null notes.

53   See *Dogmatic Constitution on the Church*, no. 28; *Decree on the Pastoral Office of Bishops in the Church*, no. 15; *Decree on the Priestly Ministry and Life*, no. 7.

54   See *Decree on the Priestly Ministry and Life*, no. 7.

55   See *ibid.*

56   *Ibid.*, no. 8.

57   *Ibid.*

58   *Ibid.*, no. 9.

59   *Ibid.*

60   See *Decree on the Pastoral Office of Bishops in the Church*, no. 27.

61   See *2 Cor.* 3, 4-12.

62   See *Jn.* 13, 6.

63   See *Phil.* 3, 13.

64   See *Eph.* 3, 19.

65   *1 Jn.* 1, 2-3.

MINISTERIA QUAEDAM, Motu Proprio of Pope Paul VI on the Ministries of Lector and Acolyte, August 15, 1972.

1   See Vat. Coun. II, *Constitution on the Sacred Liturgy*, no. 62: *AAS* 56 (1964), 117; see also no. 21: loc. cit., 105-106.

2   See Ordo Missae, *Institutio Generalis Missalis Romani*, no. 58, definitive edition (1969), p. 29.

3   Vat. Coun. II, *Constitution on the Sacred Liturgy*, no. 28: *AAS* 56 (1964), 107.

4   Ibid., no. 14: loc. cit., 104.

5   See Vat. Coun. II, *Decree on the Missionary Activity of the Church*, no. 15: *AAS* 58 (1966), 965; ibid., no. 17: loc. cit., 967-968.

6   Vat. Coun. II, *Dogmatic Constitution on the Church*, no. 10: *AAS* 57 (1965), 14.

7   See Vat. Coun. II, *Constitution on the Sacred Liturgy*, no. 24: *AAS* 56 (1964), 107; *Dogmatic Constitution on Divine Revelation*, no. 25; *AAS* 58 (1966), 829.

AD PASCENDUM, Selection from Motu Proprio of Pope Paul VI on the Role of Deacons, August 15, 1972.

22   *AAS* 59 (1967), 697-704.

23   *AAS* 60 (1968), 369-373.

24   See Vat. Coun. II, *Dogmatic Constitution on Divine Revelation*, no. 21: *AAS* 58 (1966), 827.

25   See *Rom* 12, 11-13.

26   See Paul VI, apost. letter *Sacrum Diaconatus Ordinem*, no. 16: *AAS* 59 (1967), 701.

Sacred Congregation for the Doctrine of the Faith, Declaration in Defense of Church Doctrine, June 24, 1973.

1   Paul VI, apost. exhortation *Quinque iam anni: AAS* 63 (1971), 99.

2   Paul VI, apost. constitution *Regimini Ecclesiae Universae: AAS* 59 (1967), 897.

3   Vat. Coun. II, *Dogmatic Constitution on the Church*, no. 8: *Constitutiones Decreta Declarationes*, ed. Secretariea Generalis, Vatican Polyglot Press (1966), p. 104. ff.

4   Vat. Coun. II, *Decree on Ecumenism*, no. 3: *Const. Decr. Decl.*, p. 250.

5   *Ibid.*, no. 4: *Const. Decr. Decl.*, p. 252.

6   Vat. Coun. II, *Dogmatic Constitution on the Church*, no. 8: *Const. Decr. Decl.*, p. 106.

7   *Ibid,: Const. Decr. Decl.*, p. 105.

8   Vat. Coun. II, *Decree on Ecumenism*, no. 4: *Const. Decr. Decl.*, p. 253.

9   See *ibid.*, nos. 6-8: *Const. Decr. Decl.*, pp. 255-258.

10   See *ibid.*, no. 1: *Const. Decr. Decl.*, p. 243.

11   See Paul VI, encyc. *Ecclesiam Suam: AAS* 56 (1964), 629.

12   Vat. Coun. II, *Dogmatic Constitution on Divine Revelation*, no. 7: *Const. Decr. Decl.*, p. 428.

13   See *ibid.*, no. 10: *Const. Decr. Decl.*, p. 431.

14   See *ibid.*, no. 8: *Const. Decr. Decl.*, p. 430.

15   Vat. Coun. II, *Dogmatic Constitution on the Church*, no. 12: *Const. Decr. Decl.*, p. 113.

16   *Ibid.*, p. 114.

17   See *ibid.*, no. 35: *Const. Decr. Decl.*, p. 157.

18   Vat. Coun. II, *Dogmatic Constitution on Divine Revelation*, no. 8: *Const. Decr. Decl.*, p. 430.

19   Paul VI, apost. exhortation *Quinque iam anni: AAS* 63 (1971), 99.

20   See Vat. Coun. II, *Dogmatic Constitution on the Church*, no. 25: *Const. Decr. Decl.*, p. 138 ff.

21   *Ibid.*, no. 18: *Const. Decr. Decl.*, p. 124 ff.; see Vat. Coun. I, dogmatic const. *Pastor Aeternus*, Prologue: *Conciliorum Oecumenicorum Decreta*, ed. *Istituto per le Scienze Religiose di Bologna*, Herder (1973), p. 812 (DS 3051).

22   Paul VI, apost. exhortation *Quinque iam anni: AAS* 63 (1971), 100.

23   See Vat. Coun. I, dogmatic const. *Pastor Aeternus*, chap. 4: *Conc. Oec. Decr.*, p. 816. (DS 3069, 3074). See also decree of the Holy Office *Lamentabili*; 6: *AAS* 40 (1907), 471 (DS 3406).

24   Vat. Coun. I, dogmatic const. *Pastor Aeternus*, chap. 4: *Conc. Oec. Decr.*, p. 816 (DS 3070). See Vat. Coun. II, *Dogmatic Constitution on the Church*, no. 25: *Const. Decr. Decl.*, p. 141; and *Dogmatic Constitution on Divine Revelation*, no. 4: *Const. Decr. Decl.*, p. 426.

25   See Vat. Coun. II, *Dogmatic Constitution on Divine Revelation*, no. 11: *Const. Decr. Decl.*, p. 434.

26   See *ibid.*, no. 9 ff.: *Const. Decr. Decl.*, pp. 430-432.

27   See Vat. Coun. II, *Dogmatic Constitution on the Church*, no. 25: *Const. Decr. Decl.*, p. 139.

28   See *ibid.*, nos. 25 and 22: *Const. Decr. Decl.*, pp. 139 and 133.

29   Vat. Coun. I, dogmatic const. *Pastor Aeternus*, chap. 4: *Conc. Oec. Decr.*, p. 816 (DS 3074). See Vat. Coun. II, *Dogmatic Constitution on the Church*, no. 25: *Const. Decr. Decl.*, pp. 139-141.

30   See Vat. Coun. II, *Dogmatic Constitution on the Church*, no. 25: *Const. Decr. Decl.*, p. 139.

31   Vat. Coun. I, dogmatic const. *Dei Filius*, chap. 3: *Conc. Oec. Decr.*, p. 807 (DS 301). See *CIC* can. 1323, § 1 and can. 1325, § 2.

32   See Council of Trent, sess. 6: decree *de Justificatione*, chap. 6: *Conc. Oec. Decr.*, p. 672 (DS 1526); see also Vat. Coun. II, *Dogmatic Constitution on Divine Revelation*, no. 5: *Const. Decr. Decl.*, p. 426.

33   See Vat. Coun. I, constitution on the Catholic Faith *Dei Filius*, chap. 3: *Conc. Oec. Decr.*, p. 807 (DS 3008); see also Vat. Coun. II, *Dogmatic Constitution on Divine Revelation*, no. 5: *Const. Decr. Decl.*, p. 426.

35   *Reflections and Suggestions Concerning Ecumenical Dialogue* IV, 4b in Secretariat for Promoting Christian Unity, *Information Service*, no. 12 (Dec., 1970, IV), p. 8.

36   Vat. Coun. I, dogmatic const. *Dei Filius*, chap. 4: *Conc. Oec. Decr.*, p. 808 (DS 3016).

37   See Pius IX, brief *Eximiam taum: AAS* 8 (1874-75), p. 447 (DS 2831); Paul VI, encyc. *Mysterium Fidei: AAS* 57 (1965), 757 ff., and *L'Oriente cristiano nella luce di immortali Concili*, in *Insegnamenti di Paolo VI*, vol. 5, Vatican Polygot Press, p. 412 ff.

38   See Vat. Coun. I, dogmatic const. *Dei Filius*, chap. 4: *Conc. Oec. Decr.*, p. 809 (DS 3020).

39   *Ibid.*

40   *Ibid.*, can. 3: *Conc. Oec. Decr.*, p. 811 (DS 3043).

41   John XXIII, address at opening of the Vatican Council: *AAS* 54 (1962), p. 792. See Vat. Coun. II, *Pastoral Constitution on the Church in the World of Today*, no. 62: *Const. Decr. Decl.*, p. 780.

42   Paul VI, apost. exhortation *Quinque iam anni: AAS* 63 (1971), 100 ff.

43   See Vat. Coun. II, *Dogmatic Constitution on the Church*, no. 10: *Const. Decr. Decl.*, p. 110.

44   *Ibid.*, no. 11: *Const. Decr. Decl.*, p. 111.

45   *Ibid.*, no. 10: *Const. Decr. Decl.*, p. 111.

46   See Pius XI, encyc. *Ad Catholici Sacerdotii:AAS* 28 (1936), 10 (DS 3735). See Vat. Coun. II, *Dogmatic Constitution on the Church*, no. 10: *Const. Decr. Decl.*, p. 110 ff, and *Decree on the Priestly Ministry and Life*, no. 2: *Const. Decr. Decl.*, p. 622 ff.

47   See Vat. Coun. II, *Dogmatic Constitution on the Church*, no. 28: *Const. Decr. Decl.*, p. 145.

48   Vat. Coun. II, *Decree on the Priestly Ministry and Life*, no. 3: *Const. Decr. Decl.*, p. 625.

49   See Vat. Coun. II, *Dogmatic Constitution on the Church*, nos. 24, 27 ff.: *Const. Decr. Decl.*, pp. 137, 143-149.

50   Vat. Coun. II, *Decree on the Priestly Ministry and Life*, no. 4: *Const. Decr. Decl.*, p. 627.

51   See *Dogmatic Constitution on the Church*, no. 11: *Const. Decr. Decl.*, p. 111 ff.; see also Council of Trent, sess. 22: *Doctrina de Missae Sacrificio*, chaps. 1 and 2: *Conc. Oec. Decr.*, pp. 732-734 (DS 1739-1743).

52   See Paul VI, Solemn Profession of Faith, no. 24: *AAS* 60 (1968), 442.

53   Council of Florence, *Bulla unionis Armenorum, Exsultate Deo: Conc. Oec. Decr.*, p. 546.

54   Council of Trent, Decree on the Sacraments, can. 9 and Decree on the Sacrament of Order, chap. 4 and can. 4: *Conc. Oec. Decr.*, pp. 685, 742, 744 (DS 1609, 1767, 1774).

55   See Vat. Coun. II, *Dogmatic Constitution on the Church*, no. 21: *Const. Decr. Decl.*, p. 130, and *Decree on the Priestly Ministry and Life*, no. 2: *Const. Decr. Decl.*, p. 622 ff.

56   See Documents of the Synod of Bishops, *I. The Ministerial Priesthood*, part one, 5: *AAS* 63 (1971), 907.

57   Vat. Coun. II, *Dogmatic Constitution on the Church*, no. 17: *Const. Decr. Decl.*, p. 123.

58   Vat. Coun. II, *Decree on the Priestly Ministry and Life*, no. 2: *Const. Decr. Decl.*, p. 621 ff. See also: 1) Innocent III, letter *Eius exemplo* with *Professio fidei Waldensibus imposita: PL*, vol. 215, col. 1510 (DS 794); 2) IV Lateran Council, Constitution 1, *De Fide Catholica: Conc. Oec. Decr.*, p. 230 (DS 802); passage quoted on the Sacrament of the Altar to be read together with the following passage on the Sacrament of Baptism; 3) Council of Florence, *Bulla unionis Armenorum, Exsultate Deo: Conc. Oec. Decr.*, p. 546 (DS 321); passage quoted on the Minister of the Eucharist to be compared with nearby passages on the Ministers of the other Sacraments; 4) Council of Trent, sess. 23, Decree on the Sacrament of Order, chap. 4: *Conc. Oec. Decr.*, p. 742 ff. (DS 767, 4469); 5) Pius XII, encyc. *Mediator Dei: AAS* 39 (1947), 552-556 (DS 3849-3852).

59   Documents of the Synod of Bishops, *I. The Ministerial Priesthood*, part one, 4: *AAS* 63 (1971), 906.

60   See Synod of Bishops (1967), *Relatio Commissionis Synodalis constitutae ad examen ulterius peragendum circa opiniones periculosas et atheismum*, II, 4: *De theologorum opera et responsabilitate*, Vatican Polyglot Press (1967), p. 11 (*L'Oss. Rom.*, Oct. 30-31, 1967, p. 3).

Homily of Pope Paul VI at a Concelebrated Mass on the Meaning of Ecclesial Power, September 22, 1974.

1   *2 Cor* 13, 13.

2   *Jn* 13, 35; see *Jn* 15, 12.

3   See *Col* 1, 24; *Eph* 1, 22.

4   *Eph* 4, 12.

5   *Lk* 22, 26.

6   *PL* 38, 1484.

7   See *AAS* (1951), 641; and see Congar, *L'Episcopat; Summa Theologiae* III, 80, 10 and 5; etc.

8   See *2 Thes* 2, 10.

9   *Mt* 28, 19.

10   See *1 Tm* 4, 6; 6, 20; *2 Tm* 1, 14.

11   See *1 Cor* 4, 1-2; *Eph* 3, 8.

12   See *Jn* 21, 15 ff.

13   See *2 Tm* 1, 6.

Sacred Congregation for the Doctrine of the Faith, Declaration on the Question of the Admission of Women to the Ministerial Priesthood, October 15, 1976.

1   *Acta Apostolicae Sedis* 55 (1963), pp. 267-268.

2   Second Vatican Council, Pastoral Constitution *Gaudium et Spes,* 29 (December 7, 1965): *AAS* 58 (1966), pp. 1048-1049.

3   Cf. Pope Paul VI, Address to the members of the Study Commission on the Role of Women in Society and in the Church and to the members of the Committee for International Women's Year, April 18, 1975: *AAS* 67 (1975), p. 265.

4   Second Vatican Council, Decree *Apostolicam Actuositatem,* 9 (November 18, 1965): *AAS* 58 (1966), p. 846.

5   Cf. Pope Paul VI, Address to the members of the Study Commission on the Role of Women in Society and in the Church and to the members of the Committee for International Women's Year, April 18, 1975: *AAS* 67 (1975), p. 266.

6   Cf. *AAS* 68 (1976), pp. 599-600; cf. *ibid.,* pp. 600-601.

7   Saint Irenaeus, *Adversus Haereses,* I, 13, 2: *PG* 7, 580-581; ed. Harvey, I, 114-122; Tertullian, *De Praescrip. Haeretic.* 41, 5: *CCL 1*, p. 221; Firmilian of Caesarea, in Saint Cyprian, *Epist.,* 75: *CSEL* 3, pp. 817-818; Origen, *Fragmentum in I Cor.* 74, in *Journal of Theological Studies* 10 (1909), pp. 41-42; Saint Epiphanius, *Panarion* 49, 2-3; 78, 23; 79, 2-4: vol. 2, *GCS* 31, pp. 243-244; vol. 3, *GCS* 37, pp. 473, 477-479.

8   *Didascalia Apostolorum,* ch. 15, ed. R. H. Connolly, pp. 133 and 142; *Constitutiones Apostolicae,* bk. 3, ch. 6, nos. 1-2; ch. 9, nos. 3-4: ed F. H. Funk, pp. 191,201; SaintJohn Chrysostom, *De Sacerdotio* 2, 2: *PG* 48, 633.

9   Saint Bonaventure, *In IV Sent.,* Dist. 25, art, 2, q1, ed. Quaracchi, vol. 4, p. 649; Richard of Middleton, *In IV Sent.,* Dist. 25, art. 4, n. 1, ed. Venice, 1499, f ° 177r; John Duns Scotus, *In IV Sent.,* Dist. 25: *Opus Oxoniense,* ed. Vives, vol. 19, p. 140; *Reportata Parisiensia,* vol. 24, pp. 369-371; Durandus of Saint-Pourcain, *In IV Sent.,* Dist 25, q.2, ed. Venice, 1571, f ° 364v.

10   Some have also wished to explain this fact by a symbolic intention of Jesus: the Twelve were to represent the ancestors of the twelve tribes of Israel (cf. *Mt* 19-28; *Lk* 22:30). But in these texts it is only a question of their participation in the eschatological judgment. The essential meaning of the choice of the Twelve should rather be sought in the totality of their mission (cf. *Mk* 3:14): they are to represent Jesus to the people and carry on his work.

11   Pope Innocent III, *Epist.* (December 11, 1210) to the Bishops of Palencia and Burgos, included in *Corpus Iuris, Decret. Lib.* 5, tit. 38, *De Paenit,* ch. 10 *Nova:* ed. A. Friedberg, vol. 2, col. 886-887; cf. *Glossa in Decretal. Lib. 1,* tit. 33, ch. 12 *Dilecta, v ° Iurisdictioni.* Cf. Saint Thomas, *Summa Theologiae,* III, q. 27, a.5 ad 3; Pseudo-Albert the Great, *Mariale,* quaest. 42, ed. Borgnet 37, 81.

12   Pope Pius XII, Apostolic Constitution *Sacramentum Ordinis,* November 30, 1947: *AAS* 40 (1948), pp. 5-7: Pope Paul VI, Apostolic Constitution *Divinae Consortium Naturae,* August 15, 1971: *AAS* 63 (1971), pp. 657-664; Apostolic Constitution *Sacram Unctionem,* November 30, 1972: *AAS* 65 (1973), pp. 5-9.

13   Pope Pius XII, Apostolic Constitution *Sacramentum Ordinis: loc. cit.,* p. 5.

14   Session 21, chap. 2: Denzinger-Schönmetzer, *Enchiridion Symbolorum* 1728.

15   Saint Cyprian, *Epist,* 63, 14: *PL* 4, 397 B; ed. Hartel, vol. 3 p. 713.

16   Second Vatican Council, Constitution *Sacrosanctum Concilium*, 33 (December 4, 1963): " . . . by the priest who presides over the assembly in the person of Christ . . . "; Dogmatic Constitution *Lumen Gentium*, 10 (November 21, 1964): "The ministerial priest, by the sacred power he enjoys, molds and rules the priestly people. Acting in the person of Christ, he brings about the Eucharistic Sacrifice, and offers it to God in the name of all the people . . ."; 28. "By the powers of the sacrament of Order, and in the image of Christ the eternal High Priest . . . they exercise this sacred function of Christ above all in the Eucharistic liturgy or synaxis. There, acting in the person of Christ . . ."; Decree *Presbyterorum Ordinis*, 2 (December 7, 1965): ". . . priests, by the anointing of the Holy Spirit, are marked with a special character and are so configured to Christ the Priest that they can act in the person of Christ the Head"; 13: "As ministers of sacred realities, especially in the Sacrifice of the Mass, priests represent the person of Christ in a special way"; cf. 1971 Synod of Bishops, *De. Sacerdotio Ministeriali* I, 4; Sacred Congregation for the Doctrine of the Faith, *Declaratio circa catholicam doctrinam de Ecclesia*, 6 (June 24, 1973).

17   Saint Thomas, *Summa Theologiae*, III, q. 83, art. 1, ad 3: "It is to be said that [just as the celebration of this sacrament is the representative image of Christ's Cross: *ibid.* ad 2], for the same reason the priest also enacts the image of Christ, in whose person and by whose power he pronounces the words of consecration".

18   "For since a sacrament is a sign, there is required in the things that are done in the sacraments not only the 'res' but the signification of the 'res' ", recalls Saint Thomas, precisely in order to reject the ordination of women: *In IV Sent.*, dist. 25, q. 2, art. 1, quaestiuncula 1a, corp.

19   Saint Thomas, *In IV Sent.*, dist. 25, q.2, quaestiuncula 1a ad 4um .

20   Cf. Council of Trent, Session 22, chap. 1: *DS* 1741.

21   Second Vatican Council, Dogmatic Constitution *Lumen Gentium*, 28: "Exercising within the limits of their authority the function of Christ as Shepherd and Head"; Decree *Presbyterorum Ordinis*, 2; "that they can act in the person of Christ the Head"; 6: "the office of Christ the Head and the Shepherd". Cf. Pope Pius XII, Encyclical Letter *Mediator Dei:* "the minister of the altar represents the person of Christ as the Head, offering in the name of all his members": *AAS* 39 (1947), p. 556; 1971 Synod of Bishops, *De Sacerdotio Ministeriali*, I, 4; " [The priestly ministry] . . . makes Christ, the Head of the community, present . . .".

22   Pope Paul VI, Encyclical Letter *Mysterium Fidei,* September 3, 1965: *AAS* 57 (1965), p. 761.

Motu Proprio of Pope Paul VI on the Council of the Laity, December 10, 1976.

1   See 1 *Cor.* 12, 5.

2   *Dogmatic Constitution on the Church*, no. 31.

3   *Decree on the Apostolate of the Laity*, no. 1

4   *Decree on the Apostolate of the Laity*, no. 26.

5   *AAS* 59 (1967) 25-28.

6   See Apostolic Letter *Catholicam Christi Ecclesiam: AAS* 49 (1967) 28.